WOMEN
WHO
RULED

WOMEN WHO RULED

Guida M. Jackson

ABC·CLIO

Santa Barbara, California
Oxford, England

Library of Congress Cataloging-in-Publication Data

Jackson, Guida M.
    Women who ruled / Guida M. Jackson.
       p. cm.
    Includes bibliographical references.
    1. Women heads of state—Biography—Dictionaries. 2. Heads of
state—Biography—Dictionaries. 3. Queens—Biography—Dictionaries.
I. Title.
D107.J33   1990   920.72—dc20   89-28282
[B]

ISBN 0-87436-560-0 (alk. paper)

97 96 95 94 93 92 91   10 9 8 7 6 5 4

ABC-CLIO, Inc.
130 Cremona Drive, P.O. Box 1911
Santa Barbara, California 93116-1911

*To my husband, William Laufer,
who made it possible*

Contents

Illustrations

Preface

The scope of this work is all women rulers, de facto rulers, and constitutional monarchs, living or deceased, of the world's kingdoms, islands, empires, nations, and tribes since the beginning of recorded history. The book is arranged alphabetically according to rulers' names, in dictionary style. The entries are supported by notes and a bibliography, and I have also included a chronological list of rulers by century.

Such a compilation could not possibly be a history based on original research of primary sources. It must rather be a gathering together from secondary souces—from the works of others from all cultures—of information pertinent to the subject at hand. As such, if it cannot be an original work of historical research, it still carries an added obligation that a history does not, and that is to provide information in some cases even beyond historical fact, so called.

Grey areas are inherent in a categorization as broad as women who ruled. In general terms, I have sought to include the name (or occasionally, when the name has not survived, the identifying clan, dynasty, or even locale) of any woman who held the reins of power, regardless of the extent to which she exercised it, and regardless of her official sanction to do so. To include only those who presided from a recognized seat of government, however, would omit certain leaders of nomadic subjects; and yet

there is a difference between "leaders" and "rulers." Joan of Arc, certainly a leader, did not preside from a recognized seat of government and would not be termed a ruler. On the other hand, Trieu Au, another leader who did not preside from any recognized seat of government, is included because she clearly ruled over the Vietnamese hill people whom she led into battle.

Far more open to controversy is my inclusion of certain women behind the throne, such as Diane of Poitiers, to the exclusion of others like Marie Antoinette and Eva Perón, both of whom doubtless influenced history to a greater degree. My inclination has been to omit these powers behind the throne unless history indicates that they dominated the designated rulers completely.

In addition, with some ambivalence, I have included the names of some legendary rulers about whom no firm historical or archeological evidence survives, whose embroidered histories may—or may not—have been based on the lives of actual (albeit far less colorful) persons. These inclusions are clearly labelled as legendary and are included because of the unique information they provide, information which in some cases may link the historical to the legendary or may contain some elements that coincide with known historical data. There are others, such as the Nitrocris of whom Herodotus writes, that I feel a responsibility to include, if only to clear up confusion concerning identity and to offer information on possible historical counterparts.

Diacritics, particularly in accounts of rulers of recent times, have been kept to a minimum for the sake of a particular fluid robustness that a clean page allows; however, in the case of certain of the more exotic and distantly removed entries, the use of diacritics seems preferable and even unavoidable. I hope that whatever fluidity is lost due to their inclusion is compensated for by the edaphic flavor they lend.

The name of each woman ruler is followed by a title or titles and, in parentheses, the year(s) during which the woman ruled. In the case of entries that give more than one title, the additional title will help to distinguish the ruler from other women in history with similar names; to designate either a title different from that which the ruler held while ruling or a title that was not the usual one held by a ruler of that particular place; or to clarify for the reader the type of title used in a certain time and place.

For material on the rulers Aelfwyn, Anna Anachoutlou, Āzarmēdukht, Berengaria, Bōrān, Jacqueline, Mei, Sati Beg, and Seaxburh, I consulted *Dynasties of the World,* by John E. Morby (Oxford and New York: Oxford University Press, 1989), a source that became available to me relatively late in the research for this book. Information used for the late-breaking additions of Nicaraguan President Violeta Chamorro and Haitian President Ertha Pascal-Trouillot was gleaned from articles in the *New York Times,* the *New York Times Magazine,* and the *Houston Chronicle.* "Opposing Ortega," by Mark A. Uhlig (*New York Times Magazine,* February 11, 1990, pp. 34–35, 62–72) was the primary source for the Chamorro entry. The Pascal-Trouillot entry was compiled from information in three reports: "Haitians Name Woman Leader as Avril Flees," by Don A. Schanche (*Houston Chronicle,* March 13, 1990, p. 8A), "Pascal-Trouillot Blazes a Trail for Women," by Michael Norton (AP) (*Houston Chronicle,* March 13, 1990, p. 8A), and "Civilian Sworn in as Haiti's President," by Joseph B. Treaster (*New York Times,* March 14, 1990, p. A3).

In this seven-year endeavor, I am indebted to those who brought rulers to my attention, who lent materials and offered editing assistance, inspiration, and encouragement: William H. Laufer, Jeffrey A. Jackson, Phyllis S. Prokop, Julia Mercedes Castilla de Gomez-Rivas, Ida H. Luttrell, William A. Jackson, Alphonsina Nswofwa, Frances McMaster, Venice Standley, Olivia Orfield, Eleana Tacciu, J. Tucker Jackson, Carol Rowe DeBender, Lynda Upchurch, Cathryn DeBruyn, Gloria Wahlen, Ocheze Nweze, Joyce Pounds Hardy, Donna Wolfe, Homer D. Johnson, Nell Harris, Kemala Motik Amongpradja, Mary Zimmeth Schomaker, Christopher Woods, Farangiz Hajizadeh, Glenda M. Lowery, Constanzia Moron, Frances Wegner, Linda S. Johnson, Tunde Agbabiaka, D. L. Hansen, S. O. Biobaku, Anna Ramos, Claire Ottenstein, Anne Heyburn, L. A. Abeyratne, Nagibee Hamady, Jasminka Posinovec, W. D. Norwood, Jr., James Hurley Miller, and my most helpful and supportive editor, Heather Cameron.

Introduction

Evidence of women rulers extends to the beginning of recorded history and throughout all geographic regions of the world. The following survey by region demonstrates the prevalence of women who ruled.

Africa

Egypt's dazzling history of ruling dynasties has so overshadowed the histories of other African cultures that we sometimes overlook the fact that there have been many other empires on the continent—and many other women rulers. Certainly Egypt's long tradition has influenced other cultures. In addition to establishing a precedent for the occasional sole woman ruler, Egypt is responsible for the concept of an "official woman" within the government of a ruling man, an office bearing the weight of co-ruler, vice-ruler, prime minister, or secretary of state.

Addressing governments other than those presided over by a woman exclusively: In ancient Egypt, full-blooded consanguineous marriage among royalty, instituted during the late 1600s or early 1500s B.C., reflected the belief in divine rule. The queen bore the title of God's Wife of Amon. Even after the practice of full-blooded consanguineous marriage was discontinued in the mid-1500s B.C., the title of God's Wife remained. It was bestowed in childhood upon the pharaoh's legitimate heiress. The incoming pharaoh, to secure his right to the throne, generally married the God's Wife. Some variation of this procedure has been practiced in many other parts of the world. Often these unions resulted in co-rule by both king and queen; other times they did not. There is at least one instance where the queen ruled the land while the king engaged himself in cultural pursuits. There are other instances where the queen was given one state, city, or principality to govern while the king took command of another.

Greek historian Diodorus Siculus, who traveled in Egypt during 60–57 B.C. and commented in his *Bibliotheca Historica* on the matriarchal character of the Egyptian royal family, also noted of the commoners: "Among private citizens, the husband by the terms of the marriage agreement, appertains to the wife, and it is stipulated between them that the man shall obey the woman in all things."[1] Diodorus noted that while every Egyptian princess of the royal house was born a queen and bore the titles and

1

dignities of the office from the day of her birth, a man acquired them at his coronation and could do so only by becoming the consort of a royal princess. Those features of the constitution of Egyptian royalty are substantially the same as in most other African kingdoms, even the Moslem ones.[2]

Ibn Batuta described the custom of joint rule in Islamic Mali where, to show obeisance to and acceptance of the queen, the noble ladies would throw earth on their heads. In Mali it was the custom for the empress to be crowned with the *Mansa* and to share the imperial power. However, her ability to rule depended upon a vote of confidence from the other noble women. Mali is not the only Islamic country that practiced liberal treatment of women. In Sudan the ruler Shehu Usman cited the *Koran* as the source of his liberalism. He pointed out that the *Koran* had not assigned to women the tasks of cooking or washing clothes, and that it was necessary for them to receive an education in order to know the teachings of God and the laws of the Prophet.[3] By contrast, in the Songhay, where a full-fledged Moslem kingdom also existed, and in the Fulani Empire, women played essentially no part at all.

West Africa is the site of several ancient kingdoms of certain sophistication and boasts the most African women rulers of record, although many others doubtless existed whose identities are not known, since detailed written history began so relatively recently. In Bornu and Haussa the queen mother and the queen held important posts in the court. The Bornu queen mother, *Maguira*, acquired great prestige and power, including veto power over the acts of the emperor. The queen mother also played an important role in the ceremonials of the court. The empress, *Gousma*, also had a role of authority. Among the Mossi, the queen was also crowned and shared in a joint rule. Among the Akan, which includes the Ashanti and Baule, the title of queen mother likewise refers to an office, not a familial role, although in fact she was invariably related to the chief. Among Ashanti she often would be the sister of the chief. Elected by the council, the queen mother acted as head of state in the absence of the ruler; at his death, she

nominated the next ruler. In addition, the queen mother was usually the instigator of all diplomatic exchange with other governments.

Some West African nations had only women rulers. The Baule tribe came into being under the rule of a woman (Awura Pokou), as did Zaria (Turunku Bakwa). At least three women in a row ruled the Hausa state of Zaria during its prime. Kanem-Bornu records at least one sole woman ruler. Since only the names of outstanding leaders have survived in this region, it is not known how many other women ruled African kingdoms.

Much of Central and Eastern Africa was matrilineal: the original inhabitants of Angola and the Kongo kingdom (as well as later Bantu people, such as the Lunda) were matrilineal. Nzinga Mbandi, who inherited leadership of the Mbundu at a time when the Portuguese and Dutch were vying for slave trade in Angola, spoke to the foreigners in a language they could understand: she put on a gory display of dance for a Dutch captain designed to make him keep his distance, and for her first humiliating audience with the arrogant Portuguese overlord who refused her the courtesy of a chair, she sat on her own slave whom she then had hacked to death when she had finished with him. All nine clans of the Gikuyu tribe were named for daughters of the original founder of the tribe. In Buganda, among the Babito people, the Babito kings perpetuated the long-held custom of adopting the clan of their mothers. The Basaigi clans of the Ababito tribe employed a system of governing similar to that prevalent in West Africa. In addition, among the families of the Babito kings of Kitara there would be many princesses—as many as 60. One would be elected *Rubuga*, official queen-sister of the king. She would have an official position and/or seat on the king's council. In Sudan also, the preeminent offices were nearly always those of the queen mother, the queen sister, and a limited number of titled ''great wives'' of the ruler. In Kitara because the queen mother was an indispensable figure in the government, in some ways more pivotal than the king, she was greeted in a special way, possibly in the same manner as the king (''You who are better than all men in this village,'' or ''The savior of the people in the country'').[4]

Madagascar has a minor tradition of women rulers—at least four in a row at one point. However, the real power in each case rested with the queen's consort, the same man in three cases.

African women have a tradition of bravery and aggression. In eighteenth-century Dahomey (Benin), a corps of women warriors was formed. Originally, women caught in adultery or found guilty of other crimes had the option of being executed or joining the army. The ruler Agaja was so impressed by the bravery of the women soldiers that he made them a regular unit of the army, called the Amazons. The group soon became a *corps d'elite*, and the criminal elements were then eliminated from the corps. A law was passed requiring every notable to present one daughter to the king for service in the Amazons, which was divided into five corps: the Infantry, the Elephant Huntresses, the Razor Women, the Archers, and the Blunderbuss Women.[5] Their strenuous training would make a U.S. Marine blanch. They became the most dreaded, terrible force in West Africa. The last Ashanti war against the British is called the Yaa Asantewaa War, named for the feisty Ohemaa of Edweso, Yaa Asantewaa, who, even though she was 50 years old at the time, led the fight. In this century, a young Senegalese queen, Aline Sitoe, mounted such a revolt against the French that she had to be deported when she was finally captured to keep her from continuing her fight even from prison. In North Africa, the Berber tribes of the Aures mountains combined under the leadership of a woman named Kahina to sweep down repeatedly on the Arabs who had taken Carthage (traditionally said to have been established, by the way, by Queen Dido) from the Byzantine forces in A.D. 695. The actions of these warriors against the Arabs were not unlike the guerrilla attacks of the Vietnamese Trung sisters in ca. A.D. 39 or those of Queen Mawia, who first battered away at the Romans and later even chilled the blood of the barbarous Goths.

Kenyatta tells the story of the Gikuyu clans which, being named originally for the nine daughters of the founder, were all ruled by all men in this village, women. (While holding a superior position in the community, the women became domineering and ruthless fighters and practicers of polyandry.) Many men were put to death for committing adultery or other offenses. Finally the men overthrew the women and took command, becoming for the first time the heads of their families. Immediately they took steps to abolish the system of polyandry and established polygamy. They planned to change the clan names as well, but the women, infuriated by this final and ultimate insult, threatened that if the clan names, which stood as proof that women were the original founders of the clan system, were changed, they would bear no more children. Frightened by the women's strong stand on this point, the men acceded to the women's demand.[6]

Acts of courage and defiance by women in South Africa did not begin with the twentieth century. When the British defeated the Zulu army in 1879, a tribal elder, Mkabi, called her people together and told them that, having seen the glory of the Zulus, she could not bear to see their king Cetewayo become a hunted fugitive. Protesting the British degradation of their illustrious and gallant leader, she cut her own throat in front of the assembled tribe.[7] Nor was her act of bravery the first of its kind in this region. The Zulu Chronicles relate at least one story of a young maiden who killed an enemy soldier and won for herself a warrior's insignia and an official praise name. The official organ of the African National Congress of South Africa perhaps most succinctly describes African women (both rulers and commoners) in what can only be termed masterful understatement: ''African women are not fragile flowers.'' [8]

India and the Middle East
The most ancient people of the Indo-European culture of which we now know, the Hittites, invaded Central Asia Minor ca. 2000 B.C. and established the Hittite kingdoms (1640–1380 and 1380–1200). Following the model of an older culture of the Middle Minoan III–Late Minoan II at Knossos, Phaistos, and Hagia Triada, in which women held a privileged position in society,[9] the queen occupied a strong central

position in this Hittite culture (Tawannanna).[10] The ruler of the feudal state was chosen by the predecessor, and after death the ruler was deified. As we saw in Egypt, deifying of rulers prevailed from every corner of Africa to Celtic Europe and across Asia all the way to Japan. Thus we are able to suppose that many legendary rulers did, in fact, exist.

Hundreds of years after the Hittites, a battling queen (Tomyrus) ended the life of Cyrus the Great, founder of the Persian Empire. Herodotus sang the praises of four outstanding women rulers (Artemisia, Semiramis, Pheretima, and Nitrocris), but he recounted the berating Darius' son Masistes gave General Artayntes: "He abused him roundly, and, to crown all, told him his leadership was worse than a woman's . . . to call a man 'worse than a woman' is, of course, the greatest insult one can offer to a Persian."[11]

Although there were other Arabian queens who acquitted themselves handily, we have the final word from the Prophet, quoted to the Mameluks by the khalif Mutawakkil when they proclaimed Spray of Pearls Queen of Egypt: "Unhappy is the nation who is governed by a woman." This, after the queen had directed all activities, including guiding the army to victory, from within the tent concealing the rotting body of the supposed ruler.[12]

Much the same attitude existed in India. Concerning Raziyya, the first Moslem woman to rule in what is now Pakistan, an ancient historian named all the virtues that made her such an outstanding ruler, then added, "She was endowed with all the qualities befitting a king, but she was not born of the right sex, and so, in the estimation of men, all these virtues are worthless."[13] However, Islamic law does not delineate the role of Muslim women in politics; in fact, in early Islamic times, according to Professor Ann Elizabeth Mayer, "Women played central active roles in political affairs. Only later, as Islamic doctrines combined with local customs that subjugated women, did a consensus develop that in Islam women should be barred from politics."[14]

The religions that preceded Islam in India were no kinder; still, women continued to emerge in Indian history. Megasthenes re-

corded that a daughter of Herakles founded the Pandyan Kingdom in south India,[15] and an ancient Ceylonese queen was called to the throne three times. Among all classes, the preference for a son emphasized the inferior status of women, but exceptional women (usually of the upper class) sometimes grabbed the reins of government intended for their husbands or sons. Nur Jahan issued her edicts and even fired her rifle without ever leaving the confines of purdah; Durgavati, during the time of the great Moghuls, and Lakshmi Bai and Hazrat Mahal, during the Sepoy War, were not quite so circumspect. In the aftermath of the Sepoy War, at least one outraged ex-leader's wife turned outlaw: the Rani of Tulsipur, apparently a widow who had escaped with her life and described only as bloodstained, joined a band headed by Babu Ram Babhsh, the Taluqdor of Dhundiakhera, who took advantage of the power vacuum to rustle and plunder everything in sight (1858). She was among those who escaped capture by the British only to die of exposure or disease in the wilds of northern Oudh or southern Nepal.[16]

The Hindu women were nevertheless indebted to the British for their attempt at reforms, such as Dalhousie's Hindu Widow's Remarriage Act of 1856 and the British Age of Consent (Sarda) Act of 1891, which raised the age of statutory rape for "consenting" brides from age 10 to 12. (The British made no concerted attempt, however, to enforce the laws.) In the Punjab under John Lawrence's leadership, incidents of *suttee* (the custom of a Hindu widow being burned upon her late husband's funeral pyre) and infanticide of female children decreased.[17]

Restraints notwithstanding, Hindu India gave us the area's most famous prime minister (Indira Gandhi), but Buddhist Sri Lanka (Ceylon) gave us the world's first woman prime minister—twice (Sirimavo Bandaranaike). And in modern-day Pakistan, Benazir Bhutto, a Moslem, was elected prime minister (1988).

But followers of her political rival, Mian Nawaz Sharif, pointed out that she is from Sind, looked down on as primitive by people in the rich province of Punjab. Punjabis will never follow a leader from Sind, they say, "let alone a Sindi woman."[18] Too, fundamentalists challenge the right or even the ability of a woman to lead. "We will never accept her in power," one said. "How can a woman deal with unemployment?"[19]

Islam has gone through spurts alternately of encouraging its women and "protecting" them. Writers in tenth-century Baghdad recounted women who had become lawyers, doctors, university professors, and public officials. However, the complete breakdown in law and order that followed made it inadvisable for women to go out unescorted.[20] In these somewhat calmer times, a courageous Benazir Bhutto tried again. Pakistani businessmen are more worldly, and they know their own history. One businessman explained to reporter Ian Buruma that the election of Benazir Bhutto was not such a break with tradition: "In feudal societies for hundreds of years, when there was no male heir, the mother or wife would take over. So it is no revolution at all. It shows the power of tradition and custom."[21]

This is precisely the model via which many women have come to power in Europe, in Turko-Mongolia, and in China, as well as in the Middle East. Even excluding Byzantium, several other Middle East kingdoms that frequently fell into the hands of women were actually European anomalies. The kingdoms of Jerusalem and Cyprus and the principality of Antioch were guided by European crusaders but frequently were governed by women, usually a titular heir whose ruling consort had died, or the mother of a minor legal heir. But such a woman was seldom dignified with a title other than regent, even if she was the legal heir. A few women who were never officially named regent (usually mothers of weak sons or wives of ineffectual husbands) simply usurped the power of the acquiescent kings and ruled in their stead. Fortunately, few would go to the lengths of Byzantine Empress Irene who, after her own abdication, still lusted for power to the degree that she finally had her own son blinded and deposed in order to become sole ruler, or of Athaliah, who seized the throne of Judah and tried to have all her grandsons put to death. In

fact, quite the opposite has been the case. As a matter of practice around the world, women appear to have attempted to make their husbands and sons look good. Much beautiful Chola art survives today to attest to that principle: several Chola kings, including Rajaraja I (985–1014), have been credited with building many beautiful temples that actually were the work of the pious Queen Sembiyan Mahadevi, widow of King Gandaraditya (949–957), but never a ruler herself. Through the reigns of Gandaraditya's two successors and well into the reign of a third, her great-nephew Rajaraja I, the queen constructed magnificent temples—many from A.D. 970 onward. (Queen Mahadevi lived until A.D. 1001.)[22]

Although women have built temples, monuments, churches, and monasteries, in the business of ruling, as in all else, it has most frequently been a woman's task to keep the home fires burning and mind the store while her man charged off into battle and, when he failed to make it back, to mop up and hold things together until the next generation could take over. Usually the latter entailed fighting off greedy neighbors or relatives anxious to usurp the throne. As a typical case in point, in the four years following the murder of Persian King Chosroes Parwiz (628), all the male heirs were killed. Nine claimants, including several women, ascended the throne only to be deposed.[23]

Central Asia
The names of some of the most colorful women have not survived. When Mo-ki-lien (the Turkish khan who ruled Mongolia from 716 to 734) was poisoned by his minister, he was succeeded first by his son Yi-jan and then by his brother Tängri khagan. During this seven-year period covering two reigns, Mo-ki-lien's widow actually ruled, but no one bothered to record her name. Another crusty Turko-Mongol dowager regent whose name did not survive, the widow of A-pao-ki (d. 926), supposedly ruled "with" her son but in fact held sole power. Her way of dealing with recalcitrant ministers was to send them to the land of the departed "to take news of her to her late

husband.'' When one wily old Chinese suggested that such a high honor should go to her instead, she expressed regrets that she was unable to oblige and lopped off one of her own hands and sent it along to be buried in her husband's tomb.[24]

Women were usually chosen as wives for what wealth or territory they could bring, and what they brought seldom remained theirs. Once he had used up her fortune to pay off his debts, King Baldwin I of Jerusalem was no longer fascinated by Adelaide of Salona. Prior to being named her father's heir (English King Henry I), "Empress Maud" was married to Holy Roman Emperor Henry V, who managed to lose her estates in his own wars before he died. But the Jewish heiress Mibtahiah was wilier. In fifth-century Egypt, Ashor took her as his wife, expecting her to forsake not only her family but her fortune (to him). Later, when she divorced him in a huff, she made certain to take along her fortune, which she promptly bestowed upon her Jewish second husband.[25]

Even though the exploits of his own mother Oelun-eke set for him an example of strong womanhood, Jenghiz-khan (whose idea of supreme joy was "to cut my enemies to pieces . . . seize their possessions, witness the tears of those dear to them, and embrace their wives and daughters!'')[26] probably did not envision how soon his empire would fall into the hands of his daughters- and granddaughters-in-law. Nor would he have sanctioned the overbearing influence upon their men of other of his progeny's wives: Sorghaqtani, for example, was called the directing spirit of the house of Tolui (Jenghiz-khan's fourth son). Hulägu married a Kerayit princess, Doquz-khatum, who was a Nestorian Christian. When he sacked Baghdad, she interceded to save the lives of all the Christians. The great Khan Mongka also respected her wisdom and advised Hulägu that he would do well to consult her in all his affairs. To please his queen, Hulägu heaped favors upon the Christians, and all over his realm new churches sprang up.[27] The history of the rule of later descendants of Jenghiz-khan is rife with Nestorian wives and mothers making Christians of their men. Jenghiz-khan owes to another queen,

Manduqhai, twice at the head of the Mongol army, the fifteenth-century renaissance of his all-but-defunct empire.

China and the Far East

Burmese women have enjoyed rare equality throughout history. In Pagan, temple inscriptions refer not only to female writers, scholars, and musicians, but to female chiefs as well.[28] In neighboring Thailand women hold a high position, and acts of courage recounted in Thai history are not confined to men. In 1549 one brave Thai queen, Suriyothai, struck out for the front lines of a Thai-Burmese battlefield to rescue her husband, King Maka Chakkraphat (1548–1569). The king survived, but she lost her life in saving his.

In Chinese Confucian times women were generally subordinate to their fathers, husbands, and then sons. A woman had no property rights except for a dowry, and in times of famine baby girls were sacrificed. Once a woman became a mother-in-law, however, all the rules changed: she could—and did—become autocratic and domineering. Nowhere is this principle more apparent than with dowager empresses. During the middle years of the Eastern Han Dynasty, the rebellion of the "yellow turbans" (A.D. 184) was triggered by the power of dowager empresses and their eunuchs.[29] For sheer wanton, bloodthirsty mayhem, few could equal Empress Wu Chao, who began by having two of her rivals killed and quickly followed that by killing her own baby almost at birth—and those were only two of the milder examples.[30]

Some of the strongest women rulers on record reigned in China, but equally strong were some of the concubines who never cared to rule. Yang Kuei-fei, a buxom concubine of the sexagenarian Emperor Ming Huang, not only had her brother installed as prime minister and infested the court with hundreds of her clansmen, but spent the empire's money lavishly: she sent relays of horsemen nearly 1,000 miles to procure litchis for her breakfast, and she ordered a new summer palace built complete with 16 marble bathing pools. However, when Yang Kuei-fei took a Tatar general as a lover, she went too far. This ambitious ingrate used her as she had used her emperor: he mounted an insurrection and drove the entire court from the capital. But the palace escort had had enough of the concubine's demands. They murdered her sister, fed her brother's head to the vultures, and, in royal fashion, strangled her with a silver cord.[31]

A change in the status of women in China occurred in the late T'ang and Sung periods. With the movement of the upper classes to the city, women became little more than playthings. Secondary wives were forbidden to talk in public, and widows were not allowed to remarry. During the Sung, the fashion of binding the feet of women—breaking the arches and turning the toes under—became a status symbol among upperclass men, demonstrating their ability to afford a completely useless appendage.[32]

The Chinese, whose historic records are generally considered more reliable than early Japanese ones, recorded the earliest Japanese ruling queen in the third century; in fact, in the Chinese *Wei* accounts Japan is described as "queen country" and a list is given of the countries (within Japan) over which she ruled. Later Japanese records show that between A.D. 592 and 770, half the rulers of Japan were women. Since that time there have been only two. During the Ashikaga period of shōguns (1338–1573), a strictly military society existed. Women were then excluded from any inheritance and relegated to the socially and legally inferior status in which they remained until this century.[33]

Polynesia and the Western Hemisphere

We know of a few Polynesian queens, such as Salote, Hinematioro, Liliuokalani, and Vaekehu, and in the northern portion of the western hemisphere native groups have occasionally had women rulers. In the 1980s two large tribes, the Seminoles and Cherokees, have been headed by women, and history records at least four others. In the nineteenth century a U.S. explorer and his wife, Augustus and Alice Le Plongeon, claimed to have deciphered Mayan hieroglyphs and unearthed the history of a Queen Moo, but only one other student of Mayan culture supported his

claims and they are generally thought to be spurious.[34]

It was a princess regent (Isabel) who freed 700,000 slaves in Brazil. A century later, Isabel Perón became the first woman to serve as president in this hemisphere; Violeta Chamorro, the first to be elected president; Ertha Pascal-Trouillot, the first appointed president; and Mary Eugenia Charles, the first elected prime minister.

Europe

By far the majority of women rulers of whom we have record ruled in Europe, where a tradition to include women has existed since legendary times. One has only to look at the ancient Arctic race still in existence, the Lapps, to imagine the attitudes of other European ancestors. The position of Lapp women has always been better than that of some women in the United States today. Lapp girls marry at about the age of 20, maintaining their maiden names and property. A suitor is expected to give presents, and in order to "earn" the right to marry his bride, he and his new wife may live with her parents for a year.[35] Even before the time of Canute, the Vikings record a Queen Asa, and Canute himself, unable to govern everything at once, left his English mistress Aelfgifu in charge of Norway. Queen Margrete united the kingdoms of Denmark, Norway, and Sweden under one rule for the only time in history. The Irish legends of Celtic queens abound, and many an Irishman will swear beyond all reason to their veracity. At the present time, Northern Europe boasts the first women to be elected president in their own right (Vigdis Finnebogadóttir and Mary Robinson), three prime ministers (Margaret Thatcher, Kazimiera Prunskiene, and Gro Harlem Bruntlandt), and three queens (Elizabeth, Margrethe, and Beatrix). A queen has held the throne of Holland for a century.

In the rest of Europe, the seventh century became a period of boy-kings and female rulers among the Franks under the Merovingians. The notoriety of the bloodthirsty Fredegond rivals the aforementioned Wu Chao. From an account of Fredegond's crimes, it is barely conceivable that she had time to think of anything else but methods of revenge. During the Middle Ages, although few women ruled in their own right, many regents, such as Blanche of Castile, made a tremendous impact upon history. Some queens, such as ''King'' Jadwiga of Poland, exercised far less personal power. Some extremely powerful women were neither queens, ''kings,'' nor regents, but duchesses and rulers of their own smaller domains. During her time, there was not much the papacy did that was not first sanctioned by the powerful Matilda of Tuscany. The Renaissance flowered under the tutelage of a number of women. It was women who ruled Europe while their men marched off on the Crusades (except those like Eleanor of Aquitaine, who insisted on going along), and it was women who ruled when their men did not return. They fought wars of conquest as well as of defense; they negotiated treaties, murdered enemies, arranged mergers, instituted reforms, squandered fortunes, inspired their countrymen—and had babies.

Attributes for Leadership

Women have always stirred many pots at once. The mention of offspring in the account of a woman's life is essential, particularly any woman born prior to this century, because throughout whatever else she was doing, the bearing of children did not stop until she could have them no longer. Today's rulers, while neglecting neither their political responsibilities nor motherhood, find time to demonstrate their creative versatility: Queen Margrethe is a renowned illustrator whose best-known work is of *The Lord of the Rings*, but whose other work is respected as well. She also wrote a book with her husband. Gro Harlem Bruntlandt is a doctor; Queen Beatrix, a sculptor; and Queen Liliuokalani wrote a song recognized around the world, ''Aloha Oe.''

The characteristic socialization of women throughout history often carries over today into their method of governing. In Iceland, where the woman president is backed by a parliament of more women than men, the all-women political party does not have a leader. The women form groups to work out a consensus on each issue. In Canada, where a large number of women worked nationwide for only one year to accomplish the passage of the Women's Equality Clause 28 (passed 23 April 1981), the 1980 conference that led to its passage was headed not by a charismatic leader, as is the case with most social reform movements, but by a team of three women. In conducting the affairs of our shrinking global village, there will be little room for large egos and great need for leaders from individual nations adept at working by consensus for the welfare of all.

Over millennia women have learned to adapt to changing conditions that were beyond their power to alter. Adaptability and the willingness to change course must be added to the ability to work in harmony with others as necessary attributes for tomorrow's leaders. As we arrive at the realization that war has become unthinkable, more of the creative skills that have made women so versatile must be the qualities we seek in our leaders. Women will continue to have a share, as always, in guiding our destiny, and perhaps that share may even grow.

Chronology

Thirty-first century B.C.
Meryet-Nit (Egypt)

Twenty-fifth century B.C.
Khentkaues (Egypt)

Eighteenth century B.C.
Nefrusobek (Egypt)

Sixteenth century B.C.
Ahhotep (Thebes)
Ahmose-Nofretari (Egypt)

Fifteenth century B.C.
Hatshepsut (Egypt)

Fourteenth century B.C.
Eji (Egypt)
Tiy (Egypt)

Thirteenth century B.C.
Deborah (Israel)
Twosret (Egypt)

Tenth century B.C.
Makeda (Axum)

Ninth century B.C.
Athaliah (Judah)
Dido (Phoenicia)
Sammuramat (New Assyrian Empire)

Eighth century B.C.
Samsia (Southern Arabia)
Zabibi (Arabian state)

Seventh century B.C.
Naqi'a (Assyria)

Sixth century B.C.
Nitrocris (Babylon)
Tomyris (Massagetae)

Fifth century B.C.
Artemisia I (Halicarnassus and Cos)
Nitrocris (Egypt)

Fourth century B.C.
Ada (Caria)
Artemisia II (Caria)

Third century B.C.
Arsinoe II (Egypt)

Second century B.C.
Cleopatra I (Egypt)
Cleopatra II (Egypt)
Cleopatra III (Egypt)
Cleopatra Thea (Mesopotamia)
Lu Hou (China)
Pāndyan Queen (Pāndya)

First century B.C.
Alexandra (Judaea)
Amanishakhete (Kush)
Anula (Ceylon)
Berenice III (Egypt)
Berenice IV (Egypt)
Cheng-Chun (China)
Cleopatra VII (Egypt)
Cleopatra of Cyrene (Cyrene)
Cleopatra Tryphaena (Egypt)

First century A.D.
Boudicca (Iceni)
Brigantia (legendary, Brigantia)
Cartimandua (Brigantia)
Julia Berenice (Southern Syria)
Sivali (Ceylon)
Tou Hsien (China)
Trung Nhi (Vietnam)
Trung Trac (Vietnam)

Second century
Liang (China)
Pimiku (Japan)
Teng (China)

Third century
Jingō-kōgō (Japan)
Julia Avita Mammaea (Roman Empire)
Julia Domna (Roman Empire)
Julia Maesa (Roman Empire)
Trieu Au (Vietnam)
Zenobia (Palmyra)

Fourth century
Mavia (Saracens)
Prābhavatī Gupta (Vākātakas)

Fifth century
Eudoxia (Eastern Roman Empire)
Galla Placidia (Western Roman Empire)
Pulcheria (Eastern Roman Empire)

Sixth century
Amalswinthe (Western Roman Empire)
Brunhilde (Austrasia and Burgundy)
Fredegund (Neustria)
Hind al-Hīrah (Lakhm)
Hu (Toba)
Pheretima (Cyrene)
Suiko-tennō (Japan)

Theodolinda (Lombards)
Theodora (Byzantine Empire)

Seventh century
Āzarmēdukht (Persia)
Balthild (Neustria)
Bōrān (Persia)
Himnechildis (Austrasia)
Jitō-tennō (Japan)
Kahina (Moors)
Kōgyku-tennō (Japan)
Seaxburh (Wessex)
Wu Hou (China)

Eighth century
Gemmei-tennō (Japan)
Genshō-tennō (Japan)
Irene (Byzantine Empire)
Kōken-tennō (Japan)
Mo-ki-lien (Mongolia)
Plectrudis (Austrasia and Neustria)

Ninth century
Asa (Norway)
Thecla (Byzantine Empire)
Theodora (Eastern Roman Empire)

Tenth century
Adelaide (German Empire)
Aelfwyn (Mercia)
Aethelflaed (Mercia)
Arsinde (Carcassonne)
Didda (Kashmir)
Drahomira (Bohemia)
Helena Lecapena (Eastern Roman Empire)
Hsiao-shih (Khitan Empire)
Judith (Abyssinia)
Ludmila (Bohemia)
Marozia Crescentii (Rome)
Mathilde (Nevers)
Matilda (Germany)
Olga (Kiev)
Shu-lü shih (Turkish Mongolia)
Sugandha (Kashmir)
Theophano (Byzantine Empire)
Theophano (Germany)

Eleventh century
Adela (Blois and Chartres)
Adele (Vendôme)

Aelfgifu (Norway)
Agnes of Poitou (Bavaria,
  Holy Roman Empire)
Anna Dalassena (Byzantine Empire)
Beatrice (Tuscany)
Ermengarde (Carcassonne)
Eudocia Macrembolitissa (Byzantine Empire)
Euphrosine (Vendôme)
Mary (Georgia)
Matilda of Flanders (Normandy)
Matilda of Tuscany (Central Italy)
Sung Dynasty Empress (China)
Theodora (Byzantine Empire)
Yüan Yu (China)
Zoë (Byzantine Empire)

Twelfth century
Adelaide of Salona (Sicily)
Agnes de Nevers (Nevers)
Alice (Antioch)
Constance (Sicily, Germany)
Constance (Antioch)
Eleanor of Aquitaine (England)
Ermengarde (Narbonne)
Ermensinde (Luxembourg)
Euphrosyne (Byzantine Empire)
Hodierna of Jerusalem (Tripoli)
Ide d'Alsace (Boulogne)
Mahaut de Boulogne (Boulogne)
Mahaut de Courtenay (Nevers)
Margaret of Navarre (Sicily)
Margareta (Flanders)
Marie (Boulogne)
Mary of Antioch (Byzantine Empire)
Matilda (England)
Melisende (Jerusalem)
Petronilla (Aragon)
Sibylla (Jerusalem)
Tamara (Georgia)
Ta-pu-yen (Kara-Khitai Empire)
Teresa of Castile (Portugal)
Urraca (León and Castile)
Ye-lü Shih (Kara Khitai Empire)

Thirteenth century
Agness de Dampierre (Bourbon)
Alix of Vergy (Burgundy)
Anna Palaeologina-Cantacuzena (Eprius)
Béatrix de Bourgogne (Bourbon)

Berengaria (Castile)
Blanche of Castile (France)
Boraqchin (Kipchak)
Constance (Sicily)
Ebuskun (Turkestan)
Eschiva of Ibelin (Beirut)
Hedwig (Silesia)
Isabella (Beirut)
Isabella of Cyprus (Jerusalem)
Jeanne de Chatillon (Blois)
Johanna (Belgium)
Juana I (Navarre)
Kalyānavati (Ceylon)
Kassi (Mali)
Lilavati (Ceylon)
Lucia (Tuscany)
Lucienne (Antioch)
Mahaut I (Bourbon)
Mahaut II de Dampierre (Bourbon)
Mahaut de Dammaratin (Boulogne)
Margaret (Belgium)
Margaret of Antioch-Lusignan (Tyre)
Margaret of Norway (Scotland)
Margaretha (the Netherlands)
Marguerite (Blois)
Marie (Brabant)
Marie (Jerusalem)
Marie de Chatillon (Blois)
Oghul Qamish (Karakorum)
Orghana (Turkestan)
Plaisance of Antioch (Cyprus and Jerusalem)
Raẓiyya (Northern India)
Russudan (Georgia)
Spray of Pearls (Egypt)
Sung Dynasty Empress (China)
Töregene (Outer Mongolia)
Yolanda (Jerusalem)
Yolande (Latin Empire)
Yolande de Bourgogne (Nevers)
Zabel (Lesser Armenia)

Fourteenth century
Agnes (Dunbar)
Anna Anachoutlou (Trebizond)
Anna of Savoy (Byzantine Empire)
Anna Palaeologina (Eprius)
Beatrice (Portugal)
Bendjou (Mali)
Catherine (Vendôme)

Catherine of Valois (Byzantine Empire)
Eleanor of Arborea (Arborea)
Elizabeth (Poland)
Isabella (Foix)
Isabella of Bavaria (France)
Jadwiga (Poland)
Jeanne I (Dreux)
Jeanne II (Dreux)
Jeanne de Castile (Vendôme)
Joanna I (Naples)
Johanna (Brabant)
Juana II (Navarre)
Leonora Telles (Portugal)
Margaret (Belgium)
Margaret (Carinthia, Tirol)
Margaret (Denmark, Norway, and Sweden)
Maria (Sicily)
Maria of Anjou (Hungary)
Sati Beg (Persia)
Tribhuvana (Java)

Fifteenth century
Aissa Koli (Kanem-Bornu)
Amina (Zaria)
Anne (Brittany)
Anne of France (France)
Bianca (Sicily)
Bianca Maria (Milan)
Blanca (Navarre)
Bona of Savoy (Milan)
Catalinda de Albret (Navarre)
Caterina Sforza (Forli and Imola)
Catherine Cornaro (Jerusalem on Cyprus)
Charlotte (Jerusalem on Cyprus)
Claudine (Monaco)
Eleanor (Navarre)
Elizabeth (Hungary)
Elizabeth of Görlitz (Luxembourg)
Isabella I (Castile)
Isabella D'Este (Mantua)
Jacqueline, or Jacoba (Holland)
Joanna II (Naples)
Mandughai (Mongolia)
Margaret of Anjou (England)
Mary (Burgundy and Luxembourg)

Sixteenth century
Catherine de Médicis (France)
Catherine of Aragon (England)

Diane of Poitiers (France)
Durgavati (Gondwana)
Elizabeth I (England)
Jane Grey (England)
Henriette de Cleves (Nevers)
Jeanne d'Albret (Navarre)
Joanna of Austria (Portugal)
Juana (Castile)
Louise de Savoy (France)
Maham Anga (Mughal Empire)
Margaret of Austria (Parma and
    the Netherlands)
Margaret of Austria (Savoy and
    the Netherlands)
Margaret Tudor (Scotland)
Maria of Austria (Hungary and the Netherlands)
Mary I (England)
Mary of Guise (Scotland)
Mary Stuart (Scotland)
Susanne of Bourbon (Bourbon)
Turunku Bakwa (Zaria)
Yelena Glinskaya (Russia)

Seventeenth century
Anne Marie Louise d'Orléans (Auvergne)
Anne of Austria (France and Brittany)
Apumatec (North American Indian tribe)
Christina (Sweden)
Christine of France (Savoy)
Hinematioro (Ngati Pirou in New Zealand)
Isabella Clara Eugenia of Austria (Spanish
    Netherlands)
Jeanne de Nemours (Savoy)
Luisa Maria de Guzmán (Portugal)
María Anna of Austria (Spain)
Marie de Bourbon Montpensier (Auvergne)
Marie de Médicis (France and Normandy)
Mary II (England)
Myōjō-tennō (Japan)
Nicole (Lorraine)
Nūr Jahān (India)
Nzinga Mbandi (Mbundu in Ndongo)
Sofya Alekseyevna (Russia)
Vittoria (Urbino)

Eighteenth century
Anna (Russia)
Anna Leopoldovna (Russia)
Anne (England)
Anne of England (Dutch republic)

Awura Pokou (Baule tribe)
Catherine I (Russia)
Catherine of Braganza (Portugal)
Catherine the Great (Russia)
Elizabeth I (Russia)
Go-Sakuramachi-tennō (Japan)
Isabella Farnese of Parma (Spain)
Louise Hippolyte (Monaco)
Maria I of Braganza (Portugal)
María Anna of Spain (Portugal)
Maria Carolina (Naples and Sicily)
Maria Christina (Austrian Netherlands)
Maria Theresa (Hapsburg Empire)
Mary Bosomworth (Ossabaw, Sapelo, and
    St. Catherines islands)
Mentewab (Ethiopia)
Sada Kaur (Śukerchakāīs in Pakistan)
Udham Bai (India)
Ulrica Eleanora (Sweden)

Nineteenth century
Afua Koba (Asante)
Cixi (China)
Elisa Bonaparte (Tuscany, Piombino,
    and Lucca)
Emma (the Netherlands)
Eugénie-Marie (France)
Hazrat Mahal (Oudh)
Hortense de Beauharnais (Holland)
Isabel (Brazil)
Isabella II (Spain)
Jindan (Sikh Kingdom)
Lakshmi Bai (Jhānsi)
Liliuokalani (Hawaii)
Luisa (Etruria)
Luise-Marie (Parma and Piacenza)
Maria II da Gloria (Portugal)
María Christina I of Naples (Spain)
María Christina of Austria (Spain)
María de la Mercedes (Spain)
Marie-Louise (France, Parma)
Mei (Cambodia)
Min (Korea)

Ranavalona I (Madagascar)
Ranavalona II (Madagascar)
Ranavalona III (Madagascar)
Rasoaherina (Madagascar)
Tz'u-an (China)
María Uicab (Tulum)
Vaekehu (Taiohae in the Marquesas Islands)
Victoria (British Empire)
Wilhelmina (the Netherlands)
Yaa Akyaa (Asante Empire)

Twentieth century
Alexandra (Russia)
Aline Sitoe (Casamance)
María Corazon Aquino (Philippines)
Sirimavo Bandaranaike (Sri Lanka)
Beatrix (the Netherlands)
Benazir Bhutto (Pakistan)
Gro Harlem Bruntlandt (Norway)
Violeta Barrios de Chamorro (Nicaragua)
Mary Eugenia Charles (Dominica)
Charlotte (Luxembourg)
Elizabeth II (England)
Vigdis Finnebogadóttir (Iceland)
Indira Gandhi (India)
Juliana (the Netherlands)
Betty Mae Jumper (Seminole Nation)
Kossamak (Cambodia)
Wilma T. Mankiller (Cherokee Nation)
Margrethe II (Denmark)
Maria Adelaide (Luxembourg)
Golda Meir (Israel)
Olga (Greece)
Vijaya Pandit (UN General Assembly)
Ertha Pascal-Trouillot (Haiti)
Isabel Perón (Argentina)
Mary Robinson (Ireland)
Salote Topou III (Tonga)
Sirikit (Thailand)
Taitu (Ethiopia)
Margaret Thatcher (Great Britain)
Yaa Asantewaa (Edweso)
Zauditu (Ethiopia)

Ada
Queen of Caria (344–341 and 334–? B.C.)

Caria was a separate Persian satrapy belonging to the Delian League. Ada was the wife-sister of Idrieus, who ruled from 351 to 344 B.C. After his death, Ada ruled Halicarnassus for three years until her younger brother, Pixadarus (341–335 B.C.), expelled her. She moved to the strong fortress of Alinda, southwest of Alabanda, where she held out for several years. When her brother Pixadarus died in 335 B.C., his son-in-law Orontobates claimed the throne, but Ada quickly disputed his claim. On the road she had met Alexander the Great, who was preparing to attack Halicarnassus. She made him her adopted son, thus assuring him her throne. Alexander soon destroyed Halicarnassus and left 3,000 mercenaries to garrison Caria, which he granted to Ada with the title of queen (ca. 334 B.C.). Soon after, Ada brought about the surrender of the Persians in the citadel of Myndus, a feat Alexander had been unable to accomplish earlier.[1]

Addagoppe (or Adda-Guppi)
See Nitrocris

Adela
Countess of Blois and Chartres, regent (ca. 1097–1109)

The daughter of William I the Conqueror of England, Adela (b. ca. 1062) inherited his strong will and an interest in politics. She married Count Stephen of Blois and Chartres and governed alone when her husband left for the Holy Land on the First Crusade, ca. 1097. In the spring of 1098, Stephen became discouraged and decided to return home. On the way, he met Byzantine Emperor Alexius and convinced him that the attempt to take Antioch was hopeless, so Alexius also turned back. Stephen's advice was to cause Alexius difficulties later, for when the remaining crusaders learned he had turned back, they felt no obligation to return Antioch to him. Stephen's return without fulfilling his crusading vows was a source of great humiliation to Adela, reared in the tradition of the great William the Conqueror. It was said that behind the doors of their bedchamber she shamed him for his cowardice and urged him to redeem his honor. Stephen could not argue that he was needed to rule Blois, for Adela had always actually ruled. Against his own better judgment, Stephen set out on another expedition in 1101. This time he survived the siege of Antioch and continued the pilgrimage to Jerusalem. The crusaders' ship was blown ashore off Jaffa where, under the command of Jerusalem's King Baldwin, they planned to attack the approaching Egyptian army, believing it to be much smaller than it was. Stephen saw the proposed attack as precipitous, but his comrades, remembering his past cowardice, ignored his advice. Too late they realized their mistake, but they went into battle bravely. Stephen redeemed his honor but lost his life (1102). After his death Adela continued to serve as regent until 1109, when her oldest son Theobald reached majority and she had him made count. During the years of her regency she worked to strengthen her fiefdom so that her son would have an increasingly important role to play in European affairs. It was due to her efforts, through her friend the Bishop St. Ives of Chartres, that her younger brother, King Henry I of England, was able to reach a compromise with the archbishop of Canterbury over the lay investiture of churchmen. The schoolmaster Hildebert of Lavardin (1056–1133), who became archbishop of Tours, earned the ardent admiration of Adela because of his classical Latin poetry. She addressed many love songs to him, as did the Empress Matilda. Adela's third son, Stephen, became king of England, based on her claim of inheritance following Henry's death. She died in 1137.[2]

Adelaide
Queen of Italy, regent of German Empire (983–995)

She was born in 931, the daughter of King Rudolph II of Burgundy and Bertha of Swabia. She married King Lothair of Italy in 947, at about age 16. Lothair died only three years later, and for a brief time Adelaide ruled alone. However, the following year, her kingdom was threatened with siege by Berengar of Pavia. She was imprisoned but, because she was a beautiful woman of strong character, she found many willing to help her. She managed to escape after a confinement of four months. She offered her hand in marriage as reward for helping her regain her Italian throne. Several nobles sought to intervene, but it was Otto (Otto the Great,

Saxon emperor of the German Empire) who stepped in to the rescue. Seeing an opportunity to expand his holdings, he came to Adelaide's aid, defeated Berengar's forces, and declared himself king of the Franks and Lombards. Adelaide, glad to have Otto's protection, and envisioning for herself a larger kingdom, married Otto and ceded Italy to Berengar in exchange for Istria, Friuli, and Verona, which became part of Bavaria. Otto and Adelaide were crowned emperor and empress of the Western German Empire in 962. Their son, Otto II, succeeded to the throne upon his father's death in 973. Only ten years later, three-year-old Otto III, son of Otto II and Theophano, inherited the throne. Adelaide, his grandmother, served as co-regent, sharing the duties with her daughter-in-law from 983 to 991, when Theophano died. She then governed alone until Otto came of age in 995. After his coronation, she devoted herself to founding churches and monasteries. She died in 999 at the age of 68 and was buried in Seltz, Alsace, where miracles were reported to have occurred. She was made a saint of the Catholic Church; her feast day is December 16.[3]

Adelaide of Salona (or Savona)
Countess, regent of Sicily (1101–1112)

Adelaide was the daughter of the Marquis Manfred and the niece of Boniface of Salona. She married the great Count Roger I of Sicily in 1089, becoming his third wife. When Roger died two years later, she assumed the regency for Simon, who died in 1105, and thereafter for her son Roger II, who went on to become one of the most remarkable rulers of the Middle Ages. Queen Adelaide's immense wealth attracted the attention of the Frankish King Baldwin I of Jerusalem, who had cast aside his dowerless second wife and was looking for a new, wealthier queen. Adelaide had just retired from more than a decade of her regency and was looking for a new husband. Baldwin sent word asking for her hand; Adelaide accepted, providing the king would agree to the terms of her contract: that if no baby was born of the union—and the ages of both suggested little possibility—the crown of Jerusalem would pass to her son,

Roger II. Her terms accepted, Adelaide sailed the Mediterranean in elegant splendor reminiscent of Cleopatra, with a fleet of gold- and silver-trimmed ships carrying all her personal treasure. Baldwin met her with equal pomp, and ordered all his kingdom adorned for her arrival. However, once he had spent her dowry to pay off his debts, his ardor cooled, as did hers, when she found that Jerusalem was a far cry from her luxurious Palermo palace. In 1117 Baldwin fell seriously ill, and his confessors reminded him that he might die in a state of sin, since he had never legally divorced his second wife. When he recovered, he announced the annulment of his marriage to Adelaide. Now alone, scorned, stripped of her wealth, Adelaide sailed back to Sicily in humiliation. Baldwin's insult would cost the kingdom of Jerusalem dearly in the ensuing years: Adelaide's marriage contract would be the basis for her son's claim upon the lands of Jerusalem. Roger II never forgot Baldwin's humiliation of his mother. In 1117, two lunar eclipses and the appearance of the aurora borealis were believed to foretell the death of princes. In the following months, in 1118, King Baldwin, his patriarch Arnulf, Pope Paschal, Iranian Sultan Mohammed, Baghdad Caliph Mustazhir, and ex-Queen Adelaide all died.[4]

Adele
Co-ruler of Vendôme (ca. 1017–1031)

She was the wife of Bouchard I, count of Vendôme, Paril, and Corbeil, ruler of Vendôme from 958 to 1012. The couple had three sons: Renaud (bishop of Paril), Bouchard II, and Foulques d'Oison. When Bouchard I died in 1012, the oldest son ruled for four years. Following his death in 1016, a nephew, Eudes, son of Landry, count of Nevers, ruled briefly because Bouchard II was too young and quite possibly Adele was again pregnant. Bouchard II assumed the rule sometime after 1016 with his mother, but apparently he died soon after. The youngest child, Foulques d'Oison, then ruled with his mother until 1031, when Adele, in financial straits, sold the duchy to Foulques' uncle, Geoffri Martel, count of Anjou.[5]

Aelfgifu (or Eligifu) of Northumbria
Regent of Norway (ca. 1029–1035)

She was the daughter of an ealderman of Northumbria who in 1006 had been murdered at the order of King Aethelred II. In ca. 1013 she met and became the mistress of Canute (the Great), son of Danish King Sven I Fork Beard, who invaded England that year. Canute became king of Denmark when his father died in 1014, was elected king of England in 1016, and became king of Norway in 1028. Aelfgifu bore two sons, Sven (Sweyn) and Harold (Harefoot). However, in 1017, to bolster English support in case of an attack by Aethelred, Canute married Emma, the mother of exiled King Aethelred's sons. Emma was also sister of Duke Richard II. After Canute became king of Norway, he assigned Haakon as his regent; however, Haakon soon died. He then put Norway in the hands of Aelfgifu as regent for their son Sven. The two, Aelfgifu and Sven, remained in Norway for some six years before they were driven out. They escaped to Denmark, where Canute had put his legitimate son by Emma, Harthcanute (Hardecanute), in charge (1035). Canute died the same year, and Aelfgifu returned to England to champion the cause of her second son, Harold I Harefoot, as king. He ruled as regent from 1035 until his death in 1040, when his half brother ascended to the throne.[6]

Aelfwyn
Queen of Mercia (918–919)

The daughter of Aethelred II, who ruled from 879 to 911, and Aethelflaed, who ruled following his death until 918, Aelfwyn briefly ascended to the throne upon her mother's death but was deposed in 919 when Mercia was annexed by West Saxony.

Aethelflaed (or Ethelfleda)
Queen of Mercia (ca. 910–918)

Mercia was an Anglo-Saxon kingdom located in central England, originally consisting of the border areas, what is now Derbyshire, Staffordshire, and northern Warwickshire, eventually encompassing an area bounded on the north by the River Humber, on the east by East Anglia, on the south by the Thames, and on the west by Wales. Aethelflaed was the daughter of Alfred the Great. She married Aethelred, ealderman of the Mercians, and became the effective ruler in his stead long before he died. When Aethelred died in 911, she anomalously succeeded him, having already become firmly established as ruler. She became known as the Lady of the Mercians. She rivaled her brother Edward the Elder, ruler of West Saxony (899–924), in both war and organization, and she assisted him in overcoming the Danish armies that controlled great portions of eastern England. While Edward spent six years (910–916) fortifying the southeastern midlands, Aethelflaed was doing the same for Mercia. In 913 she erected the great earthen mound near present-day Warwick Castle as a fortress. By 917 the two of them had amassed large forces for a joint assault against the Danes. She captured Derby easily and went on to occupy Leicester in 918. She had already extended her boundaries into Wales on the west and Northumberland on the north. She gained a promise of submission from the Danes in Northumberland; however, before she could gain complete victory, she died (918) in Tamworth, now in Staffordshire, leaving Edward to win the final victory against the Danes. With his sister gone, Edward claimed her lands, and thus nearly all of what is present-day England was united under his control.[7]

Afua Koba
Asantehemaa, queen mother of the Asante Empire (ca. 1834–1884)

Asantehemaa comprised at that time most of the present-day West African nations of Ghana and Togo and portions of the Ivory Coast and Dahomey. The office of *asantehemaa,* or queen mother, was an elected position of great importance and influence. The holder of this office nominated the *asantehene,* or leader of the chiefs, and she might serve during several administrations in some cases. Accession to the Golden Stool (or throne) was matrilineal. Afua Koba—whose second husband, Boakye Tenten, occupied the Boakye Yam Panin okeyeame stools—was the mother of Kofi Kakari, occu-

pant of the Golden Stool from 1867 to 1874, and Mensa Bonsu, occupant of the Golden Stool from 1874 to 1883. She was a powerful and influential figure in a troubled period in the history of Asante. During the reign of her first son, the British general asked Kofi Kakari, as a condition of his not advancing to Kofi's city, that the queen mother and Prince Mensa, next heir to the throne, be sent to him as hostages. The general did not understand that in the eyes of the Asante these were the most important persons in the kingdom, and that it was not within Kofi Kakari's power to surrender them even had he been so inclined. In 1881, her intervention in the interest of peace with the British invaders was instrumental in preventing bloodshed for a time. She held the office of queen mother during the reign of several of her royal family members. In 1884, after Kwaku Dua was poisoned and the governmental system was in disarray with several outlying areas threatening to secede, she put forth for the office of the Golden Stool Kwasi Kisi, an unpopular candidate she knew had no chance of winning. This nomination was a gesture to win British assistance and to bring the outlying rulers into the capital for council deliberations. The ploy was unpopular; she was deposed in late 1884 and was succeeded by Yaa Akyaa.[8]

Agnes de Nevers
Countess, ruler of Nevers (1181–1192)

Nevers was located in the modern-day *Departement* of Nivre in central France, south-southeast of Paris. Agnes succeeded Count Guillaume V, who ruled from 1175 to 1181. She married Pierre de Courtenay and they had a daughter, Mahaut, who succeeded her mother in 1192.[9]

Agnes of Dunbar (Black Agnes)
Countess (of March), ruler of Dunbar (ca. 1338)

She was the daughter of the great Randolph, earl of Moray, who had been fighting off the British for years. In 1338 the English troops of Edward III attacked Dunbar castle; Edward had never been happy about the Treaty of Northampton (1028) making Scotland an independent realm, and he intended to bring it back under English control. Agnes held out triumphantly for five months, successfully defending the castle until the English retreated. Fortunately for the Scots, Edward, attempting also to gain the French throne, took his army to France.[10]

Agnes of Poitou
Empress, duchess of Bavaria (1056–1061), regent for Holy Roman Emperor Henry IV, (1056–1062)

She was born ca. 1024, the daughter of William V The Pious, duke of Aquitaine, a descendant of the kings of Italy and Burgundy. She married Henry III on November 1, 1043, becoming the second wife of the holy Roman emperor, and forming an allegiance cementing the empire's relations with its western neighbors. She and Henry III had a son, Henry IV, for whom Agnes assumed the regency when her husband died in 1056. However, although she was descended from kings both of Italy and Burgundy, she had no talent for leadership; she was, in fact, characterized as being pious and colorless. She gave away the duchies of Bavaria, Swabia, and Carinthia to relatives. An opponent of church reform, she allied herself with Italian dissidents and helped elect Cadalus as Antipope Honorarius II to oppose Pope Alexander II, elected by the reformers. In 1062 Archbishop Anno of Cologne, with the help of several princes, succeeded in kidnapping the young king and bringing him to Cologne, out of his mother's grasp. He jumped overboard but was rescued and recaptured. As ransom for her son, Agnes resigned as regent and Anno took her place. She spent the rest of her life in a convent.[11]

Agness de Dampierre
Baroness, ruler of Bourbon (1262–1287)

Agness ruled Bourbon during that period in French history in which so-called "feudal anarchy" existed. The French kings actually ruled a small area around Paris and Orleans while the heads of the great duchies and baronies maintained their independence. Agness was the daughter of Dame Mahaut I and Gui II de Dampierre and the sister of Baroness Mahaut II,

who ruled from 1249 to 1262. Mahaut II married Eudes de Bourgogne and Agness married his brother, Jean de Bourgogne. She succeeded to the barony when her sister died in 1262.[12]

Ahhotep
Queen of Thebes (1570–1546 B.C.)

She was the mother of Egyptian rulers: King Kamose, who died in 1570; Ahmose I, who succeeded him and is generally given credit for founding the Eighteenth Dynasty in Egypt; and Ahmose-Nofretari, their younger sister. While her son Ahmose I was driving the Hyksos kings out of Egypt, Ahhotep ran the government in Thebes, which is near modern-day Luxor. She helped to quell an uprising until her son could arrive with reinforcements. Her efforts, added to his, reunited Egypt under one rule.[13]

Ahmose-Nofretari
Co-ruler of Egypt (ca. 1570–1546 B.C.)

During the Second Intermediate Period of Egyptian history (1783–1550 B.C.), characterized by turbulence and regional rulers, the Hyksos, from Asia, invaded. Ahmose I, Nofretari's brother, continued the fight against these invaders, which his brother King Kamose had begun, eventually defeating the Hyksos and founding the Eighteenth Dynasty. He married his sister, Ahmose-Nofretari, who was given the title of God's Wife of Amon, through which the matrilineal dynasty would succeed. They had a son, Amenhotep I, who succeeded to the throne upon his father's death, and a daughter, Ahmose, who received the title God's Wife as her mother did. Ahmose-Nofretari was an influential and highly honored queen, as evidenced by depictions at Thebes of later pharaohs making offerings to her as a goddess.[14]

Aissa Koli
Queen, ruler of Kanem-Bornu (1497–1504), located in West Africa

She was the daughter of Ali Gaji Zanani, ruler of Kanem-Bornu. When he died, he was succeeded by Dunama, a relative, who also died in 1497. Aissa Koli ruled alone for seven years because it was believed that there was no male heir. However, she was unaware of the existence of a brother, sent to the Bulala court by his mother, a Bulala, because the interim ruler had threatened to kill all the former king's sons. The boy, Idriss, was five years old at the time that Aissa Koli's rule began. When he reached the age of twelve, he wrote his mother and his sister the queen, informing them of his existence. Aissa Koli's term being up—the rulers of many of the African nations had a fixed term of seven years—she asked him to come home. He was crowned king in 1504. Aissa Koli continued in a position of influence and authority, advising her long-exiled brother on governmental procedures and on the ways of his subjects.[15]

Alexandra
Empress of Russia, became absolute ruler in her husband's absence (1915–1917)

She was born in 1872 in Darmstadt, the daughter of Alice, Queen Victoria's daughter, and Louis IV, duke of Hesse-Darmstadt. Darmstadt was located in present-day West Germany. Alexandra was often unbending and firm-willed with a strong and proud appreciation of her Teutonic blood. She married Nicholas II of Russia in 1894 and dominated their entire married life. She was not popular with the Russian people, who considered her a German interloper. As consolation, she immersed herself in religion; however, her interest in religion did not prevent her from exerting her influence to undo the 1905 reforms, which limited the powers of the monarchy. The couple had four daughters before their son Alexis, a hemophiliac, was born. The boy's perilous health also put the future of the dynasty in peril. Alexandra turned for advice to Grigory Yefimovich Rasputin, a self-proclaimed holy man upon whom she came to rely so heavily that her conduct became a public scandal. In August of 1915, when Nicholas left for the front to assume command of Russian troops, Alexandra moved quickly to consolidate her own power. She dismissed valuable ministers and replaced them with puppets, choices of Rasputin. The government soon became paralyzed, and Alexandra was further alienated from an already suspicious and mistrusting pub-

Empress Alexandra. The Beinecke Rare Book and Manuscript Library, Yale University.

lic. Alexandra apparently believed that she was safely beyond justice, and even when Rasputin was murdered, she continued her despotic rule, giving public opinion no quarter. After the October Bolshevik Revolution, the entire family was imprisoned. On 29 July 1918, she was shot to death at Yekaterinburg, now Sverdlovsk, Russia. It might be concluded that she alone precipitated the collapse of the military government in March of 1911 and thus hastened the beginning of the Bolshevik Revolution.[16]

Alexandra (also called Salome Alexandra)
King, ruler of the Maccabees (Judaea)
(76–67 B.C.)

She was the wife of King Alexander Jannaeus of the Asmonean, or Hasmonean, dynasty of Syria, who ruled from 103 to 76 B.C. during one of the brief periods of Judaean independence. The couple had two sons, John Hyrcanus II and Aristobulus II. When Alexander died in 76 B.C., she became king, not queen, and her eldest son was appointed high priest. She died in 67 B.C. and was succeeded by her son Hyrcanus II, who three months later was driven from power by her other son Aristobulus II. Hyrcanus eventually regained the throne but was a puppet in the hands of various Roman factions.[17]

Alice
Princess, regent of Antioch (1130 and 1135–1136)

Born ca. 1106, the second daughter of Jerusalem's King Baldwin II and Queen Morphia of Melitene, Alice counted herself fortunate to marry tall, fair-haired, handsome Prince Bohemond II of Antioch in 1126. They had a daughter, Constance, who was only two years old when her father died in 1130. Without waiting for her father to appoint a regent, Alice at once assumed the regency for her daughter. But her ambition to rule as more than a regent—as a reigning sovereign—drove her to rash measures. When she heard that her father was on the way to Antioch to claim a regency, she sent an envoy to the atabeg Zengi, offering to pay him homage if he would guarantee her possession of the throne of Antioch. But Baldwin intercepted the envoy and had him hanged. When Baldwin reached Antioch, he found the gates locked. After three days of negotiations, he entered the city where Alice had barricaded herself in a tower, waiting for guarantees of her safety. When she and her father finally met, she knelt in terror and begged his forgiveness, which she received. However, Baldwin removed her from the regency, which he himself assumed, and banished her to her dower lands of Lattakieh and Jabala. After Baldwin's death (1131), Alice reasserted her claims for the regency. She gathered a sizable following against King Fulk, her brother-in-law, who sailed from Jerusalem to claim the regency. Alice's revolt (1132) was put down, but she remained unharmed at Lattakieh. In 1135, the Latin Bishop of Mamistra, Radulph of Domfront, assumed the patriarchal throne without benefit of canonical election. Not wishing to be dominated by the crowns of Jerusalem, he opened negotiations with Alice, who saw an opportunity to regain power in Antioch. She appealed to her sister, Queen Melisende, Fulk's wife, who arranged for Alice to return to Antioch. Although Fulk retained the title of regent, the governing power was actually shared by Alice and Radulph in what was characterized as an uneasy alliance. However, Radulph soon quarreled with his clergy, and Alice seized the opportunity to govern Antioch alone. She endeavored to strengthen her rather tenuous position by offering the hand of her nine-year-old daughter, the heir Princess Constance, to the Byzantine Emperor's son Manuel. Radulph, fearing he would be replaced as patriarch by a Greek if such a union occurred, sent an urgent secret message to King Fulk advising him to find a suitable husband for Constance at once. Fulk realized that neither Alice nor his wife Melisende must know of his plans. He chose as Constance's consort Raymond of Poiters. The patriarch Radulph then requested an audience with Alice to tell her that a handsome stranger had approached him as a candidate for marriage to her. Alice was most receptive to the proposal, but while she waited for the arrival of her future husband, Constance was kidnapped and brought to the cathedral, where Radulph quickly performed the wedding ceremony uniting the child and Raymond. Alice, seething at the betrayal and seeing that she had no more claim to the rule of Antioch, retired again to Lattakieh. At the time of her retirement, she was still under 30 years old.[18]

Aline Sitoe
Queen of the Diola Tribe, Casamance (ca. 1936–1943), in modern-day Senegal, West Africa

She was born ca. 1920 in Kabrousse. Beginning in 1942, she turned her people against the French who ruled her country. She gained renown as far away as Mauritania, Mali, and Guinea-Bissau for her battle cry, ''The white man is not invincible.'' She instigated a boycott of French products, encouraging local artisans to produce more. She discouraged use of the French language and exhorted her people to develop their intellectual capacities and resurrect their own culture. She sought to strengthen community life by giving women a more vital role. She announced a return to the use of the Diola six-day-week calendar, which was based on the annual rainy season, harvest season, dry season, and prerainy season. When Diola warriors ambushed a truck and killed four men, three of them soldiers, the French advanced upon Kabrousse and held it under siege from 13 to 29 January 1943, when the queen surrendered to prevent the French from burning the town to the ground. She was arrested and condemned to ten years in exile in Timbuktu; however, she died on 22 May 1944 after a long bout with scurvy. She was buried in Timbuktu's Sidi el Wafi Cemetery, but plans were made in 1983 to return her remains to Senegal, which became independent from France 19 years after her death. Legend has it that Queen Sitoe could change herself into a bird whenever she wished.[19]

Alix of Vergy
Countess, ruler of Burgundy (1248–?)

She was the daughter of Count Otto II and his wife, Countess Beatrix, daughter of Count Otto I. Alix's brother, Otto III, became count in 1234, and she inherited Burgundy, located in present-day eastern France, upon his death in 1248. She was married to Hugh of Chalon, and their son, Otto IV, inherited Burgundy upon her death sometime before 1290. Otto IV, in financial straits after protracted conflicts with the emperor, concluded two treaties (1291 and 1295) with King Philip IV of France wherein he ceded Burgundy to France.[20]

Amalswinthe (or Amalsuntha)
Regent of the Ostrogoths (526–534), then co-ruler (534–535)

She was born in 498, the daughter of King Theodoric the Great of the Ostrogoths and Audofleda, sister of King Clovis. Even by today's standards, she was an extremely well-educated woman. She studied both Greek and Latin and became a lifelong patroness of literature and the arts. In 515 she married Theodoric's distant relative, Eutharic. They had a son, Athalric, and a daughter, Matasuntha. Eutharic died in 522 and Theodoric died four years later, after which Amalswinthe served as regent for her ten-year-old son. She chose to continue the pro-Byzantine policies of her father, even though they were

Amalswinthe. The Granger Collection, New York.

unpopular with the Ostrogoth nobility. Recognizing the danger her policies put her in, she took the precaution of arranging with Byzantine Emperor Justinian that if she were deposed she would transfer herself and the entire Ostrogothic treasury to Constantinople. In 533 she successfully quelled a rebellion and put to death three of its instigators, Ostrogoth noblemen. Upon her son's death in 534, she shared the throne with her cousin Theodahad; however, he fell under the influence of the forces that opposed her, and ordered her banished to an island in the lake of Bolsena (Tuscany, Italy), where, at the instigation of the Empress Theodora, relatives of the three noblemen she had put to death strangled her in her bath in 535.[21]

Amanishakhete (also called Candace)
Queen, ruler of Kush (ca. 24–23 B.C.)

Queens were called ''Candace'' in Kush, which gave rise to the assumption by conquering Romans that Candace was her name. When the Romans under Petronius attacked the northern Kushian city of Napata, they were met by a ''one-eyed lady of masculine status'' who retreated to a neighboring fort, probably Merowe, and sent envoys to negotiate, hoping to dissuade them from destroying the religious capital. Petronius brushed aside her pleas and destroyed the town and the great temple of Amun at Jebel Barlal. Two years later she returned to attack Petronius, but the Romans held their ground. The Romans then withdrew to Nubia, finding nothing more to interest them. Amanishakhete was succeeded by Queen Amantari and King Natakamani (Nelekamani), probably not only husband and wife but brother and sister as well, Amanishakhete's offspring. These two were able to carry on some measure of restoration of Napata.[22]

Amina
Queen of Zaria (or Zazzau), West Africa
(ca. fifteenth or sixteenth century)

One source postulates that she was the daughter of Turonku Batwa, who founded the city of Zaria in 1536, and therefore gives her rule as the end of the sixteenth century. Amina succeeded her mother as ruler, but she had no husband. Under her remarkable leadership, Zaria became the most powerful state in Haussaland. Eventually her holdings stretched down to the sea. The Chronicles of Kano speak of her with great respect: "At this time Zaria under Queen Amina conquered all the towns as far as Kwarafara and Nupe. Every town paid tribute to her. The Sarikin Nupe sent forty eunuchs and ten thousand kolas to her. She was the first to have eunuchs and kolas in Haussaland. Her conquests extended over thirty-four years." The kola nut which she introduced is one of the great luxuries of Western Sudan; it is prized for its bitter taste, slightly aphrodisiac properties, and its ability to quench thirst. It was said that, although she never married, she took a new lover every night. After Amina's death, her sister Zaria succeeded to the throne, but the kingdom Zaria soon faded from history as a great West African power.[23]

Anga
See Maham Anga

Anna
Empress of Russia (1730–1740)

She was born in 1693, the daughter of Ivan V, nominal tsar of Russia but a chronic invalid. She was the niece of Peter the Great. Her marriage to the Duke of Courland was short-lived; he died in 1710 on their wedding trip to Courland. After the death of Peter the Great, she was offered the throne by the Privy Council, which expected her to act as figurehead while it continued to govern. However, when she came to the throne in 1730, she dismissed the Council and made herself absolute ruler. Soon, however, the tedium of her office began to bore her; she found that she had no interest in governing, and she was untrained for the position. She left the government in the hands of her lover, Ernst Johann Biron, a ruthless and greedy man who brought in his clique of German friends as advisers. They exploited the country for their own self-interests while Anna held extravagant court in St. Petersburg. On the day before she died in 1740, she named her nephew Ivan as her successor and her arrogant lover Biron as regent.[24]

Anna Anachoutlou
Queen of Trebizond (1341) and (1341–1342)

Trebizond was located in what is now northeastern Turkey. Anna, the daughter of King Alexius II, who ruled from 1297 to 1330, was brought to the throne twice in 1341, first following the deposition of Irene Palaeologina. She was briefly deposed in favor of Michael, son of former King John II (1280–1284), but was restored to the throne that same year and ruled until 1342.

Anna Dalassena
Acting regent of Byzantine Empire (ca. 1081)

The mother of the Emperor Alexius I, Anna exercised great influence over him. She served as regent during his absence from Constantinople at the time of the war against Robert Guiscard.[25]

Anna Leopoldovna
Regent of Russia (1740–1741)

Born in 1718, she was a niece of Anna, empress of Russia. In 1739 she married Prince Anton Ulrich, a nephew of Charles VI, holy Roman emperor. They had a son, Ivan, born in 1740, the year Empress Anna died. Empress Anna had named the retarded two-month-old boy heir to the throne and made her lover Biron his regent. However, the unpopular Biron was arrested a few weeks later by members of his own ruling German coalition, who then named Anna Leopoldovna regent. The Germans expected to continue to play important roles in Anna's government; however, they were unpopular with the people and were unable to maintain order even among themselves. In 1741, Elizabeth I, the daughter of Peter the Great, who also aspired to the throne and was a palace favorite, took advantage of the disorder in Anna's administration to mount a palace revolution. She borrowed a guard's uniform and marched with the palace guards into the winter palace, personally woke Anna and her sleeping family, and had them imprisoned. In 1744 she exiled them to Kholmogory, where Anna died two years later in childbirth.[26]

Anna (or Anne) of Savoy
Empress, regent of Byzantine Empire (1341–1347)

She was the wife of Andronicus III, by whom she had a son, John V Palaeologus, in 1331. When Andronicus died in 1341, John V was only nine years old. A dispute broke out between Anna and John Cantacuzenus, chief minister under Andronicus and the late ruler's nearest friend. Even during Andronicus III's reign, the Grand Domestic, John Cantacuzenus, had been the real ruler. He therefore asserted his claim to the regency. John Cantacuzenus left Constantinople to battle the Serbs in Thrace, and in his absence Anna had him declared a traitor and imprisoned his supporters. For a time Anna was formally recognized as senior sovereign in Constantinople. Her likeness appears on seals and coins of the period. During her reign she made vigorous attempts toward a reunion of the churches of Rome and Constantinople, efforts even more decisive than those of her late husband, but without lasting results. John Cantacuzenus had himself declared emperor in 1341, but he held to the principle of legitimate succession, placing the names of Empress Anna and Emperor John V before those of himself and his wife Irene. At the beginning of the civil war that followed, Anna pawned the crown jewels in Venice for a loan of 30,000 ducats with which to defend her throne. The loan was never repaid. In 1345 John Cantacuzenus, giving Empress Anna the office of despot, asked the Ottoman Turks to come to his aid, even marrying his daughter Theodora to the sultan Orhan. By 1346 John was confident enough of victory to have himself crowned emperor in Andrianople. Although Empress Anna's power was now limited to Constantinople and the immediate vicinity, the ambitious empress would not give in. She negotiated with the Turks for assistance. However, instead of attacking John Cantacuzenus, the Turks invaded and plundered Bulgaria, then did the same to outlying Constantinople on the way home. Despite last-minute appeals to the *hesychasts* (a sect of mystics), Anna was forced to surrender in 1347. John was crowned co-emperor with John V in 1347, and he ruled alone for seven years until John V came of age. To assure that Anna would wield no further influence over her son, John Cantacuzenus married his daughter Helena to John V.[27]

Anna Palaeologina
Despina, regent of Eprius (1335–1340)

She was the wife of John Orsini, despot of Eprius from 1323 to 1335, and had a son, Nicephorus II. In 1335 Anna poisoned her husband and, with her son, took over the government. She immediately entered into negotiations with the Byzantine emperor, hoping that by recognizing Byzantine suzerainty she would be allowed to continue to rule unmolested. However, the emperor did not want anyone so closely tied to Eprian independence to rule Eprius, so Byzantine troops marched into Eprius and replaced Anna with an imperial governor. Anna and her son were compelled to move to Thessalonica. Much later, Nicephorus II attempted to win back his rule and undertook an extensive and fairly successful campaign in both Eprius and Thessaly, but he died in 1358 while fighting the Albanians.[28]

Anna Palaeologina-Cantacuzena
Despina, regent of Eprius (1296–ca. 1313)

She was the daughter of Princess Eulogia (Irene), sister of Byzantine Emperor Michael VIII. Anna married Nicephorus I, despot of the Greek principality of Eprius from 1271 to 1296. They had two children: Thomas of Eprius and Thamar (Tamara), who married Philip of Tarento. Anna became regent for their son Thomas when Nicephorus died in 1296. With her close ties to the Byzantine Empire, the pro-Byzantine party of Eprius gained control. In 1306 anti-Byzantine forces under the leadership of Philip of Tarento joined forces with the Catholic Albanians, seized Dyrrachium, and were intent upon overthrowing Anna, but their campaign failed. Anna ruled until Thomas reached majority, ca. 1313.[29]

Anne
Duchess, ruler of Brittany (Bretagne) (1488–1514)

She was born in 1477, the daughter of François II (1458–1488). Anne inherited the duchy of Brittany upon her father's death, whereupon a French army invaded. Various countries sent aid, but the French forces prevailed. Anne was then forced to promise to marry only with the consent of the king. But she married Maximilian of Austria without such consent, touching off a new French invasion, after which the crown annulled her marriage. In 1491 she married Charles VII, king of France. When he died in 1498, King Louis XII obtained a divorce from his wife Jeanne, and married Anne in order to keep this duchy for the crown. They had a daughter, Claude, who married King Francis I of France. Anne died in 1514.[30]

Anne
Queen of England and Scotland (1702–1714)

Anne (b. 1665), the second daughter of King James II and Anne Hyde, did not impress her father as a particularly promising offspring. For one thing, she did not embrace his Catholicism. For another, her father and indeed her public considered her particularly dull and common, partially due to the fact that she was sickly, plump, and plain—in later life, she was to bear a close resemblance to Queen Victoria who would live a century later. From Mary Queen of Scots the Stuart line had inherited the blood affliction called porphyria, which plagued Anne all her life. During her childhood, at the insistence of her Protestant uncle, King Charles II, Anne lived away from court, estranged from her father, who himself has been described as arrogant, unattractive, humorless, and boorish. She developed an abiding friendship with Sarah Jennings Churchill, who wielded huge influence over her for more than 20 years and who convinced her to favor William III of Orange over James when William arrived on England's shores to claim the throne from Anne's Catholic father. William and Mary, Anne's sister, became constitutional monarchs in 1683, and Anne was placed in line for succession to the throne. That same year, at age 18, Anne married a handsome, fair-haired, blue-eyed prince, who soon became as fat and phlegmatic and as fond of drink as she. He was Prince George of Denmark, by whom she subsequently had 17 pregnancies, most ending in miscarriage or infant death. Only one child survived, living to age 11. During the six-year reign of her sister, with whom she quarreled bitterly—primarily over Anne's devotion to Sarah Churchill—Anne continued to live in exile from court. However, following Mary's death in 1694, William welcomed her and her unpopular husband, and Sarah as well, at court. Shortly before his death, William embarked on the War of the Spanish Succession, which was his legacy to Anne. When Anne came to the throne at age 37 (1702), she suffered from obesity, gout, and premature aging brought about by her blood disorder. Too ill to walk to her coronation, she made a heavy burden for the bearers of her sedan chair. Despite her obesity, or possibly because of it, her subjects perceived her as good-natured and dubbed her "Good Queen Anne." Her husband Prince George attempted to assist

Queen Anne. The Granger Collection, New York.

tablished a receptive climate for the arts. Anne was also the last monarch to practice "touch healings" of her subjects for the lymphatic tubercular condition called scrofula. She died in 1714 leaving no heirs, a widowed and friendless old woman at age 49, the last of the Stuart line.[31]

Anne of Austria (or Anne d'Autriche)
Queen, regent of France (1643–1651),
governor of Brittany (1647–1666)

Anne was born in 1601 in Madrid, the daughter of Philip III of Spain. In 1615, at the age of 14, she became the wife of Louis XIII of France. The royal couple had two sons, the future Louis XIV and Philippe, future duc d'Orléans, but they lived apart for 23 years as a result of the meddlings of Cardinal Richelieu who, for political reasons, wished to alienate the king from his wife. In 1636 she was named governor of Paris. When the king died in 1643, Anne had his will—which deprived her of the right of sole regency—annulled, and became the queen regent for her son Louis XIV. She immediately exercised shrewd judgment by choosing as her minister Cardinal Mazarin, a wise and diplomatic manager who helped her maintain the absolute power of the monarchy that Richelieu had established for Louis XIII. Louis XIV was only five years old when his father died, and thus Anne served as regent for almost a decade, preserving a close relationship with the cardinal, her favorite (some have concluded that they were secretly married), thereby establishing on firm ground her young son's throne. In 1647 she became governor of Brittany, the second female to govern a major province. She continued to exercise influence over her son's decisions and to govern Brittany until the time of her death in 1666.[32]

Anne of England
Regent of the Dutch Republic (1751–1766)

Also called Anne of Hanover, she was the eldest daughter of King George II of Great Britain and Caroline of Ansbach. She was married to William IV of Orange-Nassau who ruled the Dutch Republic from 1748 to 1751. When he died, their son, William V, was only five years

her in her royal duties, but he was unpopular with the English people. In 1704, partly due to her friendship with Sarah but also due to John Churchill's illustrious victories in the continuing war, Anne named Sarah's husband the first duke of Marlborough. Eventually, however, Sarah became more queenly than Anne, even throwing a royal tantrum in Kensington Palace. Queen Anne dismissed her and, soon after, the duke as well. The death of her beloved George in 1708 left her with few personal allies. But her political future was bright: When the war ended in 1713, England towered as the world's greatest power with many new, far-flung acquisitions. England forged a legislative union with Scotland, forming the nucleus of the United Kingdom. In addition, Anne accepted the principle of a constitutional monarchy, a system that England maintains to this day. She was the last monarch to veto an act of Parliament, or to preside over the majority of the Cabinet meetings. Although she showed no interest in the literature, drama, and art that flourished during her reign—she felt taxed, in fact, by prolonged attempts at intellectual conversation—she es-

old. Queen Anne acted as regent until William turned 18.[33]

Anne of France
De facto regent of France (1483–1491)

She was born in 1461, the daughter of King Louis XI of France. She was more intelligent and politically astute than her brother Charles (VIII), nine years her junior, and than the man she married, Pierre de Bourbon, seigneur de Beaujeu. The couple had a daughter, Suzanne (or Susanne), who was named heir to her father's Bourbon lands. When King Louis died in 1483, Charles was singularly unfit to ascend to the throne. He was 13 years old, with modest intellectual capacities and delicate health. Anne and her husband assumed the reigns of power in an effort to surmount problems with many wealthy noblemen caused by her late father. To mollify these noblemen, she restored lands that had been confiscated under her father's rule, and she dismissed many of her father's court favorites who had been responsible, in the eyes of the noblemen, for their grievances. In 1483, by negotiations already begun before the death of Louis XI, Charles was betrothed to Margaret of Austria, duchess of Savoy. From this betrothal, he received Artois and the Franche-Comté; however, Anne had a more profitable union in mind: one that would bring the duchy of Brittany under France's dominion. In 1491 she persuaded Charles to repudiate his engagement to Margaret in favor of marriage to Anne of Brittany. After the marriage, Charles' wife and his friend Étienne de Vesc persuaded him to free himself from the influence of his sister. In addition to holding the reigns of government for seven years, Anne had been the effective overseer of her husband's Bourbon lands during the whole of their marriage. When he died in 1503, she continued to administer her daughter Suzanne's lands, knowing from her own experiences the penchant of royalty for expanding their domains. Anne died in 1522.[34]

Anne Marie Louise d'Orléans
Mademoiselle de Montpensier, ruler of Auvergne (1617)

She was the daughter of Marie de Bourbon Montpensier and Jean Baptist Gaston, duke of Orléans, who ruled from 1608 to 1617. She was the granddaughter of Henri de Bourbon, who ruled from 1602 to 1608. She was the last ruler of Auvergne, which became part of France.[35]

Anula
Queen of Sri Lanka (Ceylon) (47–42 B.C.)

She was the wife of King Darubhatika Tissa, whose death in 47 B.C. threw the country into a period of great turmoil. For short periods during that year, three people—Siva, Vatuka, and Niliya—tried briefly to rule. Eventually Queen Anula was called upon to restore order. She ruled for five years and was succeeded by her son, King Kutakanna Tissa in 42 B.C.[36]

Apumatec
Queen of North American Indian tribe (1607)

She was encountered in Virginia by Captain Newport's expedition on its first exploration inland from Jamestown, which did not proceed beyond the present site of Richmond. She was described by Gabriel Archer: "She had much copper about her neck; a crownet of copper upon her head. She had long black haire, which hanged loose downe her back to her myddle; which only part was covered with a deare's skyn, and ells all naked. She had her woemen attending on her, adorned much like herselfe (save they wanted copper) . . . Our captain presented her with guyfts liberally; whereupon shee cheered somewhat her countenance. . . ."[37]

Aquino, María Corazon (Cory)
President of the Philippines (1986–)

She was born in 1933, the daughter of José Cojuangco, the wealthiest man in Tarlac Province. She was educated at elite girls' schools in Manila, Philadelphia, and New York before attending Mount Vernon College in New York. She married Benigno S. Aquino, Jr., in 1954 and became his political helpmate. They had five children: Elena, Victoria, Aurora, Christina, and Benigno S. Aquino III. Her husband entered politics and rose to become the most popular opponent of President Ferdinand Marcos, who declared martial law in 1972 to prolong his presidency. Marcos jailed Benigno

María Corazon Aquino. Reuters/Bettmann Newsphotos.

Aquino, whom he considered his greatest threat. When Aquino was released, the family sought refuge in the United States, where they lived in exile from 1980 to 1983. In August 1983, Aquino attempted to return to the Philippines but was assassinated in the Manila airport. This assassination was the rallying point that united the opposition and forced Corazon Aquino to choose a political career. She led the dissidents calling for Marcos' resignation. In 1986 she ran for president on the Unido party ticket, and abandoning the speeches that had been prepared for her, she spoke simply of her own victimization by Marcos. She was elected president and immediately attempted to forge unity, bring about order, and commence economic reform, all the while fending off attacks by political foes. In September of 1986, she traveled to the United States seeking support for her government and for the country. Although President Reagan refused to give her an audience, she received assurance that the United States would retain its two military bases in the Philippines. Following her speech to the joint session of Congress, which Speaker Thomas P. (Tip) O'Neill, Jr., labeled ''the finest speech''

he had heard in his congressional career, Congress approved $200 million additional aid to her country. Although she has instituted an economic growth program, much of her presidency has been marked by unrest among citizens who want quicker results. On one occasion her palace troops opened fire and killed 20 demonstrators. She has weathered numerous crises, including several coup attempts, with surprising aplomb. Although untrained in politics, she is a member of the class of wealthy oligarchs who have long ruled the Philippines. She speaks English, French, Spanish, Japanese, and Tagalog, the native language. Eschewing Marcos' elaborate Malacanang Palace as too opulent in a country where wealth has too long been kept in the hands of a few, she lives in a more modest home/office nearby. She repeatedly denied Marcos permission to return to the Philippines in an effort to still opposition before it developed, buying time for her economic programs to work.[38]

Arsinde

Countess, ruler of Carcassonne (934–957)

She was the daughter of Acfred II, count of Carcassonne, which was located in what is now southwestern France. Arsinde ruled during a time when Carcassonne went its own way. It was not until the reign of Philip III the Bold (1270–1285) that walls were built (1272) and royal power firmly established in southern France. Arsinde married Arnaud de Comminges. The couple had a son, Roger, who succeeded his mother, ruling as Count Roger I in 957.[39]

Arsinoe II

Queen (first of Thrace, then of Macedonia, then of Egypt), co-ruler of Egypt
(277–270 B.C.)

She was born ca. 316 B.C., the daughter of Berenice and Ptolemy I Soter of Egypt. In 300 B.C. she married Lysimachus, king of Thrace. Thrace was located in Asia Minor, bounded by the Aegean and Black seas on the east and south, and by the Danube River on the north. Arsinoe was leaving her homeland far behind when she married the king of Thrace. But as she was not his first wife, she had little prospect of furthering the futures of her offspring. Lysimachus already had an heir to the throne, his son Agathocles. In an attempt to advance the rights of succession of her own three sons, Arsinoe accused Agathocles of treason, hoping to discredit him. An angry Lysimachus ordered his son Agathocles executed, and in the outbreak of violence that followed, which escalated into a war involving Agathocles' avenging allies in Selucia, Lysimachus was killed in battle (281 B.C.). Arsinoe took her sons to safety in Cassandrea, where her exiled half brother and new king of Macedonia, Ptolemy Ceraunus, cajoled her into marrying him, then murdered two of her sons. When Ptolemy Ceraunus died fighting the Gauls in 279, Arsinoe attempted to have her remaining son Ptolemaeus installed on the Macedonian throne, but she failed and was forced to flee to Egypt. There, in ca. 276, she married her brother, Ptolemy II, and became in every sense co-ruler. It was due largely to her diplomatic skill that Egypt won the First Syrian War (ca. 274–271 B.C.), and following it, she was deified as Philadelphus (meaning "brother-loving") and displayed on the coinage of the realm. The new queen ruled the empire and managed its wars, meanwhile gathering around her such notable men of letters as the poet Callimachus. Ptolemy reigned among the chiefs and scholars of the court, while Arsinoe, a woman of great intelligence and mature experience, is thought to have played the dominant role in the formulation of royal policy so long as she lived. Her interest in cultural pursuits led her to found the museum at Alexandra. She died in 270 B.C., but even before her death she was being worshipped as a goddess.[40]

Artemisia I
Queen, ruler of Halicarnassus and Cos
(ca. 480 B.C.)

Halicarnassus was a Greek city-state in southwestern Anatolia and Cos was an island off the coast. As a tribute-payer to Xerxes, king of Persia, Artemisia participated in his war of invasion against the Greeks in 480 B.C. She ably commanded five ships during the naval battle off the island of Salamis. Herodotus, a great admirer of her accomplishments, claimed that Xerxes, who was badly defeated, had sought Artemisia's advice. Artemisia advised him to retreat, which he did.[41]

Artemisia II
Queen, ruler of Caria (352–350 B.C., or 353–351 B.C.)

Caria was located in Asia Minor, in southwestern Anatolia. Artemisia was the daughter of King Hecatomnos of Caria, and wife and sister of King Mausolus, who succeeded him. She was, in her own right, a botanist and a medical researcher. A plant genus, a sagebrush, is named for her. Artemisia and her husband were extremely devoted. When he died in 352 or 353 B.C., Artemisia succeeded him as sole ruler. During her approximately three-year reign, the Rhodians, believing that the reign of a woman offered them an excellent opportunity to free themselves from Caria's dominion, charged the capital. Artemisia, apprised that they were coming, ordered the citizens of Halicarnassas to pretend surrender. Even as the Rhodians landed and began plundering the marketplace, the

Queen Artemisia II. The Mansell Collection.

hidden Carian fleet emerged from a man-made channel connected to a hidden harbor and seized the empty Rhodian ships. Soldiers hiding along the city walls shot down the plunderers. Then Artemisia wreathed the captured ships in laurel, signifying victory, and with her own forces aboard, sailed the Rhodian ships back to the island. Before her ruse was discovered, the Carians had entered the Rhodian harbor. The Rhodian leaders were executed and Artemisia erected two monuments in Rhodes commemorating her conquest of the island. In the capital of Halicarnassus, which is modern-day Bodrum, Turkey, she had erected for her late husband a magnificent tomb for which all subsequent tombs that are splendid edifices are named. It was called the Mausoleum of Halicarnassus, considered one of the Seven Wonders of the World. Tradition holds that she never recovered from the death of her husband and died of grief ca. 350 B.C. A statue of Artemisia in Museo Archeologico Nazionale, Naples, shows her to have been a beautiful woman with a purposeful stride and an aura of strength.[42]

Asa
Queen of Norway (mid–ninth century)

Queen Asa is known to have lived in Viking Norway in the middle of the ninth century and to have died at about age 25 or 30. In 1904 the bodies of two women were found in an elaborate burial ship in a grave in Oseberg, South Norway. The highly decorated vessel was the kind probably used by a king or chieftain, so one of the bodies was believed to be that of Queen Asa. With her was buried an older woman of about 60 or 70, possibly a bondswoman who sacrificed herself so as to serve her mistress in the afterworld.[43]

Athaliah
Ruler of Judah
(ca. 844–837 B.C. or 845–839 B.C.)

She was the daughter of Queen Jezebel and King Ahab, seventh king of the northern kingdom of Israel, according to the Old Testament. She married Jeham (or Joram or Jehoram), King of Judah. Their son, Ahaziah, became the

Athaliah. The Granger Collection, New York.

sixth king of Judah upon his father's death in 841. Athaliah served as queen mother in court, a position of honor, while her son went off to war. After a reign of only one year, Ahaziah was killed in battle by Jehu. Athaliah seized the throne and tried to put to death all her own grandsons, heirs to the throne, in order to destroy the line of David and keep the throne for herself. One of the infants, Joash, was hidden away by followers loyal to Ahaziah. Athaliah reigned tyrannically for seven years. She eliminated the Omrites from Judah and eradicated the House of David. She also introduced the worship of Baal. When Joash was of age, he came out of hiding and in the revolution that followed, Athaliah was overthrown. She was executed ca. 839 or 837 B.C.[44]

Awura Pokou (also called Aura Pokou)
Queen of the Baule tribe (ca. 1730–1750)

She ruled over one branch of the Akans' great Ashanti kingdom, which moved into the southeast part of the Ivory Coast region early in the eighteenth century. Following a dispute over leadership, in which she refused to join the Ashanti confederacy in what is now Ghana, she led her group south to the banks of the Komoe River. When she questioned her priest about the hazardous crossing of the river, he informed her that if she offered a sacrifice, all would go well for her tribe's crossing. She offered her own son as a sacrifice, calling out, "Baouli—the child is dead." To this day, her descendants are called Baoules. Queen Pokou and her tribe crossed the river and cultivated the savanna that lay on the other side. This was the beginning of the Baule (Baoule) tribe, which populates the area between the Komoe and Bandama rivers. Eventually her tribe assimilated many of the pre-existing tribes of the area to become the largest, most powerful tribe on the Ivory Coast. Although the tribe lost much of its political power during the nineteenth century, it remains the largest tribe in the Ivory Coast today.[45]

Āzarmēdukht
Sasanid queen of Persia (631–632)

The younger daughter of King Khusrau II, who ruled Persia from 590 to 628, she succeeded her sister Boran on the throne. Her reign was marred by pretenders and rival kings in various parts of the empire. She was succeeded by her nephew, Yazdgard III. Sasanid monarchs used the oriental title Shahanshah, or king of kings.

Bai
See Lakshmi Bai

Bakwa (Bazao)
See Turunku, Bakwa

Balkis
Legendary name of the Queen of Sheba.
See Makeda[1]

Balthild
Regent of Neustria (657–664)

Neustria was located in the northeastern portion of present-day France. The daughter of Anglo-Saxon royalty, Balthild, being a Christian, was kidnapped as a child and made a slave. She escaped and eventually married King Clovis II (Chlodwig), ruler of Neustria and Burgundy (639–657). When he became deranged, she ruled in his stead. He died in 664, and Balthild became regent for Clothar III (Lothair), king of Neustria (657–673), king of all Franks (656–600), until he came of age in 664. Balthild, remembering her own tragic childhood, forbade the sale of Christians as slaves. She founded a monastery and made efforts to establish communication between Christian converts in Neustria and those across the English Channel.[2]

Bandaranaike, Sirimavo Ratevatte Dias
Prime minister of Sri Lanka (1960–1965 and 1970–1977)

She was born in 1916 in Ratnapura, Balangoda, in southern Ceylon (now Sri Lanka). Although she received a Catholic education, she remained a Bhuddist. In 1940 she married Solomon West Ridgeway Dias Bandaranaike, an Oxford-educated attorney already committed to a life in politics, which Sirimavo loved as well. In 1956, as leader of the People's United Front, a coalition of four nationalist-socialist parties, he was appointed prime minister. Three years later he was assassinated by a Buddhist monk, and Sirimavo became president of the Sri Lanka Freedom Party that her husband had founded in 1952. In 1960, with no previous political experience, she became the world's first female prime minister, elected with the understanding that she would continue her husband's socialist policies. She followed a neutral policy with both communists and noncommunists. She attempted to stabilize the economy by extending the government into various businesses, but worsening economic conditions and racial and religious clashes led to her party's ouster in 1965. Sirimavo did not retire from politics, however, and in 1970 her party again regained power. During her second term as prime minister she took more radical steps to bring the country's economic and ideological difficulties under control. Much of the turmoil of her administration had to do with ethnic problems that she failed to address adequately and that continue into the 1990s. The dominant population is Sinhalese; the minority Tamil group, Indian in origin, has agitated for years for a separate state. When Sirimavo nationalized key industries, a court determined that she had gone too far. It expelled her from Parliament and stripped her of her civil rights (1977). The election of 1977 decimated her power base. The United National Party, under President Junius R. Jayewardene, was no more successful than she in solving the island's worsening problems.[3]

Beatrice
Duchess, regent of Tuscany (1052–1076)

Tuscany was located in present-day northwestern Italy. Beatrice was married to Count Boniface of Canossa, Marquess of Tuscany. They had three children, two of whom died early. Boniface was considered by Holy Roman Emperor Henry III to be his most dangerous enemy in Italy. When Boniface was assassinated in 1052, the youngest child, Matilda, age six, became heiress to the house of Attoni, founded by her grandfather Atto Adalbert. Beatrice ruled Tuscany alone until 1054, when she married Godfrey the Bearded, duke of Upper Lorraine. Godfrey stood in no better stead with Henry III than Boniface, and in 1055 Henry arrested Beatrice and Matilda and sent them to Germany, while Godfrey went into hiding. In time, Godfrey made peace with Henry, and in 1056 Beatrice and Matilda were released, Beatrice returning to Tuscany to rule over her daughter's lands. In 1069 Godfrey died. Matilda, who had meanwhile married Godfrey's son and settled in Lorraine, returned to Italy in 1070 to rule with her mother until Beatrice's death in 1076.[4]

Beatrice
Minority ruler in name only of Portugal (1383–1384)

She was the daughter of Ferdinand I (the Handsome), ruler of Portugal (1367–1383), and Leonora Telles. Henry II, king of Castile, coerced Ferdinand to accept an arranged marriage between his infant daughter and John I of Castile in order to bring Portugal under the eventual dominance of Castile. When Ferdinand died in 1383, Leonora acted briefly as Beatrice's regent, but she was forced to acknowledge John I as king of Portugal under the terms of the marriage agreement. In 1387, to strengthen a claim for the Castilian crown, John was married a second time to Phillipa of Lancaster, daughter of Duke John of Gaunt. Thus from infancy onward Beatrice remained a helpless pawn in the drive for Castilian power.[5]

Béatrix de Bourgogne
Ruler of Bourbon (1287–1310)

The daughter of Agness de Dampierre and Jean de Bourgogne, Béatrix married Robert de France, comte de Clermont, and succeeded as ruler of Bourbon when her mother died in 1287. She died in 1310.[6]

Beatrix Wilhelmina Armgard
Queen of the Netherlands (1980–)

Beatrix was born in 1938 in Baarn, the Netherlands, the oldest of four daughters of Queen Juliana and Prince Bernhard. Because of the hardships of Nazi occupation of their country during World War II, the royal family was sensitive to public sentiment against unnecessary extravagances by the monarchy, even though the royal family continued to be much loved by the Dutch people. As a result, the four daughters were reared in a democratic fashion, much more so than their counterparts in Great Britain. Beatrix attended Baarn grammar school and the State University of Leiden, where in 1961 she earned a doctor of law degree. In 1966 she made an unpopular marriage to Claus von Amsberg, a German diplomat whose participation in the Hitler Youth Movement and in the German Army during World War II did not make him a prime candidate in the eyes of the people. That he had been exonerated by an Allied court did not clear him in the opinion of the Dutch subjects. However, the union produced the first male heir to the House of Orange since the time of William III (d. 1890) when Willem-Alexandre was born in 1967, and much of the public opposition to von Amsberg disappeared. Two other sons were born in 1968 and 1969. At the age of 42, when her youngest son had reached the age of 11, Beatrix succeeded her mother upon Queen Juliana's abdication (1980), taking an oath as "king." Beatrix describes a woman's role in Holland as being much like her own: "She can do a lot but she can't decide. There's a traditional limit on all women." Described as having a "strong handshake" and as "stylish, magnetic with plumbline posture," the queen does not engage in social controversy, understanding that her main function is to be a symbol of unity and of continuity with the past. Her concern for historic preservation led her to take great care in equipping the room in her seventeenth-century palace that she uses for her sculpture studio. The royal family, which engages in a certain amount of foreign diplomacy on an informal level, has enjoyed wide popularity throughout Europe. The Netherlands has now had a woman ruler for 100 years.[7]

Bendjou
Empress, joint ruler of Mali (ca. 1345)

Bendjou was a commoner and the second wife of Emperor Suleymon, who ruled Mali from 1341 to 1360, and who had divorced his first wife, Kossi, in order to marry Bendjou. However, either because of her commoner origins or because of the popularity of Kossi, when Bendjou met the noble ladies in the audience chamber, none would pay homage to her by throwing earth on their heads. They threw it only on their hands, a sign of disrespect. Bendjou complained to the emperor, whose anger was incited against his ex-wife. The incident, a reflection of a greater struggle for political power in Mali, escalated into a minor civil war that pitted Suleymon against the relatives of his ex-wife. Suleymon and his chiefs defeated the opposition spearheaded by Kossi, and Bendjou assumed joint rule of Mali without further incident.[8]

Berengaria
Queen of Castile (1217)

The daughter of King Alfonso VIII, ruler from 1158 to 1214, Berengaria succeeded her brother Henry I, who ruled from 1214 to 1217. She was married to Alfonso IX, ruler of Leon from 1188 to 1230, and the couple had a son, Ferdinand III. Berengaria abdicated in 1217 in favor of her son, who ruled the combined thrones of Castile and Leon until 1252. Berengaria died in 1246.

Berenice
See Julia Berenice

Berenice III (or Cleopatra Berenice)
Queen of Egypt (81–80 B.C.) and co-ruler (101–88 B.C.)

She was the daughter of Ptolemy Lathyrus (Ptolemy IX), who ruled from 88 to 81 B.C., and either Cleopatra IV or Cleopatra Selene. In ca. 100 she married her father's brother, Ptolemy Alexander (Ptolemy X). In 101 Alexander reputedly murdered his own mother, Cleopatra III, and he and Berenice ruled Egypt until her father returned from Cyprus in 88 to defeat Alexander and reunite Cyprus and Egypt. Lathyrus then ruled jointly with his daughter Berenice until he died in 81 B.C., when Queen Berenice became the sole ruler of Egypt. Young Ptolemy Alexander, son of her late husband Ptolemy X, arrived upon the scene shortly afterward, intent upon marrying Berenice and thus sharing the throne. However, Berenice had no intention of dividing her power and refused his proposition; he subsequently had her assassinated (80 B.C.). The enraged populace, with whom Berenice had been very popular, killed Alexander, thus eliminating the last Ptolemaic ruler of Egypt.[9]

Berenice IV
Queen, ruler of Egypt (58–55 B.C.)

She was the eldest daughter of Ptolemy XII Auletes (called "the flute player" because of his frivolous pursuits), Macedonian king of Egypt, and Cleopatra V Tryphaena. Berenice was the older sister of the famous Cleopatra VII. When her father went to Rome in 58 B.C. to seek military aid against an Alexandrian insurrection, he left the government in the hands of Berenice and her mother. However, the mother died shortly thereafter, and Berenice was proclaimed queen of Egypt, ruling alone for three years. In 56 B.C. the Alexandrians, anxious to replace the absent Ptolemy XII Auletes, found a suitable marriage candidate for Berenice in Archelaus, a Pontic prince. However, in 55 B.C. her father returned with Syrian reinforcements, regained control of the throne, and executed Berenice and her supporters.[10]

Bhutto, Benazir
Prime minister of Pakistan (1988–1990)

She was born in 1953, the eldest child of Zulfiqar Ali Bhutto, a Berkeley- and Oxford-trained Pakistani lawyer, and his second wife Nusrat, an Iranian. Ali Bhutto became a cabinet member at the age of 32, when Benazir was only 5 years old; thus she and her younger siblings were reared in proximity to power. When she was 16 she entered Radcliffe, continuing her studies at Oxford where she was elected president of the Oxford Union. Her father became leader of the new truncated state of Pakistan in 1971. In 1979, in a U.S.-supported coup, Ali's rival, General Zia ul-Haq, sent

Benazir Bhutto. Reuters/Bettmann Newsphotos.

tanks to surround the prime minister's house. Ali was dragged away before his family's eyes and sentenced to be hanged by a court rigged by Zia. Ali immediately became a national martyr and his wife and daughter became symbols of resistance to Zia's military dictatorship. They were imprisoned and mistreated until their health failed, and in 1983 Benazir received permission to be sent abroad for medical treatment. In 1984 Indira Gandhi personally intervened in behalf of Nusrat, believed to be suffering from cancer. The family was reunited in London, where Benazir began to organize her supporters. Zia lifted martial law in 1985 and Benazir returned the next year to a tumultuous welcome. However, she was promptly imprisoned and several of her supporters were shot. But Zia's popularity was waning: his generals had grown wealthy from heroin money, and the whole country was weakened by heroin. Benazir was released one month later, when Zia realized that public sentiment was in her favor. That year she consented to an arranged marriage with Asif Zardari who came from a wealthy landed family like her own. In 1988, Benazir was several months pregnant when the plane upon which Zia and most of his high command were traveling exploded and crashed. Her People's Party won the election that followed despite the discriminatory practices against women and the poor that prevented them from voting. Benazir was sworn in as prime minister of Pakistan, the world's second Moslem woman ruler, and her mother, Nusrat, became a member of the Parliament. Benazir faced enormous problems of a bankrupt economy, a heroin mafia, 1.35 million heroin addicts, and thousands of Afghan refugees. Of her political struggles she said, "You can never survive on your fears. Only on your hopes." On August 6, 1990, she was ousted by her old rival, Mian Nawaz Sharif.[11]

Bianca
Queen, vicar of Sicily (1410–1412)

She was the wife of Martin I, king of Aragon from 1395 to 1410. On the death of John I, who ruled Sicily from 1387 to 1395, Martin I, ruler of Aragon (1395–1410) and regent of Sicily, left his only son, also named Martin, as king, or viceroy, of Sicily. The latter, then also called Martin I, died in 1409, willing the kingdom to his father just like any other item of personal property. The kingdom went to King Martin I of Aragon, who then also became known as Martin II, king of Sicily. The following year he too died, and as neither Martin had left an heir, the vacant throne of Sicily fell to Martin II's widow Bianca. Count Cabrera of Modica, Grand Justiciar, defied Queen Bianca, hoping to secure the throne for himself. In addition, in each region powerful feudal barons reasserted their rights and withheld revenues, so Queen Bianca had to resort to private borrowing to keep the kingdom running. Even the citizens of Messina, who supported her rule, took advantage of the situation by occupying the royal castles at Syracuse and Catania. A committee was appointed to select a candidate for king. Out of a list of six, the committee chose Ferdinand, king of Castile, who in 1412 proclaimed himself king of Sicily before the citizens of Sicily had even been consulted.[12]

Bianca Maria
Duchess, regent of Milan (1466–1468)

She was the illegitimate and only child of Duke Filippo Maria Visconti of Milan and Maria of Savoy. In 1433 she became betrothed to Francesco Sforza, whom she married in 1441. The couple had a son, Galeazzo Maril Aforza, born in 1444. When her father died in 1447, Bianca thought she was the legal heir of Milan, but instead her father had named Alfonso of Aragon, king of Naples, as his successor. Francesco battled Naples, Venice, Montferrat, and Savoy for the right to rule Milan in his wife's name. In 1450 he achieved that right and ruled until his death in 1466. Bianca ruled with her son for the first two years of his rule, but following his marriage in 1468 to Bona of Savoy, she retired and became a patron of the arts.[13]

Blanca, Doña
Queen of Navarre (1425–1441)

In the Middle Ages, from 1134 to 1458, Navarre was an independent kingdom in present-day northern Spain. In ca. 1420 Blanca married Juan II of Portugal of the house of Aragon. They had a son, Carlos de Viana, and two daughters, Leonore (Eleanor of Navarre) and Blanche of Aragon. In 1425 Blanca succeeded her father, Capetian King Carlos III the Noble (who ruled from 1387 to 1425) as queen of Navarre. When she died in 1441 she was succeeded by her son Don Carlos (d. 1461) and then by her daughter Leonore.[14]

Blanche of Castile
Queen, regent of France (1226–1236 and 1248–1252)

Blanche was born in 1188 in Palencia, Spain, to Alfonso VIII of Castile and Eleanor, daughter of Henry II of England. In 1199, when Blanche was only 11 years old, her grandmother, Eleanor of Aquitaine, arranged for her marriage to the future Louis VIII of France; in fact, the elderly Eleanor traveled from England to Spain to deliver Blanche to France herself, a gesture designed to emphasize the importance of the union for peace with both Spain and England. In 1214 Blanche and Louis had a son who would eventually become Louis IX. In 1216 when her uncle John of England died, Blanche tried to seize the English throne. Louis stormed England on her behalf but was defeated, and John's son was crowned Henry III. In 1223 Louis VIII succeeded to the throne of France, but he died three years later. Blanche then became regent of France and guardian for their son, Louis IX, who was 12 years old. She proved to be a strong and able ruler. To quell rebellious nobles, Blanche rode into battle at the head of her own troops. When the nobles tried to abduct her son, she expelled them and replaced them with commoners. It was Blanche who was responsible for the Treaty of Paris, which ushered in an era of peace and prosperity. When her son reached 21, Blanche was relieved of the regency, but she remained a large influence on his life and upon affairs of state. When Louis and his wife Margaret determined to embark on a crusade in 1248, Blanche, whose ability to rule had been proved during her son's minority, was once again made regent of France. There were foreign problems to solve: she had to persuade the English to keep the

Blanche of Castile. The Granger Collection, New York.

peace as well as maintain a delicate balance of relations with Holy Roman Emperor Frederick. Louis was captured by the Turks in 1250 and most of his troops were shot. He was ransomed and sent home, but Blanche died in 1252 while her son was still out of the country.[15]

Bona of Savoy
Duchess, regent of Milan (1476–1479)

Bona was the wife of Galeazzo Maria Sforza, ruler of Milan from 1466 to 1476. They had a son, Gian Galeazzo. After her husband was assassinated in 1476, Bona served as regent, governing for her son. In 1478 she supported Florence against Naples after the Pazzi family conspiracy, an unsuccessful attempt to overthrow the Medici rulers of Florence. The Duchy of Milan was usurped in 1479 by Bona's brother-in-law, Ludovico il Moro.[16]

Bonaparte
See Elisa Bonaparte

Bōrān
Sasanid queen of Persia (630–631)

Boran was the daughter of King Khusrau II the Victorious, ruler of Persia from 590 to 628. During two chaotic years following his death,

two of her brothers, Kavad II and Ardashir III, and a usurper, Shahrbaraz, each held the throne briefly. Bōrān was then placed on the throne, but the following year her sister, Āzarmēdukht, succeeded her.

Boraqchin
Khatum, regent of the Mongolian khanate of Kipchak (1255–1257)

She was the wife of Batu, khan of Kipchak from 1227. When he died in 1255, his son and heir Sartaq had gone to pay court to Grand Khan Mongka, his father's friend. But before Sartaq could return home and be crowned, he died. Mongka nominated a young prince, Ulaqchi, either Sartaq's younger brother or his son, to succeed to the throne of Kipchak, and he made the widow Boraqchin regent. She served until Ulaqchi died in 1257.[17]

Boudicca (or Boadicea)
Queen of the Iceni (ca. A.D. 60)

Born ca. A.D. 26 of a royal family, Boudicca was married to King Prasutagus, who ruled the

Queen Boudicca. The Granger Collection, New York.

Iceni in what is now Norfolk, England, by special arrangement under Roman suzerainty. Tall with a commanding presence, tawny-haired and possessing what was described as a "harsh voice," she had produced two daughters but no male heirs when King Prasutagus died. According to the terms of his will, he left his holdings to his daughters and to Nero, Emperor of Rome, believing that he could count on the crown's protection of his family's holdings. However, the Romans immediately seized his kingdom, ousted his family, plundered his chief tribesmen, and installed Suetonius Paulinus as provisional governor. Boudicca was publicly flogged and she watched her daughters, legendarily named Voada and Voadicia, being raped by the legionnaires. She immediately began organizing opposition and, while Paulinus was away, she initiated a determined revolt throughout East Anglia. During her brief reign of terror, her followers managed to sack Camulodunum (Colchester), Verulamium, Londinium (London), and various military installations, and reportedly took the lives of 70,000 Romans and Roman sympathizers. She left the Roman Ninth Legion in shambles. However, her victory was short-lived, for Paulinus retaliated with fresh troops and met the Britons somewhere near Fenny Stratford on Watling. After a bloody standoff, the exhausted Britons were cut down and Roman rule was restored. Boudicca, unwilling to live under Roman rule and certain, at any rate, that she would be executed, poisoned herself ca. A.D. 60.[18]

Brigantia (or Brigit)
Legendary queen of the Brigantes (A.D. 51)

Brigantia is mentioned in inscriptions both in Britain and in Gaul. According to Cormac, she was the daughter of the Dagda (or lord of diverse talents, or good-at-everything god). The patron of poets, she was called *banfile*, meaning "female poet." She is believed to be Christianized as St. Brigid.[19]

Brunhilde (or Brunichildis)
Queen regent for Austrasia and Burgundy (575–581 and 595–613)

She was born ca. 550, the daughter of the Visigothic king, Athanagild, and Goiswinth.

She was the sister of Galswintha, who became the second wife of the Merovingian king Chilperic I, ruler of the area now known as Belgium. Brunhilde married Chilperic's half-brother, Sigebert I, king of the eastern kingdom of Austrasia from 561 to 575. Between them, the two brothers and their two sister wives controlled the whole Frankish world. However, when Galswintha was murdered at the instigation of Chilperic to please his mistress Fredegund, Brunhilde vowed revenge, and thus began a feud that lasted and escalated for 40 years amid plots and counterplots resulting in several murders. Sigebert was murdered by Fredegund's emissaries in 575, and Brunhilde's son Chilperic II was made king. During his minority, Brunhilde was made regent, and she soon married Merovech, Sigebert's nephew. In 581, Chilperic II was adopted by his uncle Chilperic I and Brunhilde was free to devote herself to venting her revenge upon Fredegund. When her son died in 595, Brunhilde was again made regent for her two grandsons: Theudoric

Brunhilde. The Granger Collection, New York.

II, king of Burgundy, and Theudebert II, king of Austrasia. She wielded tremendous power, and her only rival was Fredegund, who by that time was ruling Neustria for her young son, Clotaire II. On Fredegund's death in 598, Brunhilde seized Neustria as well, and so united the entire Merovingian world under her dominion. Her grandson Theudebert incurred her wrath in 612 and she persuaded his brother Theudoric to overthrow him. In 613, the Austrasian nobles who opposed her and favored Theudebert united under Clotaire II and were able to overthrow her government. Brunhilde was sentenced to death by being dragged behind a wild horse. Brunhilde probably inspired some of the ancient German heroic myths concerning a beautiful amazonian queen.[20]

Bruntlandt, Gro Harlem
Prime minister of Norway (1981 and 1986–)

Born in 1939, the daughter of Oslo of Grundmund and Inga Harlem, Gro Harlem Bruntlandt received an M.D. degree from Harvard University and became a practicing physician by profession and a cross-country skier by avocation. In 1960 she married Arne Olav Bruntlandt with whom she had three sons and one daughter. From 1965 to 1970 she served as consultant to the Ministry of Health and Social Affairs in Norway, serving in various other governmental capacities until 1974, when she became minister of environment, a post she held until 1979. In 1981 she became leader of the Labour Parliament Group. Her party was in power for nine months in 1981, during which time she served her first term as prime minister. She was returned to the post in 1986. She is a strong proponent of a more active role for women in politics, and women outnumber men in her cabinet. She was quoted in the *China Daily* on the subject of women in politics and in the work force in general: "Men and women should have equal opportunity to fulfill their roles in society as well as at home . . . Husbands will have to increase their domestic participation."[21]

Cahina
See Kahina

Candace
Traditional name of several queens of
Ethiopia and Kush. *See* Amanishakhete,
whom Romans called "Candace."[1]

Cartimandua
Queen, ruler of Brigantia (A.D. 41–60)

The Brigantes were a large northern British
tribe who lived during the time of the Roman
invasion of Britain. Cartimandua's consort and
sometime adversary was Venutius, who had
ambitions to rule on his own. In A.D. 43, when
the Romans invaded Britain, in a Celtic practice
known as *celsine* Cartimandua signed a treaty
placing herself under Roman protection. Her
decision was very unpopular with the Brigantes, who launched a series of revolts against
her. In A.D. 48 she was forced to call on her
Roman protectors to quell a rebellion. When
Caratacus, Welsh leader of an unsuccessful
anti-Roman rebellion, approached Queen Cartimandua seeking asylum and an alliance, the
queen, in a display of loyalty designed to buy
Roman favor, had him arrested and turned him
over to the Romans in chains. Her husband
called her a traitor and began rallying support
for her overthrow. In A.D. 57 he attempted to

seize control of the government, but the Romans again intervened on her behalf. The couple eventually reconciled and ruled jointly for a
short period. Then Queen Cartimandua ran off
with Vellocatus, the royal armor-bearer. Venutius and his troops gave chase, but again her
Roman allies came to her rescue. Eventually in
ca. A.D. 69, she abandoned the Brigantes alto-
gether, and without her tie with the Romans,
Vellocatus was powerless to prevent a takeover.
In A.D. 71, in a battle against the Roman general Venutius, Vellocatus and the Brigantes
were defeated, and Rome annexed Brigantia.[2]

Catalinda de Albret (also called Catherine de Foix)
Queen of Navarre (1481–1512)

Catalinda de Albret succeeded Francesco Febo,
who had married her mother Eleanor (Leonore),
grandaughter of John II of Aragon and Doña
Blanca of Navarre. She married Jean d'Albret
ca. 1502, and in 1503 they had a son, Henry II.
In 1512 King Ferdinand's troops succeeded in
forcing Navarre to be annexed to Aragon and
Castile, thus eliminating the throne of Navarre
entirely. Catalinda remarked to her husband at
the time, "If we had been born you Catherine
and I Don Jean, we would not have lost our
kingdom." Catalinda died in 1516 and Henry
became heir to the house of Albret claim. He

gathered French forces and in 1521 invaded Navarre, intent on freeing it. He was defeated in his attempt; however, in 1530 Charles I of Spain, of his free will, ceded portions of Navarre back to Henry.[3]

Caterina Sforza
Effective ruler of Forli and Imola
(1488–1500)

Born in 1462, the illegitimate daughter of Galeazza Maria Sforza, later duke of Milan, and his mistress. Reared by her grandmother, Bianca Vistonti-Sforza, she received an excellent education. Her father was assassinated in 1476. In 1477 Caterina was married by proxy to Girolamo Riario of the Ordelaffi family, a nephew of Pope Sextus IV. When Venetian forces attempted to occupy her husband's lands in Forli, Caterina defended them in his absence (1483). When Sextus died, Caterina, seven months pregnant, held the fortress of Sant' Angelo until the new pope could arrive to take possession. During her husband's illness, she ruled Forli for him. In 1488 her husband was killed by the Orsi family, but she made the Orsi pay dearly in public executions, mutilations, and dismemberments. While ruling on behalf of her son, she had to fight off neighbors, papal claims to the throne, and even the French. Her children were held hostage at one time, but she (again pregnant) refused to yield the castle, explaining that she could always make more babies.

Caterina took many lovers over the years. In 1489 her affair with Mario Ordelaffi so scandalized the pope that he used her conduct as an excuse to attempt to award her lands to his own son, whose conduct was no better. One of her lovers, Giacomo Feo, of whom her legitimate son was jealous, had been speared to death and mutilated by a cohort of her son's. She had the killer, his wife, and sons thrown down a well to drown (1495). Her second husband was Giovanni d'Medici (not the pope), son of Pierofrancesco d'Medici. In 1498 she had a son by Giovanni, Giovanni Della Banda Nera (John of the Black Bands), who became the greatest military leader of all the d'Medicis. In 1499, following the Treaty of Blois between France and Venice, the controversial and notorious Pope

Caterina Sforza. The Granger Collection, New York.

Alexander VI, citing a papal bull designating Caterina as a ''daughter of iniquity,'' decided that was grounds for giving her lands to his son, Cesare Borgia. Caterina did not plan to give up without a fight; Borgia was acting captain general of the papal army and was aided by a large contingent of French troops, so she was aware that her chances of holding them off and surviving were slim. She wrote her uncle, ''Should I perish, I want to perish like a man.'' Instead, she was captured in 1500 and repeatedly raped and sodomized for a year by Borgia's soldiers. She was released in 1501 and died in 1509.[4]

Catherine
Countess, ruler of Vendôme (1374–1412)

Catherine was the daughter of Count Bouchard VI and Jeanne de Castile. When her father died in 1366, her mother and her brother, Count Bouchard VII, ruled Vendôme jointly until his death in 1374. Catherine married Jean de Bourbon and bore a son, Louis I de Bourbon. She succeeded her brother and ruled until her death in 1412. Her son Louis I succeeded her.[5]

Catherine I
Empress of Russia (1725–1727)

Born Marta Skowronska, the daughter of Lithuanian peasants in ca. 1683 in Marienburg (now Malbork), Poland, Catherine was orphaned when she was three years old and subsequently reared by a Lutheran minister who later made her his servant—an inauspicious beginning for a future empress. Her chief attribute was her beauty, and that, plus a misfortune of war, changed her fortunes. However, her more durable attributes were her intelligence, her diplomacy, and her ambition, which would prove more valuable as she rose to prominence. During the Great Northern War, Russian troops swept through Marienburg, and Marta was taken prisoner by Marshal Boris Sheremetev, who made her his mistress. When he tired of her, she was handed over to a close advisor to Peter I, Prince Aleksandr Menshikov. Peter had put aside his wife Eudoxia, banishing her to a nunnery, and it was not long before he took notice of Marta. She became his mistress in 1702 and the following year bore a son. The tzar set about making his heir more palatable to the court by having Marta received into the Orthodox Church and rechristened Catherine Alekseyevna. For the next nine years Catherine was Peter's companion, bearing many children, only two of whom, Elizabeth and Anna, survived past infancy. Peter, already having a legitimate heir in Alexis, his son by Eudoxia, and having no sons by Catherine, felt no need to marry her. In addition, his first wife still loomed in the background, having taken vows and then rescinded them. However, in 1712, after pressure from the outside, Peter and Catherine were married. In 1718 Alexis was implicated in a conspiracy against the crown, and Peter had him condemned to death, possibly by torturing. When Peter was well past 50, he consented to allow Catherine to be crowned empress consort of Russia (1724).

When he died nine months later without naming an heir, Menshikov and his other advisors, whose cases Catherine had often supported before Peter, now backed her candidacy. She was declared empress by the Senate and the Holy Synod, which had controlled the government during her husband's reign. She soon began to transfer control into a new governing body of her own design, the Supreme Privy Council, which effectively robbed the Synod of

its power. During her reign Menshikov, her former lover, was the most influential member of the government. Shortly before her death, urged by her advisors, she named Peter's 12-year-old grandson, Pyotr (Peter) Alekseyevich, as heir to the throne and sanctioned his marriage to Menshikov's daughter. She died in 1727 in St. Petersburg. Her daughter Elizabeth would later become empress and Anna's son, Peter III, would later become tzar.[6]

Catherine Cornaro
Regent ruler of Jerusalem (on Cyprus)
(1473–1489)

Catherine was a Venetian noblewoman married to James II, bastard of the house of Lusignon, who ruled Cyprus from 1460 to 1473, and who had also become archbishop of Nicosia. When Jerusalem's ruling Lusignon family was driven from the mainland in 1291, it had retreated to Cyprus, but still claimed to be rulers of the kingdom of Jerusalem. Catherine and James had a son, James III, who was too young to rule when his father died in 1473. Catherine and her son remained in Venice, from whence she ruled for her son, who died only a year later. She continued to rule in the queen's name from Venice until 1489 when, partly by gift and partly by extortion, she deeded Cyprus to Venice and abdicated. Cyprus remained a Venetian possession until 1570.[7]

Catherine de Foix
See Catalinda de Albret

Catherine de Médicis
Regent of France (1552, 1560–1563, and 1574)

Born in 1519, the daughter of Lorenzo de' Medici, duke of Urbino, and Madelaine de la Tour d'Auvergne, a Bourbon princess, Catherine de Médicis was the great-granddaughter of Lorenzo II Magnifico, one of the greatest Italian leaders of all time. She was also the niece of Pope Clement VII. Her parents died when she was very young, and Catherine was reared by nuns in Florence and Rome, who provided her with an excellent education. At the age of 14, in 1533, she married Henry, duke d'Orléans in a prearranged marriage. Catherine had no children until she was 24, and Henry took a mistress, Diane de Poitiers, who had a great influence on him and his affairs for the rest of his life. Catherine remained in the background from that time onward until his death and only made her influence felt on the occasion of his absence when she received her first appointment as regent. In 1543, Catherine gave birth to a son who later became Francis II. She bore nine or ten children in all, seven of whom lived. Three of her sons became kings of France, and two of her daughters became queens of Spain. In 1547 Henry became King Henry II, ruler of France, and in 1552 he went off to continue his father's war against the Holy Roman Emperor Charles V, and Catherine was appointed regent. In 1559 Henry was killed by the splinter of a broken lance while jousting. Francis II came to the throne, but ruled less than two years. He was succeeded by his brother, Charles IX, a boy of ten, in 1560. Catherine, a devout Catholic, became regent of France, to the despair of the Protestant Huguenots. Her greatest problem was the animosity between Catholics and Protestants, which her Edict of Toleration aimed at alleviating. In 1562 the first of the Wars of Religion erupted in France. Catherine presided over three civil wars in a decade. Charles was declared of age when he reached 13, but he remained under her domination for the rest of his life. She tried playing off the parties of the Protestant Condes against the Catholic Guises, entering into a plot with the Guises to rid the country completely of the Huguenots. She is credited with inducing Charles to order the Massacre of St. Bartholomew's Day in 1572 in which nearly all of the leading Huguenots in Paris were killed. All of Europe was scandalized by the bloodthirsty loss of life. Charles himself was guilt-ridden over the ghastly massacre and died within two years, the victim of tuberculosis. In 1572 Catherine proposed her third and favorite son, Henry, for the throne of Poland, and in 1573 he was crowned. After Charles' death in 1574, Catherine again assumed the regency for three months until Henry could be induced to return and be crowned Henry III. Henry was easily persuaded; he abandoned Poland at once. Catherine did not try to dominate her favorite

Catherine de Médicis. The Granger Collection, New York.

son, who was considered a fop and a disgrace by the French people. She remained close and did his bidding, including making arduous diplomatic journeys on his behalf even in her later years. In 1589 he died as a result of a stab wound. Catherine died the same year at the age of 70.[8]

Catherine of Aragon
Regent of England (1512–1514)

Catherine was born in 1485, the second daughter of King Ferdinand II of Aragon and Queen Isabella of Castile. She received an excellent education, particularly for a woman of her day, and was called a "miracle of learning." In 1501 she married Arthur, oldest son of King Henry VII of England, but he died a year later. In 1509 she became the first wife of Arthur's brother, Henry VIII. Unlike many royal couples of arranged marriages, the two appeared devoted on the many occasions when they entertained lavishly, and all might have gone well if

Catherine of Aragon. The Detroit Institute of Arts.

Catherine had produced a male heir. During the next nine years she bore six children, but all died except Mary, who later became queen of England (1553–1558). Meanwhile, in 1512 Henry joined his father-in-law in a war against France, and Catherine served as regent in his absence. By 1527, since Catherine had produced no male heir, Henry appealed to Rome for an annulment on the grounds that she was his brother's widow. Catherine countered with an appeal, arguing that her first marriage had never been consummated. The pope delayed making a decision for years. In 1531 Henry separated from his wife and two years later—after his marriage to Anne Boleyn—he had his own archbishop of Canterbury annul his first marriage. Parliament then passed the Act of Supremacy making the king, not the pope, the head of the Church of England.[9]

Catherine of Braganza
Regent of Portugal (1704–1705)

Catherine of Braganza was the daughter of King John IV and Luisa Maria de Guzmán, who married her in 1662 to King Charles II of England.

In the next two decades Catherine was frequently pregnant. She had a number of miscarriages and produced no heir, although Charles had 13 illegitimate offspring by a parade of mistresses. Catherine eventually returned to Portugal, ashamed of her own inadequacy and unable to tolerate Charles' philandering. When he lay dying in 1685, he asked for his wife, but she sent a message asking that her absence be excused and "to beg his pardon if she had offended him all her life." He answered, "Alas, poor woman! She asks my pardon? I beg hers with all my heart; take her back that answer." Back in Portugal, Catherine made herself useful to the court: in 1704, while her brother was fighting in the War of Spanish Succession, she acted as regent on domestic matters.[10]

Catherine of Valois
Titular Byzantine empress (1313–1346), sole ruler (from 1331)

She was the daughter of Emperor Charles of Valois and Catherine of Courtenay. As a child, in 1313, she was given in marriage to Philip of Tarentum (or Tarento). They became co-rulers

Catherine of Braganza. The Granger Collection, New York.

upon Charles' death in 1313, and Catherine gave birth to three sons. Philip died in 1331 and Catherine ruled alone. In 1337, she also became ruler of the principality of Antioch. At her instigation, the governor of Dyrrachium stirred up a revolt in favor of the deposed despot Nicrophoros. Upon her death in 1346, her second son, Robert II, succeeded her.[11]

Catherine the Great
Empress of Russia (1762–1796)

Born Princess Sophia Augusta Frederica in 1729 in Stettin, Anhalt-Zerbst, a small kingdom in Prussia, Catherine was the daughter of Prince Karl Augustus and Joanna Elizabeth—an indifferent mother who, being vain and envious of the bond between father and daughter, convinced Sophia that she was far homelier than she actually was. A smart, astute, and energetic girl, Sophia concentrated on other interests besides attracting suitors. Elizabeth I of Russia, looking for a suitable mate for her scrawny, pocked 15-year-old nephew/heir Peter, chose Sophia when she was only 14 and not the beauty she was later to become. In the winter of 1743, Sophia, ill-prepared to become a tzarina by education or possessions, which consisted of three shabby dresses in a half-filled trunk, but possessed of intelligence, self-discipline, and ambition, traveled secretly with her mother to meet her future husband. At the Russian border, the party was met with a welcoming escort that paraded all the way to Moscow with much fanfare. In the beautiful Elizabeth, Sophia found the kindness her own mother had never shown; the young girl idolized the empress and from the very first tried to emulate her. She converted to Russian Orthodox and took the name of Catherine. She threw herself enthusiastically into preparing for her role, studying and mastering Russian, a language her future husband never bothered to learn.

The couple was married a year later and Elizabeth personally escorted them to the marriage chamber and dressed the bride for bed. But the groom did not respond to the challenge, then or for years to come; desultory and immature, he spent much of his time playing with toy soldiers. Eight years later, Catherine had become a tall

and slender beauty but was still an untouched maiden. Elizabeth, convinced that Peter was impotent, arranged for a clandestine lover for Catherine. However, once she had become pregnant and delivered a son, Catherine was ignored, and for years was allowed to see her child only by appointment. At the age of 30, she took a lover, Gregory Orlov, a handsome war hero five years her junior and an officer in the imperial guard. Eventually she bore a child by him.

Upon Elizabeth's death, Peter, who refused to observe a period of mourning, began a disastrous reign of six months, during which he ended the war against his beloved Prussia and forced France and Austria to do likewise, restoring to Frederick the Great the lands he had lost. Still obsessed by his toy soldiers, he dressed his guards in Prussian-like uniforms. During Orthodox church services he would stick out his tongue at the priests. He then decided to have Catherine arrested, and to divorce her so that he could marry his mistress, Elizabeth Woronotsov.

Catherine, near to term with Orlov's child, delivered the baby in secret while a servant distracted Peter, who loved fires, by setting fire to his own cottage. Word spread of Peter's intentions, so Orlov spirited her away to an army barracks, where Catherine begged for protection. The soldiers rushed to kiss her hands, calling her savior. She was sworn in as empress on the spot. Peter was arrested and killed by a brother of Orlov.

Catherine II assembled more than 500 leaders and scholars, gave them each extracts from Montesquieu's *The Spirit of Laws,* and charged them with reform of the government. However, she later disbanded the commission and actually increased her own power. Her action was probably the direct cause of the 1917 revolution, although she was to become more lenient in the later years of her reign. Under her rule Russia became a world power. As a result of two wars with Turkey, Russia gained the Crimea and an outlet to the Black Sea. Its image as a barbaric state further receded as she established the Russian Academy and encouraged the arts, belatedly bringing the Renaissance to Russia. She became the protectoress of the philosopher

Catherine the Great. The Granger Collection, New York.

Diderot—chief editor of the *Encyclopédie,* the most important publishing enterprise of the century. She had Voltaire to visit in Russia; he had, in fact, advised her to take up arms and drive the Turks from Europe.

During the time of the Turkish wars, Catherine took a Crimean general, Gregory Potemkin, as lover. Well into old age, she took yet another lover, Platon Zubov, who was 40 years younger than she. She ruled for 34 years. Her son Paul I, who should have been Peter's successor, did not come to the throne until he was 44 years old and ruled only five years. The other rightful heir, Ivan VI, who held the crown briefly as an infant before Elizabeth's rule, was imprisoned, never knowing his real identity. Catherine gave orders that if he became ill, he was not to be given medical treatment. He was eventually stabbed by a jailor during an escape attempt. She died in 1796 of a stroke at the age of 67. Among her papers was found her credo: "Be gentle, humane, accessible, compassionate and liberal-minded. Do not let your grandeur prevent you from being condescending with kindness toward the small and putting yourself in their place. . . . Behave so that the kind love you, the evil fear you, and all respect you."[12]

Chamorro, Violeta Barrios de
Elected president of Nicaragua (1990–)

Born Violeta Barrios in 1929 in Rivas, Nicaragua, the daughter of a wealthy cattle baron and his wife, Violeta received her education in women's colleges in Texas and Virginia. At the age of 20 she married Pedro Juaquín Chamorro Cardenal, who became editor of the family newspaper *La Prensa* in 1952. His crusades against the Somoza regime resulted in his imprisonment in 1956. After he was exiled to a remote village, he escaped to Costa Rica, where Violeta joined him and where they lived for several years.

In 1978, while his wife was in Miami, he was assassinated. The following year Violeta Chamorro became one of five members of a revolutionary junta that brought Sandinista Daniel Ortega Saavedra into power. Two of her four children, Claudia and Carlos Fernando, took an active part in the revolution. But after nine months, Violeta Chamorro left the government, claiming that what had promised to be a pluralistic democratic government had instead become a Marxist Communist government. Part of her husband's family broke away from *La Prensa* to form a progovernment newspaper, *El Nuevo Diario,* and Mrs. Chamorro assumed the leadership of *La Prensa,* which became the focus of opposition to the Sandinista government. Two of her children, Pedro Juaquín and Cristina, followed her, while the other two remained in the Sandinista camp.

In 1990 a 14-party coalition chose Violeta Chamorro to be its candidate in a democratic election for president of Nicaragua. On February 25, 1990, she became the first woman to be elected president of a nation in the western hemisphere.

Charles, Mary Eugenia
Prime minister of Dominica (1980–)

The granddaughter of former slaves, the daughter of John Baptiste and Josephine Delauney Charles was born in 1919 in Pointe Michel,

Dominica. Dominica, an island in the Caribbean, was a British possession at that time. Her father, who lived to be 107 years old, was founder of the Penney Bank. She received a B.A. from the University of Canada and studied law at the London School of Economics and Political Science. In 1949 she returned to Dominica to become the first woman lawyer on the island. She became interested in politics in 1968 while fighting a sedition law that stifled dissent, and was appointed to the legislature in 1970 and to the house of assembly in 1975. There she became leader of the opposition. It was partly through the efforts of the Dominica Freedom Party, which she cofounded, that Dominica gained independence from Great Britain in 1978. In the election of 1980 her party gained the majority and she became prime minister. Charles instituted immediate measures of economic reform. She set about to corral the tax evaders and to put an end to governmental corruption. In 1985 she won a second five-year term and was also made minister of foreign affairs, finance, economic affairs, and defense. Her primary concern was improving the quality of life for her people. "We should give the people not luxury but a little comfort—a job, the means to build a house, assistance for agricultural pursuits," she said in an interview. "We will never be rich, but I think we can be a self-reliant nation with a little thrift and a little development." To that end Charles has sought to encourage tourism to some extent, but she has been adamant about preserving the island's ecology and national identity. Dominica has no casinos, no night clubs, no duty-free shops, and Charles has no intention of encouraging them. "We want to bring in the kind of tourists who like what we already have here. We especially are encouraging naturalists . . . We don't want hordes of tourists who expect to go to night clubs every night," she told an interviewer. She has been described as a no-nonsense leader and a pragmatist. A strict constitutionalist, her colleagues consider her a brilliant lawyer and a savvy politician "with considerable charm." Of women's rights on her island, Charles said, "In Dominica, we really live women's lib. We don't have to expound it." It was Eugenia Charles who

petitioned President Ronald Reagan's help against Cuban infiltration of Grenada, which led to the U.S. invasion of Grenada in 1983.[13]

Charlotte
Grand Duchess, ruler of Luxembourg
(1919–1964)

She was born Josephine-Charlotte, the daughter of Duke William IV and the younger sister of Maria Adelaide, whom she succeeded in 1919. Maria Adelaide had been forced to abdicate during the German occupation of Luxembourg during World War I. In December of 1918 the Chamber voted to continue the existence of the grand duchy of Luxembourg, and Charlotte became its ruler, thwarting a coalition of Liberals and Socialists that attempted to bring an end to the dynasty and unite it with Belgium. Luxembourg then joined the League of Nations. Charlotte married Prince Felix of Bourbon, and in 1921 the future Grand Duke Jean was born. In 1922 Luxembourg concluded economic union with Belgium, but it was not until 1925 that French occupation troops were finally withdrawn from the land. In 1932, an agreement was made at the Ouchy Convention for the gradual reduction of economic barriers between Belgium, Luxembourg, and the Netherlands. Luxembourg enjoyed a period of relative prosperity under Charlotte until May of 1940, when the Germans again invaded and occupied it. Charlotte and her family fled to England and then to Canada, where they remained until U.S. troops liberated their country in September of 1944. It was a more worldly Charlotte who returned to rule. In 1947 the grand duchy joined the Benelux union and the following year it officially abandoned its long-held policy of "eternal neutrality." The country joined the North Atlantic Pact in 1949 and participated in the European Economic Community. On 26 May 1964, in one of her last official duties, she joined with President Charles de Gaulle of France and President Heinrich Luebke of Germany in opening the Moselle Canal. In 1964 she abdicated in favor of her son, Grand Duke Jean, who presided over a duchy now firmly committed to cooperation with the rest of the European community.[14]

Charlotte

Queen of kingdom of Jerusalem (on Cyprus)
(1458–1487)

Charlotte was the elder daughter of John II, who ruled the remnants of the kingdom of Jerusalem, located on Cyprus, from 1432 to 1438. She married Louis of Savoy. When her father died in 1458 she ruled alone for two years and then shared the rule with her younger brother, James II. James died in 1473, and his wife Catherine Cornaro ruled from Italy, but Charlotte continued to share the rule until her death in 1487.[15]

Cheng-Chun (also called Wang Cheng-Chun)

Empress, de facto co-ruler of China
(48 B.C. to A.D. 13)

She was a member of the Wang family, which had come to dominate the 200-year-old Han Dynasty. She was married to Emperor Yuan Ti and came to the throne in 48 B.C. The couple had a son, Ch'eng Ti. When Yuan Ti died in 32 B.C., she was given the title of empress dowager, which carried much power and influence. She exercised her powers not only through her own office, but also through those of her relatives. Ch'eng Ti reigned from 32 to 7 B.C., during which time the empress dowager appointed four of her relatives as his regents. She had eight brothers or half-brothers, five of whom were appointed in succession to the equivalent of prime minister. She also bestowed titles of nobility upon a number of other relatives. She introduced changes in the state religious cults in an effort to secure blessings from various spiritual powers. Ch'eng Ti had several wives and, to please his favorite, he had his two sons by two other wives put to death. Therefore, he had no heir at the time of his own untimely death—probably murder—in 7 B.C. With her son's death, Cheng-Chun's influence waned, for Ai Ti, who succeeded him, was not of the Wang family. Against Cheng-Chun's judgment, he tried to appease other families, primarily the Ting and Fu families, by assigning them court appointments. The influence of the Wang family was thus diluted but was saved from further dilution by Ai Ti's death in 1 B.C.,

following only a five-year reign. After Ai Ti's death, the empress summoned her nephew Wang Mang to the capital. A young boy, Ping Ti, had been chosen to become emperor, and the empress dowager chose Wang Mang to serve as regent. Wang Mang was an astute politician and, when Ping died five years later—probably from poisoning—he selected, from more than 50 possible candidates, all legal heirs, a one-year-old baby so that he could be named acting emperor. Three years later he made himself emperor, declaring that heaven had mandated that he establish a new dynasty, the Hsin Dynasty. Empress Cheng-Chun died in A.D. 13, distressed to see what she believed to be the end of the Han Dynasty, but confident that the Wang family name and influence would live on.[16]

Christina

Queen of Sweden (1632–1654)

Born in 1626 in Stockholm, the daughter of King Gustavus Adolphus and Maria Eleonora of Brandenburg, Christina succeeded her father when she was only six years old, although she was not crowned until 1644. Her chief regent was Axel Oxenstierna. Witty and bright, she was particularly well schooled: Descartes, for example, taught her philosophy. Under her reign education flourished, the first newspaper was established (1645), local rule was broadened, and industry was encouraged. Over the objection of Oxenstierna, she sought an end to the Thirty Years' War and was instrumental in concluding the Peace of Westphalia in 1648. She was easily persuaded to delegate her duties and give away crown lands. In 1654 she secretly became a convert to Roman Catholicism—forbidden in Sweden—and shocked her constituents by abdicating in favor of her cousin Charles X Gustavus. She moved to Paris and immersed herself in the literate and scientific communities and became a popular patroness of the arts. In such a stimulating atmosphere, she began taking a belated interest in affairs of state. She made vain attempts to obtain the crowns of both Naples and Poland, and when her cousin Charles X died in 1660, she vainly attempted to regain the Swedish throne. But the

Queen Christina. The National Swedish Art Museums.

firmly entrenched state's ministers were set against her, primarily because of her Catholicism. She continued her associations with a brilliant entourage of friends and wrote a number of works, including her autobiography. She formed an intimate liaison with Cardinal Decio Azzolino, even naming him her heir. She died in Rome in 1689 at the age of 63. Azzolino died only two months later.[17]

Christine of France
Duchess, regent of Savoy (1638–1648)

Christine was the daughter of Henry IV, king of France from 1589 to 1610, and his second wife, Marie de' Medici. She married Victor Amadeus I of Savoy and bore three children: Francis Hyacinth; Henrietta, who married Ferdinand of Bavaria; and Charles Emmanuel II. Savoy was an independent state whose rulers also governed Piedmont. Victor Amadeus I ruled the two from 1630 to 1637. Following his death in 1637, their son Francis acceded to the throne, but civil war broke out. At the end of one year, Christine's younger son Charles Emmanuel came to the throne under her capable regency. Although the regency officially ended when he came of

age in 1648, in reality Christine continued to dominate him until her death in 1663.[18]

Cixi (also called Tz'u-hsi)
Empress of China (1862–1873, 1875–1889, 1898–1908)

Cixi was born in Peking in 1835 and first came to court as a minor concubine to Emperor Xian Feng, who reigned from 1851 to 1862. In 1856 she bore his only son, Tong Zhi, and contrived, with the emperor's senior consort, Tz'u-an, to become Tong's co-regent when Xian Feng died in 1862. Cixi immediately assumed the dominant role, setting the groundwork for a remarkable career that brought China under her control for 50 years. Ruthless, politically astute, and power hungry, she continued, even after her son attained his maturity, to wield her power over affairs of state. The young emperor was completely dominated by her. He led a dissolute life, which she probably encouraged so as to have a freer rein herself. He died at the age of 19, the victim of his own excesses. Cixi engineered the ascension of her four-year-old nephew Guang Xu by adopting him and naming him heir. The

Empress Cixi. The Empress seated on the Imperial Throne. Courtesy of the Freer Gallery of Art, Smithsonian Institution, Washington, DC. SC-GR 256.

tradition of ancestor worship dictated that the succeeding emperor should be of the next generation, which her nephew quite obviously was not, but this fact did not deter Cixi. The two empresses again served as regents until Tz'u-an's sudden death in 1881, possibly by poisoning. Prince Gong, the principal court official, had instituted some crucial governmental reform measures which Cixi sabotaged whenever she could. In 1884 she dismissed him in favor of Li Hongzhang, who would cooperate with her more fully. She was particularly fond of the theater and often attended accompanied by one or both of her two favorite palace eunuchs who, with her patronage, soon became wealthy and powerful in their own rights to the disgust of Prince Gong in particular. In the late 1880s, urged on by her favorite eunuch, and with the help of Li Hongzhang, Cixi appropriated funds from the navy to construct a magnificent summer palace northwest of Peking, where she briefly retired in 1889. The only new ship constructed during that time was a marble one that was placed at the edge of an ornamental lake. Thus the Chinese navy was ill-prepared when Japan struck Korea in 1894. China went to the aid of its ally but suffered a humiliating defeat. In 1895 Li Hongzhang was forced to sue for peace.

In 1898 the new young emperor Guang Xu was prevailed upon to institute the far-reaching Hundred Days of Reform. Opposition to the reform rallied around Cixi and in 1898 she came out of retirement as head of a military coup, had the emperor seized and six of the reformers put to death. She confined the emperor to his quarters for good and again assumed the regency. By 1900 the Boxer Rebellion had reached its peak, and when foreign troops invaded Peking the court was forced to flee west to Xian. Before she left, out of pure spite, Cixi arranged for one of the emperor's favorites, the Pearl Concubine, to be drowned in a well. She was forced to accept heavy peace terms before she was allowed to return to Peking two years later. Although the emperor Guang was not allowed to participate in the government, Cixi continued to rule, belatedly attempting to implement some of the proposed reforms in an attempt to salvage a crumbling dynasty. The day before she died in

1908, she issued an order for Guang's poisoning and from her deathbed named three-year-old Pu Yi as the new emperor, unable to relinquish the reigns of power even at her death.[19]

Claudine
Titular sovereign of Monaco (1457–1465)

She was born in 1451, the daughter of Catalan Grimaldi. In 1419 her grandfather John Grimaldi of the prominent Genoese family had succeeded in retaking Monaco from the French for the final time. The title of prince or princess of Monaco was not assumed by a Grimaldi until 1659. Claudine became sovereign at the age of 6, when Catalan died. While still a minor, she married Lambert Grimaldi, who became seigneur. The couple had three sons who ruled: John II (1494–1505), Lucien (1505–1523), and Augustin (1523–1532). Claudine died in 1514.

Cleopatra I
Regent of Egypt (180–176 B.C.)

She was the daughter of Antiochus III, Seleucid king of the Hellenistic Syrian Empire, which had long been at war with Egypt. She was given in marriage to Ptolemy V Epiphanes in 193 B.C., when he was 16. The marriage, a political move as a result of a peace treaty with Antiochus, also made Egypt a protectorate of Seleucia. In ca. 189 B.C. the couple had a son who was to become Ptolemy VI Philomater (meaning ''loving mother'') and later, a daughter, Cleopatra II. Philomater was still a child when his father died in 180 B.C. Cleopatra I became regent and kept an iron grip on the government until her death in 176 B.C. She also taught her son well; Ptolemy VI is mentioned in the Egyptian ruin Kom Ombo as a kind, wise, and tolerant ruler.[21]

Cleopatra II
Co-ruler of Egypt (176–130 B.C. and 118–116 B.C.), sole ruler of Upper Egypt (130–118 B.C.)

She was the daughter of Ptolemy V Epiphanes. In 176 B.C. she married her brother, Ptolemy VI Philomater, who ruled Egypt from 180 to 145 B.C. She became co-ruler and bore him a daughter, Cleopatra III, and a son, Neos Philopater.

During the war with Antiochus IV (171–168 B.C.), Philomater displayed such cowardice that thereafter the people of Alexandria insisted that the couple share the rule with their younger brother, Ptolemy VII Euergetes (Physcon). This arrangement lasted until 164 B.C., when Euergetes expelled Philomater. To settle the quarrel between the two brothers, the Roman senate restored Philomater, giving Egypt to him and his wife to rule, and Cyrene and Cyprus to Euergetes. In 145 B.C., while on a campaign in Syria, Philomater died. Their son was to share the throne with Cleopatra, but Euergetes came back to Egypt, killed Neos Philopater, and married Cleopatra II. Thus the empire was united, but only briefly. Euergetes divorced his sister and married her daughter, Cleopatra III. In 130 B.C. Cleopatra II revolted against him and became queen of parts of Upper Egypt, which she ruled alone until 118 B.C., when she and her brother signed a peace and amnesty agreement. They both died in 116 B.C.[22]

Cleopatra III
Co-ruler of Egypt (116–101 B.C.)

Cleopatra was the daughter of Cleopatra II and Ptolemy VI Philomater, who was also her mother's brother. She married her uncle, Ptolemy VII Euergetes II, and had two sons, Soter II Lathyrus and Alexander. When her father died in 116 B.C., he bequeathed the throne jointly to her and her sons. Soter II, being the elder, ruled with his mother from 116 to 110 B.C. as Ptolemy VIII. However, Cleopatra favored her younger son and doubtless encouraged him to expel his brother. Alexander, as Ptolemy IX, ruled briefly with his mother in 110 B.C., but Soter II gathered his forces and returned the next year to oust his brother. Two years later Alexander was again able to expel his brother and join Cleopatra in ruling Egypt until her death in 101 B.C.[23]

Cleopatra VII
Queen of Egypt (51–31 B.C.)

She was born in 69 B.C., the daughter of Ptolemy Auletes. Although probably born in Egypt, she was not Egyptian, but Macedonian, Persian, and Greek. When she was 14, Mark

Queen Cleopatra VII. Relief in Temple of Hathor. Courtesy of the Oriental Institute of the University of Chicago.

Antony visited Alexandria and the couple may have met then for the first time. Her father had previously been forced to flee an incensed populace in Egypt because of high taxes he had imposed, and he had only just been restored to the throne at the time of Mark Antony's visit. When her father died in 51 B.C., as the oldest surviving daughter, she became, at 18, joint ruler and bride of her younger brother Ptolemy XII, the oldest surviving son. Their father's will made Rome the guardian of Egypt, for by this time the dynasty of the Ptolemys had become weak. Plutarch described the young queen as the epitome of beauty, and she obviously also possessed great powers of persuasion. The chief ministers, Pothinus and Achillas, plotted to get rid of Cleopatra so that they could rule in her younger brother's name, and for two years they thwarted her attempts to rule, finally succeeding in expelling her to Syria. There she raised an army and set out for Egypt. Her forces met the opposition at Perlusium in 48 B.C., but before a battle could be waged Julius Caesar arrived in Alexandria, and Cleopatra decided on a new tack. She concealed herself in a rolled-up rug and had herself delivered to Caesar's headquarters so that she could petition him to intervene in her behalf. The old general—he was 56—was charmed by the young queen, and he quickly ordered that Cleopatra be restored to the throne. Pothinus, believing that he was too far away from Caesar to be challenged, instigated a rebellion against Caesar's forces that lasted three months and resulted in Pothinus' death. During the final battles, Ptolemy drowned while trying to escape down the Nile on a barge. Caesar, who had originally traveled to Egypt to do battle with his former son-in-law Pompey, whom Pothinus had already killed, had no further reason to remain in Egypt except for his infatuation with the young queen, who even bore him a son. Caesar chose another of her younger brothers, Ptolemy XIII, then ten, to be her co-ruler. Although there is not complete agreement on the activities of Cleopatra, at least one legend claims that she followed Caesar back to Rome, arriving in 46 B.C. with a large retinue that included her brother and her baby. She moved into Caesar's villa and entertained him frequently, by this account. He was assassinated in 44 B.C., and one version of the reason for that murder was that he asked the senate to pass a special law enabling him to divorce his wife so that he could marry Cleopatra, declare himself king, and make their son heir to the Roman Empire. He also placed a gold statue of her in the temple of Venus, an unpardonable sacrilege, since Cleopatra was a barbarian.

In the civil war that raged after his death, Cleopatra fled to Egypt. She did not remain neutral in that struggle, however. She sent a fleet and four legions against Brutus and Cassius, Caesar's murders, but her forces were intercepted and conscripted for Cassius. Again she raised a fleet, but it was turned back by a storm. The three victors of that war divided their spheres of influence such that Octavian stayed in Rome, Lepidus took Spain and France, while Mark Antony took the east. On arriving in Tarsus, Mark Antony immediately summoned Cleopatra to answer charges of conspiracy, since her troops had been used by Cassius. Cleopatra was prepared; she had not been idle. Before her younger brother could reach the legal ruling age of 14, she had had him poisoned and had named her son Caesarion as her co-ruler. At 28, she had gained great confidence and theatrical timing. She took her time answering Mark Antony's summons and eventually arrived, just as he was holding audience, dressed as Venus aboard a gaudily festooned boat. The crowds turned from him and rushed to the bank of the Nile where she waited, like a hostess, for him to come to her. Mark Antony did indeed come to her, and she gave him a queenly reception and proposed a great feast. By the time the revelry ended, Cleopatra had even managed to convince him to order the death of her one remaining sister, Arsinoe, so that no other threats remained to her sovereignty. The relationship between Antony and Cleopatra lasted for 12 years, although in its midst he returned to Rome and in 40 B.C., as a political move, married Octavian's sister, Octavia. He probably also married Cleopatra in 36 B.C. in order to legitimize the couple's three children.

Together the couple ruled Egypt and most of Asia Minor. Mark Antony designated her "Queen of Queens" and appointed her and Caesarion as joint rulers of Lybia, Cyprus, and Coelesyria. They parceled out other lands to their children: Alexander, the older son, was made ruler of Armenia, Media, and Parthia; while his twin sister Cleopatra was made ruler of Cyrene, and their brother Ptolemy Phoenicia was made ruler of Cilicia and Syria. Octavian then denounced Mark Antony in the Senate and in 32 B.C. declared war on Cleopatra. The couple ignored the threat and spent the winter in feasting and revelry on the island of Samos. Octavian advanced across their lands, claiming them for Rome until he met Antony's troops near Actium in Greece in 31 B.C. Although Antony had superior troops, Cleopatra persuaded him to fight a naval battle against Agrippa, Octavian's naval commander. During the battle, Cleopatra's boat sailed away, and Antony, thinking that she had fled, was so distraught that he left his command and sailed after her. His forces were defeated, so Cleopatra left for Alexandria to raise another fleet.

There Cleopatra met Octavian. She offered to abdicate in favor of Caesarion, but Octavian was not interested. He offered her favorable treatment if she would kill Antony. After yet another losing battle, Cleopatra retreated to a mausoleum she had built for her own death and sent a messenger to tell Antony that she was dead. Distraught, he stabbed himself, but he didn't die immediately. When he learned that Cleopatra was still alive, he had servants carry him to her mausoleum, where they raised him by ropes so that he could see her looking out the window. Plutarch said, ''Those who were present say that there was never a more pitiable sight than the spectacle of Antony, covered with blood, struggling in his death agonies and stretching out his hands towards Cleopatra as he swung helplessly in the air.'' She pulled him up through the window and Antony died in her arms. The year was 30 B.C.

At age 39 when Antony died, Cleopatra again tried to beguile Octavian, but she could see that he was not easily entranced by a middle-aged woman. Fearing poor treatment as a hostage in Rome, she attempted suicide, but Octavian removed all knives and weapons and threatened to harm her children when she went on a hunger strike. Legend maintains that loyal servants smuggled an asp into her mausoleum in a basket of figs. She held it to her breast until it killed her. To the Egyptians, the asp was the divine minister of the sun god. The symbolic meaning of an asp bite was that the sun god had rescued his daughter from humiliation and taken her to himself.[24]

Cleopatra of Cyrene
Ruler of Cyrene (ca. 33–31 B.C.)

She was the daughter of Mark Antony and Cleopatra VII and the twin sister of Alexander,

who ruled Armenia, Media, and Parthia. Another brother, Ptolemy Phoenicia, ruled Syria and Cilicia. Her parents gave her Cyrene to rule ca. 33 B.C., but Octavian restored the lands to Roman rule after the battles of 31 B.C. Octavia, his sister and a wife of Mark Antony's, arranged a marriage for the deposed Cleopatra with Juba, the king of Numidia, one of the most gifted rulers of his time.[25]

Cleopatra Thea
Ruler of Mesopotamia (125–120 B.C.)

She married Demetrius II Nicator who ruled the Seleucid Empire and the kingdom of Pergamum in Mesopotamia from 145 to 139 B.C., when he was captured by Mithridates by treachery. Cleopatra Thea and Demetrius had two sons, Seleucus V and Antiochus VIII Epiphanes Philomater Callinicus Grypus. She also had at least one son by Antiochus VII Euergetes Eusebes Soter Sidates, who ruled while Demetrius was held prisoner. That son was Antiochus IX Philopater Cyzicenus. In 129 B.C. Demetrius II was released and sent back to Syria to rule for four more years, but he was murdered by Alexander Zabinas, a pretender to the throne. Cleopatra and her son Seleucus V assumed the throne, but she soon had him put to death. She ruled with her second son, Antiochus III Epiphanes, until her death in 120 B.C. Three years later, her youngest son Antiochis IX, forced his brother to abdicate, and he ruled briefly. Later the two half-brothers divided the realm.[26]

Cleopatra Tryphaena
Co-ruler of Egypt (58 B.C.)

Cleopatra Tryphaena was married to Ptolemy XII Auletes (the flute player), who ruled from 80 to 58 B.C. and from 55 to 51 B.C. Ptolemy had an illegitimate claim to the throne, so he faced much opposition to his rule. When he was driven into exile in 58 B.C., Cleopatra Tryphaena and his daughter Berenice IV took turns ruling. Cleopatra died shortly after he left, and Berenice was elected queen.[27]

Constance

Holy Roman Empress, queen of Sicily
(1194–1198) and regent of Germany
(1197–1198)

She was born in 1154, the daughter of King
Roger II (of Apulia) and his third wife Beatrice
of Rethel. In 1186 she became the future holy
Roman empress by marrying the future Henry
VI, the Lion, of the house of the Hohenstaufen
(ruled from 1190 to 1197). When her nephew
William II died in 1189, Constance, as legal
heiress, claimed the throne of Sicily, but she
was opposed by Count Roger and another of her
nephews, Tancred of Lecce, son of her older
brother Roger. The Sicilian people did not want
Constance's husband, a German, for a ruler,
and neither did the papacy. Tancred grabbed the
crown briefly in 1190, and while his enemies
cried, ''Behold, an ape is crowned!'' Henry
sent troops to unseat him. Tancred took his aunt
Constance captive, but the pope induced him to
set her free. Tancred's death in 1194 cleared the
way for Constance and Henry to assume the
thrones of Sicily. Constance was installed as
governor of the regno. That same year, their
son Frederick II was born. The people of Sicily
hated the German Henry, who was a harsh
ruler. Constance, and even Pope Celestine, may
have been aware of a plot to assassinate him.
When Henry discovered the plot, he took terrible vengeance, blinding all prisoners, even German ones. His death in 1197 of a fever was
celebrated throughout the land. As regent ruler,
Constance exercised particular political skill.
She consolidated her power and secured the
protection of Pope Innocent III in preserving
her son's claim to the throne. She managed to
have her son crowned king in April 1198 before
she died in November of that same year.[28]

Constance

Queen of Sicily (1282–1302)

She was the daughter of King Manfred of Sicily, who ruled from 1258 to 1266, and his first
wife Beatrix of Savoy. She was the granddaughter of Emperor Frederick II. She married
Peter III, king of Aragon, who ruled from 1276
to 1285. Charles I of Anjou, son of Louis VIII
of France, was out to create his own Mediter-

ranean empire, and to that end he invaded
Sicily, defeating King Manfred in 1266. The
papacy awarded Charles the kingdom of Sicily.
In 1282, Constance's husband King Peter
launched a long-planned campaign to recapture
the throne in Constance's name, disguising his
trip as an African crusade. He landed at Callo in
1282, defeated Charles, placed himself and
Constance upon the throne of Sicily, and refused to do homage to the pope. The pope nat-
urally opposed their rule and endeavored to
have them deposed, and even the local nobility
was opposed to the Aragonese takeover. The
struggle to maintain their family's right to ascendancy continued even after Peter's death.
Constance acted as regent for their 11-year-old
son James until he reached 18. The couple had
four children: Alfonso III, who succeeded to the
throne of Aragon; Isabella, who married Diniz,
king of Portugal; James I, who succeeded to the
throne of Sicily under his mother's regency
and, as Jaime II, succeeded to the throne of
Aragon in 1291; and Frederick III, who also
ruled Sicily. James ruled for 10 years, then exchanged Sicily for Corsica and Sardinia. He appointed his younger brother, then 17, as regent
in 1291, when he took over Aragon from his
brother. Four years later Frederick was elected
king and eventually the pope recognized him as
such. Thus Constance's heirs were finally
firmly established as rulers of Sicily.[29]

Constance

Co-ruler of Antioch (1130–1163)

Constance was born in 1127, the daughter of
Bohemund II, ruler of Antioch (1126–1130)
and Alice of Jerusalem. When her father died,
Constance was only two years old. Instead of
waiting for King Baldwin, Alice's father, to
appoint a regent, Alice assumed the regency for
Constance at once. But rumors spread that Alice planned to immure Constance in a convent
so that she could rule, not as regent, but as
reigning sovereign. When Baldwin arrived, he
removed Alice from the regency and banished
her to Lattakieh. He placed Constance under the
guardianship of Joscelin. A year later Joscelin
died, and Alice reasserted her claim to be her
daughter's regent. Late in 1135 Alice, who had

been allowed to return to Antioch and rule the city in her daughter's name but who did not have the regency, thought of a plan to enhance her own power. She offered the hand of the 8-year-old Constance to the Byzantine emperor's younger son, Manuel. Quickly the patriarch Radulph notified King Fulk that he must find a husband for Constance. In 1136 Fulk decided on handsome 37-year-old Raymond of Poitiers, son of Duke William IX of Aquitaine. In a disguise, Raymond reached Antioch, while Constance was kidnapped and brought to the church for a quick wedding while Alice, deceived into believing Raymond was coming to ask for her hand, waited at the palace. Constance, once married, was then considered a legitimate ruler. The couple had at least three children: Bohemund III, Maria, and Philippa. Raymond died in 1149 when Constance was only 22.

The throne was Constance's by right, but it was thought, since Moslems threatened and times were treacherous, that a man was needed at the head of government. Her elder son Bohemund III was only five. King Baldwin of Jerusalem, her nearest male relative, tried to find her a husband and offered her what he considered three suitable choices. Constance was not interested in any of them. Baldwin had no choice but to return to Jerusalem and leave Constance in charge of the government. Constance then sent word to Constantinople to ask the overlord, Emperor Manuel, to find her a suitable mate. Manuel chose his middle-aged brother-in-law John Roger, but Constance, whose first husband had been dashing and handsome, sent the older man packing. Her own choice was a young knight named Reynald of Chatillon. She married him in 1153, probably before she asked permission of King Baldwin. She did not ask Emperor Manuel's permission at all. The choice was not a popular one, since it was generally believed that she had married beneath her station. Reynald, ambitious but lacking in funds, embarked on an unpopular

expedition against Cyprus, while Constance stayed at home and bore at least one child, Agnes (who later married Bela III, king of Hungary). Reynald, after a humiliating groveling in the dirt at the feet of Emperor Manuel for his brash attack on Cyprus, never gained the prestige he longed for. In 1160 he made a raid into the Euphratesian valley and was taken prisoner by Nur el-Din. He was bound and sent on camelback to Aleppo, where he remained in gaol for 16 years, for neither King Baldwin nor Emperor Manuel was in any mood to ransom him. Constance claimed the power to rule Antioch which was hers, but public opinion leaned toward her son Bohemund, age 15. King Baldwin came back to Antioch, declared Bohemund III king and appointed the patriarch Aimery as regent. Constance was immensely displeased, and the overlord, Emperor Manuel, was displeased that Baldwin had taken the decision into his own hands without consulting him. Constance appealed to Emperor Manuel to restore her, and in addition proposed her daughter Maria as wife for the widowed emperor. Baldwin, fearing a closer tie between Manuel and Antioch would diminish his own authority over Antioch, suggested Melisende of Triploi as Manuel's wife instead. Miffed by Baldwin's effrontery in appointing Constance's son as ruler and acting amid rumors of Melisende's illegitimacy, Emperor Manuel chose Constance's daughter Maria as his wife and sent his emissaries to Antioch to establish Constance as ruler.

Again, when Bohemund III reached 18, he wanted to take over the throne from his mother; but Constance believed that the throne should be hers until she died. She appealed to General Constantine Coloman for military aid to protect herself from being bodily removed from office by her son, the news of which provoked a riot in Antioch. She was exiled and died soon after, ca. 1163.[30]

Crescentii
See Marozia Crescentii

Deborah

Judge who ruled Israel (ca. 1224–1184 B.C.)

Deborah lived during a time when Israel was ruled by judges (as was Sardinia 2,500 years later), when the term implied more than simply legal advisor: judges were local and national leaders, chieftains, and battle commanders. The wife of Lapidoth (about whom nothing is known), Deborah was also a prophetess and lived in the hill country of Ephraim, on the road between Ramah and Beth-el. Possessing wisdom, she became a counselor to passersby. She was also a keeper of the tabernacle lamps, and eventually she was elevated to a judgeship to become Israel's only woman judge.

Although Athaliah is mentioned in the Bible as a ruler of Judah, Deborah is the only woman listed in the Bible who was raised to political power by the common consent of the people. Her chief concern became dealing with marauders. For 20 years the king of neighboring Canaan, Jabin, had raided the camps of Israel using iron chariots, pillaging homes and vineyards, and raping and murdering women and children. (The Canaanites are believed to have been a Celtic tribe.) Deborah sent a message to neighboring Kedesh, home of Barak, a man noted for his military skill. Jabin's army, under the command of Sisera, was said to possess 900 iron chari-

ots—a formidable force for a people to face who still fought on foot, using arrows, slings, and swords. Deborah commanded Barak to raise an army and go to meet Sisera's forces near Mount Tabor, which rises 1,000 feet above the Plain of Jezreel. But General Barak announced that unless Deborah accompanied him, he would not

Deborah. The Granger Collection, New York.

go. Deborah consented to accompany him, and they led the troops to the foot of Mount Tabor, near the Kishon River. They arrived in a cloudburst of hail, sleet, and rain that changed the Kishon into a raging torrent. Sisera's iron chariots became mired in the mud, making the charioteers easy marks for the foot soldiers. Sisera escaped and fled on foot. A woman named Jael, wife of Heber the Kenite, saw him and invited him to hide in her tent. Since the Kenites were at peace with the Canaanites, this tent seemed to offer safe refuge. However, after Sisera fell asleep, Jael drove a tent stake through his temple. When Barak arrived, searching for the retreating general, he found him dead. Without a commander, the Canaanites were defeated and retreated in disarray. To celebrate the victory, Deborah and Barak sang a duet, the ''Ode of Deborah,'' one of the most ancient pieces of writing in the Old Testament, and certainly the lengthiest: it runs through 31 verses in the fifth chapter of Judges. It was also one of the earliest military songs in history. Deborah's story and song are recorded in the fourth and fifth chapters of the book of Judges in the Old Testament.[1]

Diane of Poitiers
Duchess, de facto co-ruler of France
(1547–1559)

Diana, duchess of Valentinois, was born in 1499 and came to court as lady-in-waiting to Louise of Savoy and later to Queen Claude. She was married to Louis de Breze, comte de Maulevrier, who died in 1531. At that time, even though she was 20 years his senior, she became the mistress of the future King Henry II, who ruled France from 1547 to 1559. She so completely dominated him that he gave her many of the crown jewels and kept her prominently at court, while his wife, Catherine de Médicis, was obliged to remain in relative obscurity, serving as regent only in Henry's absence and after his death. Although Diane had absolute power over Henry's decisions, she did not usually concern herself with the larger affairs of state but focused her interests upon arts and letters, becoming a patron of both. However, it is doubtful that she refrained from expressing her preferences and dislikes of Henry's advisors, or that she refused to express an opinion when Henry unburdened himself to her. His complete enthrallment of and dependence upon her suggests that she represented far more than a lover or companion; rather, that she was the mother authority he never outgrew. Henry died accidentally in 1559, after which Diane retired to her chateaux at Anet where she died in 1566.[2]

Diane de Poitiers. The Granger Collection, New York.

Didda
Queen, regent of Kashmir (tenth century)

Having defeated the powerful Tantrins, the *damaras,* or feudal landlords, had become so powerful that they threatened several rulers. When Queen Didda assumed the regency for her son, the landlords saw an opportunity to refuse payment of tribute and to assert their independence. The era was rife with feudatories vying for power and Turks threatening the borders. In spite of much opposition, Queen Didda conducted affairs of state.[3]

Dido

Queen of Phoenicians, legendary founder of Carthage (ca. 825 or 814 B.C.)

Dido is also called Elissa in Greek mythology and is associated with Tanit, tutelary goddess of Carthage. Dido was said to be the daughter of Mutton, King of Tyre, and the sister of Pygmalion. She married Acerbas, who was killed by her brother. To escape her brother, Dido fled to northern Africa, near modern-day Tunis, where a local chief, Iarbus, sold her a piece of land upon which she founded the settlement that was to become Carthage, eventually the most important outpost of Phoenician civilization in the western hemisphere. In the sixth century it was the wealthiest city in antiquity. To keep from having to marry Iarbus, Dido stabbed herself in the presence of a host of witnesses atop her own funeral pyre, which she herself had caused to be constructed.

In its broadest sense, the word "legend" may be used as a general term as can the word "myth." Often, however, it is defined as analogous to the word "saga" and made to refer to stories inspired by actual persons and events. Virgil's version of the legend of Dido is that Dido met Aeneas when he landed in Africa, killing herself with his sword when he abandoned her. She cursed him and his descendants, swearing that they would always be enemies of Carthage. Ovid tells the story of Dido's sister Anna who came to Italy after Dido's death and many other misfortunes. There she was welcomed by Aeneas, but his wife, Lavinia, was jealous. Warned of Lavinia's jealousy by Dido's ghost, Anna left and disappeared in the Numicus River. Morford and Lenordon suggest this story may have some validity.[4]

Drahomira (or Dragomir)

Queen, regent of Bohemia (926–928)

Born Drahomira von Stoder, Drahomira married Duke Rastislav (Vradislav) I, ruler of Bohemia from 912 to 926. (Rastislav's parents, Borivoj and Ludmila, were the first Czech rulers to adopt Christianity.) Drahomira and Rastislav had two sons, Wenceslas (b. 908) and Boleslav the Cruel. Ludmila took it upon herself to educate Wenceslas, as heir to the throne, in the ways of Christianity, while Drahomira, a pagan, saw to Boleslav's upbringing. When Rastislav died in 926, Wenceslas was only 14. His Christian grandmother became his regent, to the consternation of anti-Christian factions throughout the land. Drahomira, an ambitious and conniving woman, is said to have been behind the plot whereby anti-Christian agents broke into Tetin Castle and strangled Ludmila. Drahomira then assumed the regency herself. Wenceslas remained a Christian and Boleslav a heathen. Civil strife between Christians and non-Christians characterized Drahomira's regime, and her intrigues at court were so flagrant that Wenceslas chose to assume the reins of government in 930 when he was barely 18. Wenceslas was a wise and beloved ruler who made the mistake of yielding to Henry the Fowler when the Germans threatened to invade, an action that further enraged the anti-Christian faction. In ca. 932 he was murdered by his brother at the door of the church. King Wenceslas became Bohemia's patron saint, the last thing that Queen Drahomira would have wanted. The Christmas carol, "Good King Wenceslas," refers to his deeds. After Wenceslas' murder Boleslav ascended to the throne as Boleslav I, and Bohemia was incorporated into the Byzantine Empire under its own dynasty. Boleslav died in 967. (Other sources give Drahomira's regency as 921 to 924 or 925, and Wenceslas' death as 929.[5])

Durgavati (or Durgawati)

Rani, queen of Gondwana (ca. 1545–1564)

Located outside the southern boundary of the Indian Mughal Empire at the time, Gondwana (also called Garha-Kalanga) had been ruled by independent and tributary chiefs. Fed by the Mahandi River, Gondwana lay on the east-central side of India north of the Deccan. The Gonds were a group of Dravidian tribes, aboriginal (pre-Aryan) people of India. To this day the Raj Gonds still remain outside the Hindu caste system, neither acknowledging the superiority of Brahmins nor being bound by

Hindu rules. Queen Durgavati was a member of the Gond Chandels, the remnants of which are now in Bundelkhand in north-central India. She was the daughter of Kirat Rai, chandella king of Mahoba and Kalanjar, who was king when Sher Shah besieged the fort in 1545. She married Raja Dalpat Sa Garha Mandala of Gondwana, ca. 1545, but was soon left a widow to rule the kingdom on behalf of her infant son, Bir Narayan. With magnificent courage she maintained its sovereignty for the better part of two decades in the face of repeated threats of both Baj Bahador of Malwa and the Afghans of Bengal. Historians have termed her one of the most able and effective female leaders in Indian history. In 1564, intent upon enlarging his empire, the Moghul Akbar sent General Asaf Khan with an army of 50,000 men to make an unprovoked invasion of Gondwana. Queen Durgavati and her son, now about 18, met the Moghul army with a seasoned force of their own in a bloody two-day battle at Narhi. On the second day, her son was wounded and had to be escorted to safety by a large contingent of the Rani's troops. Withdrawal of the escort so weakened her army that it was quickly overpowered. Durgavati, wounded by two arrows, stabbed herself to death to escape the disgrace of capture. Akbar then annexed her kingdom.[6]

Ebuskun
Khatun, regent of Turkestan (1242–1246)

Ebuskun was the wife of Mütügen, eldest son of Jagatai. Jagatai was one of the four sons of Jenghiz-khan who shared in their father's empire, and Mütügen would inherit the land of Jagatai when he died. However, Mütügen was killed in 1221 at the siege of Bamian, leaving his wife Ebuskun and their son Qara-Hulägu, who inherited the throne upon Jagatai's death in 1242. Ebuskun served as regent for four years, when the new grand Khan Güyük intervened and replaced Qara-Hulägo with a personal friend—Jagatai's younger brother, Prince Yissu-Mangu (Mongka).[1]

Eji (also called Metnedjenet)
Ruler of Egypt (1351–1350 B.C.)

Eji was the sister of Queen Nefertiti, wife of King Akhenaton, who ruled ca. 1375–1358 or 1379–1362 B.C. Nefertiti had either died or fallen out of favor with her husband about the twelfth year of his reign. Toward the end of his reign, their oldest daughter Meritaton's husband Sakere (or Smenkhkare) was asked to co-rule, probably because of an infirmity of Akhenaton's. When Sakere died, at either 57 or 61, his child-brother Tutankhamen ruled (ca. 1362–1352 B.C.). He was also married to a daughter of Akhenaton, Ankhesenpoaten. During Tutankhamen's rule, the actual power rested with his elderly regent Ay and with General Horemheb, the royal deputy. When King Tut died ca. 1352 or 1351 B.C., the elderly Ay continued to hold power while the widow queen looked for a husband-successor. It is likely that Horemheb had a hand in the void that led to his own ascension, since the widow's husband-to-be was murdered. Ay died, and so, apparently, did Tut's widow. During this void, Queen Eji, as the sister of the late queen, was left as ruler for only a year or two. Horemheb married her to secure a claim to the throne, and Eji seemed to play little part in the government following the marriage. Although he was an elderly man, Horemheb ruled for over a quarter of a century, but he and Eji had no children. This rule marked the end of the Eighteenth Dynasty.[2]

Eleanor (or Leonor)
Queen of Navarre (1479–1481)

Eleanor was the daughter of King John of Aragon and Queen Doña Blanca of Navarre, who ruled Navarre until her death in 1441, when Eleanor's older brother Charles de Viana succeeded his mother and ruled until 1461. Charles and his father had serious disagreements; when he died suddenly in 1461 it was assumed that he had been poisoned. King John continued to rule in his late wife's name. Meanwhile, Eleanor married Francesco Febo and they had a daughter, Catalinda. When Eleanor's father died in 1479, she succeeded to the throne of Navarre. She died two years later, in 1481. Febo died two years following, and Eleanor's daughter claimed the throne.[3]

Eleanor of Aquitaine
Duchess (of Aquitaine), Countess (of Poitiers), Queen (of both France and England), Regent of England (1189–1199)

To cite only the regency of this remarkable woman is to disregard the tremendous and far-reaching impact she had on the affairs of Europe during her lifetime. Born ca. 1122, the daughter of William X, duke of Aquitaine and count of Poitiers, upon her father's death in 1137 Eleanor inherited Aquitaine and Poitiers and married Louis VII the Young, who became king of France that year. She and Louis had two daughters: Marie, who married Henry of Champagne; and Alice, who married Thibault of Blois.

Eleanor was considered far more intelligent than Louis. In 1148 she and her retinue, dressed in battle garb, accompanied him on the Second Crusade. They went first to Antioch, where Eleanor's uncle Raymond of Tripoli sought Louis' help in recovering Montferrand from the Turks. Louis, however, was not quite ready to fight, or perhaps Raymond's proposal did not sound prestigious enough; at any rate, he said that he wanted to make a pilgrimage to Jerusalem before he began any military campaigns. Eleanor, the more sensible of the two, pleaded her uncle's cause; in fact, she and Raymond were in each other's company so much that tongues began to wag and Louis, growing jealous, announced that he would set off for Jerusalem at once. Unwilling to be bullied, Eleanor announced that she would stay in Antioch and get a divorce, whereupon Louis dragged her by force from her uncle's palace.

Louis lost all in the crusade—honor, the battle, and, for all practical purposes, his wife—and he returned home in 1149 a temporarily chastened man. After a brief attempt at reconcilia-

tion, the couple separated and the marriage was annulled (1152)—no male heir had, after all, been produced. Eleanor saw to it that her lands were returned to her and then promptly married Henry, duke of Normandy, who in 1154 became Henry II, king of England. During her marriage to the English king, she continued to administer her own lands, Aquitaine consisting of Guienne and Gascony. The couple had eight children: William; Henry; Richard I the Lionhearted (ruled 1189–1199); Geoffrey; John Lackland (ruled 1199–1216); Matilda, who married Henry the Lion; Eleanor, who married King Alfonso VIII of Castile; Joan, who married both King William II of Sicily and Count Raymond VI of Toulouse. In 1168 Queen Eleanor gave her favorite son Richard the duchy of Aquitaine and in 1172 made him duke of Poitiers. In 1173 her sons revolted against their father, with not only Eleanor's blessing, but also her military support. Although her sons were defeated in 1174, it was Eleanor whom her husband sent to prison for 15 years. She was released upon her husband's death in 1189.

A few months after Richard became king, he left on the Third Crusade, and Eleanor was given vice-regal powers. (Although she would have much preferred to sail with her son, rules of the Third Crusade specifically barred the participation of women). After three years away from his throne, Richard was on the way home when he was captured by Duke Leopold of Austria and held for ransom of 150,000 marks, an astronomical sum even for Eleanor to raise. However, she rounded up the money and traveled in person to escort home her son, who by this time (1194) had been gone five years. The queen arranged for him to be crowned again, but a month following his coronation, he left again for Normandy, leaving the Archbishop of Canterbury in charge, never going to England again. When he died in 1199, the great Richard the Lionhearted had actually served only six months as king of England.

To solidify relations between England and France, Eleanor quickly arranged a marriage between her granddaughter, Blanche of Castile, and the Dauphine of France; in fact, to ensure its success, in 1200, at almost 80 years of age, she traveled to Castile to fetch Blanche and deliver her personally to France. She then returned to Aquitaine, which her son John had inherited from his brother, and defended it against her grandson, Arthur of Brittany, who tried to claim it for France. She continued to be on hand to thwart Arthur during the campaign at Mirebeau in 1202, when at last John could take him prisoner. Triumphant but exhausted, she retired to the monastery at Fontevrault, Anjou, where she died in 1204.

Historian William of Tyre assessed Eleanor as a "fatuous woman," but in the light of her long and illustrious career, his assessment would appear to be short-sighted and biased. Other historians have described her as possessing good looks, charm, courage, passion, self-will, a hot temper, sound sense, and a taste for poetry and romance.[4]

Eleanor of Arborea
Ruler of Arborea (1383–1404)

Arborea, located in the center of Sardinia, was one of the four territorial divisions of that island, one of the largest in the western Mediterranean. Eleanor succeeded her father as queen or "judge" of Arborea and is famous as a warrior queen. Her small realm had been invaded first by Pisans and then by Alfonso IV of Aragon, who drove out the Pisans. Eleanor fought valiantly against the invaders but did not succeed, dying in 1404 without securing her realm. Another of her endeavors, however, was more successful: it was due to her efforts at codifying the laws, completing work begun by her father, that in 1421 her Carta de Logu was adopted by the Sard Parliament, to be effective for the entire island. It remained in effect until the Treaty of Utrecht in 1713.[5]

Elisa Bonaparte (or Elisa Lucca)
Duchess of Tuscany, princess of Piombino
and ruler of the principality of Lucca
(1805–1814)

Elisa was born in 1777 on the island of Corsica, the oldest daughter and one of eight surviving children of Carlo Maria Buonaparte, a lawyer, and Maria Laelitia Ramolini. Her father's family, of ancient Tuscan nobility, had emigrated to Corsica in the sixteenth century. Elisa married Felix Bacciochi. She was the younger sister of Napoleon, who was born in 1782. Napoleon was generous with his brothers and sisters; he first made Elisa the duchess of Tuscany. In 1905 he made her ruler of the principality of Lucca, in the Tuscany region of north-central Italy, and princess of Piombino. Elisa, like her famous brother, demonstrated remarkable administrative abilities. A woman of strong convictions, she occasionally found herself at odds with her family, even with Napoleon. At one point near the end of Napoleon's life he noted that all but Elisa had disappointed him. In 1815, following Napoleon's defeat, the Congress of Vienna assigned Lucca to the Spanish infanta Queen María Luísa of Etruria. Elisa withdrew to Bologna and later to Trieste, where she died in 1820, a year before her exiled brother.[6]

Elissa
See Dido

Elizabeth
Queen, ruler of Hungary (1439–1440)

Elizabeth was the daughter of Holy Roman Emperor Sigismund, king of Hungary from 1387 to 1437, and his first wife Barbara of Cilli. She married Albert V, duke of Austria, who became King Albert II of Hungary upon her father's death. As Albert was also crowned king of Germany and Bohemia, Elizabeth became queen of those realms as well. The couple had a daughter, Elizabeth.

Albert II had the makings of a strong leader and immediately set about ending territorial feuds by appointing arbiters. He also divided Germany into governable administrative districts. However, he died after only two years (May of 1439) while on an unsuccessful campaign against the Turks. Elizabeth was pregnant at the time and in 1440 gave birth to their son, whom she named Ladeslav V Posthumus. In May 1440, to prevent Hungary from falling permanently under Polish rule, she compelled the primate to crown her baby king, exactly one year after her husband had died. She then made her cousin Frederick V of Styria (later Emperor Frederick II) his guardian. However, from 1440 to 1444 Hungary was nominally ruled by Vladislav VI of Poland. Elizabeth was supported in her struggle to win her son's throne by some influential Croatian magnates and by the Serbian despot, George Branković, who had been granted large estates in Hungary. Elizabeth's forces met Vladislav's General Hunyadi in 1442 and were defeated. All might have been lost but for Vladislav's death in 1440, which cleared the way for Elizabeth's baby son to "rule." Her daughter Elizabeth married Casimir IV, king of Portugal, Vladislav's brother.[7]

Elizabeth I

Queen of England (1558–1603)

Born in 1533, the daughter of Henry VIII and his second wife, Anne Boleyn, Elizabeth spent a childhood and early adulthood that were fraught with danger and disaster. Her mother was beheaded when she was three years old. During the reign of her brother Edward VI, his protector, Edward Seymour had his own brother Thomas, accused of plotting to marry Elizabeth and usurp the throne, tried for treason and executed. Elizabeth, a nominal Protestant, was considered a constant threat to her Catholic sister Mary, who ruled from 1553 to 1558. For a while during Mary's reign, Elizabeth was imprisoned in the Tower of London, suspected of having aided Sir Thomas Wyatt in a rebellion against the queen. These early experiences, whereby she was often saved by cautious circumspection, helped her perfect a technique which was to hold her in good stead throughout her reign: the technique of giving "answerless answers." In addition, Elizabeth schooled herself well; during her teens she could already speak six languages. In later years this facility with languages would place her at an advantage with foreign dignitaries.

Elizabeth came to the throne in 1558, at the age of 25, when her sister Mary died. In later years of her 45-year reign, she would become known as "the Virgin Queen" and still later as "Good Queen Bess." The greatest threat to her throne was posed by her cousin Mary Stuart, queen of Scots, a threat Elizabeth ended by consenting to Mary's beheading once her involve-

Queen Elizabeth I of England. The Granger Collection, New York.

ment in an assassination plot by Anthony Bolington was clearly proved. In 1588 she raised a fleet and forces to defend against the Spanish Armada. She rode out to the mouth of the Thames to address her troops, saying in part, ". . . I am come amongst you . . . not for my recreation and disport, but being resolved, in the midst and heat of the battle, to live or die amongst you all . . ." Her presence and her speech so inspired Drake's pitifully small fleet that the Spanish Armada was routed and forced to retreat to the North Sea, where it was destroyed by storms. Elizabeth dabbled more frequently in foreign affairs after that, endeavoring to undermine, wherever possible, the Catholic influence. She assisted the Netherlands in gaining independence from Spain, and she helped the Protestants gain a foothold in France. The trait that exasperated her ministers and foreign rulers alike (one they considered a terrible womanly weakness) was perhaps her greatest strength—indecisiveness. However, what they considered to be indecisiveness was, instead, caution and circumspection. Elizabeth seemed to rule by instinct, knowing just when to withhold a decision, often until the need for decisive action had passed and a crisis had thus been averted. For years she used this trait to keep the nations of Europe guessing concerning her marriage plans. Half the monarchs of Europe curried her favor, hoping for a beneficial union. In her innate wisdom, she kept her plans to herself, neither rejecting nor accepting overtures. This technique was her special ploy to manipulate affairs of state. When it became apparent that she would not marry, would not produce an heir, she kept the world guessing, until she lay on her deathbed, about whom she would name as her successor.

At the end of her reign, England was poised to become a major world power and a colonial giant. During the latter years of her reign, literature flowered as did, to a lesser degree, art and architecture. She personally attended the premier of the new playwright Shakespeare's *Twelfth Night*. Even today, Elizabeth is generally considered to be one of England's greatest monarchs. In 1603, almost 70 years old, she named from her deathbed James VI of Scotland, the Protestant son of her cousin Mary, queen of Scots, as James I of England, first of the Stuart line.[8]

Elizabeth I
Tzarina of Russia (1741–1762)

Elizabeth was born in 1709, the daughter of Peter the Great, who ruled Russia from 1682 to 1725, and Catherine I, who ruled from 1725 to 1727. When her mother was on her deathbed, she named her late husband's grandson, Peter II, to succeed her. Elizabeth was 18 at the time, a beautiful, vivacious, and popular young woman at court. When Peter died in 1730, the throne was offered to Anna, a niece of Peter the Great. Anna ruled for ten years and on her deathbed named her grandnephew Ivan as her successor and her niece Anna Leopoldovna as regent. By this time Elizabeth was 31 and still very popular at court, particularly among the guards. Believing that Elizabeth's popularity would make it more difficult for her to conduct her regency, Anna Leopoldovna had decided to banish Elizabeth to a convent, but the French ambassador and other anti-German factions in the court learned of the plan and approached Elizabeth with the idea of staging a coup d'état. One night late in 1741, Elizabeth dressed as a palace guard, stole into the palace, and arrested the infant emperor, his regent-mother, and her advisors. Elizabeth was then proclaimed empress of Russia.

She immediately reinstated the Senate, which had been created by her father but abolished by his successors, leaving control of most state affairs to her ministers while she turned her attention to westernizing her country. She established Russia's first university in Moscow and founded the Academy of Arts in St. Petersburg (now Leningrad). The privileged classes prospered in her reign while the lot of the serfs worsened. The government's financial base deteriorated, although the country itself grew in stature as a European power. Russia fought a war with Sweden and gained a portion of Finland. She joined with France and Austria in the Seven Years' War against Prussia's Frederick the Great, but by choosing her nephew Peter III as her successor, she was paving the way for Peter to undo all the gains made against Prussia. She realized he was not a strong choice, so she carefully chose a wife for him and groomed her for her future role herself. That young girl would become Catherine the Great. Elizabeth died in 1762.[9]

Elizabeth II
Queen of England (1952–)

Elizabeth Alexandra Mary was born in 1926, the elder daughter of Prince Albert, duke of York (later to become King George V who ruled from 1936 to 1952) and Lady Elizabeth, daughter of Claude Bowes-Lyon. She and her younger sister Margaret Rose spent their early childhood never expecting to be thrust into the limelight. In 1936 her uncle Edward VIII abdicated, her father became king, and Elizabeth suddenly found herself next in line for the throne. At age 13 she met her distant cousin, Lieutenant Philip Mountbatten, prince of Greece and prince of Denmark. Eight years later they were married. Their first son, Charles, was born the following year, 1948. Subsequently the couple had a daughter, Anne, and two more sons, Andrew and Edward. Eliz-

Queen Elizabeth II of England. The Bettmann Archive.

abeth acceded to the ostensibly symbolic position of queen in 1952. However, as queen, she has exercised more than ceremonial power, according to the London *Economist:* "Any prime minister who thinks that the weekly audition is a mere formality is in for a shock. The queen's experience tells . . . She has seen every cabinet paper and important Foreign Office dispatch of the past 35 years and has held weekly meetings with eight consecutive prime ministers. She has met most foreign heads of state and has complained to the Foreign Office that its briefings are too simple. The queen is not only powerful but also popular. . . ." Both Winston Churchill and Harold Wilson were embarrassed to find that the queen was sometimes more up to date than her prime ministers. Wilson said when he retired, "I shall certainly advise my successor to do his homework before his audience." It has been speculated that the queen has performed her job so well that she would be unlikely to abdicate at age 65. The queen lives in 600-room Buckingham Palace in London, a dozen rooms of which are the royal apartment. Although the palace and its 51.5-acre grounds require a staff of 346 employees, the queen is thrifty at that. One authority, Robert Lacey, says the apart-

ment is "visibly frayed at the edges." Yet the government allowance of $6.3 million for maintenance is usually inadequate and the queen must make up the shortfall from her private funds.

The queen is one of the wealthiest women in the world and owns 52,000 acres of prime land. As alternate residences she has at her disposal Windsor Castle on the Thames near London and Holyroodhouse in Scotland. She also has estates at Sandringham in Norfolk and Balmoral in Scotland, both of which she maintains at her own expense. The British people regard the queen as a symbol of unity, stability, and tradition, and although liberal British press occasionally criticizes the wealth of some of the royal family, the queen herself remains above criticism.[10]

Elizabeth of Görlitz (also called Elizabeth of Luxembourg)
Co-ruler of Luxembourg (1412–1415) then sole ruler (1415–1419 and 1425–1444)

Elizabeth was the second wife of Antoine of Burgundy, duke of Brabant, who in 1406 had been named successor to Limburg and Brabant by the childless Duchess Joanna, his great-aunt. Elizabeth and Antoine had two sons, John IV, later duke of Brabant (1415–1427), and Philip, later duke of Brabant (1427–1430). During the reign of Holy Roman Emperor Wenceslas IV (also king of Bohemia), the ruler spent so much time attending peace conferences in Prague trying to bring an end to the many internal conflicts that plagued his realm, that the various princes of Germany began to demand some degree of separate rule for Germany. Anarchy reigned in much of the outlying areas of his realm. Wenceslas was eventually imprisoned as a heretic and Antoine and Elizabeth, as heirs of the house of Limburg, saw the opportunity to become pretenders to the duchy of Luxembourg. Wenceslas managed to escape prison and restore himself briefly in ca. 1411, but in 1412 he returned to prison and Antoine and Elizabeth claimed the throne of Luxembourg. Wenceslas was executed in 1415, but Antoine also died the same year. Although Wenceslas' brother Sigismund became king of Germany, Elizabeth managed to hold onto Luxembourg. She ruled alone for five years while her son John IV became duke of Brabant. In 1419 Duke Johann of Bavaria assumed rule of the duchy until he died in 1425. Elizabeth then ruled alone again from 1425 until 1443 or 1444. In the meantime, her son John had died in 1427 and her younger son Philip became duke of Brabant until 1420, when he also died. Elizabeth, having outlived her heirs, continued as sole ruler of Luxembourg until ca. 1443, when she ceded it to Philip the Good, her husband's nephew. Luxembourg then joined the house of Burgundy.[11]

Elizabeth of Luxembourg
See Elizabeth of Görlitz

Elizabeth of Poland
Queen of Hungary, regent of Poland
(1370–ca. 1377)

She was the daughter of King Vladislav IV, king of Poland from 1305 to 1333. In 1320 she married Charles Robert of Anjou, king of Hungary (1310–1342), and they had two sons: Andrew, who married Joanna I, queen of Naples, and Louis I, king of Hungary (1342–1382) and king of Poland (1370–1382). Her brother, Casimir III, succeeded their father as king of Poland in 1333 but died in 1370 leaving no male heir, so Elizabeth's son Louis I was named king of Poland. Louis had no interest in governing Poland and appointed his mother Elizabeth as regent. She ruled Poland until she died ca. 1377.[12]

Emma
Queen, regent of the Netherlands
(1889–1898)

Born Emma of Waldeck Pyrmont, she became the second wife of King William III, ruler of the Netherlands from 1849 to 1890. In 1880 they had a daughter, Wilhelmina, who became second in the line of succession, the king's elder son by his first wife Sophia having died the previous year. In 1884 his other son, Alexander, died, making Wilhelmina heir apparent. During King William's final illness, Queen Emma served as regent. William died in 1890, and Emma continued as regent for 10-year-old Wilhelmina until she reached the age of 18. During her rule, Emma was faced with putting

down two serious revolts in the Dutch East Indies (1894 and 1896). The Liberal party, in power at the time, passed a new electoral law in 1896 that more than doubled the number of citizens allowed to participate in the electoral process, but workers would not be satisfied with anything less than universal suffrage. The Liberal ministry continued to pass social legislation for the next five years. Queen Emma retired at the time of her daughter's majority.[13]

Ermengarde
Countess, ruler of Carcassonne (1067–1070)

Carcassonne was located in the southwestern section of modern-day France. Ermengarde was the daughter of Count Roger II, who ruled Carcassonne until his death in 1060. Her brother, Roger III, succeeded his father but died in 1067. Ermengarde married Raimond Bernard, vicomte d'Alby. She inherited the realm in 1067 from her brother and ruled until her death in 1070.[14]

Ermengarde
Viscountess, ruler of Narbonne (1143–1192)

Narbonne was located in the southeastern section of modern-day France. Ermengarde was the daughter of Aimery II who ruled from 1105 to 1134. When he died, he was succeeded by her brother, Alfonse Jourdain, count of Toulouse, who ruled from 1134 until he died in 1143. Ermengarde then presided over Narbonne for almost 50 years. She was the leader of the French Royalist party in the south of France, which was in opposition to the English. She has been described as a nobly born Joan of Arc. She was married several times, but her husbands took no part in the government of Narbonne. Ermengarde fought numerous wars defending her domain, and was a patron of troubadours and a protector of the Church. She gained renown as an arbiter and judge in complex cases of feudal law. She had no children and named her nephew, Pierre de Lara, as her heir when she died in 1192.[15]

Ermensinde
Countess, ruler of Luxembourg (1196–1247)

She was of the house of Namur, originally a medieval county in present-day southeastern

Belgium. Around the year 1100 the low-country territories began to expand and form principalities, weakening the hold of the German kings so far away. With the decline of the power of German kings, emperors could do little to enforce their influence in the lowlands. Ermensinde inherited rule of the principality of Luxembourg in 1196 from Count Henry IV the Blind, who ruled from 1136 to 1196. Count Henry V, who was born in 1217, inherited the rule when Ermensinde died in 1247.[16]

Eschiva of Ibelin
Lady, queen of Beirut (1282–ca.1284)

She was the younger daughter of John II of Beirut and Alice de la Roche of Athens. Her older sister Isabella became queen of Beirut following their father's death in 1264. Eschiva married Humphrey of Montfort, younger son of Philip of Montfort, lord of Toron and Tyre. The couple had a son, Roupen. When her sister Isabella died in 1282, the fief of Beirut passed to Eschiva. When Humphrey's brother John of Montfort died ca. 1283 leaving no issue, Humphrey inherited Tyre. But he died ca. 1284, so Tyre then went to John's widow, Margaret. After a suitable interval, Eschiva was married (by King Hugh III of Cyprus and Jerusalem) to King Hugh's youngest son, Guy. When the Mameluk sultan Qalawun was preparing to attack those Franks who were not protected by the truce of 1283, Eschiva hastened to ask him for a truce, which was granted. (Mameluks were former slaves from Russia and Central Asia who founded a dynasty in Egypt and Syria in 1250 that lasted almost 300 years. Mameluks made up an important part of Islamic armies from 833 onward.) However, in 1291, the truce did not keep the Mameluks—under a later leader, Shujai—from tearing down not only the walls of Beirut, but the Castle of the Ibelins as well, and turning the cathedral into a mosque.[17]

Eudocia Macrembolitissa
Empress, regent of the Byzantine Empire (1067), then co-ruler (1071)

She was born in 1021, the daughter of John Macrembolites. She was also the niece of the patriarch of Constantinople, Michael Cerularius. She married Emperor Constantine X Ducas and they had three sons: Michael VII, Andronicus, and Constantine; and two daughters, Zoe and Theodora Anna (also called Arete). When Constantine died in 1067, by Michael Psellus' own account, Eudocia succeeded him as supreme ruler in accordance with the wishes of her late husband. She assumed control of the administration in person, instructing her two sons (Andronicus had died earlier) in the nature of political affairs. Psellus said, "I do not know whether any other woman ever set such an example of wisdom or lived a life comparable to hers up to this point." After a series of setbacks from the Turks who threatened along the frontier, Eudocia was convinced of the need for a strong military government. Psellus recalled praying aloud that she might enjoy power as long as she lived and Eudocia's calling the prayer a curse: "I hope it will not be my fate to enjoy power so long that I die an empress," she told him. Despite the opposition of her advisors, Psellus and Caesar John, her brother-in-law, Eudocia married General Romanus IV Diogenes, who became ruler in 1068. He was an unpopular choice with the people. He fought the Turks with valor but was defeated in 1071 and taken prisoner. Again the throne was vacant. Some preferred that Michael succeed his stepfather, while others favored the complete restoration of Eudocia's rule to the exclusion of her sons. It was Psellus' suggestion that Eudocia and her son Michael assume joint and equal rule, which they did for a while. Meanwhile, Romanus concluded a treaty with the Turks that freed him if he paid an annual tribute to them. Romanus, intent on regaining the throne, wrote to Eudocia that he was free and wished to return. Eudocia, caught in an embarrassing situation, did not know what to do. Michael did not want to lose his reign, so he decided to cut himself off from his mother and assume sole control. His advisors decreed that Eudocia should leave the city and live in a convent that she herself had founded. Michael refused to ratify such a decree. But with Romanus threatening, a constant stream of propaganda was directed against Eudocia. It was feared that she would allow Romanus to return and assume the throne. At length a second decree was issued stating that she must take the veil of a nun. In 1071 she was immured in a nunnery and Michael was declared sole ruler. When Romanus returned, before he ever reached Constantinople he was set upon by agents of Psellus and his eyes were put out with hot irons. He died soon after, in 1072, as a result of his horrible injuries. Eudocia died in the nunnery in 1096, having been granted her wish not to die an empress.[18]

Eudoxia (or Eudocia)
Augusta, de facto co-ruler of the Eastern Roman Empire (400–404)

The daughter of a mercenary general, the Frankish chief Bauto, in 395 Eudoxia married Arcadus, emperor of the Byzantine Empire from 383 to 408. The marriage was engineered by a corrupt court eunuch, Eutropius, in an effort to weaken the status of a political rival. Eudoxia soon found that she was married to a weak and ineffectual ruler who let Eutropius dominate him. In time she decided to join Eutropius' opposition in order to bring about his ouster (399). Eudoxia and Arcadus had four children: Theodocius II, weak like his father; Pulcheria, strong like her mother; and two other daughters. Despite the fact that she was frequently pregnant, Eudoxia exercised enormous influence over her husband's affairs. The period of her greatest influence dates from her designation as augusta in January, A.D. 400. The patriarch of Constantinople, John Chrysotom, openly criticized and publicly reproached her and her court. She retaliated, after several bitter quarrels, by appealing to a rival archbishop for help in expelling him from his see (403) and permanently exiling him (404). She died shortly afterward of a miscarriage (404).[19]

Eugénie-Marie
Countess (of Teba), Empress, regent of France (1859, 1865, 1870)

She was born in a tent, to escape falling ceilings, during an earthquake in 1826, the daughter of a Spanish grandee, Don Cipriano de Guzmán y Palafox y Portocarrero, count of Teba, and Doña María Manuela. Her full name was María Eu-génia Ignacia Augustina de Montijo de Guzmán. Her uncle Eugenio was the count of Montijo, and her father was his heir if Eugenio died childless. In 1853 she married Louis Napoleon who had been elected president of the republic of France, but who the year before had become Emperor Napoleon III when the monarchy was reestablished. The new red-haired empress was strikingly beautiful, brilliant, and charming, but pious, naive, and unschooled in affairs of state. Two events altered the degree of her involvement in the political life of the country: an assassination attempt against her husband in 1855 and the birth of their son Napoleon-Eugene-Louis in 1856, whom she hoped to see become the next emperor. Eugénie-Marie, a devout Catholic, became intent on fostering Catholicism. While her husband attempted to liberalize domestic policy, she worked for conservative causes, becoming the leader of the Clerical Party at the palace. Napoleon III used much of his energies concentrating on war with Austria and on the Franco-Prussian War. In addition, he was afflicted with bouts of ill health throughout his reign. On at least three occasions, 1859, 1865, and 1870, possibly more, Eugénie-Marie served as regent while he was out of the country.

Eugénie-Marie was first appointed regent in 1859 during the war against Italy. In 1861 she was instrumental in the decision to create a Mexican Empire and to make Austrian Archduke Maximilian its emperor. In 1862 she suggested that a united Italy was a threat to French security; she wanted Victor Emmanuel's kingdom broken up into four states of an Italian federation. But she was determined that Victor not take Rome and insisted that French troops stay in Rome for fear that the pope might excommunicate her and Napoleon both if the French abandoned Rome. In 1869 she officially opened the Suez Canal with the Turkish Khedive and Franz Joseph. In a time when entrance into medical school was denied women, she interceded in behalf of promising women applicants to gain them admittance. In 1870 she was appointed regent while Napoleon took supreme command of the army against the Prussians in the Franco-Prussian War. When Napoleon's defeat and surrender following the Battle of Sedan (1870) left him a prisoner of war, Eugénie-Marie as regent refused to negotiate with the Prussians, who wanted her to cede them Alsace and Lorraine. She did, however, write a personal letter to King William of Prussia asking him not to annex those territories. In a courteous reply the king wrote that Prussia's security required their possession. Napoleon's defeat made the likelihood of his reassuming his reign highly problematic, so Eugénie-Marie sought exile in England. The deposed emperor died in 1873 following an operation for bladder stones, but Eugénie-Marie continued to play a part in politics, because her son was immediately proclaimed Napoleon IV by the Bonapartists. In 1879, hoping that her son would capture the imagination of the French people, that he might return to claim the crown much as her husband had done a generation before, Eugénie-Marie encouraged him to embark on an expedition to Africa to gain notoriety and military experience. But he was killed by Zulus, and Eugénie-Marie's aspirations died with him.

Eugénie-Marie was not completely out of politics, however; she was 88 at the outbreak of World War I, and from her vantage in England, she saw France pitted against her old friend Franz Joseph. She offered her yacht to the British Admiralty; it became a mine sweeper. She then contacted the British War Office and offered to convert a wing of her 41-room mansion, Farnborough Hill, into a hospital. She continued to live in exile, becoming a well-loved celebrity wherever she went. She died at the age of 94 in 1920 while on a visit to Madrid.[20]

Euphrosine
Countess, ruler of Vendôme (1085–1102)

She was the sister of Bouchard III, who began his rule with the help of his guardian uncle, Gui de Nevers, and ruled from 1066 to 1085. She married Geoffroi Jourdain, sire de Previlly. When Count Bouchard III died in 1085, Euphrosine became countess and ruler. When she died in 1102, she was succeeded by Count Geoffroi Grisegonella.[21]

Euphrosyne
Empress, de facto co-ruler of the Byzantine Empire (1195–1203)

She was the wife of Byzantine Emperor Alexius III Angelus, who wanted to rule so badly that he blinded and deposed his own brother in 1195. Alexius, a weakling with a lust for power, adopted the name Comnenus after the great Comneni emperors, because he thought Angelus didn't sound distinguished enough. The couple had three children: Irene, whose grandson became Michael VIII Palaeologus; Anna, whose husband became Theodore I Lascaris; and Eudocia, or Eudokia, whose second husband became Alexius IV. Alexius III busied himself with diplomatic affairs, at which he showed some aptitude, but home affairs were left to Euphrosyne, who proved to be extravagant and as corrupt as her brother-in-law Isaac had been.[22]

Finnebogadóttir, Vigdis
President of Iceland (1980–)

In Iceland surnames are a combination of the father's first name and the suffix *dóttir* (daughter) or *sson* (son). People are called by their first names, since surnames are usually lengthy and complex. A woman does not take her spouse's name when she marries but is known by her maiden name all her life. Vigdis was born in 1930 in Reykjavík to Finnbogi Ruter Thorvaldsson, a civil engineer and professor at the University of Iceland, and Sigridur Eriksdóttir, a nurse, chairman of the Icelandic Nurses Association for 36 years. Interested in the theater, Vigdis attended junior college in Reykjavík, then studied abroad at the University of Grenoble and at the Sorbonne. She also attended the University of Copenhagen, where she studied theater history. Married in 1953, she divorced after nine years and returned to Iceland, where she taught French both in college and on television. As a single woman, she adopted a daughter, Astridur. In 1972 she became director of the Reykjavík Theater Company, which flourished under her direction.

Vigdis first became interested in politics in 1974 when she helped organize a petition campaign for the removal of the U.S. naval base at Keflavík. According to Washington columnist Betty Beale, Vigdis first ran for president in 1980 on a dare, opposed by three men. She was elected, the first popularly elected woman president in history, and she easily won reelections in 1984 and 1988. Although her post is largely ceremonial, with governing power vested in the prime minister, Vigdis does have some authority in the government. She signs all bills passed by the Althing, or parliament. If she vetoes a bill, it goes before the people in a national referendum. In times of crisis, i.e., the death of the prime minister, she oversees the forming of a new government. As cultural ambassador for her country, Vigdis makes state visits to other countries to educate the world to the fact that Iceland is not a place of snow and ice. On a five-city U.S. tour in 1987 called the "Scandinavia Today" celebration, she took along the "gourmet ambassador," founder of Iceland's only gourmet magazine, Hilmar Jonsson, to prepare typical Icelandic foods to illustrate how far Icelanders have come from the days of eating large chunks of raw cod.

Although Vigdis encourages the modernization of her country, and has been particularly interested in bettering the status of women, there are some areas of Icelandic life that are sacred and that she hopes progress will not alter. She is proud of the Norse heritage of her people and is unwilling to see Iceland become too worldly. The state-run television does not operate on Thursday night, for example, because that is family night. Until 1989, the manufacture and sale of beer were prohibited on the island. Vigdis described her position in an interview: "The role of the president is to be a symbol for the nation of unity and identity."[1]

Fredegund (or Fredegond)
Queen, regent of Neustria (584–597)

A study of the life of Fredegund should put to rest for all time the argument that if women ruled, peace would reign. She was at least the third wife of Merovingian King Chilperic I, who ruled the western Frankish kingdom of Soissons from 561 to 584. Soissons was located in present-day western Belgium, an area that has been called by several names. When the Frankish kingdom was divided among Chlotar I's four sons at the time of his death in 561, Chilperic's part, the smallest part, was called Tournai, or the kingdom of Soissons. When Chilperic's half brother died in 567, Chilperic received a large portion to the south, and later this entire area was designated as Neustria. Chilperic was possibly the most barbaric of the Frankish kings. Gregory of Tours claims that he had many wives, but the first of record were Audovera and Galswintha, sister of Queen Brunhilde. Fredegund, a former servant and Chilperic's mistress, induced him to repudiate Audoveda and to garrote Galswintha. This murder began a 40-year feud between Brunhilde and Fredegund. Fredegund and Chilperic married, and if the account of Gregory of Tours is accurate, she became one of the most bloodthirsty queens in history. She and Chilperic had many children, at least six known ones, most of whom died, and it was their deaths that motivated many of her bloodthirsty acts. Another motivation was the desire to rid the Frankish world of Brunhilde and her husband Sigebert. She sent two emissaries to assassinate Sigebert, who was also planning an attack on Chilperic, his brother. The entire Frankish world was infected with an epidemic of dysentery during Chilperic's reign. When her young son Samson became ill, Fredegund rejected him and wanted to have him put to death. She failed in her attempt, but he died anyway. When two more of her children were near death, she decided the disease was God's punishment because Chilperic had amassed so much wealth by taxing paupers. She ordered him to burn the tax demands. Chilperic sent messages to the people promising never to make such assessments again, but the children died anyway. She attempted to have two of her stepsons killed. She had the girlfriend of her stepson Clovis and the girl's mother tortured before she had him stabbed for making "unforgivable remarks" about her. When she lost a fourth child to dysentery, she tortured and killed a number of Parisian housewives as alleged witches, charging that they had caused the death. She and Chilperic had Leudast, count of Tours, tortured to death for scurrilous behavior and perfidious talk. She had at least one daughter left, Rigunth, who in 584 was sent off to Toulouse with 50 carts of wealth as her dowry, which she claimed was not from the country's treasury.

That same year, their baby Lothar was born, and shortly afterward, Chilperic was assassinated. Fredegund knew that she must preserve the child's life at all cost, as it was her last tie to power—although she did claim to be pregnant again at the time of Chilperic's death, just as a precaution. She gathered her wealth and took refuge in a cathedral, but she and the chief advisors of Chilperic's reign were removed to the manor of Rueil so that a new regime could be formed around the baby Lothar. But Fredegund was far from finished. She sent a cleric from her household to gain Queen Brunhilde's confidence and then assassinate her. When he failed, she murdered him. She then sent two priests to assassinate King Childebert II and his mother, Queen Brunhilde, but they were intercepted and executed. In 586, after she had had a bitter argument with Bishop Praetextatus, he was stabbed, apparently at her instigation. She came around to his room to watch him slowly die. She then poisoned a man who dared to berate her for murdering the bishop. She tried, but failed, to murder the bishop of Bayeux for investigating her part in the bishop's murder.

Her daughter Rigunth, back home after all

her wealth was plundered, often insulted her mother, and they frequently exchanged slaps and punches. After a particularly vexing exchange, Fredegund tried to murder her daughter by closing the lid of a chest on her throat. She sent 12 assassins to murder King Childebert II, but they were all caught. She had three men decapitated with axes at a supper she gave for that specific purpose, because their constant family quarreling was causing a public nuisance. Other members of the victims' families wanted the queen arrested and executed, but she escaped and found refuge elsewhere. Later, in Paris, she sent word to King Guntram of Burgundy that was more a command than a request: "Will my lord the King please come to Paris? My son is his nephew. He should have the boy taken there and arrange for him to be baptised . . . and he should deign to treat him as his own son." The king took Fredegund, as regent, and Lothar (Clothar II) under his protection, but he had to be convinced by a large body of sworn depositions that the boy was Chilperic's legitimate son, since Fredegund had taken a few lovers in her time. King Guntram died in 592, and Brunhilde's son King Childebert II of Austrasia tried to take both Burgundy and Neustria, since he did not think that Fredegund and Lothar would be strong enough to resist an attack. This kind of attack and counterattack continued until Childebert's death three years later, and then the struggle was left to the two aging women, Fredegund and Brunhilde, who kept it up until Fredegund's death in Paris in 597.[2]

Galla Placidia
See Placidia, Galla

Gandhi, Indira
Prime minister of India (1966–1977 and 1980–1984)

Born Priyadarshini Nehru in 1917, she was the only child of Jawaharlal Nehru, India's first prime minister, and his wife Kamala. As leaders of the movement for India's independence, her parents were frequently imprisoned by the British during her childhood, but Nehru wrote his daughter many letters that inspired her to follow in his footsteps. As a girl of 12, she organized the Monkey Brigade, an association of thousands of children who assisted the National Congress Party. Sporadically she attended boarding schools in India and Switzerland, then college in West Bengal and Oxford. At 21 she joined the National Congress Party and became actively involved in the revolution. Against her father's advice, she married a childhood friend, Feroze Gandhi—lawyer, economist, and member of Parliament—and Parsi. The mixed marriage raised a public furor. The couple had two sons, Rajiv and Sanjay, in the ten years before they separated.

In 1947 India was free to choose its own leader, and Nehru was the obvious choice. Since his wife had died in 1936, his daughter Indira served as "First Lady." In 1959 she was elected president of the Congress Party, the second highest political position in India. In 1960 her husband died, but she never remarried. Her father died in 1964. His successor, Lal Badahur Shastri, brought her into his cabinet as minister of information and broadcasting. In 1966 Shastri died and Gandhi was elected prime minister, the first woman ever to lead a democracy, the world's largest. In the 1967 election, her win was less than an absolute majority and she had to accept a right-wing deputy prime minister. In 1971 India annexed the kingdom of Sikkim, exploded its first nuclear device, and sent a satellite into orbit. Gandhi then called for another election and won handily, running on the slogan, "Abolish poverty." Her party won two-thirds of the seats in parliament. At that point she was probably the most popular leader in the world. U.S. Secretary of State Henry Kissinger said of her at that time, "The lady is cold-blooded and tough," although Indians called her *Mataji*, "respected mother." However, she could not both abolish poverty and please the rich, to whom she owed her power. A voluntary sterilization program she had instituted was attacked by her right-wing opponents as being a compulsory program. In 1975, amid riots and protests, she declared a state of emergency and severely limited personal freedoms with new laws and with

Indira Gandhi. UPI/Bettmann Newsphotos.

prison terms for political opponents. In effect, she suspended the democratic process in which she professed to believe. Two years later, having restored democratic practices, she was voted out of office and replaced by the right-wing Janata party. She was charged with abuse of office by the new administration and even spent a week in jail. In December of 1979 she was reelected by a large plurality with the help of her younger son Sanjay, who was her heir-designate. When he died in a plane crash in 1980, there was speculation about the future of the Congress Party and Indira's rule, but her popular support remained strong for a long time. She began to groom her other son, Rajiv, to be her successor. In 1983 she told the World Energy Conference, "We are opposed to nuclear weapons and do not have any," but that India was developing a nuclear program for peaceful purposes. Gandhi could not begin to solve India's economic, social, religious, linguistic, and cultural problems and contend with a devastating drought that affected 2.7 million Indians. She said in a 1982 interview, "Can democracy solve such vast

problems, especially when we have this constant opposition in the way? People are hitting at our feet and still saying, 'You must go further, you must go faster.' But we believe in democracy; we were brought up with those ideals. And in India we simply cannot have another way. . . . Only a democracy will allow our great diversity. . . . The only danger to democracy is if the people feel it is not solving their problems."

Indira's chief detractors were the right-wing and the two Communist parties. In 1984, after she had again placed restraints on personal freedoms and ordered a raid on a Sikh temple, she was assassinated. Her son Rajiv Gandhi became the new prime minister of India. In her autobiography, Indira Gandhi, the most powerful woman India has ever known, wrote simply, "To a woman, motherhood is the highest fulfillment."[1]

Gemmei-tennō
Empress of Japan (708–714)

Originally named Abe, she was born in A.D. 662, the daughter of Emperor Tenchi, who ruled Japan from 662 to 673. Following his abdication in 673, two other rulers, his brother Temmu (673–686) and Tenchi's daughter and Temmu's consort Jitō (687–696), followed before Gemmei's son Mommu, Jitō's nephew, became emperor. He had been born in 682 and was 20 years old when he ascended to the imperial throne. He ruled for 11 years. At his death, Abe became Empress Gemmei-tennō at the age of 46. She proved to be an exceptionally able ruler. It is due to her foresight that the early traditions of Japan have survived. At her instigation, the *Kojiki* (712) and the *Fudoki* (713) were written to preserve the ancient traditions. In keeping with the ancient belief that a dwelling place was polluted by death, it was customary upon the demise of a sovereign for the successor to move into a new palace. Emperor Tenchi had enacted an edict to regulate the capital in 646, but the edict was not carried out until 710, when Empress Gemmei moved the court from Asuka to Nara, or Heijo, as it was then called, in the province of Yamato in central Japan. She also ordered the coinage of the first copper money. She abdicated in 714 in favor of her daughter, Hitaka (Genshō-tennō) and died in A.D. 723 at the age of 61.[2]

Genshō-tennō
Empress of Japan (715–723)

She was born Princess Hitaka in 779, the daughter of Empress Gemmei-tennō and the older sister of Emperor Mommu. She emulated the work of her mother by encouraging the arts, letters, science, and agriculture. The *Nihongi*, chronicles of Japan to the year A.D. 697, were completed and published during her reign (720). When her nephew Shomu reached age 25, she abdicated, at the age of 45, in favor of him. She died in 748 at the age of 69.[3]

Go-Sakuramachi-tennō
Empress of Japan (1763–1770)

She was born Princess Toshi-ko in 1741, the daughter of Emperor Sakuramachi-tennō, who after a reign of 11 years during which the Shōgun Yoshemune held actual power, abdicated in favor of his 11-year-old son Momosono. During the boy's reign, power rested with the Shōgun Ieshige. When her brother died in 1763, Go-Sakuramachi-tennō, two years his junior, succeeded to the ceremonial position and permitted Ieshige to continue his government. She abdicated at the age of 30 in favor of her nephew Hidehito. She died in 1814 at the age of 73.[4]

Grey, Jane
Lady, queen of England for nine days (1553)

Jane was born in 1537, the daughter of Henry Grey, marquess of Dorset, later duke of Suffolk, and Lady Frances Brandon, sister of Henry VIII. Jane was the great-granddaughter of Henry VII. She led a short and unhappy life. At the age of 16, at the instigation of the duke of Northumberland, she was married to his son, Lord Guildford Dudley, and went to live with Dudley's parents, whom she found disagreeable. A few weeks later, the duke, an ambitious man who had plans to make his son the king, persuaded the dying King Edward VI to name Lady Jane as heir to the throne, bypassing the legal heirs, Edward's sister Mary Tudor, daughter of Henry VIII, and after her, his sister Eliz-

Lady Jane Grey. The Granger Collection, New York.

abeth, then his cousin Mary of Scots. When Jane first learned of the scheme to name her queen, she fainted. Nevertheless, when Edward VI died in July of 1553, she allowed herself to become a pawn in the political intrigues against Mary Tudor. She and Guildford were escorted to the Tower of London where she was proclaimed queen on July 10, 1553. But Mary had gained great popular support, and realizing this, the duke of Northumberland left town, leaving his son and daughter-in-law to their own devices. The mayor of London announced Mary as queen, and the duke of Suffolk, Jane's father, convinced Jane to step down. She left the Tower in relief, saying that she never wanted to be queen in the first place. Northumberland was executed, but Queen Mary "could not find it in her heart to put to death her unfortunate kinswoman, who had not even been an accomplice of Northumberland but merely an unresisting instrument in his hands."

However, in 1554, when Jane's father was involved in an insurrection led by Sir Thomas Wyatt, Queen Mary became convinced that her throne would be threatened so long as Jane lived. Jane, her father, and her husband were all executed in 1554.[5]

Hatshepsut (or Hatasu)
Queen of Egypt (1503–1482 B.C.)

Other sources list 1505–1484, 1501–1480, or 1473–1458, Eighteenth Dynasty. Hatshepsut was the daughter of King Thutmose I and Queen Ahmose I. She married her half brother, King Thutmose II, and when their father died in ca. 1512 B.C., the couple ascended to the throne. Thutmose II died ca. 1504, before Hatshepsut could bear him a son, and a boy of six by a minor wife of his became Thutmose III.

Hatshepsut assumed the regency, but very shortly usurped the throne and ordered herself crowned pharaoh, as selected by the god Amon-Re. She adopted the false beard signifying wisdom worn only by pharaohs, and occasionally she was depicted wearing masculine garb as well. An extraordinary and able monarch, she forswore the military conquests of her forebears and concentrated instead on commercial enterprises. She sent a trade expedition to Punt that brought back many treasures with which to adorn the impressive edifices and monuments built during her approximately 20-year reign. The military leaders chafed under her indifference and lack of military ambitions and rallied around Thutmose III, waiting for him to grow to manhood. Encouraged by them, Thutmose III became bent on acquiring a reputation as an empire builder, and he rose to become head of

Queen Hatshepsut. Colossal red granite kneeling figure from her Temple at Deir el Bahri, Thebes. The Granger Collection, New York.

the army, occupying himself with foreign wars, while Hatshepsut busied herself constructing monuments. Monuments that have survived from her reign include small chapels dedicated to the great architect of the day, Senmut, who rose to a position of eminence in her court. Their location within her temple suggests that Senmut must have been her lover. However, if he had the memorials placed there without her knowledge, as some suggest, she must have discovered them and hacked them from the walls of niches. Five years prior to the end of her reign, all record of Senmut's activities ceases.

In the last five years of her reign, Hatshepsut's power began to wane. Prince Thutmose III, doubtless irked by the usurpation of his aunt, either came to the throne in a coup d'état or acceded at the time of her death. Evidence of his vendetta against her memorials is irrefutable. According to the various Egyptologists, Hatshepsut died as late as 1458 B.C. or as early as 1484 B.C.[1]

Hazrat Mahal
Begam, regent of Oudh (1856–1858)

Until 1856 the kingdom of Oudh in northern India, with its capital of Lucknow, had been ruled by a nominally independent king. But the exile of King Wajid Ali Shah and the annexation in 1856 of his kingdom were two of the causes of the Sepoy War or Indian Mutiny of 1857. Hazrat Mahal, a concubine of the harem, was the only member of the harem willing to commit herself to the rebellion. Raja Jai Lal visited her and made a bargain: he would present her young son, Birjis Qadr, to the army as the son and rightful heir of the deposed king if she, as new queen regent, would appoint him as military leader. Hazrat Mahal agreed, although it was common gossip in Lucknow that the boy was really the son of her paramour, Mammu Khan.

Birjis Qadr was accepted by the army and enthroned in 1857, and Hazrat Mahal appointed her lover chief of the high court. The new queen fought valiantly against the British, and worked hard to retain the leadership of the revolt by fiery personal speeches to the troops, but during the final assault by the British in 1858, she could sense that she was losing control. People were leaving Lucknow in search of safety. She considered suing for a compromise peace, but the British were having none. As the British advanced on Lucknow, the rebels escaped; Hazrat Mahal, her ailing son, and her court went northeast to Bithavli where they attempted to regroup for a pitched defense. The British demanded surrender, but Hazrat and her party refused and tried to escape to Nepal. Among her party were the Rani of Tulsipur, Raja of Gonda, and Beni Madho. By that time Hazrat had come to realize that she and her son had been virtual prisoners of the sepoys; she berated them, saying they had made goats of her and her son, although the queen had never sought their support. The British tried to prevent the retreat of the rebels and many were killed or captured. Although Hazrat and her party escaped capture, it was presumed that they died of exposure or disease soon after. Reporters at the time likened her to Penthesilea, queen of the Amazons, who in post-Homeric legends fought for Troy; hence, a strong commanding woman.[2]

St. Hedwig
Duchess of Silesia (ca. 1236, 1241–1243)

She was the daughter of Bertold III of Andrechs, marquis of Meran, count of Tirol and prince (or duke) of Carinthia and Istria. Her mother was Agnes, daughter of the count of Rotletchs. At a very young age, Hedwig's parents placed her in a monastery. At the age of 12, she became the wife of Henry I, duke of Silesia from 1201 to 1238. The couple had six children: Henry II the Pious, Conrad, Boleslas, Agnes, Sophia, and Gertrude. At Hedwig's suggestion, after the birth of their sixth child the couple agreed not to cohabit, so as to remain pure, and never to meet except in public places. At her persuasion, and with her dower, Henry built the monastery of Cistercian nuns at Tretnitz, the construction of which took 16 years.

In 1163 Silesia (now primarily part of Poland) was divided into Upper and Lower Silesia, each ruled by a Piast prince. Henry and his son tried unsuccessfully to reunite the territory, while Hedwig ruled Silesia. When Henry was taken prisoner by the duke of Kirne, his son Conrad raised an army to rescue him. However Hedwig, who placed great faith in her prayers, dissuaded Conrad from attempting the rescue, saying she was sure that in due time he would be released. In 1238 Henry I died, but Hedwig remained duchess of Silesia, although she concerned herself only with matters of the Church. In 1241 Henry II was killed in the battle of Liegnitz, which pitted the Silesian Knights of the Teutonic Order against the Mongol army under the command of Baider, son of Jagatai. Hedwig died in 1243 and was canonized in 1266.[3]

Helena Lecapena
Co-ruler of Eastern Roman Empire (945–959)

Helena was the daughter of Romanus Lecapenus, the regent of the Roman Empire. In 919 she married the young Emperor Constantine VII Porphyrogenitus, who wore the crown from 913 to 959, and who raised her father to the rank of caesar and the status of co-emperor of the Eastern Roman Empire. Romanus dominated Constantine and became one of the most important rulers in Byzantine history. But in 944, as he began to age noticeably, two of his sons, anxious that Constantine VII not gain control upon Romanus' death, staged a coup d'état and sent their father to a monastery. However, the coup did not have popular support. The brothers were executed and Constantine VII was left in reluctant control of his throne.

Helena and Constantine had at least six children, one of whom was Romanus II, who became emperor of the Eastern Roman Empire from 959 to 963, and another of whom was Theodora, who married John I Tzimisces, emperor of the Western Empire from 969 to 976. Constantine VII, a scholarly man who was more interested in intellectual pursuits, did not come into his full rights as sole ruler until he was nearly 40 (945), although by that time he had worn the crown for 33 years. Even during the period of his sole rule, however, he was apt to follow the lead of Helena.

Of great historical importance was the visit of the Russian Princess Olga, who came to Constantinople to cement Byzantine and Russian relations. As a measure of her esteem, Olga, a Christian, took at her baptism the name of the Byzantine Empress Helena. This honor by the regent of the Kievan state and her stay with Helena and Constantine at the Imperial Palace at Constantinople ushered in a new era between the two nations and gave fresh impetus to the missionaries of the Byzantine church in Russia. In 959 Constantine VII died and their son Romanus assumed the throne. He had married the beautiful and ambitious Theophano and was completely under her spell. To please Theophano, Helena had to retire from court, and her five daughters were forcibly removed to convents.[4]

Henriette de Cleves
Duchess, ruler of Nevers (1564–1601)

Henriette de Cleves was the daughter of François II, duke of Nevers from 1562 to 1563, and the sister of Jacques, duke of Nevers from 1563 to 1564. As was frequently the case with minor rulers, Henriette inherited the financial problems of several of the men in her family. By the time of her grandfather, François I, the concept of provincial governors had been well established (although actually the term "governor" had come into usage for royal provincial agents as early as 1330). Originally, governors were appointed when there was no male heir. Four of the 142 major governors of the period from 1515 to 1560 were dukes of Nevers, the first being Henriette's grandfather, François I, who was appointed governor of Champagne. He dissipated much of his fortune in the discharge of his duties, particularly on military campaigns. When he died early in 1562, he left Henriette's father François II, the new governor of Champagne, bankrupt. François II died in battle only ten months later, leaving the guardian of Henriette's young brother Jacques de Cleves the job of liquidating the debts. Henriette's dowry was lowered, and to protect her jewels from creditors, she hid them at the Paris townhouse of the president of the parlement, Pierre de Seguier. Seguier's wife eventually filed a protest: "Since the day that the said lady left her family jewels (with us) . . . a merchant has not ceased to bother us . . . We plead to be freed from the charge of keeping the jewels.''

Before the liquidation process had begun, however, Jacques also died in 1564. Since there was no male heir in the Cleves line, the property could have been dispersed among others as was often the case. But in 1565 King Charles IX issued extraordinary permission for the family property and titles to pass to Henriette, and a marriage was arranged for her with the prospective heir of some large estates, Ludovico Gonzaga, or Louis de Gonzague. The two succeeded to the duchy and guided it for 37 years. The marriage did not solve Henriette's financial problems completely, for Gonzague had debts of his own, and his inheritance wasn't as large as the Cleves'. In addition, Henriette had to provide dowries for her two sisters. Each received £700,000 worth of land and dowries totalling another £600,000. Louis sold many properties, but much of the estate administration fell to Henriette. Louis was in the prime of his military career, serving as mobile army commander and courtier, and had to borrow money to pay his men. Despite this, the Nevers were the chief creditors of the monarchy during this period. Henriette had at least one daughter and, in 1581, a son, Charles II (Charles de Gonzague), who succeeded upon her death in 1601, but who actually had become co-governor of Champagne with his father in 1589 and succeeded as duke when his father died in 1595.[5]

Himiko
See Pimiku

Himnechildis
Queen, guardian/regent of Austrasia (662–675)

She was the wife of Sigibert III, king of the eastern Frankish kingdom of Austrasia from 632 to 656. She had at least one child, a son, Dagobert II, who, when her husband died, was shorn of his long royal hair and sent to an Irish monastery by Grimoald, father of the pretender Childebert. Sigibert's nephew Childeric II, age 13, was then proclaimed ruler of Austrasia under the joint guardianship of Queen Himnechil-

dis and the mayor of the palace, Ebroin. Childeric II was assassinated in 675 and Himnechildis and the Austrasian mayor Vulfoald, with the help of Wilfrid, bishop of York, traced her son Dagobert, age 26 by that time, and restored him to his throne.[6]

Hind al-Hīrah
Queen, regent of the kingdom of Lakhm in the Syrian desert (554–?)

A Christian princess of either Ghassan or Kindah, Hind al-Hīrah married Mundhir-al Mundhir III, whose mother was Mariyah or Mawiya. Al Mundhir III, the most illustrious ruler of the Lakhmids, ruled ca. A.D. 503 to 554. He raided Byzantine Syria and challenged the kingdom of Ghassan, possibly the homeland of Queen Hind. They had a son, 'Amr ibn-Hind, who inherited the throne in A.D. 554 when his father died and ruled until A.D. 569. Queen Hind, an independent and resourceful queen, served as regent for her son. Although she has been described as bloodthirsty, she founded a convent in the north Arabian capital. She reared her son 'Amr ibn-Hind to appreciate the finer things of life; he became a patron of the poet Tarafah and other practitioners of the art of Mu'allaqāt, or suspended odes.[7]

Hinematioro
Paramount chieftainess of the Ngati Porou (seventeenth or eighteenth century)

The Ngati Porou is a Maori group of some 40 tribes in New Zealand. The Maori are a Polynesian people that migrated to New Zealand in two waves, ca. the ninth and fourteenth centuries. The largest social division is the tribe, based on common ancestry. The subtribes are the principal landowners. Unlike other tribes, the Ngati Porou have retained most of their ancestral lands and the *mana*—prestige and power—that comes with them. Hinematioro was one of the rare women who attained lofty status, due in part to the prestige of her ancestors. The Maori not only record their ancestors in the ''treasured book,'' but also memorize these genealogies, and the most skilled orators relate them to guests. All that remains to attest to Hinematioro's ferocity and her status are ornately carved wooden openwork prows and figureheads outfitting her 100-foot-long war canoe.[8]

Hodierna of Jerusalem
Countess, regent of Tripoli (1152–1164)

Hodierna was one of the four popular daughters of King Baldwin II of Jerusalem (1118–1131) and Queen Morphia. Her sisters were Melisende, who married King Fulk of Anjou and bore King Baldwin III; Alice, who married King Bohemond IV of Antioch; and Joveta, who, because she had been captured by Turks as a child, was considered too tainted to make a suitable marriage and was sent off to become abbess of Bethany.

Hodierna was married in 1133 to Count Raymond of Tripoli, a man of strong passions who was jealously devoted to her. In 1140 their son Raymond III was born, and they also had a daughter of great beauty, Melisende. Hodierna and Raymond's marriage was not entirely happy; gossip circulated concerning the legitimacy of Hodierna's daughter Melisende, and Raymond, wildly jealous, attempted to keep his wife in seclusion. Their relationship worsened to the point that early in 1152 Hodierna's sister, Queen Melisende, felt it her duty to intervene. She persuaded her son, King Baldwin III, to accompany her to Tripoli to try to achieve a reconciliation between the two. Raymond and Hodierna agreed to call off their quarrel, but it was decided that Hodierna should take a long holiday in Jerusalem. Queen Melisende and Hodierna set off southward for Jerusalem, accompanied for the first mile or so by Raymond. As he returned to the capital, he was attacked by a band of assassins as he entered the south gate and stabbed to death. King Baldwin III, who had remained behind at the castle playing dice, marshalled the garrison, which rushed out and killed every Moslem in sight but did not find the assassins. Baldwin sent messengers to bring back Queen Melisende and Hodierna and tell them the grim news. Hodierna then assumed the regency in the name of her 12-year-old son Raymond III, but since the Turks were a constant threat, it was thought that a man was also needed as guardian of the government and

Baldwin, as nearest male relative, obliged. The Turks attacked Tortosa and were driven out, but with Hodierna's consent, Baldwin gave Tortosa to the Knights of the Temple and returned to Jerusalem. In 1164 King Amalric assumed the regency for Raymond III. Hodierna's daughter's questionable parentage cost her the opportunity to become the bride of Byzantine Emperor Manual.[9]

Hortense de Beauharnais
Queen, regent of Holland (1810)

She was born in 1783, the daughter of Alexander, vicomte de Beauharnais, and Joséphine Tascher de la Pagerie of Martinique. Reared in Paris, she spent the years from age five to ten on Martinique after her parents separated. When Alexander died, Joséphine married Napoleon I (1797), and that marriage was to change Hortense's future. Attractive, intelligent, and cultured, she later wrote in her memoirs, ''My life has been so brilliant and so full of misfortune that the world has been forced to take notice of it.'' Hortense was a gifted pianist and composer of popular songs, at least two of which were sung by French troops. In 1802 she married Louis Bonaparte, Napoleon's brother, and became, so to speak, sister-in-law to her stepfather Napoleon. She bore three sons: Charles Napoleon, born in 1802, died in 1807; Napoleon Louis, born in 1804; Louis Napoleon (later Napoleon III), born in 1808, possibly fathered by someone other than Louis. She became queen of Holland in 1806 when Napoleon gave her husband Louis the crown. In 1809 she took a lover, the comte de Flahault. In 1810 Louis abdicated in favor of his elder son and appointed Hortense as regent of Holland. In 1811, nearly a year after her husband had gone into exile at Teplitz, she became pregnant. She went into hiding and gave birth to a son who was placed into the charge of his paternal grandmother, the novelist Madame de Souza. However, word of the pregnancy may have reached her husband because the two separated when he returned. After the surrender of Napoleon, Hortense received 400,000 francs per year and the title of duchesse de Saint-Leu, although she lost the rank of queen. Her husband received a lower title, the comte de Saint-Leu, which annoyed him. In 1814 her husband sued for separation, demanding custody of their older son. The principle of paternal authority was enshrined in French law, and her lawyers told her it was pointless to contest, but she did. Although her lawyer made a brilliant impassioned appeal for the rights of a mother against the archaic laws that considered only the rights of the father, the court ruled in favor of the father. Although he did not comply immediately, Napoleon Louis eventually went to live with his father. During the restoration and the Hundred Days, Napoleon stayed in Hortense's home for four days. She once received the protection of Alexander I, tzar of Russia, but after she had accepted the pension and title from King Louis XVIII and the friendship of the tzar, her support of Napoleon during the Hundred Days seemed traitorous. The tzar said of her, ''She is the cause of all the troubles which have befallen France.''

Napoleon Louis married his cousin Charlotte, daughter of King Joseph, and opened a paper factory, designing the machinery himself. He experimented with mechanical flight as well. Hortense and her younger son Louis Napoleon sought exile in England. Louis Napoleon joined the Bonapartists and, after an unsuccessful attempt or two, gained election as president of France. Later, the republic reverted briefly to an empire, and Louis became Napoleon III. Hortense died of cancer in 1837 with her son at her side.[10]

Hsiao-shih
Queen, regent of Khita (A.D. 983–?)

Hsiao-shih was the wife of the Khitan khan Ye-lü Hsien, who died in 983. Their son Ye-lü Lung-sü, born in 971, acceded to the throne upon his father's death with Hsiao-shih as regent. The appearance of a minor ruler under the guardianship of a female regent generally sparked an attempt by neighboring foes to usurp the throne. In 986 the kingdom was attacked by the army of the second Chinese Sung Emperor T'ai-tsung, but Khitan General Ye-lü Hiou-ko defeated the Chinese, then threw the retreating troops into the Sha River to drown. In 989 the Chinese tried again to overcome the Khitans but were defeated near Paoting.[11]

Hu
Queen, ruler of the Toba in Central Asia
(A.D. 515–528)

The wife of King Toba K'iao, who ruled Toba from A.D. 499 to 515, Hu reigned for 13 years upon the death of her husband. A descendant of the old Tabatch Dynasty, Hu was a forceful leader and the last member of the Tabatch to display the ancient strength. Described as a woman of exceptional energy, with a passion for power that led to bloodthirstiness on occasion, Hu was nevertheless a devout Buddhist. She added to the adornment of the Lungmen sanctuaries and dispatched the Buddhist pilgrim Sung Yun on a mission to northwest India (518–521). He returned with Buddhist documents that she prized.[12]

Ide d'Alsace
Countess of Boulogne (1173–1216)

Ide was the daughter of Countess Marie of Bou-logne (1159–1173) and Matthieu d'Alsace. When her mother died in 1173, Ide became ruler of Boulogne. She married four times. When she died in 1216, she was succeeded by Mauhaut de Dammaratin.[1]

Irene
Empress, co-ruler of the Byzantine Empire (780–790 and 792–797), then "emperor" (797–802)

Irene was born ca. 752, the daughter of Athe-nian parents. In ca. 769 she married Leo IV, surnamed the Chazar (or Kahzar) for his bar-barian mother. Leo ruled the Byzantine Empire from 775 to 780. They had a son, Constantine VI, in 770. The following year, the infant was crowned co-emperor to prevent Leo's step-brother Nicephorus from claiming the throne. When Leo IV died prematurely in 780, Irene became co-emperor with her ten-year-old son. A concealed iconodule with a lust for power, Irene could justify all her actions because she believed she was the chosen instrument of God. Her efforts were focused on gaining and keep-ing power, not on improving the welfare of the state. Her first test came immediately when Caesar Nicephorus, supported by the icono-clasts, attempted to overthrow her regime. She rapidly suppressed the rebellion and made it known that she was firmly in control. With cun-ning, diplomacy, and intrigue, she was instru-mental in restoring the use of icons in the Eastern Roman Empire when the Seventh Ecu-menical Council met in Nicea in 787. This ac-tion earned her the devotion of the Greek Church, and all her actions to follow could not deny her eventual sainthood. She forced a wife, Maria, on her son Constantine VI, who grew resentful of his mother's power as he matured. A first attempt to wrest control from her was quelled, Constantine was flogged, and Irene de-manded to be recognized as senior ruler, with her name placed above Constantine's. Finally, in 790, the army, with whom she was unpopu-lar, rejected the ambitious demands of Irene and proclaimed Constantine sole ruler. She abdi-cated and was banished from the court.

But Constantine VI proved disappointingly weak. In 792 he allowed his mother and her faithful lieutenant, the eunuch Stauracius, to re-turn, and Irene was even allowed to resume the position of co-ruler. She incited her son to blind Alexius, the general who had led the attack against her on Constantine's behalf, and to mu-tilate his uncles, who had plotted against her. In 795 she encouraged him in his lust for his mistress Theodote and persuaded him to divorce his wife, Maria. In marrying Theodote, he violated all ecclesiastical laws, outraging public opinion. With Constantine in such general disfavor, she was free to have him arrested, blinded, and deposed. In 797 she proclaimed herself sole reigning emperor, not empress.

Irene was the first woman to control the empire as an independent ruler in her own right and not as a regent for either a minor or an emperor unfit to rule. The monks praised their benefactress, who bestowed large gifts upon them. She lowered taxes while raising endowments, making everyone happy but ruining the finances of the Byzantine state. In 798 she opened diplomatic relations with Charlemagne. In 802 he was said to be contemplating marriage to Irene, but the plan never reached fruition. In the same year a conspiracy led by the Logothete-General Nicephorus seized the throne, and Irene was exiled to the island of Principio, then to Lesbos, where she died in 803. She is a saint of the Greek Orthodox Church.[2]

Empress Irene. Byzantine Visual Resources, Dumbarton Oaks, Washington, DC.

Isabel

Princess, regent of the Brazilian Empire (1871–1872 and 1876–1888)

Isabel was born in 1846, the daughter of Dom Pedro de Alantara, Pedro II, second and last emperor of the Brazilian Empire, who ruled from 1840 to 1889. King Pedro was a wise and able ruler, and his daughter was educated to become one as well. She married a Frenchman, Gaston d'Orléans, comte d'Eu. In 1871, 1876, and 1888, King Pedro, anxious to improve Brazil's relations with Europe, personally made extended visits to European heads of state. He also visited the U.S. president in 1876. During those protracted absences, Isabel acted as regent. Although Pedro and Isabel as his regent did much to enhance education, remove corruption, abolish slavery, and enhance revenues, their popularity waned. In 1888 Isabel decreed complete emancipation without compensation to owners, and about 700,000 slaves were freed, causing the slave owners to withdraw their support of the king. Advocacy for a republic grew, as did dissatisfaction with Isabella and her French husband. The army, which Pedro had barred from dabbling in politics, hatched a conspiracy and revolted in 1889. Pedro abdicated and he and Isabel and their family sought exile in Europe. Isabel died in Europe in 1921.[3]

Isabella

See Zabel

Isabella

Countess, ruler of Foix (1398–1412)

Isabella was the daughter of Gaston III Phebus, who ruled Foix from 1343 to 1391, and the sister of Matthieu de Castelbon, who succeeded upon the death of his father in 1391 and ruled until 1398. She married Archambaud de Graille, and they had at least one son, Jean de Graille. She acceded upon her brother's death in 1398 and ruled until her own death in 1412. Her son Jean then became count of Foix.[4]

Isabella

Queen of Beirut (1264–1282)

She was the daughter of John II of Beirut, who died in 1264, and the sister of Eschiva of Ibelin, queen of Cyprus. Isabella remained a figure-head all her life. She was first married to the child king of Cyprus, Hugh II, who died in 1267 before the marriage could be consummated. She then married an Englishman, Hamo L'Étranger (Edmund the Foreigner), who soon died, leaving her under the protection of the Sultan Baibar. King Hugh of Cyprus tried to carry her off and remarry her to the candidate of her choice, but the Sultan Baibar, citing the pact that her late husband had made with him, demanded she be sent back to Beirut, where a Mameluk guard "protected" her. She married twice more, to Nicholas L'Aleman and William Barlais. When she died in 1282, Beirut passed to her sister, Eschiva.[5]

Isabella I the Catholic
Queen of Castile (1474–1504)

She was born in 1451, the only daughter of Juan II, ruler of Castile from 1406 to 1454, and his second wife Isabella of Portugal. Her half brother was Enrique IV (Henry IV), who ruled Castile after his father died, from 1454 to 1474. Because Isabella was Enrique's heir, he had plans for her marriage to which she violently objected, for Isabella had larger ideas for a po-litical match with the possibility of uniting Spain. In a furtive ceremony in 1469, Isabella married her second cousin Ferdinand II, heir of the king of Aragon. This secret union would prove to be one of the most important events in Spanish history, for their heir would inherit both the kingdom of Aragon and the kingdom of Castile, thus forming Spain as we know it. Although theirs was not a love match, they grew to be the most devoted of couples, even insisting on being buried together. The couple had five children: John, Isabella, Juana, María, and Catherine. In 1474 Enrique died and Isa-bella became queen of Castile. Enrique's daughter Juana contested the claim and a civil war followed. When it ended in 1479, Isabella was the undisputed queen. That same year King Juan II of Aragon died, and Ferdinand became King of Aragon. The two countries were ad-ministered separately during the lifetimes of the couple.

Following a flagrant breach of the truce be-

Isabella I the Catholic. The Granger Collection, New York.

tween the Moors in Granada and Castile, Isa-bella became determined to drive the Moors from her land in a battle that lasted a decade (1482–1492). When she was well into her fourth pregnancy and prepared to join her hus-band in Cordoba, she was warned that it was foolish to travel so close to the Moorish capital, but she told her advisors, "Glory is not to be won without danger." Throughout the cam-paign, the king rode at the head of her army and Isabella became quartermaster and financier. She also visited camps to encourage the soldiers and established field hospitals and front line emergency tent hospitals. The latter became known as Queen's Hospitals. The truce in 1492 made Spain an all-Christian nation again after 781 years.

In 1486 Christopher Columbus, seeking fi-nancial backing for his search for a shorter route to Asia, knew that he stood a better chance of impressing the intuitive and enthusiastic Isa-bella than her cautious husband. However, although Columbus' proposition excited her imagination, all her funds were being funneled into the war with Granada. It was not until 1492, when Santangel, Ferdinand's Keeper of the Privy Purse, reminded Isabella that her goal had been to make her country preeminent in Europe, that she summoned Columbus to return to make a contract. During the next ten years she funded four voyages to the new world. Isabella is remembered for her support for Columbus, but she also was a great patron of literature, the arts, and the Church. She died in 1504, shortly before Columbus returned from his fourth voyage.[6]

Isabella II
Queen of Spain (1833–1868)

She was born in 1830, the elder daughter of King Ferdinand VII, who ruled Spain from 1814 to 1833, and his fourth wife, María Christina of Naples. Three months before he died, at the urging of his wife, Ferdinand set aside the Salic Law, or male succession law, to assure the succession of his infant daughter, thereby depriving his brother, Don Carlos, of the throne. Isabella was proclaimed queen at age three with her mother as regent. Don Carlos' dispute of her claim culminated in the first Carlist War (1834–1839). In 1840 General Baldomero Espartero, a Progressist, seized power, forced María Christina to leave the country, assumed the regency himself, and became dictator. In 1843 he was deposed by the military and Isabella was declared of age to rule, although she was only 13. In 1846 she married her cousin, Francisco de Asíz de Borbón, the duke of Cádiz. She had four children: Isabella, María de la Paz, Eulalia, and Alfonso XII. In 1847 the second Carlist War and republican uprising weakened the liberal system that was in place. A new prime minister, O'Donnell, engaged the country in war against Morocco from 1859 to 1860. Isabella was separated from her husband, and it was rumored that she took lovers, including an actor and son of a cook, Carlos Marfori, whom she made minister of state. Her reign continued to be plagued by political unrest and uprisings. In 1868 a revolution forced her to flee to France and she was declared deposed. How-

ever, in 1870 she took the formal step of abdicating in favor of her son, Alfonso XII, who, after much shuffling of leadership in Spain, declared for a constitutional monarchy when he came of age in 1874. Isabella died in Paris in 1904.[7]

Isabella Clara Eugenia of Austria
Co-ruler of the Spanish Netherlands (1598–1621), then sole governor (1621–1633)

She was born in 1566, the daughter of King Philip II, who ruled Spain from 1556 to 1598, and his third wife Elizabeth of Valois. In 1587 Philip unsuccessfully proposed Isabella as successor to the English throne after the execution of Mary Queen of Scots and, in 1598, to the throne of France after the assassination of her uncle Henry III. She married Albert, archduke of Austria, and received as dowry the ten southern Spanish Netherlands provinces to rule (1598). The rule of Isabella and Albert signaled a change in policy: Flemish Catholics were treated in a conciliatory manner rather than driven to hostility. Under their rule the Southern Netherlands regained part of its earlier pros-

Isabella Clara Eugenia of Austria. The Granger Collection, New York.

perity. The seven provinces of the Northern Netherlands had a measure of autonomy, and Isabella and Albert attempted to reunite the provinces, first by diplomacy and later by force, but they failed. Albert died in 1621, and the Netherlands became a Spanish sovereignty, but Isabella remained and ruled as governor for her nephew the king (Philip IV) until her death in Brussels in 1633.[8]

Isabella d'Este
Marquessa, regent of Mantua (1495 and 1509)

Isabella received the kind of education usually reserved for a noble boy. At 16 she married Francesco II Gonzaga, the marquis of Mantua. She administered his lands during his absence, while he led Venetian forces against Charles VIII in 1495. They had a son, Federico, born in 1500. In 1509, when her husband was taken prisoner by the Venetians, Isabella ruled Mantua and held it against the threatening forces of the Venetians. Her husband was released by intervention of the pope. As a reward for his support of Emperor Maximilian I against Venice, their son was named duke of Mantua. Isabella, a great patron of the arts and letters, presided with her husband over a splendid and impressive court.[9]

Isabella (or Elizabeth) Farnese of Parma
Queen and de facto co-ruler of Spain (1714–1746)

She was born in 1692 in Parma, Italy, the niece and stepdaughter of the duke of Parma. In 1714 she married Philip V of Spain after the death of his first wife, María Louisa Gabriela of Savoy. Isabella was a handsome, ambitious woman who immediately dismissed the royal favorite and took complete control of her husband. They had seven children: Charles, Francisco, Philip, Luís Antonio, Mariana, Teresa, and Antonia. Since Philip had two sons by his first wife, Isabella had not much hope that her children would sit on the Spanish throne, and therefore spent much of her reign attempting to supplant Austrian power in Italy, securing Italian thrones for her children. She was shrewd in her choice of ministers, selecting only those who would carry out her foreign policy to the ends that

Spain's imperialistic gains in Italy were significant. She also made improvements in the country's economy and enacted reforms in the military and administrative branches of the government. Her husband abdicated briefly in 1724 in favor of his oldest son Luís but returned when Luís died of smallpox that same year. Her husband died in 1746 and was succeeded by his other son by his first wife, Ferdinand VI. Isabella then retired from court. She died in 1766.[10]

Isabella of Bavaria
Regent of France by reason of her husband's insanity (1392–1422)

Isabella was born in 1371, the daughter of Stephen III, duke of Bavaria-Ingolstadt. In 1385 she married Charles VI, king of France, who ruled from 1380 to 1422. Her husband's first attack of insanity occurred in 1392. The following year the first of their six children was born. In the ensuing years she was frequently regent as Charles' seizures of insanity worsened and grew more protracted. She chose Philip of Burgundy as an advisor, and later the king's brother Louis, duke of Orléans, became her constant advisor. When Louis was killed in

Isabella of Bavaria. The Granger Collection, New York.

1407, she turned to John the Fearless, the new duke of Burgundy as of 1404. In 1415 Henry V of England invaded France and defeated the French at Agincourt, reconquering Normandy for the English. In 1417 her son Charles, who would rule later as Charles VII (1422–1461), was determined to gain control and had his mother imprisoned. She was rescued by John the Fearless, who assisted her in establishing a new seat of government, first at Chartres and then at Troyes. In 1419, as the English continued to advance, John the Fearless was assassinated. The following year King Charles, with Isabella's support, accepted the Treaty of Troyes, in which he repudiated the dauphin as illegitimate and adopted Henry V as heir. Henry V continued his steady conquest of France until his death in 1422. Isabella's husband died the same year. She faded from the political arena as the dauphin schemed to regain his rightful throne. She died in 1435 in Paris.[11]

Isabella of Cyprus
Regent of Jerusalem (1263)

The eldest sister of King Henry of Cyprus, Isabella married Henry of Antioch, youngest son of Bohemond IV. In 1253 the couple had a son,

Hugh II of Cyprus. In addition, Isabella reared her late sister's son, also named Hugh (of Brienne). Much information that remains about Isabella concerns her efforts to attain her rightful regency. When Queen Plaisance of Cyprus died in 1261, a new regent was required for Cyprus and Jerusalem, as Isabella's son, Hugh II, was only eight years old. Plaisance's late husband was Isabella's brother, leaving Isabella as the next in the line of succession as regent. The High Court of Cyprus refused Isabella as regent in favor of her young son, but in 1263 the High Court of Jerusalem named her regent de facto, refusing to administer the oath of allegiance because King Conradin was not present. Isabella appointed her husband Henry as *bailli*. In the thirteenth century the *bailli* was much more powerful than the English bailiff. The *bailli* had authority to act for the monarch in collecting and dispensing funds, raising an army, defending the area, maintaining order, holding court, and overseeing minor officeholders. Isabella died in 1264 and her son, who was by then 11, became regent, although her nephew Hugh of Brienne put in a counterclaim. But as Isabella had been accepted as the last regent, the vote was unanimous that her son should succeed her.[12]

Jacqueline (or Jacoba)
Countess, ruler of Holland, Zeeland, and Hainault (1417–1433)

The daughter of William VI of the house of Bavaria, ruler of Holland from 1404 to 1417, Jacqueline ascended to the throne upon his death. In 1415 she married John of Touraine, dauphin of France, who died two years later. The German king Sigismund refused to recognize Jacqueline's right to rule, so in 1418 she married her cousin John IV, duke of Brabant. When John mortgaged Holland and Zeeland the following year, Jacqueline repudiated their marriage and in 1421 went to England and married Humphrey, duke of Gloucester. The couple returned with an army in 1424 to retake her lands; however, Humphrey deserted and retreated to England the following year and Jacqueline was taken prisoner by Philip the Good, duke of Burgundy, who had his own designs on Holland. In 1425 she escaped and marshalled English forces to combat Philip; however, in 1428 the Pope intervened, declaring her English marriage null. Jacqueline was forced to make peace with Philip and to promise not to marry without his consent. In 1430 she secretly married Francis, lord of Zulen and St. Maartensdijk, with an eye to overthrowing Philip. But Francis was taken prisoner in 1432 and Jacque-line was forced to abdicate the following year. She was made duchess of Bavaria and countess of Ostrevant, and she publicly remarried Francis in 1434. She died two years later.

Jadwiga (or Hedwig)
"Maiden king" of Poland (1384–1399)

Jadwiga was born ca. 1373, the third daughter of Louis I of Anjou, king of Poland (1370–1382) and of Hungary (1342–1382), and Elizabeth of Bosnia. Polish nobility had made a special agreement to accept any one of Louis' daughters as their next ruler. Louis did not have serious concerns about Poland, which he governed through his regent-mother Elizabeth until her death, and thereafter through a council of regents. But he was concerned that the succession to the Hungarian throne should be secure. He had appointed Jadwiga as his successor and had betrothed her and formally celebrated her marriage at the age of five to William of Hapsburg, anticipating by such a union a closer relationship between Hungary and Austria. But after Louis died in 1382, the Hungarian nobles elected her sister Maria as "king of Hungary." Maria, who had been married to Sigismund, son of Emperor Charles IV, had been designated by Louis to inherit the throne of Poland after the oldest sister Catherine died in 1378. But the Polish nobles, who did not want the holy Roman emperor to have a hand in their future, urged Queen Elizabeth to name her younger daughter Jadwiga as successor to the Polish throne. However, they did not approve of Jadwiga's Austrian husband and decided that she should marry the new grand duke of Lithuania, Jagiello, hoping that he would reclaim their territory lost to Hungary.

During the interregnum following Louis' death (1382–1384) Poland suffered through civil wars and upheavals, while Polish nobles vied to increase their own power and privileges. In 1384 Jadwiga was formally elected and crowned ''king.'' After trying unsuccessfully to defend his right by attempting to occupy Wawel castle in Cracow, William of Hapsburg, Jadwiga's former ''husband,'' returned to Vienna. In 1386 at age 12, Jadwiga, who had been genuinely fond of William, had to content herself with marrying the 35-year-old Jagiello ''for the good of her country.'' Jagiello, who had converted to Catholicism and taken the name Władysław II, never intended to play the role of prince consort, but the young Jadwiga, being the hereditary claimant, had the right to rule on her own if she wished; therefore the ruling class of Poland did not wholeheartedly accept his attempts to rule. Frustrated in his ambitions, he was nevertheless able to unite his dukedom of Lithuania, three times the size of Poland, with Poland and to convert the country to Catholicism. Jadwiga remained somewhat intimidated by her older husband. She bore no children and died at the age of 29 in 1399. Only then did Jagiello become ruler of Poland in his own right. He married again three times. His last wife, Sonia of Kiev, bore two sons who became kings of Poland.[1]

Jane
Queen of England. *See* Grey, Jane

Jane
Queen of Naples. *See* Joanna I

Jeanne I
Countess, ruler of Dreux (1345–1346)

Jeanne was the wife of Count Robert, who ruled Dreux from 1309 to 1329. She succeeded her brothers Jean II, who ruled from 1329 (when

their father died) to 1331 and Pierre, who ruled from 1331 (when his brother died) to 1345. When she died a year later, her aunt succeeded her.[2]

Jeanne I
Countess of Champagne (1274–1304). *See* Juana I, queen of Navarre

Jeanne II
Countess, ruler of Dreux (1346–1355)

Jeanne was the second daughter of Count Jean II, who ruled Dreux from 1282 to 1309, and the sister of Count Robert, who ruled from their father's death in 1309 to 1329. She married Louis, vicomte de Thouars, and bore a son, Simon. When her niece, Countess Jeanne I, died in 1346, she succeeded to the reign. Her son Simon succeeded her in 1355.[3]

Jeanne d'Albret
Queen of Navarre (1555–1572)

Jeanne was born ca. 1528, the daughter of Henry II, king of Navarre from 1516 to 1555, and his second wife, Margaret of Angoulême. From 1521 until he died, Henry warred with France for the return of his Navarre territories lost by his parents in 1514. In 1548 Jeanne married Antoine de Bourbon, duke of Vendôme. They had a son, Henry, born in 1553, who had scant prospects of becoming King Henry IV of France because there were so many in the line of succession ahead of him. In 1555, Jeanne became queen of Navarre when her father died. In a series of religious wars in France, Antoine, at first a leader of the Protestant faction, eventually changed his mind and became a champion of the Catholics. Queen Jeanne, however, publicly announced her Calvinism on Christmas in 1560. In 1562 her estranged husband Antoine was killed fighting the Calvinists. In 1568 Queen Jeanne, who had remained neutral during the first two religious wars, entered the third war. When her brother-in-law Louis I, head of the army, was killed in Jarnac, she hurried to the scene and proclaimed her son Henry, age 15, the head of the army. When the war ended in 1570, Jeanne and Catherine de Médicis began arrangements for a marriage between Henry and Catherine's daughter, Margaret of Valois. The marriage occurred two years later. Queen Jeanne traveled to Paris to prepare for the event but died of a respiratory infection two months before the ceremony took place. Henry not only became king of Navarre, but also, in 1589, King Henry IV of France.[4]

Jeanne de Castile
Co-ruler of Vendôme (1366–1374)

Jeanne was married to Count Jean VI, who ruled Vendôme from 1336 to 1366. They had two children: Catherine and Bouchard VII. When her husband died in 1366, Jeanne served as co-ruler with her son, for whom she was guardian. Bouchard died in 1374, and her daughter assumed the reign.[5]

Jeanne de Chatillon
Countess, ruler of Blois (1279–1292)

She was the daughter of Jean de Chatillon, count of Blois and Chartres, who ruled from 1241 to 1279. She married Pierre, count of Alençon. She succeeded to the rule of Blois on her father's death. She died in 1292, leaving no offspring, and was succeeded by her German cousin, Hugues de Chatillon.[6]

Jeanne de Nemours (also called Marie de Savoy-Nemours)
Duchess, regent of Savoy (1675–1684)

Jeanne was the wife of Charles Emmanuel II, ruler of Savoy from 1638 to 1675. In 1666 they had a son, Victor Amadeus II, who succeeded as ruler when his father died in 1675. Jeanne acted as regent not only until he attained majority, but until 1684. Savoy, located between France, Austria, and Italy (and now a part of Italy), had once been occupied by French forces, and although it had long since regained its sovereignty and had even expanded its holdings, it constantly had to play diplomatic dodgeball between the two powers, France and the Hapsburg Empire. Jeanne inherited a Francophile orientation of Savoy's policy, which she thought it wisest to continue. After Savoy had acquired Sicily and following the Treaty of Utrecht in 1713, Jeanne encouraged her son to

trade, through diplomatic maneuvering, his title of duke of Savoy by exchanging Sicily for Sardinia. He then became the king of Sardinia-Piedmont. Jeanne died in 1724.[7]

Jindan
Rani, regent of the Sikh Kingdom of the Punjab (ca. 1843–1846)

The daughter of a chieftain of the Kanhayas and of the domineering Sada Kaur, in 1795 Jindan became the first wife of Ranjit Singh, age 15, who had been chief of the Śukerchakīās since he was 12. For the first few years of their marriage, the Rani's mother directed all of Ranjit's affairs, but in 1801 he proclaimed himself maharajah of the Punjab. In 1838 the British viceroy persuaded him to assist in placing a British choice on the throne of Kabul in Afghanistan. Following the victory in Afghanistan, Ranjit fell ill and died (1843). He was succeeded by his youngest son, Dalip or Dulop Singh, with his widow, Jindan, as regent. In 1845 British encroachment on the Punjab made it necessary for the rani, the chief minister, and the commander in chief of the army, to agree to attack the British. Their defeat in 1846 led to the Treaty of Lahore whereby they lost a number of territories, including Kashmir. Jindan was deposed as regent and a council was appointed to govern, but a second Sikh revolt erupted in 1848. The new government was powerless to stop it, and the insurrection was put down by the British. This time the British deposed the young king and sent him and Rani Jindan to England. He became a Christian and a landowner in Norfolk. A final bloody encounter in 1849 between the Sikhs and the British ended with British annexation of the Punjab.[8]

Jingō-kōgō
Empress, regent of Japan (ca. A.D. 200–269)

She was born ca. 169, the daughter of Prince Okinaga no Sukune and Katsuraki no Taka-nuka-hime. She married Chūai-tennō (Tarashi-Naka-tsu-hiko), fourteenth Emperor of Japan, who ruled from 192 to 200. The emperor had planned an expedition to conquer Korea but

Jingō-kōgō. William H. Laufer.

died in A.D. 200 before he could undertake it. The empress, although pregnant with their son at the time, conducted the expedition to Korea and brought the kings of Koryo, Pekche, and Silla (Kōrae, Hakusai, and Shinra) under her suzerainty. (Some discrepancy can be seen between Japanese and Korean dating of the expedition. According to Korean records, the expedition occurred in A.D. 346.) She returned to Japan in time to give birth to Homuda, the future Emperor Ōjin. Two sons of one of her husband's concubines revolted, claiming succession by right of primogeniture. Jingō sent General Taki-shiuchi no Sukune to put them to death, thereby ending all threat to her reign. She refused to ascend to the throne but ruled as regent for 69 years. She died in 269 at the age of 100 and was honored with the name Kashi-dai-myōjin, meaning first, most distinguished, mighty as an oak. (According to Korean histories, the empress died in 380.)[9]

Jitō-tennō
Empress, ruler of Japan (686–697)

She was born in A.D. 625, named Hironu hime, or Uno no Sasara, a daughter of Emperor Tenchi, who ruled Japan from 662 to 671, and a sister of Kōbun-tennō, who ruled from 671 to 672. When their father fell ill, he shaved his head and retired to Yoshino-zan. Kōbun-tennō assumed the throne, but a civil war broke out. Tenchi's brother, Ō-ama no Ōji, revolted and claimed the succession. Ō-ama defeated the imperial troops, so Kōbun-tennō killed himself after a reign of only eight months. Ō-ama ascended the throne and ruled for 14 years as Temmu-tennō, marrying his niece, Jitō. When he died in 687, Jitō succeeded him, at the age of 42. During her reign Jitō made important administrative reforms, encouraged the development of agriculture, and had the first silver coin struck. Sensitive to the religious plurality over which she reigned, she endeavored to remain impartial in her religious devotions and contributed to both Buddhist and Shintō temples. After a reign of 11 years, she abdicated in favor of her nephew (and grandson) Mommu. Upon her retirement she was the first to take the honorary title for past emperors, Dajō-tennō. She was also the first monarch to be cremated. She died in A.D. 701.[10]

Jitō-tennō. William H. Laufer.

Joanna I (or Joan I or Giovanni I; also called Jane)

Countess (of Provence), queen of Naples (1343–1381)

She was born in 1326, the daughter of Charles of Calabria and Maria of Valois, and the granddaughter of Robert the Good, king of Naples from 1309 to 1343, whom she succeeded upon his death, becoming the first queen of Naples. Queen Joanna, intelligent and politically astute as well as beautiful, married her cousin, Andrew of Hungary, brother of Hungarian King Louis I (or Lewis), as a political ploy to reconcile Hungarian claims upon Naples. The influx of Hungarians brought by Andrew into Naples angered many, including Joanna, who feared that the Hungarians intended to take over Naples. Andrew was assassinated in 1345, if not by her instigation, at least with her consent. In 1347 she married Louis of Taranto but was forced to take exile in Avignon when her former brother-in-law, King Louis I, invaded Naples to avenge his brother's death, accusing her of strangling him. During her five-year exile, she sold Avignon to Pope Innocent VI in return for his declaration of her innocence of the assassination. Her second husband died ten years after her return, and in 1362 she married King James of Majorca. He died in 1375, and the following year she married Otto of Brunswick, a military man. At one time she named her niece's husband, Charles III of Durazzo, as her heir, but later she repudiated him and adopted as her heir Louis, duke of Anjou, brother of France's King Charles V. Durazzo appealed to Pope Urban VI, who in 1381 crowned him king of Naples in Rome. Durazzo then invaded Naples, imprisoned Joanna and, a year later (1382), had her murdered by suffocation.[11]

Joanna II (or Joan II or Giovanni II)

Queen of Naples (1414–1435)

Joanna was born in 1371, the daughter of Margaret of Durazzo and Charles III, who ruled Naples from 1382 to 1386 and Hungary from 1385 to 1386. She was the sister of Ladislas I, who succeeded as king of Naples after their father was murdered in 1386. She first married

William of Austria, but after he died in 1406, her amorous escapades kept Italian diplomacy in an uproar. When her brother Ladislas I died in 1414, Joanna succeeded to the throne and appointed her current lover Pandolfello Alopo grand chamberlain. The following year she married Jacques de Bourbon, comte de la Marche, who had her lover executed and then attempted to wrest the throne from her. But Italian barons, not wanting a French takeover, ousted him and sent him back to France. Joanna used the succession unmercifully as a maneuvering device. She adopted, then renounced, Alfonso V of Aragon (the Magnanimous) as her heir; adopted, then disinherited, Louis III of Anjou as her heir; readopted, then redisinherited, Louis; and, when Louis died, finally named his son René as her heir. She died in 1435, leaving Alfonso and René to fight it out. Alfonso was the victor and became the next king of Naples.[12]

Joanna of Austria

Regent of Portugal (1557–1562)

She was the daughter of Holy Roman Emperor Charles V, and Isabella, daughter of King Manuel I of Portugal. She married John of Portugal, second son of King John III (the Pious) of Portugal, who ruled from 1521 to 1557. In 1554, months before their son was born, John died. The boy, Sebastian I, succeeded to the throne three years later when his grandfather died. Joanna served as regent for five years. During her regency Portugal's overseas dominions frequently erupted in rebellions. In 1562 King John's brother, Cardinal Henry, was appointed to replace her for the remaining six years of the regency.[13]

Johanna (or Joanna)

Countess, ruler of Belgium (Flanders) (1206–1244)

The daughter of Baldwin IX, emperor of Constantinople from 1171 to 1195, Johanna became regent of Belgium in 1206 and was married to Ferdinand of Portugal in 1212. He served as co-regent until his death in 1233. She then ruled alone during a difficult period of Belgian history when the country was devastated by war. Upon her death in 1244, she was succeeded by her sister Margaret. Flanders, a great center of economic activity and a much fought-over territory, was ruled by women for 65 years.[14]

Johanna
Duchess, ruler of Brabant (1355–1406)

Johanna, of the House of Burgundy, was the daughter of John III, who ruled Brabant from 1312 to 1355. She succeeded him at his death in 1355. She married Wenceslas, duke of Luxembourg. On a ceremonial visit to Brabant in 1356, she tendered upon her subjects a new constitution, called *Joyeuse Entrée,* which conferred broad liberties to her subjects. Johanna had no children, and on her deathbed she named as successor her great-nephew Antoine of Burgundy, the grandson of her youngest sister Margaret and the son of Philip the Bold. She died in 1406.[15]

Juana (the Mad). Musées Royaux des Beaux-Arts de Belgique.

Juana (the Mad)
Queen of Spain (Castile) (1504–1509)

Juana was born in 1479, the daughter of Isabella I of Castile and Ferdinand II of Aragon She was married to Philip (the Handsome) of Burgundy and became archduchess of Burgundy. Philip became Philip I in 1504 when, upon Isabella's death, Juana inherited her mother's throne. Juana bore two sons: Charles, who became Charles I, king of Spain, and later was known as Charles V, holy Roman emperor; and Ferdinand, who succeeded his brother as holy Roman emperor. She had four daughters: Eleanor, who married King Manuel I of Portugal; Isabella, who married King Christian II of Denmark; María, who married King Louis II of Hungary; and Catherine, who married King John III of Portugal. When Philip died in 1506, Juana lost her sanity. She toured the country with his coffin and finally retired three years later to Tordesillas, still accompanied by his embalmed corpse.[16]

Juana I
Queen of Navarre (1274–1305)

She was born in 1273, the daughter of Henry (Enrique) I, king of Navarre from 1270 to 1274. She succeeded to the throne upon his death in 1274. From the mid-thirteenth century onward, the counts or countesses of Champagne were also kings or queens of Navarre. In 1284, Queen Juana I married Philip IV the Fair, who ruled France from 1285 to 1314. They had three sons who became kings of France: Louis X, Philip V, and Charles IV. Louis inherited Champagne from her, and it was subsequently annexed to France. He also inherited Navarre, but when he became king of France, he passed Navarre to his brother Philip. Juana's daughter Isabella married Edward II of England. In 1304 Queen Juana founded the College of Navarre. She died in 1305.[17]

Juana II
Queen of Navarre (1328–1349)

She was born in 1312, the daughter of Margaret of Burgundy and King Louis X, who ruled France from 1314 to 1316. She inherited the kingdom of Navarre at the death of her uncle, King Charles, who died in 1328. She married Count Philip of Evreux. Philip died in 1343. Their son, Charles (Carlos) II the Bad, inherited her throne when she died in 1349.[18]

Judith (or Esato or Yehudit)
Queen of the Falasha Agaw of Abyssinia
(tenth century)

Historical records do not make it clear when the Agaw became the monarchs of old Abyssinia (now Ethiopia). However, it is fairly certain that the Zagwe Dynasty of the Agaw of Lasta held power in Abyssinia from A.D. 1137 to 1270. In the south of Ethiopia, between the fault of the lakes and the loop of the Blue Nile, lay the great Damot kingdom. The Damot are possibly identical to the Demdem people, who are known to have been near Lake Abaya, the homeland of the Galla people. A part of these turbulent populations, who to some degree converted to Judaism, launched frequent attacks against the Amhara-Tegre power, the Christian provinces of Ethiopia. The most serious of these attacks, led by a queen named Esato (Judith) in ca. A.D. 976, devastated the Christian empire as far as the mountains of Tigre. The Ethiopians saw Esato's invasion as a heavenly punishment for their having failed to be obedient to their Coptic patriarch. Once they were delivered of Esato's terrible wrath, they tightened their bonds with the Egyptian Church. While the Agaw held political control, the Amhara and Tegre culture entered what has been described as a "dark age" about which little is known. A large part of the Ethiopian civilization was lost or destroyed during this time.[19]

Judith
See Zauditu

Julia Avita Mammaea
Augusta, regent, Roman Empire (222–235)

She was the daughter of Julia Maesa and Julius Avitas and the sister of Julia Soaemias. She married Gessius Marcianus, and in 208 they had a son, Severus Alexander, a personable and intelligent child. Julia's mother persuaded her grandson Emperor Elagabalus to adopt Alex-

ander as his heir. When Elagabalus was murdered, Julia Mammaea's son Alexander, age 14, became emperor. His mother acted as regent with a senatorial advisory council. After the death of her mother in 226, Julia Mammaea emerged as the real power, totally dominating the young emperor. In 232 she even accompanied the army in the Persian campaign, the failure of which was then ascribed to her interference. While on campaign in 235, she and her son were slain at Mainz by mutinous Roman soldiers led by Maximus Julius Verus.[20]

Julia Berenice
Jewish co-leader (ca. A.D. 52)

Julia Berenice was born ca. A.D. 28, the daughter of King Herod Agrippa I, who ruled Judaea from A.D. 37 to 44. In ca. 52 she shared the Chaleis throne and the business of the kingdom, in Batanala and Trachonites in southern Syria, with her brother Agrippa II, who succeeded as King of Judaea in A.D. 44. She lived with Agrippa, causing a scandal among the Jews, and continued to live with him even after a brief marriage to another eastern prince. She became a Flavian sympathizer. Roman Emperor Titus' (A.D. 79 to 81) infatuation with her and his contemplation of marriage to her, a Jewish princess 13 years his senior, so scandalized the court in Rome that he had to dismiss her.[21]

Julia Domna
Empress, regent of the Roman Empire
(211–217 intermittently)

Julia Domna was born in Emesa, Syria, the daughter of the prominent high priest Bassianus. Renowned for her intelligence and beauty, she was the elder sister of the famous and equally well-endowed Julia Maesa. In A.D. 187 she married the governor of Gallia Lugdunansis, Lucius Septimius Severus, who became Roman emperor in 193. She had two children in Gaul: Caracella (born in 188) and Geta (born in 189). Devoutly religious, she introduced the Semitic goddess Tanit (as Caelestis Dea) into the Roman world. In 203 she began gathering about her in Rome a group of philosophers and other literary figures. Her life was to change drastically in 207, when Severus mounted an expedition to Britain, taking Julia and their sons with him. He died in 211 while in Britain, and his sons became co-emperors and bitter antagonists. In 212 Caracella persuaded Julia to act as intermediary to bring the two together for a reconciliation. When Geta appeared, Caracella had his brother stabbed to death in his mother's arms. Caracella then ruled alone and was frequently gone on military campaigns, leaving Julia in charge of the administration of civil affairs. In 217 he was murdered by his praetorian prefect Macrinus, who was then proclaimed emperor. On news of her son's death, Julia starved herself to death (217), either voluntarily or upon Macrinus' orders.[22]

Julia Maesa
Augusta, de facto regent of Roman Empire (217–226)

She was born in Emesa, Syria, the daughter of the high priest Bassianus and the younger sister of Empress Julia Domna. She married a Roman senator, Julius Avitus, and they had two daughters: Julia Soaemias, who became the mother of Emperor Elagabalus (218–222); and Julia Mammaea, who became the mother of Emperor Severus Alexander (222–235). Her older grandson resembled his late kinsman Caracella, so after Caracella was murdered by Macrinus, she engineered a scheme to overthrow Macrinus whereby Syrian troops passed off Elagabalus as Caracellas' bastard son and proclaimed him emperor. Elagabalus succeeded to the throne, but his grandmother was the real power of the realm. She introduced the Syrian cult of Bael at Rome. Elagabalus was bisexual and had a tendency toward transvestism. He took three different wives and had many casual sexual encounters with various other partners. His conduct so disgusted his soldiers that by 221 it was clear to Julia that he would soon be murdered. She persuaded him to adopt his cousin Alexander as his son and caesar. The 14-year-old Alexander was so popular that Elagabalus became jealous and tried to have him killed. The outraged soldiers murdered Elagabalus and his mother Julia Soaemias in 222. Julia Maesa continued to exercise her power until her death in ca. 226.[23]

Juliana
Queen of the Netherlands (1948–1980)

Juliana Louise Emma Marie Wilhelmina was born in The Hague in 1909, the only child of Queen Wilhelmina and Prince Henry of Mecklenburg-Schwerin. As a teenage princess, she met her cousin Edward, Prince of Wales (the late duke of Windsor), and it was hoped in some circles that the two would be attracted to each other. Instead, the prince said, "Juliana, you have heavy legs," to which she retorted, "If the House of Windsor had been standing as long as the House of Orange, your legs wouldn't be so skinny." She studied at the University of Leiden from 1927 to 1930. In 1937 she married Prince Bernhard of Lippe-Biesterfeld. The couple had four daughters: Beatrice (1938), Irene (1939), Margaret (1943), and Marijke (1947). During World War II, she and her children took refuge in Ottawa, Canada, returning to the Netherlands in 1945. In 1947 and 1948 she acted as regent during her mother's illness and became queen in September 1948, following her mother's abdication; however, Juliana was not crowned because in Holland the crown belongs to the people. In 1947 she freed from Dutch rule all the Netherlands East Indies except New Guinea, which later became the Republic of Indonesia.

In the 1950s Juliana became interested in faith healing, and the news that she had put a faith healer on the payroll was met with public indignation. The marriage of her daughter Princess Irene to a Spanish Carlist and of Princess Beatrix to a German ex-Nazi aroused political controversy, as did the prince consort's acceptance of a large sum of money from Lockheed Aircraft Corporation in 1976. Juliana abdicated in 1980 in favor of her daughter Beatrix.[24]

Jumper, Betty Mae
Chief of Seminole Nation (1960s)

Betty Mae Jumper was born ca. 1927 in Florida and graduated from a reservation high school in Cherokee, North Carolina. She studied nursing in Oklahoma and went into fieldwork with the U.S. Public Health Service. She then returned to Florida to the state Seminole reservation, the Big Cypress Reservation, and has been active in the affairs of the tribe ever since. In the Seminole Nation the clans are perpetuated through the women. She was elected chief in the 1960s. An interviewer in 1969 described her as bright, jolly, and vivacious. As chief, her main concern was to raise the living standards of her tribe through education. She once cited the government-funded Head Start Program as the most important boost for Seminole children's education. She said, ''Many of the kids went into the first grade without knowing English. So they couldn't learn much, and they never did catch up. With Head Start they start out even.'' The program was dismantled by President Ronald Reagan.

Of her people, Jumper said, ''We don't want to be white people; we want to be Seminoles. We want the modern things, and we want to live nicely, but we want to do it among friends.'' Jumper claimed that the greatest trial of Indian youths who go away to college or military service is loneliness.[25]

Kahina (also called Cahina)
Priestess, queen of the Moors (ca. 695–703)

Prior to the capture of Byzantine-held Carthage by the Arabs and the establishment of the new Arab city of Tunis, the pastoral Berbers (the original inhabitants of northern Africa) had remained aloof from the struggle between Muslims and Christians, probably in the hope of benefiting from the aftermath. But around A.D. 695, the independent Berber tribes of the Aures Mountains in northern Africa joined under the leadership of a queen called Kahina, meaning priestess. Shortly after the capture of Carthage, Kahina and her tribes swept down upon the Arabs with savage ferocity. In 703 the Berbers defeated the Arabs under Hassan ibn No'man near Mons Aurasius (Aures Mountains) and drove the Saracens back to Egypt. After the victory, Queen Kahina assembled the Moorish chiefs and, according to Gibbon, suggested that, because the gold and silver in their cities attracted the Arabs, they should burn the cities and bury the "vile metals" in their ruins. The fortifications from Tangier to Tripoli were burned and even the fruit trees were cut down, leaving a desert. The populace was so devastated that the general of the Saracens was welcomed back. Queen Kahina was killed in the first battle against him.

Thereafter the Berbers became allies of the Arabs.[1]

Kalyānavati
Queen of Sri Lanka (1202–1208)

Kalyānavati was a member of the non-Sinhalese faction of the Kaliṅga Dynasty. She ruled during a chaotic period in Ceylonese history following the reign of Parākramabāhu I, who for the first time had united the island under one rule (1153–1186). Following his death, the country was ruled by a succession of relatives of his Kaliṅgan wife, none of whom ruled for very long. Queen Kalyānavati was the fifth ruler to take the throne in 16 years. She succeeded King Sahassamalla, who had ruled for only two years. Following her six-year reign, she was succeeded by another relative, King Dharmasaka, who ruled for only one year.[2]

Kassi
Empress of Mali (1241–?)

Kassi was the principal wife and paternal cousin of Emperor Suleyman, who ruled Mali from 1341 to 1360. According to Mali custom, the emperor and his principal wife ruled jointly. Kassi was extremely popular with the royal court, many members of which were her relatives. She was not, however, as popular with her husband as was a commoner named Bendjou, and eventually the emperor divorced Kassi in order to marry Bendjou. Kassi rallied support of the noble ladies of the court who refused to pay homage to the new empress. Instead, Kassi was still regarded as empress by the noble ladies, who would do obeisance by throwing earth on their heads and who showed their disdain for Bendjou by throwing earth on their hands. This insubordination angered both Bendjou and the emperor, and Kassi was forced to seek sanctuary in the mosque. From this vantage, she incited the nobles, particularly her cousins, to revolt. The ensuing struggle was actually a fracture of the larger division into two ideological factions vying for ascendancy. One party in the empire supported Suleyman, while the other supported the sons of the former ruler, Mansa Maghan I, Suleyman's nephew. The latter faction also supported Kassi. Suleyman and his military chiefs eventually defeated Kassi and her cousins, discrediting her with her party by proving that she was intriguing with her cousin Djathal, who had previously been expelled for treason. Suleyman was succeeded by Kassi's son, Kassa, who ruled only nine months before his cousin Mari Diata seized power.[3]

Khentkaues (or Khamerernebti II)
Co-ruler of Egypt (ca. 2494 B.C.)

She was the daughter of Khafre (also called Cephren), who ruled ca. 2520 to 2494 B.C. Her mother was most likely Khamerernebti I, the king's sister and his first wife. She was the sister and wife of Mycernius (also called Menhaure or Menkure), fifth ruler of the Fourth Dynasty, who ruled from ca. 2494 to 2472 B.C. Mycernius began construction on the third and smallest pyramid of Giza. Although the king was supreme, the surviving sculpture indicates that Khentkaues shared the rule. In the Fourth Dynasty, kingship in Egypt reached the peak of centralized authority. According to Herodotus, Mycernius (and Khentkaues?) had only one child, a daughter, who died. The king had a wooden cow made, hollow inside and plated with gold, to hold his daughter's body. The cow was still standing during Herodotus' time (ca. 490–425 B.C.). In a chamber adjoining the one housing the cow were some statues representing, by one account, concubines of Mycernius. By a second account, the daughter hanged herself because her father had violated her, so her mother cut off the hands of the servants who allowed the king access to her. The statues in the adjoining chamber, with missing hands, represent by this account the servants.[4]

Kōgyku-tennō
Empress, twice ruler of Japan (642–645) and as Saimei-tennō (655–ca. 662)

She was born in A.D. 594, the daughter of Prince Chinu no Ōji and Princess Kibi, and the granddaughter of Shōtoku-taishi, a Japanese regent from 593 to 621. Her birth name was Ametoyo-takara-ikashi-hitarashi hime, or Hitarashi-hime, or Tarashi for short. She first married Emperor Yōmei-tennō, who ruled from 586 to 587, and bore the Imperial Prince Aya. After her first husband died in 587, she then married her uncle, Emperor Jomei-tennō, who ruled from 629 to 641. She bore two more sons and a daughter. She succeeded her husband upon his death in 642, when she was 48, having been chosen by the Soga clan, which planned to wrest the ultimate control.

During Kōgyku-tennō's first reign, she was influenced by two powerful Soga ministers, Iruku and Emishi, who, at the instigation of her younger brother, Kōtoku, were assassinated in her presence in ca. 644. The next morning she abdicated in his favor. When he died ten years later, she reascended the throne at the age of 62. This time she did not allow herself to be influenced by her ministers. She built a palace at Yamato, the first to be covered with tiles. The feast of the dead was first celebrated during her second reign. She sent a force to Ezo to subdue the Ebisu. In 660 China attacked the two Korean kingdoms of Koma and Kudara, which asked for Japan's help. The empress prepared to lead an army bound for Korea personally but died unexpectedly on the way, at the palace at Asakura, at the age of 68. For her second term as empress, she received the posthumous name of Saimei-tennō.[5]

Kōken (also called Shōtoku-tennō or Takano-tennō)

Empress, twice ruler of Japan (749–758) and as Shōtoku-tennō (764–770)

She was born Abe-naishinnō in 716, the daughter of Shōmu-tennō, who ruled Japan from 724 to 748. In 749 he shaved his head and abdicated in favor of his unmarried daughter Kōken, then age 33. An ardent Buddhist like her father, Kōken assembled some 5,000 bonzes (Buddhist priests) in the Tō-daiji Temple, the Eastern Great Monastery, to read the sacred books. She exacted severe penalties for the killing of any living things. More interested in religion than government, she was eventually persuaded by an advisor, Nakamaro, to abdicate in favor of a kinsman, Junnin, whom Nakamaro then dominated completely. Kōken shaved her head and took the name of Takano-tennō. She allowed herself to be dominated by the bonze Dōkyō, who may also have been her lover. Dōkyō was a bitter rival of Nakamaro. In 764 the latter raised an army and marched against Dōkyō, but Nakamaro was killed in the fighting. Dōkyō persuaded Kōken, now age 48, to return to the throne, while Junnin-tennō was banished to the island of Awaji, where he died a year later. The empress bestowed favors and titles upon Dōkyō, but he aspired for more: he wanted to be emperor, and in 768 he tried to persuade the empress to abdicate in his favor. However, the throne had been held by the same lineage for 14 centuries, and before the empress could bring herself to step down in favor of a usurper, she consulted an oracle. The oracle brought an answer from the god Hachiman to the effect that a subject should never become emperor. She kept the throne but died the following year. Because of her second term, she received the posthumous name of Shōtoku-tennō. Her amorous abandon with the ambitious Dōkyō prompted Japanese nobles to vow that no more women would rule. Since her time, only two women have ruled.[6]

Kossamak

Queen, joint ruler of Cambodia (1955–1960)

She was born Kossamak Nearirath, the daughter of King Sisowath, who ruled from 1904 to 1927, and the sister of King Monivong, who ruled Cambodia from 1927 to 1941. She married Prince Norodom Suramarit, and they had a son, Sihanouk, born in 1922. When Monivong died in 1941, Sihanouk was placed on the throne by the French Governor General of Indochina, Admiral Jean Decoux. In 1952 Sihanouk dissolved the cabinet, declared martial law, and fled into voluntary exile to dramatize Cambodian demands for complete independence from France. In 1954 the Geneva Conference confirmed complete independence. A referendum the following year approved King Sihanouk's rule, but he abdicated in favor of his father and became prime minister. According to Egan et al., Queen Kossamak ruled jointly with her husband until his death in 1960, when her son Sihanouk reassumed the position of head of state.[7]

Lakshmi Bai
Rani, regent ruler of Jhānsi (1853 and 1857–1858)

She was born Manukarnika ca. 1833 in Benares, the daughter of Moropant Tambe, a Brahmin official. She married Ganyadhar Rao and took the name of Lakshmi, the wife of the god Vishnu, on her wedding day. The couple had one son who died at the age of three months. When Rao became seriously ill in 1853, they adopted five-year-old Damodar Rao, a descendant of Rao's grandfather, to assure the continuation of their line. Rao died the same year, and through his will Lakshmi assumed the reign for their adopted son. The British, however, seeing the opportunity to annex Jhānsi, declared that Damodar was not a legal heir. For over a year Lakshmi battled in the courts, but ultimately she was deposed by the British East India Company. However, in 1857, when the Indian Mutiny escalated into a Jhānsian uprising against the British, Lakshmi was hastily recalled by the same people who had deposed her and was requested to restore order: "We suggest that you take your kingdom and hold it, along with the adjoining territory, until the British authority is established. We shall be eternally grateful if you will also protect our lives." Lakshmi resumed the reins of government with her father as minister.

Later in 1857 the British moved to recapture Jhānsi, and Lakshmi's forces, with Lakshmi at their head dressed in male attire, resisted. The rebel leader Ramchandra Panduranga, who called himself Tantia Topi, rode to assist her, but the British defeated their combined forces. Lakshmi and her father escaped and were welcomed by Topi at Kalpi. They all proceeded to Gwalior and recaptured it from the British; but in 1858 the British again took Gwalior, and Lakshmi's father was captured and hanged. The rani, who was still leading her troops, died a soldier's death on the battlefield.[1]

Leonora Telles
Queen, regent of Portugal (1383–1384)

Kings usually married for political gain and seldom for love. Leonora's marriage to King Ferdinand I the Handsome, who ruled Portugal from 1367 to 1383, followed the love-smitten Ferdinand's repudiation of a previous betrothal to a Castilian princess and precipitated a war between Portugal and Castile. Leonora and Ferdinand had a daughter, Beatrice, who was later married to John I of Castile. When Ferdinand died in 1383, Queen Leonora became regent for her daughter for the Portuguese throne. This arrangement led to strong opposition among the people, who detested both the regent and her Galician lover-advisor, John Fernandes

Andeiro, count of Ourem. An illegitimate brother of Pedro I, John of Aziz, led a successful revolt and murdered Andeiro. Queen Leonora fled the country and appealed to the king of Castile for help. The Castilian army marched upon Lisbon in May 1384, but an outbreak of plague forced it to retreat four months later. John was proclaimed king in 1385, becoming the first ruler of the Aues Dynasty.[2]

Liang
Empress, regent of China (A.D. 144–150)

Liang was the first of six powerful empresses from three great families who, with court eunuchs, managed to keep the court's wealth and power in their hands by seeing to it that infants and young children were appointed to the throne. Of the twelve emperors of the Eastern Han Dynasty, eight were between the ages of 3 months and 15 years. In A.D. 132, Empress Liang secured influence for her father, and the Liang family captured control of the court. Empress Liang's father held power for 12 years until he died in 144. Beginning with that year, three young emperors were appointed for whom Empress Liang served as regent; one was her brother, Liang Chi. She died in 150, to be replaced by another young empress. In 159 Emperor Huan Ti put Liang Chi to death and wiped out the last of the Liangs.[3]

Lilavati
Queen, ruler of Sri Lanka three times (1197–1200, 1209–1210, 1211–1212)

During a period of political instability in Sri Lanka, Queen Lilavati was called to the throne on three separate occasions. Frequent incursions from South India kept the island in turmoil. In addition, political factions would frequently break away to form a separate feudal state. Lilavati, a Kalingan, married Parākramabāhu I, who ruled from ca. 1153 to 1186. Following his death, her brother Nissankamalla reigned for approximately ten years. Briefly the island fell into the hands of Codaganga before Queen Lilavati came to the throne on her own in 1197. She ruled for three years. Her first reign was followed by the two-year reign of King Sahassamalla, the six-year reign of Queen

Kalyānavati, and the one-year reigns each of King Dharmasoka and King Anikanga. In 1209 Queen Lilavati was restored for one year. In 1210 she was replaced by King Lokesvara but reinstated for another brief reign the following year. In 1215 a South Indian fortune-seeker named Māgha invaded, seized power, and ruled dictatorially for over two decades.[4]

Liliuokalani
Queen, ruler of Hawaii (1891–1895)

She was born Lydia Paki Kamekeha Liliuokalani in 1838. Her mother was Keohokalole, an advisor to King Kamehameha III, who ruled from 1825 to 1854. Before his death in 1854, the king adopted his nephew, who ruled as Kamehameha IV from 1855 to 1862. When King Kamehameha IV's only son died, he withdrew from public office, grief-stricken. He was replaced by Lunalilo, who had the support of the ex-king and his wife, Queen Emma. Lunalilo died in 1874 without appointing a successor. The contest that followed pitted the partisans of Dowager Queen Emma against the supporters of the lineage of Keohokalole, Lydia's mother. The latter faction was victorious. Lydia's brother, David Kalakaua, reigned from 1874 to 1891. In 1877 her younger brother, Prince Regent W. P. Leleiohoku, died and Lydia was named heir presumptive.

She succeeded to the throne at the age of 53 on the king's death in 1891. In 1862 she had married John Owen Dominis, who died shortly after her succession. American colonists led by Sanford Dole, who controlled most of Hawaii's economy, revolted when the queen attempted to restore some of the monarchy's power dissipated during her brother's reign. Dole's faction asked for her abdication in 1893, and she had to appeal to U.S. President Grover Cleveland for reinstatement. Dole defied the president's orders and established a republic of his own. The royalists revolted, but Dole's forces squelched the revolt and jailed the queen's supporters. She abdicated in 1895 in order to win pardons for them. In 1898, the year the islands were formally transferred to the United States, she composed ''Aloha Oe,'' which quickly became the for her country. She died in

Louise ~ avoy
Duchess, regent of France (1515–1516 and 1525–1526)

She was born in 1476, the daughter of Philip II, duke of Savoy, and Marguerite de Bourbon. She married Charles de Valois-Orléans, count (later duke) of Angoulême, and had two children: Margaret, who became queen of Navarre; and Francis, who married Claude, daughter of King Louis XII, and became King Francis I in 1515. A strong and ambitious woman with great diplomatic skills, Louise, who was never a queen, was appointed regent during both her son's expeditions to Italy. When Holy Roman Emperor Charles V captured Francis I and held him prisoner, Louise kept the country running, negotiated Francis' release, and was able to convince England's King Henry VIII to sign a treaty of alliance with France, Venice, and Pope Clement VII against Charles V. In 1529, when the wars between Francis and Charles threatened to bankrupt both, they were forced to negotiate. Again Louise was called upon, this time to negotiate the peace with Charles' aunt, Margaret of Austria. The two arranged the Treaty of Cambrai, called the "Ladies' Peace." She died in 1531.[6]

Louise Hippolyte
Princess, titular ruler of Monaco (1731)

She was born in 1697, the daughter of Prince Antoine I of the House of Grimaldi. She married Prince James I and bore a son, Honoré III. Her father died in 1731. Princess Louise, heir to the throne, died the same year, and the prince consort ruled for two years. He abdicated in 1733 in favor of their son.[7]

Lu Hou
Empress, regent of China (195–180 B.C.)

Lu Hou was married to a former peasant named Gao Zu (or Kao Tsu), whom she had goaded into power and who ruled as first emperor of the Han dynasty from 206 to 195 B.C. Over the centuries it became the custom that, when the child of an emperor was made heir apparent, the mother was then recognized as empress, and on accession of her son she, as dowager empress, often became the real ruler.

This tradition began with Lu. Having ambitions of her own, she saw to it that her son, Hui Ti, was formally named heir apparent. After her husband's death, the child Hui Ti ascended, and Lu was able to ignore the more important members of the imperial clan who were located in various kingdoms and marquisates some distance from the seat of government. She dominated the palace by replacing her husband's relatives with members of her own family in all positions of power. When her son died, Empress Lu designated another young child to succeed him. When the new young emperor began to question her authority, she simply had him imprisoned, seized absolute power, and designated a third child as emperor. Her efforts to usurp the throne for her family posed a serious threat to the central government, which the late emperor's kinsmen eventually recognized. His loyal ministers put her to death in 180, massacred the whole Lu clan, and placed Wen Ti, Gao Zu's son by another wife, on the throne.[8]

Lucia
Countess, titular ruler of Tuscany (1288–1289)

The daughter of Prince Bohemond VI, ruler of Antioch and Tripoli from 1252 to 1275, and Sibylla of Armenia, Lucia was the younger sister of Bohemond VII, who ruled from 1275 to 1287. She married Narjot of Toucy, the former grand admiral under Charles of Anjou, and went to live in Apula. Her brother died childless in 1287, naming Lucia as his heir. Her mother fought bitterly to obtain the rule; meanwhile, a Commune was established that was to be the real sovereign authority. But with help and maneuvering, Lucia was able to garner acceptance by opposing factions of Tripoli and was given supreme authority by the nobles and the Commune. Foes had traveled to Cairo to ask the Sultan Qalawun to intervene against Lucia's reign. In 1289, the Sultan brought a huge army and launched a general assault on Tripoli. Countess Lucia was able to escape to Cyprus, but the majority of the men were massacred and the women and children captured as slaves.[9]

Lucienne
Princess, regent of Antioch
(ca. 1252–ca. 1258)

She was born Lucienne of Segui, a great-niece of Pope Innocent III and a cousin of Pope Gregory IX. When Prince Bohemond V of Antioch and Tripoli divorced Alice of Cyprus by reason of consanguinity and began looking for a second wife, he asked Pope Gregory to choose her. Gregory chose his kinswoman Lucienne. This choice pleased Bohemond, for he could thus claim ties with the papacy; however, the number of her Roman relatives and friends that flocked to visit Tripoli at her invitation irritated both Bohemond and the local barons. The couple took little interest in Antioch, but held court at Tripoli.

Lucienne had two children: Plaisance, who married King Henry of Cyprus; and Bohemond VI, who was 15 years old when his father died in 1252 and Lucienne assumed the regency for her son. She was described as a feckless woman who never left Tripoli and who left the governing of Antioch to her Roman relatives. In ca. 1258 members of the Embriaco family gained control of Tripoli. Louise was removed from the regency but managed to keep many of her Roman relatives in high places. The irate local barons, who had long resented interference by foreigners, marched upon Tripoli and actually wounded Bohemond in an effort to rid the city of Lucienne's relatives. Later Bohemond arranged for the murder of Bertrand, head of the younger branch of the Embriaco, and the rebels withdrew. This murder precipitated a long blood feud between the houses of Antioch and Embriaco.[10]

Ludmila
Regent of Bohemia (ca. A.D. 921)

She was born ca. A.D. 860 in what is now Czechoslovakia. She married Prince Borivoj, ruler of Bohemia, and they converted to Christianity, becoming the first Czech sovereigns to do so. They built Bohemia's first Christian church, near Prague. Their son Ratislav married Drahomira, a pagan; Ludmila's grandsons from this union were Wenceslas and Boleslav. Ludmila reared Wenceslas as a Christian, while her daughter-in-law reared Boleslav as a pagan. When Ratislav died in 920, the anti-Christian faction attempted to seize control of the government, but Ludmila urged Wenceslas, who was then about 13 years of age, to take over the reigns of government in the name of Christianity. Ludmila acted as regent when Wenceslas became ruler of Bohemia in ca. 921. However, at Drahomira's instigation, agents stole into Tetin Castle and strangled Ludmila in 921. She became a martyr and a saint, as did Wenceslas some eight years later. The carol "Good King Wenceslas" sings his virtues.[11]

Luisa
Regent of Etruria (1803–1807), duchess of Lucca (1815–1824)

Etruria was a kingdom that existed only from 1801 to 1807 by terms of the Treaty of Luneville between Austria and Napoleon. Located in Tuscany in present-day Italy, it was created especially for the House of Bourbon-Parma by Napoleon Bonaparte.

Luisa was born in 1782, the daughter of Charles IV, who ruled Spain from 1788 to 1808, and Maria Luisa of Parma. She married Louis, ruler of Etruria from 1801 to his death in 1803. They had two children, Luisa and Charles, king of Etruria (1803–1807), for whom she served as regent. In 1815, after the fall of Napoleon, Luisa was awarded the duchy of Lucca, which she ruled until her death in 1824.[12]

Luisa Maria de Guzmán
Regent of Portugal (1656–1662)

She was the wife of John IV of the house of Braganza, king of Portugal from 1640 to 1656. They had three children: Catherine, who married Charles II of England; Alfonso IV, who ruled as king of Portugal from 1656 to 1667; and Pedro II, who ruled as regent from 1667 to 1683 and as king from 1683 to 1706. When John IV died in 1656, Alfonso, age 13, ascended to the throne with Luisa Maria serving as regent during his minority. Alfonso proved to be both frivolous and vicious. Some also characterized him as feeble-minded. His outrageous conduct prompted his brother Pedro, considered to be wise and just, to imprison him and set himself up as regent in 1667. When Alfonso died in 1683, Pedro II could legally ascend to the throne.[13]

Luise-Marie (or Louise of Bourbon-Berry)
Duchess, regent of Parma and Piacenza (1854–1859)

Luise-Marie was born in 1819, the daughter of Ferdinand, the last duke of Berry, and Caroline of the Two Sicilies. She married Duke Charles III, ruler of Parma from 1849 to 1854. Within five years they had four children: Margarita, Robert, Alicia, and Enrico. When Duke Charles was assassinated in 1854, their son Robert, age six, became duke of Parma. Luise-Marie served as regent until 1859, when she transferred her powers to a provisional government. Parma was incorporated into Piedmont-Sardinia in 1860 and into Italy in 1861. Luise-Marie died in 1864.[14]

Maham Anga
De facto regent of Mughal Empire
(1560–1562)

Maham Anga was Akbar's chief nurse prior to his becoming emperor at age 13 (Kalanaur, 1556). Her own son, Adham Khān, as Akbar's foster brother, was regarded as almost one of the family. Maham Anga, shrewd and ambitious and very much in charge of the household and the harem, sought to advance her own authority and that of her son. In 1560 the two tricked Akbar into coming to India without his chief minister and guardian Bairam, and they were able to convince Akbar that now that he was 17, he didn't need Bairam. Akbar dismissed his minister and sent him on a pilgrimage to Mecca. Months later Bairam was murdered by an Afghan, and much of his former power passed to Maham Anga. Her son was sent to invade Malwa, but his conduct following victory was reprehensible. He kept the treasure and the harem for himself and had the other captives butchered while he and his fellow officers sat jesting. Akbar, enraged when he heard of the outrage, set off for Malwa at such speed that Maham Anga had no chance to send a warning to her son. Adham Khān, chastened but not dismissed, handed over the booty to Akbar and was forgiven, but he secretly kept

back two young girls for himself. When Akbar heard rumors of this treachery, Maham Anga had the girls murdered before they could testify against her son. Her power began to wane in 1561, however, when Akbar appointed Atkah Khān, a man outside her sphere of influence, as his new chief minister. Five months later (1562), her son attempted to assassinate the new minister and was thrown off the parapet—twice—as execution. Akbar himself informed Maham Anga of her son's death, and she died shortly afterward. The emperor, age 19, was then completely in charge.[1]

Mahaut I
Dame, ruler of Bourbon (1215–1242)

The heir of Archambaud V, ruler of Bourbon from 1116 to 1171, Mahaut I first married Gautier de Vienne, who ruled Bourbon upon Archambaud's death in 1171 until his own death in 1215. Mahaut then ruled in her own right from 1215 to 1242. She was married a second time to Gui II de Dampierre and had two daughters, Mahaut II de Dampierre and Agnes. Mahaut I was succeeded by Archambaud VII in 1242.[2]

Mahaut II de Dampierre
Countess, ruler of Bourbon (1249–1262),
ruler of Nevers (1257–1266)

The daughter of Gui II de Dampierre and Dame Mahaut I, who ruled Bourbon from 1215 to

1242, Mahaut II succeeded Baron Archambaud VII, who ruled from 1242 to 1249. She married Eudes de Bourgogne, and they had a daughter, Yolande de Bourgogne. Mahaut II was the granddaughter of Countess Mahaut de Courtenay, who ruled Nevers for over half a century (1182 to 1257) and whom she succeeded as ruler of Nevers upon her grandmother's death in 1257. In 1262 she was succeeded by her sister Agness as ruler of Bourbon, but she ruled Nevers until her death in 1266. She was succeeded in Nevers by her daughter Yolande.[3]

Mahaut de Boulogne (Matilda)
Countess, ruler of Boulogne (1125–1150)

Her father, Eustache III, who ruled Boulogne from 1095 to 1125, retired to a Cluniac monastery in 1125, leaving Boulogne to his daughter to rule. Mahaut married Étienne de Blois, who in 1135 became (by usurpation from his cousin, also named Matilda, and called Empress Maud) King Stephen of England (1135–1154). Mahaut, who was also sometimes called Empress Maud by the British, was much more popular with the English people than Empress Maud, the other Matilda who, to further confuse matters, was also Mahaut's cousin on the other side of the family. Thus Mahaut and Étienne were both cousins to England's Empress Maud, but not to each other.

Mahaut and Étienne had five children, three of whom succeeded her sequentially as rulers of Boulogne: Eustache IV, Guillaume, and Marie. Eustache IV succeeded Mahaut upon her death in 1150.[4]

Mahaut de Courtenay
Countess, ruler of Nevers (1192–1257)

She was the daughter of Pierre de Courtenay and Countess Agnes de Nevers, who ruled from 1181 to 1192, and whom she succeeded in 1192. In 1199 she married Count Hervé de Donzy. He died, and in 1226 she took a second husband, Guy de Forez. Upon her death in 1257 her granddaughter Mahaut II de Bourbon succeeded her.[5]

Mahaut de Dammaratin
Countess, ruler of Boulogne (1216–1260)

Mahaut de Dammaratin succeeded the Countess Ide d'Alsace (1173–1216) upon her death. She married Philippe Hurepel, the son of Philip Augustus, and died in 1260.[6]

Makeda (also called Balkis)
Queen, ruler of Axum; believed by some to be the Queen of Sheba (tenth century B.C.)

Although Arabist Sir John Glubb believes the Queen of Sheba was from Yemen, an African legend states that in the tenth century B.C., an Ethiopian king on his deathbed named his daughter Makeda as his successor, and that Makeda ruled as the Queen of Sheba. According to fourteenth-century Ethiopian manuscripts now in the British Museum, an Ethiopian merchant named Tamrin took building materials to Jerusalem for King Solomon's temple. When he returned home, Solomon sent with him

An illuminated manuscript showing scenes from the life of Solomon. Upper right: Solomon welcomes Makeda. Walters Art Gallery, Baltimore, MD.

valuable gifts for the queen. She was so impressed by the merchant's account of Solomon's court that she organized a large caravan laden with precious gifts and visited the court of King Solomon. A romance developed between them, resulting in the birth of a son, whom Makeda named Menelik. By another account, Solomon recognized Menelik as his firstborn son and decreed that only Menelik's male heirs would rule Ethiopia. Emperor Haile Selassie claimed direct lineage from Menelik.[7]

Mandughai
Khatun, regent of Mongolia (1470–ca. 1492)

Mandughai was the very young widow of Grand Khan Mandaghol, Jenghiz-khan's twenty-seventh successor, who was killed in battle in 1467. His great-nephew and heir Bolkho succeeded him, but was assassinated in 1470 before he could be proclaimed khan. The mother of Bolkho's five-year-old son Dayan had deserted the child, so Mandughai took him under her protection and proclaimed him khan. She herself then assumed command of the Mongol troops and defeated their enemy, the Oirat. In 1481 she married her young charge Dayan, who was then 16, and in 1491–1492 she again led the army to fend off the Oirat. History credits her with abolishing Oirat supremacy and restoring that of the eastern Mongols. She (and after her Dayan) gave new life to the fading authority of the Jenghiz-khanate.[8]

Mankiller, Wilma T.
Chief of Cherokee Nation (1984–1986)

She was born in 1944, the daughter of Charlie and Irene Mankiller. Her father is a fullblooded Cherokee; her mother is Dutch. She and ten brothers and sisters grew up in a fourroom frame house with no plumbing. When she was ten years old the family was moved to San Francisco with the help of the Bureau of Indian Affairs. She went to junior college in San Francisco, where she became interested in bettering the plight of Indians. She married a wealthy Ecuadorian man and toured Europe with him. Their first daughter was born in 1963 and the second in 1965. In 1971 her father died and his body was returned to Oklahoma for burial.

When Wilma divorced three years later, feeling that she must return to her roots, she moved back to Oklahoma and completed her degree in 1975 at Flaming Rainbow University. In 1977 she began working for the 65,000-member Cherokee tribe as an economic coordinator and commuted to the University of Arkansas to work toward a master's degree in community planning. An auto accident en route to classes in 1979 resulted in 17 surgeries in 12 months, and the following year she contracted myasthenia gravis. Despite her difficulties, she was elected deputy chief of the Cherokee Nation in 1983. In 1984 she became the first female chief when Chief Ross Swimmer became head of the Bureau of Indian Affairs. She lives in Tahlequah, Oklahoma, the tribal headquarters. Of her duties, she said, "It is sort of like running a small country and sort of like running a middle-sized corporation."

Mankiller attributes her resilience to her Cherokee blood. She notes that most Cherokees were marched from their southeastern U.S. homeland by soldiers in the 1838 Trail of Tears. Although 4,000 died along the way, those who survived quickly established themselves as a literate nation. They opened the first school west of the Mississippi and established several newspapers in the Cherokee language. Mankiller said in an interview, "We are fighters and survivors. We were not shy about war, but we also fought a lot of battles in court. We were devastated, uprooted and driven like cattle to this land, but we made the best of it."[9]

Margaret
Duchess of Carinthia, countess of Tirol
(1335–1362)

Born Margaretha Maultasch in 1318, the daughter of the duke of Carinthia and count of Tirol, she was married to John Henry of Luxembourg, age nine, in 1330. When her father died in 1335, she inherited Tirol but was forced to cede Carinthia back to Germany, Carinthia having been given to her family by Rudolph I in 1286. After 11 years Margaret's marriage was still childless. She acted in collusion with the Tirolese to expel John Henry, whose brother Charles (later Emperor Charles IV) had stepped in to rule. In 1342 Holy Roman Emperor Louis IV the Bavarian annulled Margaret's previous marriage and married her to his son Louis, margrave of Brandenburg. This marriage displeased not only the pope and the Luxembourgians, but the Tirolese as well, who did not want to be ruled by the Germans. An uprising against Margaret and her new husband had to be suppressed, and there remained considerable doubt that she would be able to maintain control. After Louis IV was deposed in 1346, however, the successor Charles IV favored the status quo for Tirol's rulers, who would remain in control as long as there was an heir; if Margaret produced no heir, she would cede Tirol to the Hapsburgs. Margaret bore one son, Meinhard, and the lineage of Tirol seemed secure. However, her husband died in 1361 and, in 1363, after she had passed childbearing age, her only son died. Holy Roman Emperor Rudolph IV persuaded her to cede Tirol to him, and she retired to Vienna where she died in 1369 at the age of 51.[10]

Margaret (Black Meg)
Countess, ruler of Belgium (1244–1280)

She was born ca. 1200, the daughter of Maria of Champagne and Baldwin IX, count of Flanders and Hainault, who in 1204 was crowned Baldwin I, first Latin Emperor of Constantinople. She was also the sister of Johanna, who ruled Belgium from 1206 to 1244. Margaret was first married to Buchard of Avenes, who had been pledged to serve the Church. His marriage led to his excommunication and imprisonment by his sister-in-law, Countess Johanna. Although she had borne him a son, Margaret was persuaded to seek a divorce or an annulment. She later married William of Dampierre and bore another son. When her sister died in 1244, Margaret acceded to the throne, naming her younger son as her successor. The older son, however, protested her decision forcefully, and the following civil war was resolved in a compromise whereby each son would rule a portion of the land. However, in the end Margaret outlived them both. She died in 1280.[11]

Margaret (or Margaret of Flanders or Margaret of Mâle)
Countess, ruler of Belgium (1384–1405)

She was born in 1350, the daughter of Margaret of Brabant and Louis II de Mâle, count of Flanders from 1346 to 1384. In 1369 she married Philip le Hardi, duke of Burgundy from 1384 to 1404. She was also heiress to Burgundy, the county, Artois, Nevers, and Rethel. The couple had four children: John, duke of Burgundy; Philip, count of Nevers; Margaret; and Antoine, duke of Brabant. Belgium had been under Burgundy rule from 1334 to 1377, so Louis II de Mâle actually ruled Flanders from 1377 to 1384. Margaret died in 1405.[12]

Margaret (or Margrete or Margarethe)
Queen of Denmark and Norway (1375–1412), regent of Sweden (1389–1412)

She was born in Denmark in 1353, the daughter of King Valdemar IV Atterdag, ruler of Denmark from 1340 to 1375, and Helvig, sister of the duke of Schleswig. When Margaret was six years old, she was married to King Haakon VI, ruler of Norway from 1343 to 1380, and spent her youth in the court in Norway. In 1370 she bore a son, Olaf V, and began to take an active interest in government soon afterward. After her father's death in 1375, she succeeded in getting her five-year-old son Olaf elected to the Danish throne with herself as regent. After her husband's death in 1380, she also ruled Norway for her son. When Olaf died in 1387, Margaret adopted her six-year-old nephew, Erik of Pomerania, as heir to the throne. She was asked by Swedish nobles to assist in an uprising against Swedish King Albert. The nobles proclaimed her queen of Sweden in 1388 and granted her a large domain consisting of lands belonging to former Chancellor Bo Jonsson Grip. Her forces captured Albert in 1389 and held him prisoner for six years until peace was concluded. In 1397 she united the three Scandinavian countries in the Union of Kalmar, which lasted until 1523. Despite her heir's coronation in 1397, Margaret remained the sole ruler for the rest of her life. She strengthened her influence over the Church and kept the ambitious German princes at bay, primarily through diplomacy. However, she was obliged to use force against Holstein in 1412, and she died suddenly during the conflict.[13]

Margaret of Anjou
Queen, Lancastrian leader (1455–1485), acting regent of England (1460–1461)

She was born in 1430, the daughter of René I of Anjou, titular king of Naples (1435–1442), and Isabella, duchess of Lorraine from 1431 to 1453. In a 1445 marriage arranged as part of a two-year truce in the Hundred Years' War, Margaret became the wife of King Henry VI, who ruled England from 1422 to 1461. The couple had one son, Edward, born in 1453. Margaret was not popular with her English subjects. Her husband suffered bouts of insanity and was declared unfit to rule. Richard, duke of York, served as lord protector. In 1455 a civil war (the War of the Roses) broke out between the houses of Lancaster and York. Richard of York asserted his hereditary claim to the throne, and the lords decided that he should be next in the line of succession, excluding Margaret's son Edward. He actually gained control of the government until Margaret ousted him in 1456. Here the qualities with which Shakespeare described her became evident: ''stern, obdurate, flinty, rough, remorseless'' (*Henry VI, Part III*, act 1, scene 4).

She was more than capable of acting in the interests of the king: both her mother and her grandmother had ruled their lands. In 1459 the second round of hostilities erupted. During the Battle of Northampton in 1460, Henry VI was taken prisoner, and Margaret refused to accept the terms for his release, which would exclude her son as Henry's heir. Instead, she raised an army in the north and defeated Richard of York, who died on the field in Wakefield, Yorkshire. But southern England had not forgotten the Hundred Years' War with France, nor that Margaret was French. Londoners rallied around York's son, also named Edward, defeated Margaret's army, and proclaimed Edward of York king in 1461. Margaret and her son fled to Scotland with Henry VI. In 1464 a fresh Lancastrian uprising brought them back to England. Henry

VI was again captured in 1465 and imprisoned in the Tower of London. In 1470 Margaret, then in France, entered into collusion with Richard, duke of Warwick, in a plot to restore Henry VI to the throne. However, Warwick was killed in battle on the day that she returned to England in 1471. Margaret and her son headed the forces at Tewksbury, which attempted to hold off Edward of York, but they were defeated for the final time. Margaret's son Edward was killed and she was taken prisoner. Henry VI was murdered in prison. In 1475 King Louis XI of France ransomed Margaret. She returned to France where she died in poverty in 1482.[14]

Margaret of Antioch-Lusignan
Regent of Tyre (1283–1291)

Called the loveliest girl of her generation, Margaret was the daughter of Henry of Antioch and Isabella of Cyprus, and the sister of King Hugh III. She married John of Montfort, lord of Tyre, who died ca. 1283. When Sultan Qalawun was preparing to attack those Franks not protected by the truce of 1283, Margaret asked for a truce, which was granted. She renewed the truce in 1290 after Qalawun invaded Tripoli. Early in 1291 she handed Tyre over to her nephew Amalric, brother of King Henry II of Cyprus.[15]

Margaret of Austria
Duchess of Savoy, regent of the Netherlands (1507–1515 and 1519–1530)

She was born in 1480, the daughter of Holy Roman Emperor Maximilian I, who ruled from 1493 to 1519, and Mary, duchess of Burgundy. Margaret was also the sister of Philip the Handsome. In 1483 she was betrothed to the future Charles VI, who later repudiated her. She then married John, heir to the Spanish throne, but was widowed that same year (1497). In 1501 she married Philibert II, duke of Savoy, but was widowed again three years later. In 1507 her father appointed her successor to her late brother Philip as regent of the Netherlands for her nephew Charles. In 1508 she also represented another young nephew, Ferdinand of Aragon (Holy Roman Emperor Ferdinand I), and her father in negotiating a settlement of the

French claims in the Burgundian Netherlands. Her nephew Charles was declared of age in 1515, but he reappointed her in 1519 while he was occupied in securing the Hapsburg throne. He ruled as Charles V from 1519 to 1556. In 1526 Margaret negotiated the Treaty of Cambrai, ''The Ladies' Peace,'' with Louise of Savoy, settling claims of France upon Italy, Flanders, and Artois, and claims of Germany upon Burgundy. Margaret continued to rule the Netherlands until she died in 1530.[16]

Margaret of Austria
Duchess of Parma, governor general of the Netherlands (1559–1567)

Margaret of Austria was born in 1522, the illegitimate daughter of Holy Roman Emperor Charles V (Charles I of Spain), who ruled Spain from 1516 to 1556 and the empire from 1510 to 1556, and Johanna van der Gheenst. In 1536 Margaret married Alessandro de' Medici, duke of Florence, but she was widowed in less than a year. In 1538 she married Ottavio Farnese, who became duke of Parma in 1547, and they had a son, Alessandro Farnese. Her half brother, King Philip II of Spain, appointed her governor general of the Netherlands in 1559. Under her regency the provinces prospered, despite heavy taxation. She presided over the three governing councils: Privy, State, and Finances, which were to see to it that the Protestants (Calvinists) were suppressed and that King Philip's demands for funds were met. She was saddled with carrying out a highly unpopular program without military backing, for her subjects had no desire to pay for a foreigner's military campaigns. The northern part of her territory (Holland) had embraced Calvinism, while the southern part (Belgium) was still Catholic. Both segments opposed Spanish rule, the Spanish garrison, the introduction of the Spanish inquisition, and the penal edicts against heretics. She rejected a petition submitted to her by 300 nobles objecting to religious persecution. An advisor referred to the signers as ''beggars,'' and soon all those opposed to Spanish rule took as their appellation, ''beggars.'' In 1566 Calvinist riots led Margaret, who still had no troops from King Philip, to call in German mercenaries. In 1567 she dealt with religious uprisings by mass executions. Philip II eventually sent in the duke of Alva with 10,000 troops to replace Margaret and to repress the uprisings. In 1580 she returned to the Netherlands as head of the civil administration under her son Alessandro. Margaret returned to Italy in 1583, where she died in 1586.[17]

Margaret of Navarre
Regent of Sicily (1166–1168)

She was the wife of William I, ruler of Norman Sicily from 1154 to 1166. It was claimed that she took as her lover the chief minister, Maio of Bari. In 1153 she had a son, William II, who succeeded his father at the age of 13. Margaret, as regent, first ruled through her favorite, Peter, a Saracen eunuch and former slave who had been freed by her husband. But barons who had earlier been exiled by William I saw the chance to regain their estates under the regency of a woman, and they began to return and rebuild their castles. Peter decided to escape to Morocco to avoid the inevitable conflict building between the barons and Queen Margaret. In 1167 she appointed her cousin Stephen of Le Perche chief minister and Peter of Blois as her son's tutor. But Stephen's harsh manner made him unpopular. When rumor spread that he was siphoning money to France, a riot quickly spread at Messina. Stephen fled to Jerusalem, and Peter went back to France. Into the void stepped an Englishman, Walter Offamillo, who seized power and used the Palermo mob to help him become archbishop, remaining the center of power for 20 years. In effect, Margaret's influence was at an end. Even after William came of age in 1172, he did not openly cross the archbishop. Offamillo effectively ended Margaret's attempt to rule.[18]

Margaret of Norway (the Maid of Norway)
Child queen of Scotland (1286–1290)

She was born ca. 1282, the daughter of King Eric II Magnusson, who ruled Norway from 1280 to 1299, and Margaret, daughter of King Alexander III of Scotland (1249–1286). Her mother died in 1283, and none of King Alexander's children survived him. When he died in

1286, Scottish nobles declared his granddaughter, Margaret, queen at age four. In 1290 her great-uncle, England's King Edward I, arranged for her marriage to his son, the future King Edward II. On the voyage to England, Margaret fell ill and died at the age of eight.[19]

Margaret Tudor
Regent of Scotland (1513–1514)

She was born in 1489, the elder daughter of King Henry VII, who ruled England from 1485 to 1509, and Elizabeth, daughter of King Edward IV, who ruled from 1461 to 1483. In 1503 she married James IV, king of Scotland from 1488 to 1513, and bore a son who became James V when his father died in 1513. Margaret ruled as regent for her son. In 1514 she married Archibald Douglas, earl of Angus and, since he was a partisan of England, the Scottish Parliament removed her from the regency. In 1527 she divorced Douglas and married Henry Stewart, whom her son made Lord Methven when he came to the throne the following year. Margaret and her third husband were James' most trusted advisors for the first six years of his majority, but James became angry at his mother for sharing state secrets with her brother, King Henry VIII of England. She retired to Methven Castle where she died in 1541.[20]

Margareta (or Margaret of Alsace)
Countess, ruler of Flanders (1191)

The sister of Count Philip, who ruled Belgium from 1157 to 1191, Margareta married Baldwin VI, count of Hainault (or Hainaut). In 1172 she bore a son, Baldwin I, who would become count of Flanders and Hainault. When her brother Philip died in 1191, Margareta succeeded him, but she died in the same year. Her husband ruled until his death four years later.[21]

Margaretha
Guardian for Otto II the Lame, ruler of the Netherlands (1229–1234)

The daughter of Duke Henry I of Brabant, in 1206 Margaretha married Gerhard III of Gelre (Gelderland), ruler of Gelderland and Zutphen. It was a marriage designed to unite two antagonistic dynasties. In ca. 1220 they had a son,

Otto II, called Otto the Lame. When Gerhard III died in 1229, Otto succeeded his father, with Margaretha serving as guardian until he came of age in 1234.[22]

Margrethe II
Queen of Denmark (1972–)

She was born in 1940, the daughter of Frederick IX, king of Denmark from 1947 to 1972, and Ingrid, daughter of crown prince Gustaf Adolf of Sweden. In 1953 her father signed a new constitution that permitted female succession to the throne for the first time in over 500 years. In 1967 Margrethe married Henri de Laborde de Monpezat, a French diplomat, who was then referred to as Prince Consort Henrik. The couple has two sons: Frederick, born in 1968, and Joachim, born in 1969. She acceded to the throne when her father died in 1972, the first queen to rule Denmark since 1412, becoming, at age 31, the youngest queen regnant in the world in the oldest existing monarchy. She is popularly called the ''queen of democracy.'' A talented artist, she is best known for her illustrations of *The Lord of the Rings*. With her husband, she wrote *All Men Are Mortal*.[23]

Marguerite
Countess, ruler of Blois (1218–1230)

She was the eldest daughter of Isabella, daughter of King Louis IX of France, and Thibault V (Theobald), king of Navarre, who also ruled Blois until his death in 1218. Marguerite acceded to the throne when her father died in 1218, marrying three times. Her third husband, Gauthier d'Avesnes, ruled with her. She died in 1230 and was succeeded by Marie de Chatillon.[24]

Marguerite
Countess, ruler of Nevers (1384–1404).
See Margaret (also called Margaret of Flanders or Margaret of Mâle), Countess, ruler of Belgium

Marguerite de Thouars
Joint ruler of Dreux (1365–1377)

She was the daughter of Simon of Dreux and the sister of Peronelle. She and Peronelle were parceners of Dreux when their father died in

1365. In 1377 or 1378 they sold it to King Charles VI of France, who conferred it on the house of Albret.[25]

Maria
Queen of Sicily (1377–1402)

Maria was the daughter of Frederick IV, ruler of Sicily from 1355 to 1377. (Until 1372, Sicily was claimed by Naples.) When he died in 1377, she acceded to the throne in name only. In 1390 she was abducted from Catania Castle and taken to Barcelona to marry her cousin, Martin the Younger, prince of Aragon, son of King Pedro IV. In 1392 he was crowned Martin I, king of Sicily. Martin and his relatives then set about to bring Sicily under Argonese control. Maria had one son, who died in 1402; she died the same year, having served her purpose, as far as the Argonese were concerned. Martin ruled for seven more years and was succeeded by his father.[26]

Maria I of Braganza
Queen of Portugal (1777–1816)

She was born in 1734, the daughter of King Joseph I Emanuel, ruler of Portugal from 1750 to 1777, and Maria Anna of Spain. Her father suffered from insanity from 1774, and when he died in 1777, Maria succeeded him. She married her uncle Pedro III and ruled jointly with him until his death in 1786, and from then on she ruled alone. She consented to the trial of the dictator Pombal, who had usurped her father's power and authority, but she pardoned him because of his old age and sent him into exile. Her reign was characterized by peace and prosperity. She and Pedro had one son, John VI. In 1792 Maria suffered a mental breakdown, and her son took over the government. In 1799 John assumed the title of prince regent. In 1807 Napoleon invaded Portugal and the family was forced to flee to Brazil. Maria remained in Brazil even after Napoleon's defeat. She died there in 1816.[27]

Maria II da Gloria
Queen of Portugal (1826–1828 and 1834–1853)

She was born in 1819 in Brazil, the daughter of King Pedro IV, ruler of Brazil from 1826 to 1831, and Leopoldina of Austria. Pedro inherited the Portuguese throne from his father, John VI, who ruled as a constitutional monarch. Pedro drew up a charter for Portugal providing for a parliamentary government similar to Britain's, but he refused to leave Brazil to implement it. After a few months he abdicated and ceded the throne to his seven-year-old daughter Maria da Gloria, with her uncle Miguel as regent. She was betrothed to her uncle but did not marry him. In 1828, Miguel led a coup d'état and proclaimed himself king. Maria da Gloria fled to England and contacted her father, asking him to come to her aid. In 1831 Pedro abdicated the Brazilian throne and traveled to England to lead the fight for the restoration of Maria to the Portuguese throne. With the help of England and France, the Miguelists were defeated. Maria was restored in 1833 and assumed power in 1834. She was first married to Auguste Beauharnais, who soon died. In 1836 she married Duke Ferdinand of Saxe-Coburg. They had five children: Pedro V, who ruled from 1853 to 1861; Fernando; Luis I, who ruled from 1861 to 1889; John; and Leopoldina. Maria da Gloria's reign was a troubled one, primarily because of her choice of chief ministers. She appointed the ambitious Duque de Saldanha, who dominated politics during much of her reign, at one point drawing Portugal to the brink of civil war. Maria died in childbirth in 1853.[28]

Maria Adelaide
Grand duchess of Luxembourg (1912–1919)

Born in 1894, the eldest daughter of Grand Duke William IV, who reigned from 1905 to 1912, Maria succeeded him at the age of 18 upon his death in 1912. Because of her reactionary policies, Maria Adelaide was not a popular ruler. In August of 1914 Luxembourg was invaded by the German fifth army under the command of Crown Prince Wilhelm and the country was occupied for the remainder of World War I. Early in 1919, when German occupation ended, Maria Adelaide was forced by popular opinion to abdicate in favor of her younger sister, Charlotte, whose cooperative economic and political policies more accurately reflected the times. Maria Adelaide died in 1924 at the age of 30.[29]

María Anna of Austria
Queen, regent of Spain (1665–1676)

She was born in 1634, the daughter of Ferdinand III, king of Hungary (1625–1657), king of Bohemia (1637–1657), holy Roman emperor (1637–1657), and his first wife, María Anna of Spain. María Anna of Austria became the second wife of Philip IV, who was king of Spain from 1621 to 1665. She had two children: Margareta Teresa, born in 1651, who married Emperor Leopold I, and Charles V, born in 1661, who succeeded to the throne at the age of four upon his father's death (1665). María Anna served as regent for over ten years, but her leadership was hampered by her dependence upon her Jesuit advisors and her preference for foreigners. In addition, she was preoccupied in combatting French King Louis XIV's attack on Spanish possessions in the Netherlands. Court nobles led by John Joseph of Austria gained the upper hand in the government and eventually forced María Anna to resign. She died in 1696.[30]

María Anna (or Mariana) of Spain
Queen, regent of Portugal (1774–1777)

She was born in 1718, the daughter of Isabella of Parma and King Philip V, who ruled Spain from 1700 to 1724 and from 1724 to 1746. She married Joseph I, who later became ruler of Portugal (1750–1777). Joseph showed no interest in affairs of state. His entire reign was dominated by Sebastião José Carvalho e Mello, who became marquês of Pombal in 1770. A ruthless dictator, Pombal nevertheless reformed finances and the army, broke the power of the nobility and the Church, and encouraged industry and trade. María Anna and Joseph had a daughter, María I, born in 1734. In 1774 Joseph was declared insane and María Anna was appointed regent. She began gradually to erode the power of Pombal. In 1777 her husband died, having never regained his health, and the reign was passed to their daughter, María I.[31]

Maria Carolina
Queen, de facto ruler of Naples and Sicily (1777–1798 and 1799–1806)

Born in 1752, the daughter of Maria Theresa, empress of Austria from 1740 to 1780, and Holy Roman Emperor Francis I, Maria Carolina was the sister of Marie Antoinette. In 1768 she married King Ferdinand IV, king of Naples (1759–1808), and later, as Ferdinand I, king of the two Sicilies (1816–1825). Ferdinand allowed Maria Carolina to assume much of the authority to rule that had hitherto been held by the regent Tanucci. Affairs of state were conducted chiefly by her. The birth of a male heir, Francis I, in 1777, gave her the authority, according to her marriage contract, to sit on the council of state. She soon brought about the complete downfall of Tanucci and allied herself, perhaps romantically as well as politically, with an English adventurer, Lord Acton, of obvious British persuasion. When her sister Marie Antoinette was executed, Maria Carolina engaged Naples in the Austro-British campaign against the French Revolution. When, in 1798, the French seized Naples and renamed it the Parthenopean Republic, Maria Carolina, Ferdinand, and their children were forced to flee for their lives. A year later, following the overthrow of the new republic, the royal family returned to Naples and ordered the execution of the republic's partisans. In 1805 Maria Carolina requested the aid of Russian and British fleets in yet another conflict with France. Again in 1806, Naples was overrun by the French and the royal family fled to Sicily. She had long since acquired a hatred of Sicilians and once wrote, "The priests are completely corrupted, the people savage, the nobility of questionable loyalty." Once she even suggested that the British buy Sicily from her for six million pounds. When the Sicilians adopted a new constitution, she could see what it took others years to see: that it was a baronial document that discriminated against the common people, and that parliament was a farce designed to divert people's attention from what the nobles were doing. After she quarreled with the British ambassador, he persuaded Ferdinand to exile her from Sicily. She returned to Austria alone in 1811, where she died three years later. In addition to her son, she was survived by five daughters: Maria Teresa, who married Emperor Francis I of Austria; Louisa Amelia, who married Ferdinand III of Tuscany; Maria Amelia, who married Louis Philippe, king of France; Cristina, who married Felix of Sardinia; and Maria Antonia, who married Ferdinand VII, king of Spain.[32]

Maria Christina (or Christina)
Duchess, governor general of Austrian Netherlands (1780–1789)

Maria Christina was born in 1742, one of 16 children of Maria Theresa, empress of Hungary and Bohemia (1740–1780) and Holy Roman Emperor Francis I, who ruled from 1745 to 1765. She married Albert, duke of Saxe-Teschen. Maria Christina governed the Austrian Netherlands (present-day Belgium) during the reign of her brother, Holy Roman Emperor Joseph II, whose edicts abolishing many religious bodies were so unpopular that Maria Christina was hesitant to implement them. In retaliation to the edicts, the estates of Hainault and Brabant refused to pay taxes in 1788. In 1789 revolution erupted, and the Austrians were forced to retreat to Luxembourg. Maria Christina died in 1798.[33]

María Christina I of Naples
Queen, regent of Spain (1833–1840)

She was born in Naples in 1806 and became the fourth wife of King Ferdinand VII, who ruled Spain from 1814 to 1833. They had two daughters: Isabella II and Luisa Fernanda. In 1833, two months before her husband's death, María Christina persuaded him to set aside the Salic Law, thus allowing his daughter to succeed him and depriving his brother, Don Carlos, of the throne. On the death of Ferdinand, María Christina became regent with absolute power. Realizing she needed the support of the liberals, she liberalized the constitution and sanctioned certain anticlerical measures. In 1833 she made a secret morganatic marriage to Fernando Muñoz that, when discovered, made her highly unpopular. In 1834 Don Carlos, determined to win the

throne for himself, instigated the First Carlist War aimed at María Christina and the liberals. The Carlists were defeated in 1837 but the war was not officially concluded until 1839. Don Carlos left the country for France. Meantime, María Christina was pressured into appointing a Progressist minister and accepting a new compromise constitution (1837). In 1840 General Baldomero Esparto, Progressist leader, revolted, forcing María Christina to resign her regency and leave the country, making way for Esparto to assume the regency. She later made an attempt to return and participate in the government, but failed; she retired in exile to France in 1854 where she died in 1878.[34]

María Christina of Austria
Queen, regent of Spain (1885–1902)

Born in 1858 in an area of Austria now contained in Czechoslovakia, in 1879 María Christina became the second wife of King Alfonso XII, ruler of Spain from 1874 to 1885. They had three children: María de la Mercedes, María Teresa, and Alfonso XIII, who was born after his father died. When Alfonso XII died in 1885, María de la Mercedes, the elder daughter, technically became hereditary queen until her brother was born in 1886. María Christina served as regent for both children until Alfonso XIII was declared of age to govern in 1902. Even then, Alfonso at first allowed his mother to continue to rule. During her regency, she alternated power between the liberals, led by Praxedes Mateo Sagasta, and the conservatives, led by Antonio Canovas del Castillo. The Spanish-American War of 1898 left Spain weakened and the Spanish Empire decimated, with the loss of Cuba, Puerto Rico, Guam, and the Philippines. María Christina resigned her regency in 1902. She died in Madrid in 1929.[35]

María de la Mercedes (or Mercedes)
Queen infanta of Spain (1885–1886)

She was born in 1880, the elder daughter of King Alfonso XII, who ruled Spain from 1875 to 1885, and María Christina of Austria. When her father died in 1885, there was no male heir, so María de la Mercedes, age five, succeeded him. However, several months later her mother gave birth to a boy, Alfonso XIII, who became the new king at birth. María de la Mercedes was married to Carlo, conti de Caserta di Bourbon, but bore no children. She died in 1904.[36]

María Estela Martínez de Perón
See Perón, Isabel

Maria (or Mary) of Anjou
"King" of Hungary (1382–1385 and 1386–1395)

Born in 1370, the elder daughter of Elizabeth of Bosnia and Louis I the Great, king of Hungary from 1342 to 1382, and king of Poland from 1370 to 1382, Maria was also the sister of Jadwiga, queen of Poland. In 1378, at the age of eight, she was married to Sigismund of Luxembourg, age ten, later to be king of Hungary from 1387, king of Germany from 1411, king of the Lombards from 1431, and holy Roman emperor from 1433. The couple had no children. When her father died in 1382, Maria, age twelve, became queen of Hungary. She ruled alone for three years, but in 1385 her position was challenged by Charles II of Durazzo and Naples, whose father, Steven V, had ruled Hungary from 1270 to 1272. Charles was assassinated in 1386 and Maria resumed her reign. In 1387 Maria's husband was finally crowned king consort. Maria continued to rule with Sigismund until her death in 1395 at the age of 25.[37]

Maria of Austria
Dowager queen of Hungary, governor of the Netherlands (1530–1555)

The daughter of Queen Juana of Spain and Philip of Hapsburg, Maria was also the sister of Holy Roman Emperor Charles V and of Ferdinand, king of Bohemia. She married Louis II, who was king of Hungary from 1516 to 1526. Following his death in 1526, and the death in 1930 of Margaret, duchess of Savoy and governor of the Netherlands, Dowager Queen Maria was appointed governor of the Netherlands by her brother, Emperor Charles. She ruled until her death in 1555.[38]

Maria Theresa
Empress of Hapsburg Empire, queen of Bohemia and Hungary, archduchess of Austria, ruler of Luxembourg, etc. (1740–1780)

She was born in 1717, the older daughter of Charles VI, king of Bohemia and Hungary from 1711 to 1740, and Elizabeth Christina of Brunswick. When her father died in 1740, Maria Theresa succeeded him in the midst of the War of Austrian Succession. That same year she married Francis Stephen of the house of Lorraine, grand duke of Tuscany from 1737 to 1765, later Francis I, emperor of the Hapsburg Empire (1745–1765). Two of their children, Joseph II and Leopold II, were emperors, and one was Marie-Antoinette. At her accession the monarchy was exhausted, the people discontented, and the army weak. Only seven weeks after her father's death, Frederick III the Great of Prussia marched in and took over the Austrian province of Silesia, precipitating the Silesian Wars of 1740–1742 and 1744. She never forgave the loss of Silesia to Frederick. The

Maria Theresa. The Granger Collection, New York.

ensuing Seven Years' War (1756–1763) was a world war, fought not only in Europe but also in North America and India, with Britain and Prussia fighting France, Austria, and Russia. Maria Theresa managed to bear 16 children in 20 years while she first established her right to rule, then negotiated an imperial crown for her husband, meanwhile introducing economic reforms and strengthening the central government and the army. She improved the economic climate of the Netherlands and enjoyed wide popularity there. She died at the age of 63 in 1780.[39]

Marie
Countess, ruler of Boulogne (1159–1173)

The daughter of Countess Mahaut de Boulogne (also called Queen Matilda of England), ruler of Boulogne from 1125 to 1150, and King Stephen I, who ruled England from 1135 to 1154, Marie was also the sister of Count Eustache IV, who succeeded their mother upon her death and ruled from 1150 to 1153, and of Guillaume II, who ruled after his brother died in 1153 to 1159. When Guillaume died in 1159, Marie succeeded him. She was married to Matthieu d'Alsace. They had a daughter, Ide, who succeeded her mother upon Marie's death in 1173.[40]

Marie (or Mary of Brabant)
Countess, ruler of Brabant (1260)

She was the second wife of Holy Roman Emperor Otto IV, whom she married ca. 1213. Otto was deposed in 1215 and died in 1218. Marie did not remarry and had no children. When Countess Mahaut de Dammaratin died in 1260, the fief of Boulogne passed to Marie. Eventually it passed to Robert VI, comte d'Auvergne.[41]

Marie (or Maria La Marquise or Maria of Montferrat)
Regent of Jerusalem (1205–1212)

She was born ca. 1192, the oldest daughter of Princess Isabella, heiress of the kingdom of Jerusalem, and her second husband, Conrad of Montferrat, who was murdered shortly after

Marie was born. In 1198 Isabella and her fourth husband, Amalric II, were crowned king and queen of Jerusalem. In the kingdom of Jerusalem, hereditary right to rule dictated that Maria would inherit the throne, but the high court preserved its claim to elect a ruler. Isabella died in ca. 1205, as did Amalric. Maria, at age 13, acceded to the throne, and John of Ibelin, lord of Beirut, was appointed regent for three years. In 1208, at the age of 17, she was married to a penniless knight from Champagne, John of Brienne, who was already 60 years old. In 1212 they had a daughter, Yolanda (also called Yolande or Isabella II). That same year Marie died. Her husband continued to rule for their daughter.[42]

Marie de Bourbon Montpensier
Duchess, ruler of Auvergne (1608–1627)

Born in 1606, the daughter of Henri, duke of Montpensier, who ruled Auvergne from 1602 to 1608, and Henriette de Joyeuse, at age three Marie succeeded her father upon his death. She married Jean Baptist Gaston, duke of Orléans, and in 1627 they had a daughter, Anne-Marie-Louise, who inherited her mother's rule when Marie died the same year.[43]

Marie de Chatillon
Countess, ruler of Blois (1230–1241)

Marie de Chatillon inherited Blois when Countess Marguerite of Navarre died in 1230. She was married to Hugues de Chatillon, count of Saint-Pol. They had one son, Jean de Chatillon, who became count of Blois and Chartres when his mother died in 1241.[44]

Marie de Médicis
Regent of France (1610–1614), de facto ruler until 1631, governor of Normandy (1612–1619)

She was born in 1573 in Florence, Italy, the daughter of Francesco de Medici, grand duke of Tuscany, and Joanna of Austria. In 1600 she married King Henry IV, who ruled as king of France from 1589 to 1610. In 1601 she gave birth to the future Louis XIII and subsequently had five more children. When Henry was

Marie de Médicis. The Granger Collection, New York.

Marie d'Savoy-Nemours
See Jeanne de Nemours

Marie-Louise
Regent of France (1812), duchess of Parma (1815–1847)

She was born in Vienna in 1791, the eldest of 12 children of Holy Roman Emperor Francis II, ruler from 1792 to 1806 and ruler of Austria as Francis I from 1804 to 1835, and his second wife, Maria Theresa of Naples-Sicily. When Napoleon, eager for a royal heir, decided to divorce his beloved Joséphine, the Austrian foreign minister, Count (later Prince) Klemens von Metternich, suggested 19-year-old Marie-Louise as Napoleon's second wife. They married in 1810 and in 1811 their son, Napoleon II, was born. In 1812, during Napoleon's Russian campaign, Marie-Louise served as regent. The marriage marked a turning point for Napoleon. According to historian Owen Connelly, "Marie-Louise made him so happy that he lost his compulsion to work." Whether Marie-Louise was equally happy is questionable. Napoleon still corresponded with Joséphine, and there were rumors that he was the father of the children of Marie-Louise's sister-in-law, Archduchess Sophie. After his first abdication in 1814, her father whisked her and his grandson back to Austria. The Congress of Vienna gave Marie-Louise the Italian duchies of Parma, Piacenza, and Guastalla, with sovereign power to rule in her own right, but they would revert to the house of Bourbon at her death. She refused to accompany Napoleon to Elba, and after he threatened to abduct her, she became completely estranged from him. At the time of his death in 1821, she had already given birth to two children by Adam Adalbert, Graf von Neipperg, and she married Neipperg shortly after Napoleon's death. She established a moderate rule in Parma and maintained the previously enacted French reforms. Neipperg died only two years after their marriage, and in 1824 Marie took a third husband, Charles-René, comte de Bombelles. In 1832 her son Napoleon II died in Vienna of tuberculosis. Marie-Louise died in Parma in 1847.[46]

assassinated in 1610, Marie was named regent for her son Louis XIII. She chose as her chief minister a Florentine friend, Concino Concini, whom she named marquis d'Ancre. In 1612 she became governor of Normandy as well, a post she held until 1619.

Marie was the first woman governor of a major province. She later traded this post for the government of Anjou. She continued to rule France even after Louis came of age in 1614. In 1619 Concini was assassinated, and Marie was banished to Blois, but she escaped and, with the help of the future cardinal, the duke of Richelieu, she set up court at Angers in 1619. In 1621, after the death of the king's favorite, the duke of Luynes, Marie and Richelieu gained control of affairs. Marie obtained a cardinal's hat for Richelieu and saw to it that Louis appointed him chief minister. When Richelieu rejected an alliance with Spain and opted to side with the Hugenots, Marie demanded that he be dismissed. Instead, Louis banished his mother again in 1631. She went to the Spanish Netherlands and then to Cologne, where she died in 1642, penniless.[45]

Marozia Crescentii
Ruler of Rome (A.D. 928–932)

She was the daughter of Roman Senator Theo-phylact Crescentii and his wife Theodora. The patrician Crescentii family was of the landed aristocracy that controlled Rome during the na-dir of the papacy. At the time of Marozia, the papacy was a local and secular institution. Italy as a whole was without effective native rule. Marozia was the mistress of Pope Sergius III and the mother of his son John, later Pope John XI. She married Alberic I of Spoleto, the mar-grave of Camerino who, with her father, re-stored Sergius III to the papacy. Alberic and Marozia had a son, Alberic II. After Alberic I died in 928, Marozia overthrew and imprisoned Pope John X, raised her illegitimate son to the papacy, and took control of Rome until her son Alberic II assumed power in 932. Following the death of her first husband, she married, succes-sively, Marquess Guido, Guy of Tuscany, and, after he died, his half brother Hugh of Prov-ence, king of Italy from 926 to 932. In 932 her son Alberic II rose up against her and drove out King Hugh.[47]

Mary
Duchess, ruler of Burgundy and Luxembourg (1477–1482)

Mary was born in 1457, the daughter of Charles the Bold, ruler of Burgundy from 1467 to 1477, and Margaret of York. In 1474, Louis XI (called the Spider) formed the Union of Con-stance (a coalition of foes of Burgundy) and opened war on Charles the Bold. Charles was killed in battle in 1477. Louis attempted to unite Burgundy with the crown, but Flanders stood firmly by Mary. However, the Union of Con-stance was a formidable foe for a widow alone; she soon married the Archduke Maximilian of Austria, ruler of the Hapsburg Empire from 1493 to 1519. The couple had two children: Philip, who married Joanna of Castile and was called Philip the Handsome, regent of Spain; and Margaret, who first married John of Spain and then Philip of Savoy. Mary died in 1482. Their son Philip became duke of Burgundy.[48]

Mary
Queen, regent of Georgia (1027–ca. 1031)

She was the daughter of Sennacherib-John of Vaspurahan and the wife of George I, Bagratid king of Georgia from 1014 to 1027. They had a son, Bagrat IV, who succeeded his father as a minor when George died in 1027. Queen Mary served as regent during a troubled time in Georgia's history. In 1031 after the *Katholikos* of Iberia, Queen Mary and the minister Melchisedech journeyed to Constantinople on a diplomatic mission on behalf of her son. Peace was concluded, and young Bagrat received the dignity of *Curopalate,* which had been denied his father. Mary also made arrangements at that time for her son to marry the Emperor's niece, Helena.[49]

Mary I (Bloody Mary or Mary the Catholic)
Queen of England (1553–1558)

She was born in 1516, the daughter of Henry VIII, king of England from 1509 to 1547, and Catherine of Aragon, whom he divorced in 1533, claiming the marriage to his brother's widow was incestuous and thus Mary was a bastard. His next wife, Anne Boleyn, forced Mary to serve as lady-in-waiting for her own daughter, Elizabeth. Mary was also coerced into admitting the illegality of her mother's marriage to her father. After Anne Boleyn was beheaded, Mary's lot became easier; she was, in fact, made godmother to Edward, Henry's son by his third wife, Jane Seymour. One by one she watched Henry's wives come and go. She secretly practiced her Catholicism and waited for a marriage partner to materialize. Her status as a bastard severely limited her mar-ital opportunities even though, in 1544, she was named in succession to the throne after Edward. When Edward died in 1553, one threat to her succession, Lady Jane Grey, had to be deposed after a nine-day "reign," and then Mary be-came, at age 37, the first queen to rule all of England in her own right. She set about restor-ing the ties to the Catholic Church severed dur-ing her father's reign. To that end, she determined to marry Philip of Spain, son of

Queen Mary I. The Granger Collection, New York.

Holy Roman Emperor Charles V. The people of Tudor England distrusted Spaniards, and his Catholicism was of grave concern to those English nobles who had profited when Henry VIII confiscated Catholic lands. Sir Thomas Wyatt led a Protestant insurrection, which Mary countered with an impassioned plea to her citizenry. Wyatt was executed, and Mary married Philip in 1554. Soon after, the papal legate absolved England from the sin of its 20-year break with Rome. The Church restored the heresy laws in 1555, and as a result some 280 heretics were burned. Thenceforth Queen Mary was known as Bloody Mary and was blamed for the slaughter. Philip returned to Spain in 1555 when his father died, and came to England only once more in all the years of their marriage; that was in 1556, to persuade her to take arms against France to assist Spain's interests. In 1558 Calais, which had been an English possession for more than two centuries, was taken by the duke of Guise. This loss was one from which she

never recovered. Ten months later she was dead.[50]

Mary II
Queen of England (1689–1694)

She was born in 1662, the daughter of James II, ruler of England from 1685 to 1688, and Anne Hyde. Although both parents were Catholic converts, Mary was reared as a Protestant. In 1677, at the age of 15, Mary was married to her cousin William of Orange, stadholder of Holland. Her initial disappointment on meeting William (who was 12 years older than she and four inches shorter) eventually disappeared. However, Mary never reconciled to William's long-standing love affair with her lady-in-waiting, Elizabeth Villiers, whom William insisted be retained in the queen's retinue.

In 1688 English bishops wrote to William, a champion of Protestant causes, inviting him to invade England, an invitation that William and Mary welcomed. William's invasion met with scant resistance, for the country wanted a Prot-

Queen Mary II. The Granger Collection, New York.

estant ruler. King James fled to France, and after a half-hearted attempt to regain his throne, retired to France permanently. Mary made it known that she had no intention of reigning alone: she was the prince's wife, she said, and never meant to be "other than in subjection to him." They were crowned joint sovereigns in 1689. However, during her six years as Queen of England, she reigned alone for much of the time, since William was abroad attending to matters of state in Holland, or was conducting his military campaigns against France or Ireland.

Mary enjoyed great popularity and ruled with vigor, sensitivity, and dynamism during William's absences, but when he was in England she quickly retired. Her chaplain wrote that if her husband retained the throne of England, "It would be done by her skill and talents for governing." Her estrangement from her father and from her adopted homeland, Holland, troubled her, but more vexing were her constant quarrels with her sister Anne, whose friends, Sarah and John Churchill, actively disliked William. She, in turn, mistrusted them and thought that Anne was entirely too much in their thrall. In 1694 Mary died of smallpox at the age of 32.[51]

Mary Bosomworth
"Princess," ruler of Ossabaw, Sapelo, and St. Catherines islands (1747–?)

A Creek Indian, she was the daughter of "an Indian woman of no note," according to one Georgia account. She served General James Oglethorpe, the founder of Georgia, as an interpreter to the Creek Indians. As her third husband she took the Reverend Thomas Bosomworth, Oglethorpe's chaplain. Together they persuaded the Creeks that Mary was their princess in the maternal line. The Creeks accepted her and honored her request to give her three islands off the Georgia coast to command: Ossabaw, Sapelo, and St. Catherines. The British attempted to recover the islands, but Mary raised an army of Creeks and marched into Savannah, threatening a massacre. The British backed down, but eventually ransomed Ossa-

baw and Sapelo for large sums. Mary kept the island of St. Catherines.[52]

Mary (or Maria) of Antioch
Empress, regent of Byzantine Empire (1180–1183)

She was the daughter of Constance of Antioch and Raymond of Poitiers, and the sister of King Bohemond III. In 1160, in an undeclared contest between Mary and Melisende, daughter of Raymond II of Tripoli, Mary was chosen by Byzantine Emperor Manuel I (1143–1180) as his second wife. The couple had a son, Alexius II, who acceded to the throne at the age of 11 with his mother as regent. Empress Mary was the first Latin to be ruler of the empire, and as such she was resented by the people. Opportunistic Italian merchants had all but gained a monopoly on trade in the city. To compound her problem with her subjects, Mary took as her advisor (and, as rumors had it, possibly her lover) her husband's nephew, the Protosebastus Alexius Comnenus, uncle of Maria of Jerusalem. He, too, was unpopular. The Porphyrogennete Maria and her husband, Ranier of Montferrat, plotted to kill her uncle Alexius, but their plan went awry. In 1182 Empress Maria's cousin-in-law, Andronicus Comnenus, invaded Constantinople; it was the opportunity the people needed to fall upon all the hated Latins in their midst. The citizens slaughtered the haughty Italian merchants who had controlled the city's trade. Andronicus then eliminated his rivals one by one, beginning with the Porphyrogennete and her husband, whom he murdered. Young Alexius II was forced to sign a warrant condemning his mother Mary to be strangled to death (1182). The boy himself was murdered two months later.[53]

Mary of Guise
(also called Mary of Lorraine)
Queen, regent of Scotland (1554–1560)

Mary of Guise was born in 1515, the eldest daughter of Claude of Lorraine, founding duc de Guise who ruled from 1528 to 1550, and Antoinette de Bourbon-Vendôme. In 1533 she married Louis d'Orléans, duc de Longueville. They had one son, François, born in 1534. In

Mary Stuart, Queen of Scots. The Granger Collection, New York.

1537 her husband died, and the following year Mary married King James V, ruler of Scotland from 1513 to 1542. Their daughter, Mary Stuart, was born a few days before James died in 1542, at which time English King Henry VIII tried in vain to gain control of the kingdom. In 1554 James, earl of Arran, was deposed from the regency for 12-year-old Mary in favor of Queen Mary. In the beginning of her regency, Mary, a Catholic, actually cultivated Protestants and ruled with such religious tolerance that the Protestants even supported her 1558 decision to marry her daughter to the future king of France, Francis II. However, heavy-handed French influence soon induced her to change her tolerant attitude toward Protestants and to attempt to suppress the growth of Protestantism in Scotland. Her actions sparked a civil war in which the Protestants were aided by England and the Catholics by France. Mary was driven from office but returned, only to be on the verge of defeat again. Her health failed, and from her deathbed she called a conference of nobles from both sides and pleaded for a compromise. She died in 1560 before she could see her request honored.[54]

Mary of Lorraine
See Mary of Guise

Mary Stuart
Queen of Scots (1542–1567)

Born in 1542, she was the only child of King James V, ruler of Scotland from 1513 to 1542, and Mary of Guise. Mary was born the year her father died. To keep Henry VIII from gaining control of the fatherless child, Mary's mother sent her to France when she was five years old, where she was reared in the household of King Henry II and Catherine de Médicis. In 1558 at age 16, she was married to their eldest son, 14-year-old Francis II, later ruler of France from 1559 to 1560. That same year, Elizabeth Tudor, a Protestant, acceded to the throne of England and Mary, a Catholic, was next in the line of succession. Two years later her husband died, and she soon returned to Scotland. For the first years of her majority rule, she refrained from interfering in religious affairs, even choosing Protestant advisors. Then she made the fatal mistake of falling in love with her cousin, Lord Darnley, who was unpopular with all factions. Despite all protests, she married him in 1565. Through plots and counterplots, including the murder of her secretary Rizzio before her eyes, Darnley tried to ensure the succession for his heirs. Mary bore a son, James VI, in 1566, but by now she was convinced that Darnley meant to kill her. One account says that Mary developed an adulterous relationship with the earl of Bothwell before he murdered Darnley in 1567, and that Mary was aware of Bothwell's plot. Whatever her foreknowledge of events, Bothwell abducted her, ravished her, and subsequently married her. But the marriage set Scottish nobles up in arms; they exiled Bothwell, imprisoned Mary on the island of Loch Leven, and forced her to abdicate in favor of her son. The following year she fled to England, but Elizabeth held her in prison for 18 years. Then, in 1586, suspecting Mary of being involved in a plot to assassinate her, Elizabeth consented to have Mary put to death.[55]

Mathilde
Countess, ruler of Nevers (992–1028)

The daughter of Otto Guillaume, count of Burgundy and Nevers from 987 to 992, Mathilde married Seigneur of Maers, Moncearx, and Auxerre. They had a son, Renaud, who succeeded his mother as Count Renaud I of Auxerre and Nevers upon her death in 1028.[56]

Matilda
Abbess, regent of Germany (996)

Matilda was the daughter of Otto the Great, Holy Roman Emperor from 962 to 972, and Adelaide of Burgundy, and a sister of Otto II, emperor from 973 to 983. From 954 to 968 she was Abbess of Quedlinburg. When her 15-year-old nephew, Otto III, went to Italy to receive his imperial crown in 996, he installed his very able aunt Matilda, described as "a woman of great wisdom and strength," as his regent.[57]

Matilda (also called Empress Maud)
Uncrowned queen of England (1141), regent of England (1154)

Matilda was born in 1102, the only daughter of King Henry I, ruler of England from 1100 to 1135, and Edith (also called Matilda) of Scotland. She was the granddaughter of William the Conqueror. Fierce, proud, and cynical, Matilda developed an early, consuming interest in politics. In 1114 at the age of 12, she was married to Holy Roman Emperor Henry V, who lost her estates in his second campaign for expansion. The couple had no children. In 1120 her brother William, heir to the English throne, died, and in 1125 her husband died. In 1131, her father recalled her to England, naming her his heir and arranging her marriage to 14-year-old Godfrey Plantagenet, count of Anjou. Matilda was then 29 years old. In 1133 the couple had a son, Henry II, destined to rule England from 1154 to 1189. She had two more sons, Geoffrey and William. When King Henry I died in 1135, her cousin Stephen of Blois, son of Henry's sister Adela, usurped the throne in a sudden coup

d'état. It took Matilda four years to gather her supporters, but in 1139 she invaded England to claim her throne from the usurper. It was two years more before her forces could capture Stephen and send him in chains to Bristol Castle. She was proclaimed *Domina Anglorum,* "Lady of the English," and queen in April, although she was not crowned at the time. By November, however, her demands for money and her quarrels with the Church had soured many of her supporters, who had second thoughts about crowning her. Hostility toward her mounted to such an extent that at one time she was forced to masquerade as a corpse to escape Stephen's supporters. Eventually Stephen was set free, and Matilda was again obliged to elude her would-be captors, this time by wearing white so as to blend with the snow around Oxford Castle. Finally, after many battles and much intrigue, Matilda could see that she was beaten, and in 1148 she retired to Normandy. Her son Henry II acceded to the throne in 1154, and she ably performed her duties as regent during the first few years of his reign. She died in 1167, having composed the words to appear on her tombstone: "Here lies Henry's daughter, wife and mother; great by birth, greater by marriage, greatest by motherhood."[58]

Matilda of Flanders
Duchess, regent of Normandy (ca. 1066?)

She was the daughter of Count Baldwin (Beaudoin) V of Flanders and the wife of William, duke of Normandy (later, William the Conqueror). William based his claim for the throne of England on the fact that Matilda was a descendant of Alfred the Great—her father was a descendant of Baldwin II, who married Alfred's daughter Aelfthryth. While William was conquering England (1066), Matilda ruled Normandy. The couple had four children: Robert Curthose, later duke of Normandy; William II Rufus (the Red), ruler of England (1087–1100); Adela, wife of Stephen II of Blois, ruler of England (1135–1154); and Henry I, ruler of England (1100–1135). Matilda died in 1083.[59]

Matilda of Tuscany
Duchess, co-ruler of Central Italy
(1071–1076), then alone (1076–1089)

She was born in 1046, the daughter of Boniface
of Canossa, marquis of Tuscany, and his wife
Beatrice. Her father's assassination in 1052 and
the deaths of her older brother and sister left her
the sole heir to an enormous fortune, including
the holdings amassed by her grandfather, Otto
Adalbert, founder of the House of Attoni. In
1054 Beatrice married Godfrey the Bearded of
Upper Lorraine, Emperor Henry III's greatest
foe in Germany. In 1055 Henry arrested Beatrice and Matilda, age nine, sending them to
Germany, while Godfrey fled. Later Henry and
Godfrey became reconciled and released Beatrice and Matilda. Godfrey died in 1069, and
Matilda married his son, Godfrey the Hunch-
back, and settled in Lorraine. In 1071 she lost
her only child, so she returned to Italy, where
she reigned with her mother until Beatrice's
death in 1076. Then she became sole ruler of a
large, wealthy and powerful domain. All her
life Matilda remained a powerful ally of the
papacy. In was at her castle of Canossa that
Emperor Henry IV stood barefoot in the snow
for three days in order to receive absolution
from the pope. There were few aspects of Italian or papal life about which her wishes did not
have to be considered. In 1089 Pope Urban II
arranged a marriage between Matilda and Welf
V, duke of Bavaria and Carinthia. She was 43
and he was only 17. Henry IV, intent on enlarging his holdings, invaded northern Italy, but
with her vast resources Matilda was able to hold
out against him in the hills. After he had seized
the crown of Italy, Matilda and Pope Urban
convinced his son Conrad to revolt against
Henry (1093). Her death in 1115 created a furor, for in 1086 and 1102 she had donated her
allodial lands to the papacy, while her will
named Henry V as the recipient. The resolution
of this dilemma was reached only after years of
strife.[60]

Maud
Empress. *See* Matilda

Matilda of Tuscany. The Granger Collection, New York.

Mavia (also called Mawia)
Queen of the Saracens (ca. A.D. 370–380)

Mavia was married to the king of the Saracens,
a Bedouin tribe living in the area around the
Sinai Peninsula, and succeeded her husband
when he died. She organized raids against
Rome's eastern frontier into Phoenicia and Palestine. Riding at the head of her army, she defeated a Roman army and made peace only on
the condition that a hermit named Moses be
forcibly consecrated as bishop of her tribe. Her
daughter was married to the Roman commander-in-chief, Victor, a Samaritan from
across the Danube. In 378 she sent her Arab
cavalry to aid the Romans in defending Constantinople; its shockingly bloodthirsty mode of
fighting intimidated even the Goths. She is
probably the person described elsewhere as
Mawia, Queen of Syria, possibly a Ghassanid.
Ghassar was an Arabian kingdom bounded on
the northeast by the Euphrates River and extending into the Sinai Peninsula.[61]

Mawia
Queen of Syria. *See* Mavia

Mehr-on-Nesā (or Mehrunissa)
See Nūr Jahān

Mei
Queen of Cambodia (1835–1847)

The daughter of King Ang Chan, who ruled from 1797 until his death in 1835, Mei came to the throne during a time of Vietnamese control, so she exercised very little power during her 12-year reign. In 1847 she was deposed in favor of Ang Duang, son of former King Ang Eng. She died in 1875.

Meir, Golda
Premier of Israel (1969–1974)

She was born Goldie Mabovitch in 1898 in Kiev, Russia, to Moshe Mabovitz and his wife. To escape persecution, the family migrated in 1906 to Milwaukee, Wisconsin, where Golda's father became a railroad worker and her mother a grocery clerk. Golda attended Milwaukee Teachers Training College. She joined the Poale Zion, a faction of the Labor Zionists Party, and in 1917 married Morris Myerson, a sign painter she met while visiting her sister in Denver. In 1921 Golda persuaded her husband to emigrate to Palestine and live in a kibbutz. In 1924, after their first child was born, they moved to Jerusalem where Morris worked as a bookkeeper and Golda took in laundry. There they had another child. By 1929 Golda had immersed herself in the Zionist movement, quickly becoming a leader. During World War II she emerged as a forceful spokesperson to the British in behalf of Zionism. While Golda was possessed by her mission, her husband hated his life in Israel and in 1945 they divorced. He died in Tel Aviv in 1951.

Golda was a signer of Israel's Proclamation of Independence, and in 1948, during the war for independence, Golda traveled to the United States to raise $50 million for the cause. In 1949 she was elected to the legislature, where she served for 25 years; Ben Gurion called her "the only man in the cabinet." In 1956, at Ben Gurion's suggestion, she Hebraized her name to Golda Meir. In 1969 she became Israel's fourth prime minister. Meir faced the hostility of Israel's neighbors, necessitating a huge defense budget in a struggling economy, and mass dis-

Golda Meir. UPI/Bettmann Newsphotos.

unity, not only within her own Labor party, but in the country as a whole, which was a mixture of occidental and oriental Jews. In 1974, after the outbreak of the fourth Arab-Israeli War late the year before, she was forced to resign, although she continued to work in politics. Her private life and her political career had been ones of constant struggle, but her ability to see humor in the bitterest of moments helped her retain perspective. She once said, "Can you imagine Moses dragging us forty years through the desert to bring us to the one place in the Middle East where there is no oil?" When she died in 1978 at the age of 80, it was discovered that she had had leukemia for 12 years.[62]

Melisende (or Melissande)
Queen of Jerusalem (1131–1152)

Melisende was the daughter of Morphia, daughter of Gabriel of Melitene, and King Baldwin II, ruler of Jerusalem from 1118 to 1131. Her chief companion before marriage was Hugh of Le Puiset, lord of Jaffy, a tall, handsome man who had lived in the court as a boy. In 1129 her parents married her to Fulk V, who was short, wiry, red-faced, and middle-aged, and for whom she never cared. After she and Fulk ascended to the throne following her father's death in 1131, she continued her intimate friendship with Hugh, now married to an older woman, Emma, widow of Eustace I of Sidon. Fulk grew jealous and soon the court was divided between Count Hugh and the king. To protect his mother's honor, Emma's son challenged Hugh to a duel. Hugh did not appear for the duel, a sign of his cowardice and guilt. Soon afterward, supporters of either Fulk or Emma, the aggrieved parties, stabbed Hugh, but he did not die. Because he was suspected of being behind the plot to kill Hugh, Fulk arranged for a public execution when the would-be assassin was caught. The assassin had his limbs cut off one by one, but while his head still remained, he was to continue to repeat his confession. Melisende was so enraged over the incident that for many months afterward, Hugh's enemies and even Fulk himself feared for their lives.

Melisende had several children by Fulk, but only two survived: Baldwin III, born in 1130, who ruled from 1143 to 1162, and Amalric I, born in 1136, who ruled from 1162 to 1174. In 1143 Fulk died, thrown from a horse while on a family picnic. Melisende appointed her older son, Baldwin, as her colleague and assumed the government herself. When Baldwin reached the age of 22 he wanted to rule alone, but Melisende, conscious of her own hereditary right, declined to hand over the power to him completely. She made arrangement for his coronation with the stipulation that she would be crowned again by his side so that her joint authority would be specifically honored. However, Baldwin secretly changed the date of the coronation and was crowned without her. The act created dissension between supporters of each side, but Melisende, stricken at her own son's perfidy, yielded to him and retired from politics. She died in 1161.[63]

Mentewab
Empress of Ethiopia (1730–1769)

Mentewab was the wife of Emperor Baqaffa, who ruled Ethiopia from 1721 to 1730, and the regent during the minorities of several of her children and grandchildren. She watched over the reestablishing of Christianity in the provinces of the south during the reigns of her husband and her children, upon whose advent she each time exercised a regency. Her son Iyasu II, who ruled from 1730 to 1755, was the most brilliant of her charges. With Mentewab, he had the splendid Abbey of Kusquan built. To free himself of his mother's rule, he married the daughter of one of the Gallas chiefs and introduced Gallas warriors into the capital. During the reign of Ioyas, who ruled from 1755 to 1769, a rival faction arose headed by Mikael Sehul. Sehul had Ioyas assassinated in 1769, removed Mentewab and put Tekle-Haimanot II on the throne.[64]

Meryet-Nit
Queen, ruler of Egypt (ca. 3000 B.C.)

According to Manetho, it was during the reign of Neteren that it was decided that women might occupy the throne; however, evidence has convinced some historians to believe that Meryet-Nit was the successor of Zir and the third sovereign of the First Dynasty. Since Meryet-Nit is the only one among the royal ladies of the dynasty to have great monuments both at Abydos and Sakkara adjacent to those of kings, it could be surmised that she herself was a reigning monarch. Her Abydos monument is one of the largest and finest of all.[65]

Metnedjenet
see Eji

Min (or Bin)
Queen, twenty-fifth regent ruler of Yi Dynasty in Korea (1882–1895)

The Yi Dynasty, with 26 monarchs, ruled Korea until the Japanese annexation in 1910. During the first few years of the reign of King Kojong, usually known as Yi T'ae Wang, power was in the hands of his father, Taewongun, who was kidnapped in 1882 and taken to China. Power then passed to his queen, Min, who opposed all efforts at modernizing or westernizing Korea. Min was characterized as "the one vital ruling spark in the effete Korean court.'' She was assassinated in 1895 in a plot engineered with the connivance of the Japanese resident, Viscount Miura, because she was suspected of being the mastermind behind the anti-Japanese attitude of the Korean government.[66]

Mo-ki-lien
Khatun and regent of Mongolia (734–741)

Although the name of this Turkish queen did not survive, we know that she was married to Turkish Khan Mo-ki-lien, who ruled in Mongolia from A.D. 716 and who was poisoned by his minister in 724. The couple had a son, Yi-jan, who succeeded his father and for whom the khatun served as regent. When Yi-jan died, Mo-ki-lien's younger brother, Tangri khagan, took the throne, also as a minor, and Mo-ki-lien's widow continued to serve as regent and advisor until Tangri khagan's death in 741.[67]

Myōjō-tenno (also called Myōshō)
Empress of Japan (1630–1643)

Born in 1623, the daughter of Emperor Go-Mi-no-o, who ruled Japan from 1612 to 1629, and his consort Tōfuku-mon-in (Tokugawa Kazu-ko), who was the sister of the Shōgun Iemitsu, Myōjō succeeded her father, who abdicated when she reached the age of six. During her reign of 15 years, the power was primarily in the hands of her uncle, Shōgun Iemitsu. In 1643 Myōjō abdicated in favor of her brother, Go-Kōmyō, and lived in retirement for 53 years. She died in 1696.[68]

Myōshō
See Myōjō-tennō

Naqi'a
Regent of Assyria (ca. 689 B.C.)

Much confusion exists over the identity of the builder queen whom Herodotus called "Nitrocris." Because of the building activity associated with Naqi'a, she has mistakenly been identified as the Nitrocris of whom Herodotus writes. However, that "queen" was probably Addagoppe, never a queen at all, or Sammuramat. Naqi'a was the wife of Sennacherib, who ruled Assyria from 705 to 681 B.C. Her name indicates that she was probably either Jewish or Aramaean. One of her sons was Esarhaddon, who ruled ca. 681 to 670 B.C. In ca. 700 B.C. Sennacherib and Naqi'a transformed the capital city of Nineveh into a city of unparalleled splendor, building for themselves an 80-room palace to overlook it. In 689, after defending the city of Babylon several times, Sennacherib sacked it. Naqi'a may have served as regent during his absences on military campaigns. In 681 B.C. he was murdered by one of his sons, and Esarhaddon ascended to the throne. Presumably with Naqi'a's help, Esarhaddon rebuilt the city of Babylon, which his father had destroyed, and placed it under the rule of his son, Shamashshumukin. In 670 B.C. Esarhaddon was killed while on campaign to Egypt, and his other son Assurbanapal ascended to the throne (669 B.C.).[1]

Nefrusobek (also called Sebeknefru or Sobekneferu)
Last queen of the Twelfth Dynasty, Egypt (ca. 1787–1783 B.C.)

She was the daughter of Amenemhet III who ruled from ca. 1844 to 1797, and the half sister of Amenemhet IV, who succeeded at an elderly age after his father's 45-year reign. When Nefrusobek's brother died approximately a decade later, the absence of a male heir made her the next in line of succession. She ruled as king and full pharaoh but did not attempt to depict herself as a man as did Queen Hatshepsut (Eighteenth Dynasty). Her father had enabled a long period of peace and prosperity for Egypt. Although White termed her "insignificant," she did maintain the peaceful and prosperous rule set by her predecessors until she was ready to choose a successor.

The kingship was inherited through the daughter of the monarch. In order to preserve the royal succession within the same family, the custom was adopted of having the oldest son of the king marry his oldest sister, which Amenemhet had done. Since he died childless, Nefrusobek was privileged to select the next king by marrying him. She was expected to marry a member of the Theban nobility and elevate him to the throne, but Nefrusobek had other ideas.

Instead, she married a commoner from Lower Egypt. Her choice so enraged the citizenry that civil war broke out, since the northerners believed that they were far superior to the southerners. However, the sides were too evenly matched and no one could gain a decisive victory. While this senseless war raged on, a tribe of nomads from Asia, the Hyskos ("shepherd kings") invaded and assumed power. Nefrusobek died ca. 1783 B.C., ending the Twelfth Dynasty of Egypt.[2]

Nicole
Duchess, ruler of Lorraine (1624–1625)

Nicole was the daughter of Henry II, duke of Lorraine (1608–1624), and in 1624 she became duchess of Lorraine upon her father's death. That same year she married her cousin Charles, son of her father's brother Francis who, in a neat bit of finagling, arranged the marriage in order to wrest the duchy out of her control. The following year Francis abolished female succession so that he could be proclaimed duke. He then abdicated in favor of his son Charles IV (sometimes called Charles III).[3]

Nitrocris (possible misnomer of Addagoppe or Adda-Guppi)
Priestess, regent of Babylon (ca. 552 B.C.)

Addagoppe was born in Haran in 647 B.C. and became a priestess of the god Sin in Haran. According to Herodotus, writing of Nitrocris, she was married to an Assyrian king named Labynetus and bore a son of the same name. According to contemporary historian Olmstead, based on datable historical facts in Herodotus' account, the son Labynetus corresponds to the ruler Nabonidus, or Nabu-naid. The true biography of Addagoppe is known from a stele found (1956) preserved in a paving stone, inscription side down, in the Great Mosque at Haran. Her remarkable career spanned the whole neo-Babylonian Dynasty down to the ninth year of its last king. She came to Babylon from Haran and managed to obtain a responsible position for her son at court. Nabu-naid eventually became king of Babylon and ruled from 555 to 539 B.C.,

although he spent little time in Babylon. Herodotus refers to the king's mother as "Queen" Nitrocris and says she left as a memorial of her reign many works. In order to strengthen the security of Babylon, she altered the course of the Euphrates and constructed tall embankments on each side. She also built a footbridge across the river that could be removed at night. In great but erroneous detail, Herodotus describes what he terms her "grim practical joke": she placed her own tomb above one of the main gates of the city and inscribed it with the message: "If any king of Babylon hereafter is short of money, let him open my tomb and take as much as he likes. But this must be done only in case of need. Whoever opens my tomb under any other circumstances will get no good of it." The tomb remained undisturbed until the reign of Darius, who opened it to find only the queen's body and the following message: "If you had not been insatiably greedy and eager to get money by the most despicable means, you would never have opened the tomb of the dead."

Legends abound about illustrious persons, especially those who were particularly long-lived. There is no historical verification of any of Herodotus' tales concerning her, even of his referring to her as queen, but it is a historical fact that when Addagoppe died (ca. 547 B.C.) at the age of 104, she was buried in Haran with all the honors reserved for a queen. It is possible that, when Nabu-naid left Babylon in ca. 552 B.C. to reside in Taima in northeastern Asia, leaving his son Bel-shar-usur (Belshazzar mentioned in the book of Daniel) in charge, he also left his mother there. It is possible and even likely that, during Belshazzar's absences, Addagoppe served as regent, which would explain her being honored as a queen at death. Nabu-naid did not return to Babylon until 542 B.C., so it is possible that she was being honored by her grandson and not her son, or that her death was the occasion of her son's belated return. After her death, Nabu-naid appointed his daughter to be high priestess of the god Sin, returning to his mother's ancient roots.[4]

Nitrocris
Queen of Egypt (prior to 454 B.C.)

According to Herodotus (born ca. 484 B.C.), who traveled in Egypt after 454 B.C. and obtained much of his information from word of mouth, Nitrocris was an Egyptian woman. To avenge the murder of her brother-king, whom she succeeded, she constructed an immense underground chamber. As an inaugural ceremony she held a banquet and invited all those who were responsible for her brother's death. When the banquet was in full swing, she opened a large concealed conduit pipe, causing her guests to drown in river water. To escape her punishment, she threw herself into a roomful of ashes. No other source supports Herodotus' account.[5]

Nūr Jahān (also called Mehr-on-Nesā, Mihn-un-Nisa, or Mehrunissa)
Empress, de facto ruler of India
(1611–1627 intermittently)

Mehrunissa was born in 1577, the daughter of a Persian, Sher Alkun (or I 'timād-ud-Dawlah), who was in the service of the Moghul Jahāngīr, who ruled from 1605 to 1627. Mehrunissa married a Persian, Sher Afkun, whom Jahāngīr posted to Bengal. She had a daughter, Lādilī Begam, who married Prince Shahiryār, a son of Jahāngīr. Sher Afkun died in 1607, possibly at Jahāngīr's instigation. The widow Mehrunissa was brought to court as lady-in-waiting to Salima, a widow of the previous Moghul, Akbar. Jahāngīr married Mehrunissa four years later and gave her the name Nūr Mahal, "light of the palace." Her brother, Āsaf Khān, was given a high-ranking position second only to that of her father, who was promoted to chief minister. Mehrunissa soon made herself indispensable to the dependent, alcoholic king, who gave her a new name, Nūr Jahān, "light of the world." Her mother discovered attar of roses and was rewarded with a pearl necklace; clearly, the family had taken over the palace. Nūr Jahān, her brother, and her father dominated the politics of the realm, with Nūr Jahān making the decisions and the others carrying them out. British Ambassador Sir Thomas Roe wrote home to the future King Charles I that Nūr Jahān "governs

Empress Nūr Jahān. William H. Laufer.

him and wynds him up at her pleasure." Jahāngīr fell ill in 1620, and from then on his poor health, compounded by asthma and his use of alcohol and opium, made it imperative for Nūr Jahān to exercise control. Her father died and her brother was occupied elsewhere during the final five years of Jahāngīr's life, and Nūr Jahān ruled alone from inside the harem.

There is no evidence that Nūr Jahān ever broke purdah. She even hunted tigers from a closed howdah on top of an elephant with only the barrel of her musket exposed between the curtains. In 1626 she rode into battle in an elephant litter, dispensing her orders through her eunuch. She also carried on a business, specializing in indigo and cloth trades. After her daughter married Shahiryār, Nūr Jahān began actively to work against Shāh Jahān, Jahāngīr's appointed heir to the throne. After Jahāngīr died, Shāh Jahān was able to seize control, and Nūr Jahān quickly accepted retirement and a pension of 200,000 rupees a year. She died in 1646.[6]

Nzinga Mbandi (also called Jinga, Singa, or Zhinga)
Queen, ngola of the Mbundu in Ndongo
(1624–1663)

Nzinga was born ca. 1580, the daughter and sister of kings. One of her predecessors was Nzinga Mhemba, baptized in 1491 by the Portuguese as Alfonso, who acceded to the throne in 1507 and ruled as an ''ardent and enlightened Christian'' until he died in 1543. In 1618 the Portuguese finally conquered the Ndongo Kingdom in Angola. (The word ''Angola'' comes from ''ngola,'' meaning ruler.) Nzinga first attempted to use the Portuguese to secure her leadership, even allowing herself to be baptized and to take the name ''Anna de Sousa,'' after the Portuguese governor. Her sister Mukumbu had become ''Lady Barbara'' and her sister Kifunji had become ''Lady Grace.'' But her attempts to become the ruler of her tribe failed, and her brother was made ngola in the early 1620s. He died in 1624 as did his son, both possibly at Nzinga's instigation, and Nzinga became queen. At her first official visit to negotiate with the imperious Governor de Sousa, the governor sat upon a throne while Nzinga was expected to stand before him. She ordered a slave to kneel so that she could sit. According to one account, when the interview was at an end, she ordered the slave slaughtered before the horrified governor's eyes to show him that she never had to sit in the same chair twice. She could be diplomatic, if it suited her purposes, or she could put on a great show of barbarism, which seemed to work more effectively to gain respect from the European intruders. In 1626 the Portuguese decided to drive Nzinga out and set up a puppet ruler. ''Lady Grace'' was taken prisoner, but from her captivity she supplied Nzinga with intelligence concerning Portuguese affairs for years. Nzinga's people remained loyal to her and refused to obey the puppet chief. In retaliation for the Portuguese attempt at a coup, Nzinga made an alliance with the neighboring kingdom of Kasanji, closing the slave routes to the Portuguese. She then moved eastward and conquered the kingdom of Matamba. From there, she developed her own powerful slave trading center. Nzinga became allied with the Dutch, who took Luanda from the Portuguese in 1641. Across the river from the Dutch she put on such a show of savagery, in the form of a gory ceremonial dance, that she could be certain of being unhindered by them. In 1643, 1647, and 1648 she attacked the Portuguese and drove them back each time. On one of these raids the Portuguese drowned their prisoner ''Lady Grace'' as they retreated, and on another ''Lady Barbara'' was captured. In 1848 the Portuguese reconquered Luanda and were thus free to reconsolidate their hold on their African possessions. In 1656 Nzinga agreed to an official peace with the Portuguese in which ''Lady Barbara'' was released in exchange for 130 slaves. Nzinga, as a Roman Catholic, continued to rule until her death in 1663, collaborating with the Portuguese in slave trade. She never married, but was said to keep as many as 30 slaves as sexual partners, killing them off when she had finished with them.[7]

Oghul Qamish
Empress, regent of Karakorum (1248–1251)

Oghul Qamish was the wife of Güyük, great khan of the Mongols, who ruled from 1246 to 1248. She was believed to be of Markit birth and had three young sons, Qucha, Naqu, and Qughu, for whom she acted as regent when their father died in 1248. Jenghiz-khan had given each of his four sons a khanate over which to rule. The four khans then elected a supreme or great khan who was head of the entire empire. Since her husband had been great khan, Oghul was not only regent of the land of the house of Ogödäi, but regent for the empire as well. In 1250, in the patrimonial lands of the house of Ogödäi, she received three envoys of Louis IX of France, who arrived by way of Persia. As an example of her avarice, she accepted their presents from King Louis as tribute and demanded that the king of France make more explicit submission to her. It would later be claimed by her rival that during her regency she was given to the practice of sorcery. Oghul Qamish wanted the throne of the great khan to pass to a member of the house of Ogödäi, either to Güyük's nephew Shirämön, whom the former khan (his grandfather Ogödäi) had groomed for succession, or better still, to her own son Qucha. However, although Qucha was

the eldest of her sons, he was too young. The head of the Jenghiz-khanite family, Batu, wanted to set the Ogödäi line aside and was persuaded to nominate as supreme khan a member of the Tolui family, Mongka, at an assembly not attended by representatives of the house of Ogödäi or their supporters from the house of Jagatai. The Ogödäis obviously refused to ratify such a nomination, and Mongka was elected by default. The relegation of the house of Ogödäi was a violation of legitimacy, and Shirämön and his cousins did not intend to let the election stand. They plotted to surprise Mongka and his supporters during the drunken feast following the inauguration ceremony, overpower them, and depose Mongka. The plot miscarried and a civil war erupted, the houses of Ogödäi and Jagatai on one side and the houses of Jōchi and Tolui on the other. After a year of bloodshed, Mongka triumphed over all his rivals. He had the sons of Oghul Qamish exiled and saved his venom for their mother. She was stripped of her clothes for questioning, convicted of sorcery, sewn up in a sack and drowned (May–July 1252).[1]

Olga
Princess, regent of Kiev (945–964)

She was born ca. 890 in Russia and became the wife of Prince Igor I and the mother of a son,

131

Svyatoslav. In 945 Igor was assassinated for exhorting huge sums from his subjects to pay for his campaigns against the Byzantines. Olga became regent of the grand principality of Kiev until her son reached his majority. She hunted down Igor's murderers and ordered them scalded to death. In ca. 955 to 957 she became an Orthodox Christian and shortly afterward ushered in a new era in Byzantine-Kievian relations by visiting Constantinople. There she was baptized, or rebaptized, taking as her Christian name "Helena," in honor of the Byzantine empress. It was through her efforts and those of her grandson Vladimir that Christianity was brought to Russia. Olga died in 969 and was canonized by the Orthodox Church; her feast day is July 11.[2]

Olga
Queen, regent of Greece (1920)

She was the wife of King Alexander I, ruler of Greece from 1917 to 1920. On 25 October 1920, King Alexander died from blood poisoning, having been bitten by a pet monkey. Queen Olga became regent until December, when former King Constantine I, Alexander's father who had previously abdicated, resumed the throne.[3]

Orghana
Princess, regent of the Mongolian khanate of Jagatai (1252–1261)

She was first the wife of Qara-Hulägu, a grandson of Jenghiz-khan's son Jagatai and the ruler of the Turkestan khanate from 1242 to 1246. She had two sons, Büri and Mobarak Sha. In 1246 the new Great Khan Güyük replaced Qara-Hulägu with Jagatai's younger brother, Yissu-Mangu, but in 1252, with the election of a new great khan, Mongka, Yissu-Mangu was deposed and Qara-Hulägu was reinstated and ordered to execute Yissu-Mangu. However, Qara-Hulägu died on the way to reclaim his throne, and it was up to Princess Orghana as regent to have Yissu-Mangu executed. Her husband's former minister Habash 'Amid took care of the matter without waiting for the executioner. Orghana took control of the khanate and held it for nine years. She was described as beautiful, wise, and discerning. Upon the Great Khan Mongka's death, one of his sons, Hulägu, became khan of Persia, while the other two, Kublai and Ariq-bögä, vied to become the supreme khan. Kublai outwitted his brother and became grand khan, but Ariq-bögä planned to dethrone him. To keep his other brother from sending reinforcements from Persia to Kublai, he decided to take over the khanate of Jagatai, sending Prince Alghu to remove Orghana from power, and become regent himself. But Alghu had ambitions of his own: to make the Jagatai khanate independent. He seized Ariq-bögä's tax collectors and executed them, keeping the wealth for himself. In the war that followed, Ariq-bögä suffered severe losses. After two years, he tried to make peace with Alghu. At the time, he had with him Princess Orghana, who had come to protest her removal from the khanate. He sent her and Mas'ud Yalavach to Alghu's camp in Samarkand with peace proposals, but upon her arrival Alghu married her and made Mas'ud his finance minister. With the money Mas'ud raised, Alghu and Orghana raised another large army. In 1264, Ariq-bögä was forced to surrender to Kublai. Alghu died in 1265 or 1266 and Orghana placed on the throne her son by her first marriage, Morabak Sha, who became the first Jagataite to be converted to Islam.[4]

Pandit, Vijaya Lakshmi
President of UN General Assembly (1953)

She was born Swarup Kumari Nehru in 1900, the daughter of Sarup Rani Nehru and Motilal Nehru, a Kashmiri Brahmin, prominent lawyer, and one of Mahatma Gandhi's lieutenants. Madame Pandit was the sister of Jawaharlal Nehru, who became the first prime minister of independent India, and the aunt of Indira Gandhi, first woman prime minister of India. She was privately educated in India and abroad and, along with the rest of her family, worked for Indian independence. In 1921 she married Ranjit S. Pandit, a co-worker. In connection with her efforts for India's independence, the British imprisoned her for one year (1931). Her husband died in 1944, three years before India achieved independence from Britain. Madame Pandit embarked on a distinguished political career, heading the Indian delegation to the United Nations from 1946 to 1948 and again from 1952 to 1953. She served as ambassador to Moscow from 1947 to 1949 and afterwards to the United States and Mexico until 1951. In 1953 she became the first woman to serve as president of the UN General Assembly. From 1954 to 1961 she served as ambassador in England and Ireland, during which time she wrote *The Evolution of India* (1953). In 1962 she became the governor of the state of Maharashtra, and two years later she accepted the seat in India's parliament formerly held by her brother Jawaharlal Nehru. In 1977 she left the Congress Party to join the Congress for Democracy, and in that same year wrote her memoirs, *The Scope of Happiness.* In 1978 she became the Indian representative to the Human Rights Committee. Madame Pandit was placed on the Board of the Mountbatten Memorial Trust in 1980.[1]

Pāndyan
Queen (second century B.C.)

The Pāndya was a Tamil dynasty in the extreme south of India first mentioned by Greek authors in the fourth century. Megasthenes mentions that the Pāndyan kingdom was ruled by a daughter of Herakles. If existing poetry and heroic ballads are any indication, the Cheras, the Cholas, and the Pāndyas were in constant conflict with one another. The Pāndyan queen is credited by Megasthenes with having an army of 4,000 cavalry, 13,000 infantry, and 500 elephants with which to fight her wars.[2]

Pascal-Trouillot, Ertha
Provisional president of Haiti (1990)

Born Ertha Pascal in 1944, she was a member of the wealthy mulatto professional elite that dominated Haitian politics prior to the rule of

François Duvalier. She married Ernst Trouillot, a prominent lawyer who presided over the Port-au-Prince Bar Association until his death in 1989. The couple had one daughter. She earned her own law degree in 1971 and soon gained respect as a legal scholar. She authored several books on law; the first and best known, *The Judicial Status of Haitian Women in Social Legislation,* was written only two years after her graduation. She worked to reform Haiti's outmoded laws affecting the rights of women. Although Haiti's constitutions have provided for women's suffrage since 1950, until the 1970s a woman was considered a "minor" and was not permitted to conduct business or have a bank account without the signature of her husband. In 1984 Ertha Pascal-Trouillot was named appeals court judge, and in 1986, after the fall from power of Jean-Claude Duvalier, Minister of Justice Francois Latortue appointed her to a ten-year term as a Supreme Court justice. Although other women had served as judges in Haiti, Mrs. Pascal-Trouillot was the first woman to sit on the Supreme Court.

On March 10, 1990, Haitian ruler Lt. Gen. Prosper Avril resigned during a popular uprising against his military regime, turning over power to acting army chief of staff Major Gen. Herard Abraham, who promised to transfer power to a civilian leader within 72 hours. According to the constitution, Chief Justice Gilbert Austin was next in line; however, the opposition coalition Unity Assembly rejected his claim on the grounds that he was a puppet of the military. Austin extracted a pledge from the other 11 justices not to accept the nomination over him, and 3 other justices did refuse the nomination. On the evening of March 11, the nominating committee visited Mrs. Pascal-Trouillot, the court's newest justice, to offer her the nomination. After a brief consultation with her sister and brother-in-law, she decided, in the interest of unity, to forego her commitment to Justice Austin, take a leave of absence from the bench, and preside over the provisional government for several months. As provisional president, she oversaw, with a 19-member advisory council, the democratic election of a Haitian president. Because roving assassination squads

threatened her life, she was taken into hiding until her inauguration. In her inaugural address, she said, "I have accepted this heavy task in the name of the Haitian woman, who for the first time in the history of our country has been called upon to go beyond her traditional daily sacrifices made with courage and true patriotism. . . . In the short time I have, I will work to clean the face of Haiti." In Haiti's first free election, Catholic priest Jean Bertrand Aristide was chosen to succeed her (January 1991).

Perón, Isabel
President of Argentina (1974–1976)

She was born María Estela Martínez in 1931, one of five children of a small-town bank manager in northwest Argentina. The family moved to Buenos Aires in 1933, and her father died four years later. Her mother worked to keep the family together, but María Estela quit school after the sixth grade to pursue a career in music and ballet. She studied ballet and piano and became a qualified piano teacher. When she was 20 she joined a professional ballet company, changing her name to Isabel, her saint's name. One story claims that in mid-tour of her dance company in 1956, she was stranded in Panama City and met the exiled Juan Perón, president of Argentina from 1946 to 1955. She became his personal secretary and traveling companion and settled with him in Madrid. In 1961, at the age of 30, she became the 65-year-old Perón's wife. Since she was not in exile, she was free to return to her homeland, so in 1964, she began to travel around Argentina, speaking on behalf of Peronist candidates. In 1973 Perón was recalled to Argentina and elected president, with his wife Isabel as vice president. Isabel had the handicap of following Perón's popular second wife, Eva (Evita).

Later in 1973, Perón, who was 78 and in poor health, fell ill, and he delegated full power to her. In 1974 he died and Isabel acceded to the presidency, becoming the first woman chief of state to serve in her own right in South America. Although the liberal unions had always been the bastions of Peronist support, the right-wing military had supported Perón as well. These two factions had warred for years. To combat the terrorism that had interrupted the government from time to time over the years, Isabel suspended constitutional rights and imposed de facto martial law. Inflation was running at 200 percent per year, so she imposed austere fiscal measures that precipitated a union strike that crippled the nation. Eventually she had to give in to union demands for large wage hikes just to get the country moving again. In 1976, Isabel's regime was overthrown by a military junta while she was suffering a gallbladder attack. She went into self-exile in Spain in 1981 but returned in 1983 for the inauguration at the request of the new constitutional president, Raul Alfonsin.[3]

Petronilla
Queen of Aragon (1137–1162)

She was born ca. 1136, the daughter of King Ramiro II, ruler of Aragon from 1134 to 1137. Ramiro was a monk, the brother of King Alfonso I, ruler from 1102 to 1134, who named Ramiro to succeed him on his death. Ramiro emerged from retirement only long enough to marry and produce an heir, Petronilla. He betrothed her to Ramon Berenguer IV, count of Barcelona, then returned to his monastery, leaving Queen Petronilla under the guardianship of Ramon, who was only six at the time. Thirteen years later, in 1150, she married Berenguer, who then became king. Petronilla was never allowed to exercise any authority. She had a son, Alfonso II, who acceded to the throne in 1162, when both Petronilla and Berenguer died.[4]

Pheretima
Queen of Cyrene, or Cyrenaica
(ca. A.D. 518)

She was the wife of Battus the Lame, fifth ruler of Cyrene, located in northern Libya. ''Battus'' was a Libyan word meaning ''king.'' The couple had a son, Arcesilaus. The misfortunes that had befallen the realm prior to Battus' reign (the murder of his father and mother and his own lameness) had prompted the people to send to Delphi to ask the oracle for advice about changing their luck. The priestess advised them to employ Demonax of Mantinea in Arcadia to make some changes in the kingdom. Once employed, Demonax segregated the people into three groups and gave them many of the privileges previously enjoyed only by the rulers. After Battus died, his son Arcesilaus acceded to the throne with the idea of rescinding Demonax's changes. His demands for a restoration of his ancestral rights led to civil war in which he was defeated. He fled to Samos, while Queen Pheretima went to Salamis in Cyprus. There she asked the ruler Euelthon for an army with which to recapture the throne. Instead of honoring her request, he sent her a golden spindle and distaff with wool on it, saying he sent her a present that, unlike an army, he thought suitable for her sex. Meanwhile, Arcesilaus was able to raise an army in Samos and returned to Cyrene and recovered his throne. Fearing a warning of the oracle, however, he was afraid to remain in Cyrene, so he went to Barca, leaving Queen Pheretima to represent him, running the government in Cyrene. But her son was assassinated in Barca, and when the queen learned of his death, she fled to Egypt for asylum. Intent on avenging her son's death, she convinced Aryandes to send troops from Egypt to Barca to assist her in laying siege to the town. They called on the citizens to surrender those responsible for Arcesilaus' death, but the people refused, claiming that everyone was equally responsible. The siege then continued for nine months. The Persians, meantime, were interested in mining operations in Barca and were eventually allowed by the Barcans to enter. The Persians then delivered to Queen Pheretima the men responsible for her son's murder. She had them impaled on stakes around the city wall. The wives of the murderers fared no better. She cut off their breasts and stuck them up on stakes, too. She gave the rest of the people, other than those of the house of Bothus, to the Persians, who pillaged their homes and reduced them to slavery. Cyrene and Euesperides were incorporated in a Persian satrapy in ca. 518. According to Herodotus, no sooner had Pheretima returned to Egypt than she died a horrible death, ''her body seething with worms while she was still alive.''[5]

Pimiku (also called Himiko or Pimisho, Pimiho, Yametsu-hime, or Yamato-hime-mikoto)

Queen, first known ruler of Japan
(ca. A.D. 190–247)

Chinese and Korean histories call her Pimiho, a corruption of Hime-ko. She was reputed to be the daughter of Suinin, who entrusted her with the sacred mirror, symbol of the sun goddess. In archaic Japanese, "Pimiko" meant "sun daughter." She was said to have built the Great Shrine of Ise, the most important Shinto shrine in Japan. She remained unmarried and, according to the *Wei chih* (ancient Chinese records considered more accurate than Japanese records), she ruled in Yamatai, which may have been Yamato. Other research indicates her realm was located in western Japan. Pimiku seems also to have been a priestess. The *Wei* records say that she bewitched her subjects with magic and sorcery. A list survives of the names of the lands over which she presided. In 234 she had a daughter, Iyo-hime. After she conquered the savage tribes in southern Tsukushi, Chinese Emperor Ming-ti awarded her a golden seal inscribed with the title of "king" of the country of Wo (A.D. 238). At her death in A.D. 247, over 100 of her servants buried themselves alive around her tomb.[6]

Placidia, Galla (or Aelia)

Augusta, regent of the Western Roman Empire (A.D. 425–433)

She was born in A.D. 390, the daughter of Emperor Theodosius I, ruler from 379 to 395, and his second wife, Galla, daughter of Valentinian I. She was the half sister of Flavius Honorius, who ruled from 393 to 423. In 410 the Goths, under the command of Alaric, sacked Rome and took Galla Placidia prisoner. In 414 she married Alaric's successor, Athaulf, in Narbonne. Athaulf was assassinated the following year. In 416 she was restored to the Romans, and the next year she unwillingly submitted to a political union, marriage to her half brother's generalissimo, Constantius. They had a son, Valentinian, born in 419, and at least one daughter, Honoria. In 421 Constantius was de-

clared Augustus and co-emperor, but Flavius Honorius died in 423 and, after a brief usurpation by Johannes during which Galla Placidia fled with her son to Constantinople, was succeeded in 425 by Galla Placidia's son, Valentinian, age six. Galla, as regent, was actively supported by Bonifatius (Boniface), who bore the title Master of the Soldiers of the eastern army. At first her influence was dominant in affairs of state, but when she tried to replace her own Master of Soldiers with Boniface, he enlisted the help of the Huns, and by 423 his commands went unchallenged. Galla Placidia then turned her attention to adorning the city of Ravenna with a number of churches. She died in Rome in 450.[7]

Plaisance of Antioch

Queen, regent of Cyprus and Jerusalem
(1253–1261)

She was the daughter of Bohemond V, prince of Antioch from 1233 to 1252, and his second wife Lucienne of Segni. Her brother was Bohemond VI, prince of Antioch from 1252 to 1287. In 1251 Plaisance became the third wife of King Henry I, ruler of Jerusalem and Cyprus, and a year later bore him a son, Hugh II. King Henry died in January of 1253. As their son was only a few months old, Queen Plaisance claimed the regency of Cyprus and the titular regency of Jerusalem. The high courts of Cyprus confirmed her position there immediately, but the Jerusalem barons required her attendance in person before they would recognize her. She was formally recognized as regent of Jerusalem upon her visit to Acre in 1258. An efficient ruler of high integrity, she was deeply mourned when she died in 1261, leaving her son Hugh II an orphan at age eight.[8]

Plectrudis

Queen, regent of Austrasia and Neustria
(714–716)

She was the wife of Pepin II of Herstol, mayor of Austrasia and Neustria from 687 to 714. (The title of mayor did not have the same connotation there as it has in the United States today.) The couple had at least one son, Grimoald, who died in 714, the same year his father died. All of Pepin's sons had died before him except one illegitimate son, Charles the Bold (Martel). Following the Frankish custom, Pepin's will divided the kingdoms among his grandsons as mayors under the regency of Queen Plectrudis. She did not rule long before civil war broke out among various rival factions. Between 716 and 719 Pepin's illegitimate son Charles overcame the Neustrians in three battles and took control of the kingdoms.[9]

Pokou, Aura
See Awura Pokou

Prabhāvatī Gupta
Regent of the kingdom of the Vākātakas
(ca. A.D. 390–410)

She was the daughter of Chandra Gupta II, who ruled Northern India from A.D. 380 to 415. To strengthen his southern boundaries, Emperor Chandra married his daughter to King Rudrasena II, ruler of the Vākātakas (ca. 385–390). The Vākātaka kingdom was based on what remained of the earlier Sātavāhana kingdom and was located in the central Deccan region of India. When Rudrasena died ca. 390 after a reign of only five years, his sons were infants. His widow Prabhāvatī served as regent from ca. 390 to 410. During her unusually lengthy regency, she made, with her Gupta culture and her ties to

the northern Indian kingdom, a significant impact on Vākātakas culture.[10]

Pulcheria
Augusta, regent of the Eastern Roman Empire
(A.D. 414–453)

Pulcheria was born in Constantinople in 399, the daughter of Eastern Roman Emperor Flavius Arcadius, ruler from 383 to 408, and his wife Eudoxia. She was the older sister of Theodosius II, born in 401, who ruled from 408 to 450. After her father died, Pulcheria was appointed augusta and made regent for her brother, although she was only two years his senior. She took her responsibilities very seriously and assumed a personal hand in Theodosius' education. A devout Christian, Pulcheria maintained her court with great piety and chastity. In 421 she arranged the marriage of her brother to Athenais (Eudocia), who eventually became her rival in court. In 443 friction between the two had mounted to such an extent that Eudocia voluntarily withdrew to Jerusalem. The eunuch chamberlain Chrysaphius gradually worked his way into the emperor's favor and eventually gained dominance, but Pulcheria recovered the initiative before Theodosius' death in 450. She selected a retired soldier, Marcian, as her brother's successor and married him to preserve the dynasty. She died in 453.[11]

Pu-su-wan
See Ye-lü-Shih

Ranavalona I
Queen, titular ruler of Madagascar
(1828–1861)

The kingdom of Madagascar, which united most of the island, lasted from 1810 to 1896, when Madagascar became a French colony. Of its six rulers four were women. The kingdom was founded by King Radama I, who, in exchange for assistance from the British governor of nearby Mauritius, agreed to cooperate in ending slave trade through his territory. He also allowed into the country European tradesmen and workers from the London Missionary Society. He was married to Ranavalona I, who did not share his romance with Europe. The couple had a son, Radama II. When Radama I died prematurely in 1828, his widow Ranavalona I succeeded him, and she quickly moved to reverse her husband's liberal Europeanization policies. Over a number of years she expelled the Europeans, and eventually she had so purged the kingdom of outsiders that the British and French joined forces to unseat her. They were defeated at Tamatave in 1845. The queen ruled unmolested until her death in 1861. Ranavalona I ruled a total of 33 years and was succeeded by her son, Radama II.[1]

Ranavalona II
Queen, titular ruler of Madagascar
(1868–1883)

She was, it is believed, the daughter of the sister of Queen Ranavalona I, who ruled Madagascar from 1828 to 1861. It is further surmised that she was the sister of Rasoaherina, wife of King Radama II, who acceded to the throne upon his mother's death in 1861 and ruled for two years. He was assassinated in 1861 at the instigation of the Merina oligarchy, tribes of a ''higher,'' pure Indonesian caste. His former army chief, Rainilaiarivony, asserted himself into the position of prime minister, marrying the king's widow and thereby holding almost exclusive power. When she died five years later, she was succeeded by Ranavalona II, whom the minister married in turn. The following year (1869), Christianity was adopted as the official religion of Madagascar, and the traditional Malagasy religion was suppressed. The kingdom soon took on many of the European characteristics once adopted by the queen's father and so long fought by her mother. Ranavalona died in 1883.[2]

Ranavalona III
Queen, titular ruler of Madagascar
(1883–1896)

Ranavalona III was born in 1861, presumably a cousin of King Radama II, ruler from 1861 to 1863, or Queen Rasoaherina, ruler from 1863 to 1868. She was the cousin of Queen Ranavalona II, ruler from 1868 to 1883; however, the relationship may have been even more complicated, since often rulers married their siblings or their parents' siblings. When Ranavalona II died, Ranavalona III ascended to the throne. In 1883 she married the prime minister, Rainilaiarivony, who had been married to the two preceding queens and who was implicated in the death of her father. In 1895 French troops forced her husband Rainilaiarivony into exile. Queen Ranavalona III signed a treaty recognizing the status of her country as a protectorate of France. She was not officially deposed but was allowed to remain on the throne as a figurehead. She died in 1916.[3]

Rasoaherina
Queen, titular ruler of Madagascar
(1863–1868)

It is believed that Rasoaherina was the wife (and possibly also the sister) of King Radama II, who ruled Madagascar from 1861 to 1863 and the niece of Ranavalona I. When Radama II was assassinated in 1863, Rasoaherina assumed the throne. Possibly involuntarily, she married her husband's chief of the army, Rainilaiarivony, whom she elevated to prime minister and who completely dominated her rule. She died in 1868.[4]

Raẓiyya (or Razia) Iltutmish (or Altamsh)
Sultana, Queen of Northern India
(1236–1240)

Raẓiyya was the daughter of Shamsudīn Iltutmish, a former slave who rose to be the third and greatest Sultan of the Moslem Slave Dynasty in Delhi. Her mother was the daughter of Quṭb-ud-Din Aybak, the second Sultan of

Delhi. Sultan Shamsudīn, realizing that his two sons were both feeble-minded, designated his daughter Raẓiyya as his successor. When he died in 1236, she became the first Moslem woman to rule northern India. Thirteenth-century historian Amir Khusrau said, "Since there were no worthy sons, worthy opinion turned to Raẓiyya."

Raẓiyya came to the throne at a difficult time in her country's history. During her reign, the two dominant sects of Islam—the Sunnis (the orthodox sect traditionally favored by the sultanate) and the Shias (a more radical splinter group)—were pitted against each other. The Shias, joining some other schismatics, revolted against the sultanate but were roundly put down by Raẓiyya's forces. After that time, the Shias ceased to be a serious challenge to Sunnis during the history of the sultanate. The historian Sirāj (Shams al-dīn Sirāj) said, "Sultana Raẓiyya was a great monarch. She was wise, just and generous, a benefactor to her kingdom, a dispenser of justice, the protector of her subjects and the leader of her armies. She was endowed with all the qualities befitting a king, but she was not born of the right sex, so, in the estimation of men, all these virtues were worthless." Courageous and intelligent, nevertheless after three and one-half years on the throne, she was toppled in a palace coup and executed by her own army. Historian Yahyā ibn Ahmad then wrote of the tragic event, "Every head that the celestial globe raises up/It will likewise throw a noose around the neck of that very same." It has been speculated that Raẓiyya had embarked on a torrid love affair with her Abyssinian Master of the Horse, thus contributing to unrest and jealousy among her ranks. She was succeeded by a grandchild of her father's.[5]

Robinson, Mary
President of Ireland (1990–)

Mary Robinson was born in 1945. She attended law school in Ireland and did post-graduate work at Harvard Law School. She practiced law, was a law professor, and became a senator at the age of 25. She asked for and received a mandate to extend the hand of friendship to Northern Ireland's two communities. Of voters who elected her to the largely symbolic but representative position of president, she said "Instead of rocking the cradle, they rocked the system." She was sworn in as Ireland's first woman president on December 3, 1990.

Russudan (or Rusudani or Rusudan)
Queen, ruler of Georgia, first alone (1223–1234), then jointly with her minor son David (1234–1247)

She was the daughter of Queen Thamar (Tamara) the Great, who ruled Georgia from 1186 to 1212, and Thamar's cousin and consort, David Soslan, who ruled jointly from 1193 to 1207. Her brother, King George III (Giorgi III Lasha, or the Brilliant, or the Resplendent), co-ruler from 1205 to 1212, then sole ruler until 1223, had many mistresses and even fathered an illegitimate child, but he had no legitimate heir to succeed him other than his sister. In 1221 the Georgian troops had been cut to ribbons at Khunani by Mongol generals of Jenghiz-khan, Jebe, and Sübötäi. Russudan, having something of the same disposition as her brother and little of her mother's Christian piety, described in fact as "an unmarried but not a virgin queen," acceded to the throne when her brother died, and was proclaimed "King of Karthalinia." Karthalinia, or Kartlia, was a section in present-day Soviet Georgia. In 1225 Jelal ad-Din Mängüberti (Jalal on-Din), heir to the Khwarizmian empire who had been driven into exile by Jenghiz-khan, invaded Georgia. Queen Russudan sent an army to meet them, but her troops had not regained their strength since their trouncing by Jenghiz-khan: they were defeated at Garnhi on her southern frontier. The invaders, after ravaging Southern Georgia, moved on into Russia. Queen Russudan wrote to the pope: "A savage people of Tartars [a play on words for the Tatars, "tartar" meaning "hell"], hellish of aspect, as voracious as wolves in their hunger for spoils and brave as lions, have invaded my country . . . The brave knighthood of Georgia has hunted them out of the country, killing 25,000 of the invaders." Learning that nearby Persia had been weakened by Mongol attack, Queen Russudan took advantage of their recent disaster and attacked Persia. But in 1225 Jelal ad-Din swooped down again and attacked the capital of Tiflis. Russudan then fled to Kutais while Jelal ad-Din occupied and sacked the capital, destroying all the Christian churches. In 1228 Russudan attempted to regain control of the provinces along the Kur River, held by Jelal ad-Din, but was driven back. In 1231 the Mongol army reappeared to challenge Jelal ad-Din under the leadership of General Chormaqan. Jelal ad-Din, who had been defeated by Mongols before, retreated hastily, to die in Kurdestan in 1231. That year, with the Mongols fighting the Turks, Queen Russudan reoccupied her capital of Tiflis, but five years later Chormaqan invaded Georgia, and she was forced to take refuge once again in Kutais. Around 1241 Chormaqan was stricken with dumbness and was replaced by Baiji. Queen Russudan soon became an irritant to him because of her stubborn refusal to give in to the Mongols. Eventually, however, in 1243 she herself became a vassal of the Mongols with the understanding that the whole kingdom of Georgia would be given to her son David Narin to rule under Mongol suzerainty. However, David Narin was in actuality only given Imeretia, while David Lasha, an heir of Russudan's brother, was given Kartlia.[6]

S

Sada Kaur
Rani, de facto co-ruler of the Śukerchakāīs, Pakistan (1795–ca. 1801)

She was the widow of a chieftain of the Kanhayas, whose daughter Jindan married 15-year-old Ranjit Singh, chief since the age of 12 of the Śukerchakāīs, a Sikh group. For many years Sada Kaur directed his affairs. Eventually Ranjit Singh proclaimed himself maharaja of the Punjab, a state he single-handedly created.[1]

Saimei-tennō
See Kōgyoku-tennō

Salome Alexandra
See Alexandra

Salote Topou III
Queen, ruler of Tonga (1918–1965)

She was born in 1900, the daughter of King Topou II, ruler of Tonga from 1893 to 1918, a member of a dynasty that had ruled from at least the tenth century. During her father's reign, Tonga became a British protectorate because of financial difficulties. Salote came to the throne at the age of 18, following her father's death. A commanding figure at six feet two inches tall—size and stateliness has characterized the ruling family for generations—the queen guided the islands with wisdom and

grace for 47 years, endearing herself to the people of Britain as well to her own. To encourage Tonga's traditional crafts, she organized a wo-

Queen Salote Topou III. Photo by Luis Marden. ©1965 by National Geographic Society.

men's cooperative, which maintains at least one handicraft shop in a local hotel. In 1917 she married Sione (John) Fe'iloakitau Kaho (Prince Viliami Tungi). Their son, Taufa (or Tung), born in 1918, succeeded his mother upon her death in 1965 as King Tafua'ahou Topou IV. The queen who ruled so long and so well did not live to see Tonga regain complete independence in 1970.[2]

Sammuramat (or Semiramis)
Queen, regent of New Assyrian Empire
(ca. 811–806 B.C.)

She was born in Babylonia and married King Shamshi-Adad V, ruler of Assyria from 823 to 811 B.C. Following the death of her husband, Sammuramat—as capable, energetic regent—ruled for five years. Proof that she clearly held the real power survives in dedications made in her own name, which was placed before that of her son. A memorial stele to her was found at Assur along with those of kings and other high officials, a singular honor for a woman at that time. The historical evidence stops there, but Greek historian Diodorus Siculus (ca. first century B.C.) credited her with rebuilding Babylon, a task historians attribute in part to a priestess, Addagoppe. Armenian legend attributes to ''Queen Semiramis'' much of the surviving construction of the kingdom of

Queen Sammuramat. The Mansell Collection.

Urartu, which also belonged to Assyria at the time; however, there is no historical evidence to suggest that Sammuramat ever intervened in the governing of Urartu.[3]

Samsia
Queen, ruler of Southern Arabia
(ca. 732 B.C.)

In 734 B.C. King Ahaz of Judah asked the help of Tiglath-pileser III, who had taken over the New Assyrian Empire (745–727 B.C.), to help defend against a coalition of the forces of Rezen of Damascus and Pekah (Pakaha) of Israel. Tiglath-pileser obliged by first demolishing Israel's forces and then, in 732, marching against Damascus. He first devastated the stately gardens outside the city, then swept through the capital and killed King Pekah. Samsia, who was the queen of Southern Arabia at the time, was forced to pay tribute to Tiglath-pileser in return for use of the harbor of Gaza, over which he had gained control.[4]

Sati Beg
Il-Khanid queen of Persia (1338–1339)

The daughter of Oljeitu of the Chingizid Dynasty, ruler from 1304 to 1316, and the sister of Abu Sa'id, ruler from 1316 to 1335, she was one of four to come to the throne in the three years following her brother's death. She was deposed after a year, and following the short rules by her two successors, the Il-Khanid state broke into petty kingdoms. The title il-khan denoted subordination to the great Mongolian khan.

Seaxburh
Queen of Wessex (672–674)

The wife of King Cenwalh, ruler of Wessex from 642 to 672, Seaxburh ruled for two years following his death. She was followed by Centwine, son of former King Cynegils.

Sebeknefru (or Scemiophris)
See Nefrusobek

Shajar Al Durr
See Spray of Pearls

Sheba

See Makeda

Shu-lü shih

Khatum, regent of Turkish Mongolia
(A.D. 926–?)

Shu-lü shih is not the empress' name; it simply means "of the Shu-lü clan"; unfortunately, although all the other names in this account are known, the empress' name was not preserved. She was the wife of A-pao-ki, chief of the Ye-lü clan of Khitan in the tenth century. The couple had two sons, T'u-yu and Tö-kuang. When her husband died in A.D. 926, the dowager empress rigged a popularity contest between her sons so that her favored second son, Tö-kuang, would win. She then governed with him for the first few years, although she in fact held sole power and had indefatigable stamina. Each time a minister displeased her, she dispatched him to "take news of her to her late husband." Guards at her husband's tomb would then speed him on his way to join the departed. One sage Chinese minister, Chao Ssu-wen, upon being named the next victim, respectfully demurred with characteristic Oriental courtesy, deferring such a high honor to the widow, who was far more deserving than he. The *khatum* (empress) acknowledged that this was so, but much as she would like to go her presence was essential to the horde. However, just to be a sport about it, Shu-lü shih lopped off one of her hands and sent it along to be buried in the tomb.[5]

Shōtoku-tennō

See Kōken

Sibylla (or Sibyl or Sybil)

Queen of Jerusalem (1186–1190)

Sibylla was born in 1160, the daughter of King Amalric I, ruler from 1162 to 1174, and his first wife, Agnes of Courtenay. She was the sister of Baldwin IV, who acceded upon his father's death in 1174 and ruled until 1183. When Baldwin IV was nine years old, his instructor realized he was a leper and might not live to reign. So special care was given to Sibylla's education and choice of a mate, since he might be called upon to act as regent or, if need be, as king. Sibylla first married William of Montferrat, count of Jaffa (1176). They had a son, Baldwin V, born posthumously, his father having died of malaria two months before. In 1180 she took as her lover Guy of Lusignan, of whom her brother the king disapproved on the grounds that he was a weak and foolish boy. When the king discovered this relationship, he wanted to put Guy to death, but at the request of the Templars, he reluctantly allowed Sibylla to marry him. The marriage produced two daughters. Guy proved the king's estimation of him to be accurate. Baldwin IV, from his sickbed, first appointed Guy regent, then rescinded the order, banished him, and proclaimed Sibylla's son Baldwin V as his heir. He died in 1185, but the child died only one year later. Of the two contenders for the throne, Sibylla and Isabella (by Amalric's second wife Maria Comnena), the public favored Sibylla, even though her husband was generally despised. Backers of Sibylla, through subterfuge, managed to trick the other side and to proclaim Sibylla queen. At the coronation, only she was crowned, because of Guy's unpopularity. She was then asked to crown whatever man she thought worthy to serve; she of course crowned her husband. As an indirect result of Guy's foibles, Jerusalem was soon embroiled in a disastrous war with Sultan Saladin. Saladin took Guy prisoner and asked for Ascalon in exchange for his release, but the people, ashamed of Guy's selfishness on numerous occasions, refused to give up Ascalon for the ransom. After Ascalon fell anyway, Queen Sibylla wrote Saladin, asking that he release her husband (1188), and he complied with her request. In 1190 the queen and her two young daughters all died of a disease that swept through the countryside.[6]

Sirikit

Queen, regent of Thailand (1956)

Sirikit was born Princess Mom Rajawong Sirikit Kitiyakara in 1932, the daughter of a titled Thai diplomat, H. H. Prince Nakkhatra Mongkol Kitiyakara and Krommuen Chandaburi

Queen Sirikit. UPI/Bettmann Newsphotos.

Suranat, and was soon noted for her striking beauty. In April 1950 she married Bhumibol Adulyadej, who one month later was crowned King Rama IX, ruler of Thailand. In 1956 Sirikit was named regent of Thailand while the king, who is considered holy by his people, performed his meditations and the duties of a Buddhist monk. At that time she took an oath before the National Assembly: "We will reign with righteousness for the benefits and happiness of the Siamese people." Although the constitutional monarchy wields little real political power, the monarch is head of state and commander of the armed forces and a stabilizing and unifying force. Queen Sirikit's special project was promoting the export of handwoven Thai silk. The queen traveled to remote provinces to promote various cottage industries and to encourage rural people to practice their traditional crafts. She then obtained markets for these crafts. In some cases, where knowledge of the crafts had been lost, Queen Sirikit sent instructors to reeducate the natives. To achieve those ends she established the Foundation for the Promotion of Supplementary Occupations and Related Techniques, which not only pro-

vides a chain of shops selling native crafts but also gives rural women the training and provides materials to set up artisans' cooperatives. Sirikit used her organizational skills for the Thai Red Cross, for aid to refugees, orphans, wounded soldiers, and flood victims. Of Thai women, she said, "They never had the feeling of being inferior to their menfolk." The royal couple had four children: Princess Ubol Ratana, an MIT graduate who renounced her title and married U.S. citizen Peter Ladd Jensen; Crown Prince Ma Ha Vajiralongkorn who, with his two wives and six children, calls himself the family's "black sheep"; Princess Maha Chakri Sirindhorn, who is president of the Foundation for Development set up by her father to improve the quality of life in Bangkok; and Princess Chulabhorn, a scientist with a doctorate in organic chemistry, married to a Thai commoner. The crown prince seemed little interested in civilian pursuits and there was speculation that he might remove himself from succession. In 1979 the popular and brilliant Princess Sirindhorn was accorded a special dynastic title by the National Assembly: Ma Ha Chakri (in effect, making her crown princess), and in the early 1980s the parliament revised royal law to permit a woman monarch for the first time in Thai history. In 1985 Queen Sirikit abruptly withdrew from public life; in a television interview much later Princess Chulabhorn made the only explanation ever to come from the royal family about the queen's retirement. The princess described her mother as an insomniac who was exhausted and who had been "ordered to rest."[7]

Sirimavo
See Bandaranaike

Sitoe, Aline
See Aline Sitoe

Sivali
Queen, ruler of Ceylon (Sri Lanka) (A.D. 35)

For a brief period following the death of King Chulabhoya, Queen Sivali, who was probably his wife, reigned. However, before the year was out, she was succeeded by King Ilanaga, most likely a usurper.[8]

Sofya (or Sophia) Alekseyevna
Regent of Russia (1682–1689)

Sofya was born in 1657, the eldest daughter of Tzar Alexis, who ruled Russia from 1645 to 1676, and his first wife, Mariya Miloslavskaya. She was the sister of Fyodor III (Theodore), who acceded to the throne upon his father's death and ruled for six years. When Fyodor died in 1682, Peter, Sofya's half brother by Alexis' second wife Natalya Naryshkina, was proclaimed tzar; however, Sofya, indignant that the rights of her younger brother Ivan had been ignored, sickly and feeble-minded though he was, incited the already discontented palace guard to riot, terrorizing and actually murdering members of Peter's clan. Sofya effected a compromise co-tzarship between Peter I and Ivan V, for which she assumed the regency. With the advice of her lover, Prince Vasily V. Golitsyn, she immediately moved to strengthen her position by arming the frontier and by removing those whom she did not trust from positions of authority, including Peter, whom she exiled from the Kremlin. Well educated by Russian standards of the day, she invited skilled craftsmen from Europe to settle in Russia. These western Europeans profoundly influenced Peter, who later introduced elements of their style and culture into his reign. Sofya took her lover's advice and engaged in two costly and disastrous military campaigns against the Tatars in exchange for peace with Poland and ownership of Kiev and territory east of the Dnieper River. Her military failures, as compared with Peter's consuming interest in military skills, led to her unpopularity among the disgruntled military, which had originally supported her but had since suffered loss of face in defeat. By 1689 Sofya had shown signs of her intention to get rid of Peter and to reign as tzaritsa. The partisans of Peter, in a surprise coup, overthrew Sofya and forced her to enter a convent. Following several riots by her supporters, in which she took no active part, she was tried and sentenced to take the veil. She died in 1704.[9]

Queen Spray of Pearls. William H. Laufer.

Spray of Pearls
Queen, regent of Egypt (1249–1257)

She was named Shajar Al Durr and was the devoted wife of Sultan Al Ṣaliḥ Ayyūb, Ayyūbid Sultan of Egypt from 1240 to 1249. When he died in his tent in Mansoora in 1249, with the Crusaders on the way, Spray of Pearls kept his death a secret. Daily she assured the officers that the sultan was much better, and she issued orders under the sultan's forged signature. Faced with a major battle against a well-armed force, this extraordinary woman commanded the army and at the same time ruled the land, all under cover, concealing a rotting corpse. The Crusaders were beaten by dysentery and starvation when the Muslims cut off their supply route. Early the next year, the sultan's oldest son, Tūrān Shāh, arrived from Syria to be proclaimed Sultan. But in May of 1250 the Mamlūks murdered him and hailed Spray of Pearls, to whom they were devoted, as queen of

Egypt. However, Syria refused to recognize the accession of Spray of Pearls: the Abbasid Khalif wrote, quoting the Prophet, "Unhappy is the nation which is governed by a woman," adding with sarcasm, "If you have no men, I will send you one." As a result, Spray of Pearls was compelled to marry a Mamlūk of the late sultan, Aybak, the commander-in-chief, who became the first Mamlūk sultan. It was not a happy union. In 1257 she arranged the murder of Aybak, but a few days later Aybak's supporters retaliated. They threw her, almost naked, off the battlements of the citadel of Cairo. Her body lay in a ditch for several days before it was buried.[10]

Sugandha
Queen, regent of Kashmir (A.D. ?–914)

During the tenth century two opposing military factions vied for ascendancy in Kashmir: the Ekangas and the Tantrins, a wild, ungovernable, and unpredictable clan. Queen Sugandha allied herself with the Ekangas in order to maintain her control of Kashmir as a whole. In a 914 clash between the two factions, Queen Sugandha's forces were defeated, leaving the Tantrins in complete control. Queen Sugandha was deposed, and none of the succeeding rulers was able to assert his authority over the Tantrins.[11]

Suiko-tennō
Empress, ruler of Japan (A.D. 592–628)

She was born Toyo-mike-kashikiya-hime in A.D. 554, the third daughter of Emperor Kimmei-tennō, who reigned from A.D. 548 to 571. Her mother was the daughter of Soga Iname. The Soga was a Samurai family of great distinction. Her half brother, Bidatsu, acceded to the throne when their father died (571) and reigned until 585. In 576 she married Bidatsu and bore seven sons. Bidatsu died in 585 and was succeeded by his brother Yōmei, who died in 587, and his brother Sushun, who was murdered in 592 by Soga Umako, the head of the

Soga family. Soga Umako then placed his own niece Suiko on the throne. Although Chinese ancient history records earlier reigning women in Japan, and although Japanese history records the earlier rule of Jingō-kōgō as regent for her son Ōjin, Suiko is the first reigning empress listed in Japanese recorded history. During her reign the total supremacy of the monarch was established. She encouraged the efforts of her nephew Shōtoku-taishi to implant Buddhism in Japan. Through her nephew, the empress invited craftsmen from Korea and China to come to Japan. The Nihongi Chronicles record not only the first embassy to be sent to China (607), but also much intercourse between Japan and the mainland, resulting in the adoption of the Chinese bureaucratic system and even the Chinese calendar. Suiko died in 628 at the age of 75.[12]

Sung
Empress, regent of China (ca. 1021?)

Since her given name is not recorded, she will be referred to as an empress of the Sung dynasty, or Empress Sung. She was the wife of Sung Chen Tsung (Tseng Tsung), third emperor of the Sung Dynasty, who ruled from 998 to 1022. When her husband became insane, she assumed power. Following his death in 1022, his teenaged son by a minor concubine of humble rank acceded to the throne with Empress Sung as regent. The dowager empress was frequently at odds with the young emperor, and his young wife sided with her against him as well. After Empress Sung died, the emperor divorced his wife for favoring the dowager empress, causing a scandal in the court, which practiced strict Confucian morality.[13]

Sung
Empress, regent of China (1274–1276)

Since the name of this empress is not recorded, she will be referred to by the name of her dynasty, Empress Sung. She was the wife of Sung

Emperor Tu-Tsung, ruler of China from 1265 to 1274. Following the death of her husband in 1274, she became regent for his son, Kung-Ti, age two, with minister Chia Ssu-tao in charge. The Mongolian general Bayan, under Kublai Khan, invaded the Sung capital city of Hang-chow in 1276. The empress regent handed over the empire to Kublai Khan, whereupon Bayan sent the young emperor, now age four, to Ku blai, who treated him kindly. How the Empress Sung was treated is not recorded.[14]

Susanne (or Suzanne) of Bourbon
Duchess, ruler of Bourbon (1503–1521)

She was born in 1491, the daughter of Pierre II, sire of Beaujeau and duke of Bourbon from 1488 to 1505, and Anne of France. Her only brother, Charles, died young. She married Charles II, count of Montpensier, and had three sons who also died young. When her father died (ca. 1503), Susanne inherited the duchy of Bourbon, which she and Charles administered until her death in 1521. Charles continued to rule, but a charge of treason against him led to the confiscation of Bourbon by the French crown upon his death in 1527.[15]

Susanne de Bourbonne. The Metropolitan Museum of Art, Robert Lehman Collection, 1975 (1975.1.130).

Taitu

Empress, de facto ruler of Ethiopia
(1906–1913)

She was the fourth wife of Emperor Menelik II,
who ruled Ethiopia from 1889 to 1913. It was
Taitu who persuaded Sahle Mariam, later
Menelik II, to construct a home near a warm
springs and to grant parcels of land surrounding
it to families of the nobility. From this
beginning, the new capital city of Ethiopia was
founded in 1887. Empress Taitu named it
Addis Ababa, meaning "new flower." In 1906
Menelik suffered the first of a series of strokes
that over the years would debilitate him
completely. Empress Taitu, who had always
been a strong woman with great influence, then
exercised her ruling power. Even after 1908,
when Ras Tessama was named regent for Lij
Iyasu, Menelik's grandson and heir, Empress
Taitu's authority remained supreme. Ras Tessama died in 1911, and Lij Iyasu was
proclaimed emperor; however, he proved to be
inept at governing. Empress Taitu's influence
waned after her bedridden husband died
in 1913.[1]

Takano-tennō
See Kōken

Tamara (or Thamar)

Queen, co-ruler (1178–1184), then "king" of
Karthalinia (Georgia) (1184–1212)

She was born ca. 1156, the daughter of King
George III (Giorgi), who ruled Georgia from
1165 to 1184. Georgia included the ancient
countries of Colchis and Iberia in the Caucasus.
In 1178, six years before his death, King
George had Tamara, "the bright light of his
eyes," crowned as co-ruler. He gave her the
official name of "Mountain of God." The most
celebrated monarch of the era, Tamara has
been described as being "remarkable for her
moderation, humanity, and personal culture."
She became sole ruler when King George died
in 1184, but she was put under the guardianship of her aunt, Rusudani, her father's sister.
In 1187 she married George Bogolyuaski of
Kiev, but the marriage remained childless after
two years. Tamara exiled him and, in ca. 1193,
married again: a cousin, David Sosland, who
was of the house of Bagrationi, as was she. She
made him co-ruler from ca. 1193 until 1207. In
1194 they had a son, Giorgi, and in 1195, a
daughter, Rusudani. A devout Christian, Queen
Tamara requested of Sultan Saladin that he
sell her the Holy Cross for 200,000 dinars, but
he refused. In 1191 her still disgruntled cast-off
first husband, with the help of the Seljuk Sultan

of Erzerum, attempted to depose her but failed. In 1200, with the aid of Turkish troops, he tried again. She fought off repeated attacks by Rukn ad-Din; by then she had built an invincible military power. In 1205 she made her son George co-ruler. She helped her nephews Alexius and David Comnenus, grandsons of the Emperor Andronicus, occupy Trebiz and establish a domain along the Black Sea shores of Asia Minor. David Comnenus was killed in 1206, but Alexius lived to become emperor and to found a dynasty that lasted 250 years. In 1207 her husband David Soslan died. Her son George IV succeeded her when she died in 1212. For her work in furthering the cause of Christianity, she was canonized by the Georgian Church.[2]

Tausert
See Twosret

Ta-pu-yen
Queen, regent of Kara-Kitai Empire (1142–1150)

The Kara-Khitai Empire was located in Eastern Turkestan and was founded by the gur-khan Ye-lü Ta-shih, who ruled ca. 1130 to 1142. This pagan Mongol line in Muslim Turkic territory was looked upon so contemptuously by Arabian/Persian historians that they did not record the names of the rulers; as a result, they are known only by the Chinese transcriptions of their names. After the death of Ye-lü Ta-shih in 1142, his widow Ta-pu-yen became regent of the empire for their son, Ye-lü Yi-li, who reached his majority in 1150. Their daughter, Pu-su-wan (Ye-lü Shih) also ruled following her brother's death in 1163.[3]

Teng
Empress, regent of China (A.D. 105–121)

During the Later or Eastern Han Dynasty, following the death of Emperor Ho Ti, ruler from A.D. 88 to 105, Teng ruled as dowager queen regent for her infant son until her own death in A.D. 121. At the time of her death, most of her prominent relatives, as befitted their noble status, chose suicide.[4]

Teresa of Castile
Countess, regent of Portugal (1112–1128)

Teresa was the illegitimate daughter of King Alfonso VI, ruler of Castile from 1072 to 1109, and Jimena Muñoz. She married Henry of Burgundy, count of Portugal from 1093. In 1109 they had a son, Alfonso Henriques, who at age three succeeded as count of Portugal upon Henry's death (1112). Soon after Teresa assumed the post as regent, she became embroiled in a struggle with Galicia and Castile. Portuguese defenses were easily overcome, and Teresa, being the daughter, half sister, and aunt of Castilian kings, agreed to accept Castilian domination of Portugal. Her son, at age 19, took command of the army, defeated the Castilians, and drove his mother into exile (1128). In 1139 Portugal became a kingdom and Alfonso was proclaimed king. He continued to rule until 1185.[5]

Thatcher, Margaret
Prime minister of Great Britain (1979–1990)

Margaret Thatcher was born Hilda Roberts in 1925, the daughter of Alfred Roberts, one-time mayor of Grantham, Lincolnshire. She attended Somerville College, Oxford, where she received a B.S. degree in chemistry and M.A. in law, specializing in taxation. She worked as a research chemist from 1947 to 1951. In 1951

Margaret Thatcher. Reuters/Bettmann Newsphotos.

Margaret married Denis Thatcher; the couple had one son and twin daughters. She was called to the bar in 1953 and elected to Parliament six years later. In 1970, after holding a number of political offices, she became Leader of the Opposition, and four years later succeeded Edward Heath as Leader of the Tories. In May 1979 the Conservatives won the election and Mrs. Thatcher, who belongs to the right wing of the Conservative party, became the first woman in history to serve as Britain's prime minister. She was to become Britain's longest continuously serving prime minister, and the longest serving leader in Western Europe. When Margaret Thatcher came into office, former deputy prime minister Lord William Whittlaw said, "England had reached an economic and social equivalent of Dunkirk." A breakdown in public services, labor unrest, and industrial decline plagued the country. By and large, Mrs. Thatcher's ultraconservative economic moves reached far into the future. Once asked what she had changed in Britain, she answered, "Everything." Preaching free market, private enterprise, the value of hard work, self-discipline, and thrift, she made respectable in Britain the spirit of capitalism that elsewhere in the world had become synonymous with greed and exploitation. However, for all her positive economic impact, a Gallup survey taken on the eve of her tenth year in office concluded that after Edward Heath she was the least popular of English leaders. The survey found public perception that under Thatcher's rule there was more poverty, selfishness, greed, and crime in Britain. Her attempt at censoring criticism of her administration was widely criticized, both at home and abroad. On November 22, 1990, urged by Conservative advisors, Mrs. Thatcher resigned, throwing her support to John Major, who was elected her successor.[6]

Thecla
Co-regent of Byzantine Empire (ca. 842)

She was the daughter of Emperor Theophilus, ruler of the Eastern Roman Empire from 829 to 842, and Empress Theodora. Thecla was the sister of Michael III, who acceded to the throne as a child of three upon their father's death, and of Constantine, who died ca. 830, and four sisters: Mary, Anna, Anastasia, and Pulcheria. When Michael came to the throne their mother, Theodora, served as regent. Apparently Thecla, the oldest surviving sister, was entitled to share in the regency of her mother, since she was portrayed on coins together with Michael and Theodora, and was named with them on official government documents of the period. But there is no indication that Thecla took any actual part in the conduct of government. When Theodora was forced to surrender control of the government in 856, her daughters were shut up in a nunnery. If Thecla was among them she apparently did not remain long, because she soon surfaced as the mistress of Byzantine Emperor Basil I, who ruled from 867 to 886, who, in a fruit-basket-turnover of wives, took as his second wife Eudoxia Ingerina, former mistress of Thecla's brother Michael. (Michael made Basil co-emperor in 866 but in 867 Basil repaid the compliment by having the drunken emperor murdered in his bedchamber.)[7]

Theodolinda (or Theodelinda)
Queen, ruler of Lombards briefly (A.D. 590), regent of Lombards (A.D. 616–622)

The daughter of Duke Garibold of Bavaria, in ca. 590 she married King Authari, Lombard king from A.D. 584 to 590. When Authari died shortly after their marriage, the nobles of Lombard allowed Theodolinda to choose a new husband who would then also be king. She selected a Thuringian, Agilulf, duke of Turin. In 602 the couple had a son, Adaloald, who acceded to the throne when his father died in 616, and for whom Theodolinda was regent during his minority. A devout Catholic, Theodolinda used her influence to help Catholicism triumph over Arianism in northern Italy. Theodolinda and Agilulf also had a daughter, Gundeberga, who married the Arian Rothari (Rother of legend), duke of Brescia, who ruled the Arians from 636 to 652 and who allowed the Catholic hierarchy to be reestablished in his kingdom. In 622 Theodolinda's son came of age, but shortly afterward, in 624, he went berserk, embarked on a killing rampage, and murdered 12 Lombard nobles. He was deposed and later poisoned (ca. 626). At that time, Theodolinda, who had devoted her life to religion and good works, retired in sorrow and died two years later.[8]

Theodora
Empress, de facto co-ruler of Macedonian Dynasty, Byzantium (527–548)

A woman of humble origins and a former actress, in 525 Theodora married Justinian, also born of peasant stock, who ruled Byzantium from 527 to 565. It is generally conceded by today's historians that the historian Procopius, who in 551, 553, and 554 wrote books on the ruler and his wife, unduly maligned them both. In fact, Theodora's unswerving will, superior intelligence, and acute political acumen lead many modern-day historians to the conclusion that it was she, rather than Justinian, who ruled Byzantium. In 527 Justinian was made co-emperor with his uncle, the Emperor Justin, and was given the rank of August. At the same time, Theodora, who exercised considerable power and influence over him even at that time, was crowned Augusta. While Justinian's entire reign was troubled by wars in both the east and the west, and by frequent attacks from the north by barbarians, Theodora's spheres of influence, although not wholly confined to domestic issues, concerned themselves with every facet of administrative, legislative, and ecclesiastical matters. Her name is mentioned in nearly every law passed during the period. She was one of the first rulers to champion women's rights, passing strict laws prohibiting white slavery and altering divorce laws to make them more favorable to women. In 531 she arranged the dismissal of the praetorian prefect, John of Cappadocia, whose collection of revenues and general attention to the financing of Justinian's military campaigns she thought inadequate. In 532 two factions (the Greens and the Blues) united against Justinian and proclaimed the late emperor Anastasius' nephew Hypatius emperor. Justinian, believing all was lost, prepared for flight. But the indomitable courage of Theodora prevented a coup. She persuaded Justinian to stand his ground, and those troops

loyal to the emperor were able to quell the revolt. In the field of foreign affairs, she corresponded with and received diplomats and in general conducted any foreign policy that did not pertain to fighting battles. Her championship of the cause of Monophysitism, the Christian teaching emphasizing the divine nature of Christ, counterbalanced the orthodox view set forth by the Council of Chalcedon in 451, that human and divine natures coexist in the Christ. She died of cancer in 548, leaving her bereft husband, toward the end of his life, to grapple with the theological mysteries and questions she had posed. Following her death, although her husband ruled almost two more decades, no notable legislation was passed.[9]

Theodora
Empress, regent of Eastern Roman Empire (A.D. 842–856)

Theodora was the wife of Emperor Theophilus, who ruled the Byzantine Empire from 829 to 842. The couple had seven children: Maria, Thecla, Anna, Anastasia, Pulcheria, Constantine, and Michael II (later called the Drunkard), who at the age of three acceded to the throne upon his father's death (842), with his mother as regent. Her ministers and her brother Bardas advised her to restore orthodoxy that had been recanted by her late husband. She did so with a vengeance: she reinstated icons (as pictures, not statues) and gave the Paulicians the choice of conversion or death. Paulicians who survived the ensuing bloodbath her edict caused in Constantinople made a mass exodus to Thrace. Her government was then forced to undertake a new campaign against the Slavic tribes in southern Greece. After a long, bitter struggle, the Slavs were subdued and forced to pay tribute and to recognize Byzantium supremacy. In 856 Theodora's brother Bardas, acting in secret agreement with her son Michael, murdered her advisor Theoctistus and had the senate proclaim Michael an independent ruler. Theodora was obliged to retire and her daughters were shut up in a nunnery. Ten years later, after she attempted an attack against her brother, she too was sent away to a nunnery.[10]

Theodora (or Augusta Theodora)
Empress, ruler of Byzantine Empire (1042 and 1055–1056)

Born ca. 981, she was the youngest daughter of Constantine VIII, ruler of Byzantium from 963 to 1028, and his wife Helena of Alypius. Psellus described Theodora as "tall, curt and glib of tongue, cheerful and smiling" and as having "a placid disposition and in one way . . . a dull one" and as "self-controlled in money matters." Her eldest sister Eudocia, pock-faced from an early age, entered a nunnery. Her second sister, Zoë, was singled out by their dying father to be married to Romanus III who, with Zoë, inherited the reign upon the emperor's death (1028). During their reign, Theodora was exiled to a convent in Petrion. She never married, but by some quirk of disposition seemed not to hold a serious grudge against her sister for her treatment. Zoë, always the adventurous one of the two, took a lover, Michael IV, and together they conspired to murder Romanus, after which Zoë married Michael and made him emperor. Although Michael IV treated Zoë poorly once he was installed, he nevertheless convinced her to adopt his nephew, Michael V, as her heir and his successor. Michael IV died, and Michael V came to the throne. But he made the mistake of exiling Zoë, arousing the populace against him. Michael quickly brought Zoë back, but the people were not appeased. They brought Theodora out of exile and proclaimed her empress (1042). She ruled alone briefly, then allowed her sister to join her and even gave her the more prominent role. But Zoë could not be satisfied; she seized power again by marrying a third time (Constantine IX, 1042–1055). Zoë died during this reign (1050), and when Constantine died (1055), Theodora was again summoned to take control. This time she superintended all affairs of state herself. She appointed all officials, dispensed justice from the throne, issued decrees, and gave orders. According to Psellus, during her reign the empire prospered and its glory increased. Theodora died in 1056 at the age of 76, having named as her successor Michael VI, an aged man of the court suggested by her advisors, when she was on her deathbed.[11]

Theophano
Empress, regent of Byzantine Empire (963)

Born the daughter of a publican, Anastaso, Theophano was an extraordinarily beautiful woman who attracted the attention of the future Byzantine Emperor Romanus II, who married her ca. 956. When Romanus became emperor in 959, she took the name of Theophano. A historian describes her as "entirely immoral and immeasurably ambitious." The couple had two sons, Basil II and Constantine VIII. Upon Romanus' death in 963, Theophano assumed the regency for the small boys. Being a shrewd student of political affairs, she knew her regency could not last long, so she came to an understanding with the elderly Nicephorus Phocas, offering herself in marriage to him. The supreme military command was entrusted to the brilliant General John Tzimisces, with whom Theophano conducted a heated affair. She cooperated with conspirators of Tzimisces who murdered her elderly husband in his bedchamber in 969, expecting that she and John would then be married. But the Patriarch Polyeuctus, in the sort of slap-on-the-wrist justice so often meted out to the powerful, demanded that before John could become emperor he should do penance for his part in the murder, and that he should expel Theophano from the palace. She died in 991.[12]

Theophano
Regent of Germany (A.D. 984–991)

Although historians have called her one of the greatest women in world history, they do not agree on her history. She was either the daughter of the Eastern Roman Emperor Romanus II, ruler from 959 to 963, and his wife Theophano, or the niece or grandniece of Emperor John Tzimisces, ruler from 969 to 976, who had a licentious affair with Romanus' wife, Theophano. In ca. 972 she married Otto II, who ruled the German Empire from 973 to 983. In 980 they had a son, Otto III, who succeeded his father at age three upon Otto II's death of a fever. Immediately revolts flared up among the Slavs on one side and the Danes and Franks on another, all intent upon wresting power from the throne. It was the genius of Theophano that saved the empire. In her castle at Quedlinburg she maintained a brilliant court attended by scholars of great note. She presided over a magnificent diet at Nijmwegen, attended by numerous princes. Her forceful and intelligent presence quelled the dissent, which did not surface again until after her death in 991. She was succeeded in the regency by her mother-in-law, Adelaide.[13]

Tiy
Queen, de facto regent of Egypt
(ca. 1370 B.C.)

She was a commoner, possibly of Asiatic blood, and possibly from a military family, who married Amenophis (or Amenhotep) III, ruler of Egypt from ca. 1405 to 1370 B.C. The king, having departed from the God's Wife concept of marrying the royal heiress (usually one's sister) who would become the chief queen, bestowed upon his commoner wife the august title of "great royal wife." Variously described as "formidable," "a woman of long-suffering character," possessing "compelling physical appeal," Tiy maintained influence over her husband despite his many other feminine distractions. The king enjoyed sailing with Tiy on the artificial lake outside the palace, while Tiy enjoyed unusual power within the palace. In the ceremonies held renewing kingly power, Queen Tiy participated as well. She was the mother of Akhenaton, who ruled from ca. 1370 to 1352. The king's last years were spent in illness, and it is possible that during those years Tiy's son was already elevated to ruler or co-ruler. Her brother was promoted to the important post of second prophet of Amon. Given the amount of evidence remaining of Tiy's influence and participation, it is safe to assume that during the waning years of her husband's life, this involvement increased, particularly on behalf of her son, so that if she was not regent so-called, she is likely to have performed many of the functions of regent.[14]

Tomyris
Queen of the Massagetae
(ca. 529 or 530 B.C.)

The Massagetae was a large, warlike, half-nomadic Sakan tribe whose land lay eastward beyond the Araxes River in Eastern Persia. Tomyris was the widow of a Sakan chief and was both queen and leader of the army. She had at least one son, Spargapises. Cyrus the Great, not content with his latest conquest of Assyria, turned his attention to adding the country of the Massagetae to his ever-expanding Persian Empire. According to Herodotus, Cyrus, camped across the river from the Massagetae, first sent word to Queen Tomyris pretending to want her hand in marriage, but Tomyris, not so easily duped, refused. She sent him the message, "King of the Medes, I advise you to abandon this enterprise . . . Rule your own people, and try to bear the sight of me ruling mine. But of course, you will refuse my advice, as the last thing you wish for is to live in peace." She then offered him an alternative: allow her army to withdraw a three-days' march from the river and then the two rulers could meet. Cyrus was at first inclined to accept this proposal until advised by Croesus against any compromise. Croesus suggested tricking the Massagetae by preparing a feast as a trap, luring the Massagetae to descend upon it. Once they had sated themselves and had drunk themselves into a stupor, his troops could come out of hiding and massacre them. Croesus pointed out, "It would surely be an intolerable disgrace for Cyrus son of Cambyses to give ground before a woman." Cyrus took his advice and the plot went off as planned, except for one small hitch: one of those captured in the plot was the queen's son Spargapises. When the queen learned of this, she sent word ordering that her son be released or she would give Cyrus more blood than he could drink. Actually, Cyrus could not return Spargapises even if he had wanted to because the boy had committed suicide in captivity. The Massagetae attacked and massacred the Persians, including Cyrus. By Herodotus' account, the queen, learning that her son had committed suicide, filled a skin with blood and stuffed Cyrus' head in it, fulfilling her promise to give him more blood than he could drink. According to other accounts, Cyrus was only mortally wounded at the time and didn't die until three days later.[15]

Töregene (or Turakina, Töragina, or Törägänä)
Khatun, regent of Outer Mongolia
(1241–1246)

A Naiman princess, Töregene has been described as energetic but avaricious. She was the wife of Ogödei (or Ogotai or Ogödäi), a son of Jenghiz-khan and ruler of the Mongolian Empire from 1229 to 1241. Jenghiz-khan had divided his realm among his four sons, making each a khan over the chieftains in his own realm; however, the khans then elected one great khan to rule over all. In 1229 Ogödei was elected great khan by the plenary Kuriltai. Prior to his death of a drinking bout in 1241, he had had a quarrel with his eldest son Güyük and had sent him disgraced into exile. He had named as his successor his grandson Shirämön, whose father Kuchu had been killed fighting the Chinese. But Töregene, determined that Güyük should have the throne, took over the regency. She summoned a Kuriltay (gathering of the official ruling body), which recognized her authority until a new great khan should be appointed. For five years she ruled while trying to convince the clan chieftains and princes of the blood to appoint Güyük. During her reign, she chose as her advisor, not a Christian like herself, but a Moslem, 'Abd ar-Rahman. Gossipers accused 'Abd ar-Rahman of aiding in Ogödei's untimely demise. Töregene eventually convinced the Kuriltai of Güyük's suitability, and she handed over the throne to him in 1246.[16]

Tou Hsien
Empress, regent of China (A.D. 88–97)

During the Later or Eastern Han Dynasty, dowager empresses and their eunuchs gained the power by choosing infants as successors to the throne. Tou Hsien, who came from a great land-owning family that dated back to the second century B.C., became all powerful at court by this ploy. Empress Tou altered the succession and, with her family, ruled as dowager empress from A.D. 88 to her death in A.D. 97.[17]

Tribhuvana
Queen, Majapahit ruler of Java (1328–1350)

She succeeded her father, Jayanagara, who was slain by his physician Tancha. Her minister Gajah Mada, instigator of the assassination plot, became the empire's most powerful figure. In 1350 she abdicated in favor of her son, Hayam Wuruk, the Majapahit empire's most famous king.

Trieu Au
Vietnamese hill-people "ruler"
(ca. A.D. 248)

Although she was not a queen, Trieu Au was a leader at a time when Vietnam was not a unified country under a central leader, but was instead a territory occupied by the Chinese. Born in A.D. 222, she was orphaned and taken by her brother and his wife, who treated her cruelly, more like a slave than a sister. Trieu Au killed her sister-in-law, who may have been Chinese, and escaped to the hills. A commanding and charismatic speaker, she took it upon herself to enumerate the indignities her people had suffered at the hands of the Chinese. There in the hills, in 248, she set up her administration and raised a thousand troops with which she launched a revolt against the hated Chinese. Wearing golden armor, she rode at the front of her troops on the back of an elephant. She was defeated in only six months and, in honorable fashion, rather than surrender, she committed suicide by throwing herself into a river. She is remembered today in Vietnam by a temple built in her honor and by her defiant declaration, "I want to rail against the wind and the tide, kill the whale in the sea, sweep the whole country to save the people from slavery, and I refuse to be abused."[18]

Trung Nhi and Trung Trac
Co-queens of Vietnam (A.D. 39–42)

Between 111 B.C. and A.D. 221, Vietnam was in the hands of the Han Dynasty overlords of China. For more than a century the Vietnamese made no serious challenge to the Han rule. Then, in ca. A.D. 39, a Chinese commander murdered a dissident Vietnamese nobleman and

Trung Nhi and Trung Trac. William H. Laufer.

raped his widow, who happened to be Trung Trac. She and her sister Trung Nhi organized the surrounding tribal lords and mustered an army that included at least one other outstanding woman, Phung Thi Chinh, who was pregnant at the time. The sisters attacked Chinese strongholds and either cleared out or massacred the enemy Chinese. Phung Thi Chinh reportedly gave birth to a baby but strapped it on her back and got back into the fray. The Vietnamese carved out an independent kingdom, purged of Chinese, that stretched from Hue into southern China. The Trung sisters were proclaimed co-queens of this new kingdom. They ruled until A.D. 42, when the Han emperor sent a large force to recapture the kingdom. Unable to meet such mighty opposition, the Trung sisters took the honorable route of committing suicide, drowning themselves in a river. The Vietnamese still venerate the sisters at temples in Hanoi and Saigon. Madame Ngo Dinh Nhu, the sister-in-law of South Vietnam's President Ngo Dinh Diem, erected statues in their honor in Saigon in 1962.[19]

Turunku Bakwa (also Bazao)
Queen, founder and ruler of Zaria (1536–?)

She was the mother of Amina and Zaria, both of whom ruled Zaria after her. An immigrant, she was a Fulani who moved into Macina, the eastern Niger region. Some argue that Turunku Bakwa might have come from the south because she had acquired guns from traders on the coast. She belonged to a matriarchal clan. In 1536 she founded the city of Zaria in north

central Nigeria, naming it for her younger daughter.[20]

Twosret (also called Tausert)
King, last ruler of Nineteenth Dynasty, Egypt (ca. 1202–1200 B.C.)

She was probably the daughter of Merneptah, who ruled ca. 1236 to 1223 B.C. She was the wife and probably also the sister of Sethos II (Seti II), ruler from ca. 1216 to 1210 B.C. Apparently Sethos II died or was murdered in 1210; a Syrian officer who had become powerful as chancellor of Egypt brought a young man named Siptah to the throne. Twosret, the matrilineal link to the throne, married him. When Siptah died in 1202, possibly at her hand, Twosret ruled as "king," appropriating her husband's regnal years and restoring her first husband's name over Siptah's. The throne was probably usurped by Selnakht in 1200 B.C.[21]

Tz'u-an
Queen, regent of China (1862–1873) and (1875–1881)

Tz'u-an was at one time the senior consort of the Hsien-feng emperor, who reigned from 1851 to 1862, until another consort, Tz'u-hsi (Cixi), bore a son and heir, T'ung-chih. When the emperor died in 1862, the five-year-old boy became emperor with a council of eight elders acting as regents. Through clever plotting with Prince Kung, brother of the late king, the two dowager empresses managed to get the regency transferred to them. They then named Kung as the prince councillor. The women gradually brought about some westernization of the government and put an end to much of the government corruption. The regency ended when T'ung-chih reached his majority in 1973; however, he died only two years later. Tz'u-hsi violated succession laws, which called for an emperor of the next generation, by adopting her three-year-old nephew as heir. Again the two empresses served as regents until Tz'u-an's sudden death in 1881, possibly from poisoning.[22]

Tz'u Hsi
See Cixi

Udham Bai
Queen, de facto co-ruler of Mughal India
(1748–1754)

She was the daughter of Farrukh-Siyar, who in
the twilight years of the Mughal Empire married Muḥammad Shāh (Rawshan Akhtar), ruler
from 1719 to 1748, the fourth in a row of weak
rulers. Under Muḥammad Shāh's leadership,
the empire lost the province of Kābul to Persia's
Nādir Shāh and the province of Katehr to another soldier of fortune, Ruhēla, and several
other provinces became practically independent. Udham Bai's son, Aḥmad Shāh Badāhur,
born in 1725, was no stronger. He had already
reached his majority when he crowned himself
king upon his father's death (1748), but his
mother knew that he was cut from the same
cloth as his four predecessors. If India was to
continue under the Mughals, someone besides
the good-natured, lackadaisical Aḥmad Shāh
would have to take the reins. It was not difficult
for Udham Bai to dominate her son completely.
She did not attempt to encourage responsibility
in her son, and in the end the weaknesses that
she encouraged sealed her fate as well as his.
She had as her cohort the emperor's eunuch
vicar and superintendent of the harem, Javid
Khān. Despite their meddling, Aḥmad Shāh,
who was easily intimidated, gave the Punjab

and Multan to Nādir Shāh's lieutenant, Abdālī.
Then, at a demonstration by the Marāthās in
Sikandrābād, Aḥmad Shāh, who invariably
chose flight to fight, abandoned the women of
his family, including Udham Bai, to captivity
by the Marāthās. He was blinded and deposed
in 1754 by a force consisting of Doab Afghans
and Marāthās. He lived in confinement until his
death in 1775.[1]

Uicab, María
"Queen" of Tulum (1871)

María Uicab was a Mayan woman living on the
Yucután Peninsula who was known as the patron saint of Tulum and was given the title of
queen. In 1871 the sacred Mayan ruins of the
city of Tulum became an Indian shrine where a
"talking cross" was set up. The city of Tulum,
especially the "talking cross," was placed in
the care of Queen Maria.[2]

Ulrica Eleanora
Queen of Sweden (1718–1720)

She was born in 1688, the daughter of King
Charles XI, ruler of Sweden from 1660 to 1697,
and Ulrica Eleanora of Denmark. Her brother,
Charles XII, succeeded their father on the
throne. Ulrica Eleanora was betrothed to Frederick of Hesse-Cassel, a Calvinist, but refused
to marry him until her brother assured her the

marriage would not jeopardize her accession to the throne in that Catholic country. The couple married in 1715 but remained childless. In 1718, while on a military expedition to Norway, Charles XII was shot and killed, and Ulrica Eleanora acceded to the throne. Charles Frederick, son of her late older sister Hedvig Sofia, challenged her right to rule. However, the riksdag accepted her reign on the condition that a new constitution be drawn up. This new document provided for a joint rule by the monarchy and the council when the riksdag was not in session. When the riksdag was sitting, principal decisions would be made by a secret committee made up of nobles, clergy, and burghers. Peasants were to have a voice in matters concerning taxes. This new constitution ushered in Sweden's so-called Age of Freedom. Ulrica Eleanora, being completely devoted to her husband, bowed to his ambitions in 1720 by abdicating in his favor. She died in 1741.[3]

Urraca
Queen Doña, ruler of León and Castile united (1109–1126)

Doña Urraca was born ca. 1081, the daughter of Constance and Alfonso VI, King of León from 1065 and King of Castile from 1072. She first married Raymond of Burgundy, a French knight who had come to participate in the Wars of Reconquista. She and Raymond had two sons before he died sometime prior to 1109. Her father spent most of his time fighting the Moslems. In his last battle with the Almoravids in 1108, his only son, Urraca's brother Sancho, was killed. Alfonso immediately began making arrangements for his widowed daughter, who would now inherit the throne, to marry someone he could count on to continue to fight the Muslims. When her father died the next year Urraca, still a widow, inherited both thrones, León and Castile. She bowed to her father's wishes and married King Alfonso I (the Battler) of Aragon, whom she detested. Evidence shows that she ruled her own kingdom and had no intention of giving up her authority to him. Their constant scrapping kept the government in a turmoil and even curtailed the progress of the Cross in Spain during the First Crusade. Eventually she sent him back to Aragon via annulment. Neither her lover, the Count of Lara, nor her confidant, Archbishop Bernardo of Toledo, held sway over her decisions. Before her death, to assure that the throne did not fall into the hands of the greedy Argonese, she had her son Alfonso VII crowned with her.[4]

Vaekehu
Queen, ruler of the Taiohae tribe (1891)

Remnants of the Taiohae tribe live in the Marquesas Islands, two volcanic clusters of islands 40 miles northeast of Tahiti. The main harbor and port on the northern island of Nuku Hiva is a town (also the administrative seat of the Marquesas) called Haka Pehi, or Taiolae, from the Polynesian tribe of Queen Vaekehu. The French annexed the whole group of islands in 1842. The French mission, backed by a military force, wiped out native culture by gradually weeding out recalcitrant chiefs, requiring that natives wear European-style clothing, and banning native songs and dances, musical instruments, and tattoos. By 1890, the time of Queen Vaekehu, the native culture was well broken, and she ruled at the French behest. The introduction by the French of venereal diseases, tuberculosis, smallpox, and leprosy all but obliterated the tribe. However, some improvement in their numbers has been made in this century, although their culture is lost forever. Queen Vaekehu's reign was documented in 1891 by F. W. Christian, who collected her genealogy for a paper entitled ''Notes on the Marquesas,'' published in the *Journal of the Polynesian Society* 4 (1895): 194.[1]

Victoria
Queen, ruler of the British Empire
(1837–1901)

She was born Alexandrina Victoria in 1819, the daughter of Edward, duke of Kent, and Princess Victore of Saxe-Coburg. Her father died eight months later and Victoria was reared by her mother, who would have been her regent but for the fact that King William IV of Hanover, Victoria's uncle and ruler since 1830, died shortly after her eighteenth birthday. Although Victoria inherited the crown of England, the crown of Hanover was barred to her by Salic law and went instead to her uncle Ernest, duke of Cumberland. For the first two and one-half years of her reign she remained unmarried, vacillating about becoming betrothed to her cousin, Prince Albert of Saxe-Coburg-Gotha. She eventually married him, and thus began one of the happiest royal marriages on record. The couple had nine children who married into all the royal houses of Europe: Victoria married German Emperor Frederick III; English King Edward VII married Alexandra of Denmark; Alice married Louis of Hesse-Darmstadt; Alfred married Marie of Russia; Helena married Christian of Schleswig-Holstein; Louise married the Duke of Argyll; Arthur married Louise of Prussia; Leopold

Queen Victoria. The Granger Collection, New York.

married Helena of Woldech; and Beatrice married Prince Henry of Battenburg. Not the most supportive of mothers, she often openly criticized her oldest son Edward in terms that would have crushed a lesser boy or man. Albert died of typhoid in 1861, and Victoria mourned him for the next 40 years. Her long association with

Benjamin Disraeli, the Conservative prime minister, and her grating relationship with his rival, William Ewart Gladstone, the Liberal leader, dominated her political concerns for many years. In a brilliant bit of public relations strategy in 1876, Disraeli secured for her the title ''empress of India,'' and she became the symbol of the national mood and enthusiasm for expansion and empire building. By the very length of her tenure during a time of unprecedented growth, she outlived her detractors and gained the devotion of the nation. She celebrated both a Golden Jubilee in 1887 and a Diamond Jubilee in 1897. By the time of her death in 1901, she had restored, as Britain's longest-reigning monarch, both dignity and respect to the crown and affection for its wearer. She was succeeded by her eldest son, Edward VII.[2]

Vittoria
Duchess, ruler of Urbino (1623)

Urbino was a dukedom in central Italy, famous for its majolica, a tin-glazed earthenware. Vittoria was the heir of Duke Federigo Ubaldo (1621–1623), of the family of Della Rovere. She married Ferdinando II de'Medici, who in 1627 became grand duke of Tuscany and who was a brilliant inventor of scientific instruments and a patron of the sciences. Vittoria acceded to the throne of Urbino upon the untimely death of Duke Ubaldo in 1623. At her death in 1631, Urbino was incorporated by reversion into the Papal States by Pope Urban VIII. In 1680 Urbino became part of the kingdom of Italy.[3]

Waizero
See Zauditu

Wang Cheng-Chung
See Cheng-Chun

Wilhelmina
Queen, ruler of the Netherlands (1890–1949)

She was born in 1880, the daughter of King William, ruler of the Netherlands from 1849 to 1890, and his second wife Emma of Waldeck-Pyrmont. When her father died (1890), Wilhelmina became, at the age of ten, queen of the Netherlands under the regency of Queen Emma. She was inaugurated (not crowned, because the crown belongs to the Dutch people) in 1898. The liberal ministry passed much social legislation during the first two years of her majority, including bills calling for improved housing, compulsory education for children, and accident insurance. In 1901 she married Duke Henry of Mecklenburg-Schwerin. The couple had a daughter, Juliana, born in 1909. Wilhelmina kept her country neutral during World War I, and after the German defeat, Kaiser Wilhelm sought and received refuge in the Netherlands. In 1920, the Dutch refused the Allied demand for his surrender. He lived in retirement, first at Amerongen, then at Doorn, where he died in 1941. Ironically, the Dutch kindness to the ex-ruler of Germany did not prevent the Nazis under Adolph Hitler from overrunning the Netherlands in May 1940. May was to become a pivotal month for the queen for the rest of the decade. She escaped to London with her family and the government the day

Queen Wilhelmina. The Granger Collection, New York.

before the Netherlands formally surrendered on May 14, 1940. Throughout the war, Queen Wilhelmina sent from England messages of hope for her people over Radio Orange. She returned May 3, 1945, after the Nazi surrender to find that her country had suffered extensive damage. Imminent large-scale famine was averted only by aid from the Allies. On May 17, 1948, the countries of the Netherlands, Belgium, Luxembourg, France, and Great Britain signed a 50-year mutual assistance pact in Brussels. Four months later, due to ill health, Wilhelmina abdicated in favor of her daughter, Juliana. She lived in retirement at her palace, Het Loo, until her death in 1962 at the age of 82.[1]

Wu Hou (or Wu Chao or Wu Tso Tien)
Empress, de facto ruler of China
(A.D. 660–684), regent of China
(684–690), "emperor," ruler in her
own right (690–705)

She was born in A.D. 625 and at the age of 13 came as a junior concubine to the court of T'ang Emperor Tai-tsung, ruler from 627 to 649. When he died, she was chosen by his heir (and possibly already her lover), Kao-tsung (649–684), first as his favored concubine and then in 655 as his empress. On her way to ultimate power, she is said to have poisoned one of her own sons, her

sister, and her niece, forced another son to hang himself, had 4 grandchildren whipped to death, ordered the execution of 2 stepsons and 16 of their male heirs, killed 4 daughters-in-law, 36 government officials and generals, and ordered another 3,000 families to be slaughtered. By 660 she had eliminated all her opponents. The emperor was often too ill to attend to affairs of state for months at a time and relied entirely on Wu Hou. For the last 23 years of his life, Empress Wu Hou ran the country with consummate ability and efficiency. Military spending was reduced, the country experienced peace and prosperity, and commerce and agriculture thrived. When Kao-tsung died in 683, Wu Hou became regent for their son Chung Tsung. But she had disagreements with the new emperor's wife almost immediately, so she deposed her son after only one month and installed her second son Jui Tsung, over whom she had more control. In 690 she simply usurped the throne for herself, naming herself "emperor," and ruled with great wisdom in her own name for 15 years. Described as self-confident and assertive, she took great pains to encourage independent thinking and bold behavior in her children. So long as she remained strong, no one dared attempt to usurp her power, but when she reached the age of 80, her opponents grew more courageous. She was deposed in a palace coup in A.D. 705 and died in retirement ten months later.[2]

Yaa Akyaa
Asantehemaa, queen mother of the
Asante Empire (ca. 1883–1896)

Yaa Akyaa was born ca. 1837 of the royal matriclan Oyoko. She was selected from among the women of the royal Oyoko dynasty to succeed Queen Afua Kobi as asantehemaa. *Asantehemaa,* meaning queen mother, does not carry the same connotation as it does in Europe. Each district or group had its own chief and queen mother, but there was one grand chief and one grand queen mother (who might not be anyone's mother) who ruled over all. It was the asantehemaa, in many ways the most vital person in the tribe, who nominated the chief and who made many of the diplomatic decisions. The asantehemaa was completely in charge during the long periods, stretching sometimes into years, when no one occupied the Golden Stool. Yaa Akyaa was married to the Akyebiakyerehene Kwasi Gyambibi. The *akyebiakyerehene* was a secretary or advisor to the chief and the council. The couple had 13 children, several of whom in their turn were to be nominated to sit upon the Golden Stool. Even prior to her election as asantehemaa, as queen mother of her own tribe or district she wielded considerable power. In 1883 two factions were vying for supremacy and the right to name the next

asantehene, or chief of the chiefs. The duty of the asantehene was to act as judge. He decided cases of extreme seriousness that could not be solved within the individual districts. The *mamponhene,* or leader of the Mampone district, sent word that he was coming to intercede in the dispute. Yaa Akyaa sent several messages instructing him to withdraw and to remove his guns from Kumase because the two factions were going to fight. The mamponhene did as he was told. The battle took place, and the Kumasi people headed by Yaa Akyaa were victorious (1883). Her son Kwaka Dua II was placed on the Golden Stool and another son, Agyemon Badu, became heir apparent. Following the premature death of Kwaka Dua II of smallpox only a few months later, and apparently the death of the heir as well, and the subsequent death of his predecessor and rival, the kingdom was plunged into confusion. As the Asante attempted to recover from the devastation caused by the outbreak of this strange disease, a lawless people, the Adansis, took advantage of the confusion to rob and plunder travelers en route to and from the coast. When the Asante retaliated, the Adansis sent false reports to the British, requesting aid to defeat the Asante. For a while, until they bothered to investigate the matter, the British intervened on behalf of the marauders. Meantime, Yaa Akyaa called a third son, Agyeman Prempe, to the stool, but a contender from another district had emerged, contesting Prempe's right since he was not the so-named heir apparent. Yaa Akyaa, in despair at the indecision, saw that there was imminent danger of the collapse of the empire and sent an urgent message to the chiefs requesting that they meet and elect a king. Still reeling from the unwarranted attacks by the British troops, the chiefs consented to come only if the British government would agree to support the man chosen. She then dispatched an embassy to the local British government requesting that a representative be present at the election to observe who became the duly elected ruler. The British took no notice of the message for two years, and it was yet another two years before the British deigned to comply. This unconscionable delay culminated in the appearance, in 1888, of the long-awaited British representative. Yaa Akyaa, by this time age 50, short, white-haired, and characterized as proud, tenacious, energetic, cunning, and intelligent, engaged in a dramatic bit of political maneuvering, demanding that the chief sponsor of the rival candidate return the 3,200 ounces of gold that a deposed chief had "deposited" in Saawua. (Actually he had sewn it in a mattress.) She was thus able to prevail over the Council of Kumase and Agyeman Prempe was duly elected. In 1890 she sent envoys about the refugee problem: many Asante had been lured to the British colony on the coast with promises of riches as servants and laborers, and they had acquired undesirable habits from the white men. She requested that the British instruct all Asante citizens residing in the Colony to return to Asante in order to "make Asante as it was in the olden days." In exchange, the Asante would affirm its policy of "peace, trade and open roads." In 1894 she led the more traditional councillors among the West African peoples in insisting that the British desist from interfering with their system of domestic slavery, which was integral to the Asante social structure and national plantation economy. The British colonial governor, Maxwell, believed that the arrest and detention of the asantehene would precipitate the collapse of the Asante government. To that end, in 1890,

the British government surrounded the town of Kumase and, in a surprise coup, took Yaa Akyaa, her son, and others in charge under British "protection." Two days later they were formally arrested. Her son, who was wrongly accused of killing people but knew that he would be proven innocent, allowed himself to be taken away without struggle, providing that the queen mother would go with him. She agreed to go. The two told the British and their people that there was no need to fight; they did not want their nation destroyed. The Asante people, instructed to be proud and not to react, nevertheless all cried. As one Asante wrote, "Kumase was a sea of tears." Agyeman told his people that he and Yaa Akyaa would return, so, in the words of another reporter, "We went to our villages quietly and waited." They would wait for a very long time, for in 1896 the two leaders, never tried but only held in captivity, were deported to Sierra Leone; in 1900 they were exiled to the remote Seychelles Islands. Ironically, Agyeman's and Yaa Akyaa's submission failed to save the sovereignty of the Asante kingdom. Agyeman was not allowed to return (as a "private citizen") until 1924; apparently Yaa Akyaa died on Seychelles in the interim. On the surface, the British succeeded in "neutralizing" the Asante nation, but in the villages the chant never ceased: "This nation is not yours, / It belongs to Nana Yaa, / This nation is not yours! / It belongs to Yaa Akyaa. / This nation is not your nation! / It belongs to Nana Prempe. / Nana Prempe is away, and you are occupying his office."[1]

Yaa Asantewaa
Edwesohemaa, queen mother of the Edweso tribe of the Asante and symbolic leader of the Asante War for Independence (1900–1901)

Yaa Asantewaa was born ca. 1850 and had been elected *edwesohemaa,* or queen mother, of the Edweso tribe. Following the arrest by the British of her son, Edwesohene (chief of the Edweso) Kwasi Afrane, the queen mother and two others ran the local administration. The Edweso was one tribe of the Asante empire. The British reported that under the new leaders, "Edweso appears to be flourishing." Following the British arrest in 1896 of Asantehene Agyeman Prempe and Asantehemaa Yaa Akyaa, the people hid the Golden Stool, symbol of Asante political sovereignty. The British levied stiff taxes to help recoup the cost of their campaigns against the Asante, and to meet costs of building a fort to house British troops and to build the resident's office and home. In addition, the Europeans had taken over the state-owned "secret" gold mines, which had provided the capital for operating the Asante government. By 1897, 13 Basel and 6 Wesleyan missionary schools had been established. But soon the missionaries were interfering in local political and domestic affairs, intruding upon the private lives of the citizens. These conditions and more led to widespread Asante unrest which the British sought to quell one way or another. The British governor then made the shocking demand that the Asante surrender the Golden Stool, and he sent a military attache, Capt. C. H. Armitage, to force the people to tell him where the stool was hidden. Armitage went to Edweso and confronted Yaa Asantewaa, but the edwesohemaa told him that she did not have the Golden Stool. The captain went from village to village demanding the stool. At the village of Bare, Armitage lost patience. By one citizen's account, when the people of Bare learned that Armitage was on the way, they left the village, leaving only the children on the streets. The children told the captain their fathers were gone hunting, and that they knew nothing about the Golden Stool. The captain ordered the children beaten, and the elderly came out of hiding to defend the children. The citizens were bound hand and foot and beaten. This brutality sparked the beginning of the Yaa Asantewaa War for Independence, so named because the outraged queen mother of the Edweso, described as feisty and gallant, inspired and directed it. But the Asante were no match for the British, who not only killed the citizens, but plundered and pillaged their farms and plantations and confiscated their lands so that the Asante were left completely dependent upon their victors for survival. The queen mother and her close companions were deported as political prisoners, along with the exiled Asantehene

Agyeman and the queen mother of Asante, Yaa Akyaa, to the Seychelles Islands.[2]

Yelena Glinskaya (or Helen Glinski)
Grand Princess, regent of Russia (1533–1538)

She was born ca. 1506 of a noble Tatar family, the daughter of Prince Michael Glinski, a converted Orthodox Lithuanian magnate who, during a dispute between contenders for the Polish-Lithuanian throne (Alexander I and Sigismund I), had switched sides, deserted, and emigrated to Russia. In ca. 1529 she became the second wife of Grand Prince Vasily III (Basil III), ruler of Russia from 1505 to 1533. Their first son, born in 1530, became Ivan IV (later called the Terrible), ruler of Russia at the age of three. Grand Princess Yelena ruled in Ivan's name with her favorite, Ivan Ovchina-Telepnev-Oblensky, acting as advisor, sparking unfounded rumors that Ivan was his son. Her late husband Basil III had engaged in territorial disputes with Poland-Lithuania without receiving asked-for assistance of the Hapsburgs. The Russians had made substantial gain in that ten-year conflict, acquiring the key city of Smolensk in 1514. In 1533 Yelena sent embassies both to Ferdinand I, king of both Hungary and Bohemia, and his brother, Holy Roman Emperor Charles V, hoping to bolster friendship with the Hapsburgs in case of another conflict with Poland-Lithuania. The dispute did flare again over the ownership of Smolensk: in 1534–1536 another war resulted in no gain for the Poles. Russia was able to keep possession of Smolensk. Meanwhile, the boyars families of Sujskij and Belskij fought among themselves for the privilege of overpowering Yelena's regency and assuming it themselves. In 1538 Yelena died of poisoning, allegedly at the provocation of the boyars. Ivan IV imprisoned Yelena's advisor Oblensky and his sister, although he did not formally accuse them of implementing the murder plot.[3]

Ye-lü Shih (also called Pu-su-wan)
Regent of Kara-Khitai (1163–1178)

The Kara-Khitai empire was located in Eastern Turkestan. Ye-lü Shih was born Pu-su-wan

(Chinese transcription), a member of a pagan Mongol line ruling in Muslim Turkic territory. She was the daughter of Ye-lü Ta-shih who ruled ca. 1130 to 1142 and his wife Ta-pu-yen. Upon the death of the king in 1142 the aggressive Queen Ta-pu-yen served as regent until their son, Ye-lü Yi-lie, reached majority. When he died in 1163, Pu-su-wan assumed the regency on behalf of her nephew, Ye-lü Che-lu-ku, son of her late brother. Although as ruler Pu-su-wan was called Ye-lü Shih, for the sake of clarity she will be referred to here by her birth name. During her reign, her army entered Khurasan to plunder Balkh (1165). In 1172 she took sides in the dispute of a neighbor, the Khwarizmian Empire. Two sons of the late shah vied for the throne. The loser, Takash, sought refuge in her country. She charged her husband with the task of leading an army into Kwarizmia to reinstate Takash and drive out his brother, Sultan-shah. Once this was accomplished, she demanded payment of tribute under extremely exacting conditions. When Takash rebelled, she reversed her policy and attempted to reinstate Sultan-shah. Although the Kara-Khitai were unable to accomplish this, they lent him an army with which he conquered another land, Khurasan (1181). When Ye-lü Che-lu-ku reached his majority in 1178, Pu-su-wan retired.[4]

Yolanda (or Isabella II or Yolanta)
Titular queen of Jerusalem (1212–1228)

She was born in 1212, the daughter of hereditary Queen Maria La Marquise, regent from 1205 to 1212, and King John of Brienne, ruler from 1210 to 1225. Queen Maria died the year Yolanda was born, and Yolanda (usually called Isabella, but here referred to as Yolanda to lessen confusion with other Isabellas) inherited the throne. Her father, who then had no legal right to govern except as regent, married Princess Stephanie of Armenia (1114).

Stephanie proved to be a malevolent stepmother. She died in 1219, reportedly as a result of a severe beating at the hands of her husband for having tried to poison Yolanda. In 1225 the young queen was sent off to Italy to become the

second wife of Holy Roman Emperor Frederick II. On her way to Italy, she stopped in Cyprus to see her aunt, Queen Alice, for the last time. Both queens and their courts were in tears as Yolanda said good-bye to her "sweet land of Syria" that she would never see again. Frederick was 31 and she was 14. Although he was handsome and intelligent, he was also said to be cruel, sly, selfish, and given to erotic conduct of the basest sort. He sent his new wife to a harem that he kept at Palermo, where she was obliged to live in seclusion. In 1228, at the age of 16, she gave birth to a son, Conrad; having given the emperor his heir, she died six days later, never having ruled the kingdom that had been rightfully hers all her short life.[5]

Yolande
Empress, regent of Latin Empire (1217–1219)

Yolande was the wife of Peter of Courtenay, emperor in name only of Constantinople from 1216 to 1217. She was the sister of both Baldwin I (formerly Count Baldwin IX of Flanders and Hainault), Latin emperor from 1204 to 1205, and Henry I, Latin emperor from 1205 to 1216. Yolande and Peter had three children: Marie, who married Theodore Lascaris; Robert, who ruled from 1219 to 1228; and Baldwin II, who ruled from 1228 to 1261. Her husband Peter was in Europe when his brother-in-law Henry died, and he set out for Rome where the pope crowned him emperor. He was then on his way from Durazzo to Thessalonica when he was captured by Theodore Dukas of Eprius (1217). He died in captivity in 1218, never having ruled a single day. Yolande, who was the legal heir, became regent for her feeble son Robert. She died prematurely in 1219.[6]

Yolande de Bourgogne
Countess, ruler of Nevers (1266–1296)

She was the daughter of Countess Mahaut II de Bourbon and Eudes de Bourgogne. She inherited the rule of Nevers when her mother died in 1266. She first married Jean Tristan de France, count of Valois; after his death, she married

Zabel (also called Isabella)
Queen, ruler of Lesser (Little) Armenia
(Cicilia) (1219–1269)

Little Armenia was located in what is now modern-day Turkey. Zabel was born in 1715, the younger daughter of Leo II the Great, ruler of Armenia from 1198 to 1219, and his second wife, Princess Sibylla of Cyprus and Jerusalem. Leo had no sons, and his older daughter Stephanie was the wife of John of Brienne, king of Jerusalem. On his deathbed (1219), he named Zabel his successor under the regency of Baron Constantine of Lambron. Since King Leo had earlier promised the succession to his niece Alice Roupen, married to Raymond of Antioch, Raymond put in a claim on behalf of his Armenian wife and their infant son. But his wife died, reputedly because of a battering he inflicted, and soon afterward the baby died as well. Raymond then had no further legal claim on the throne.

Zabel first married Philip of Antioch, but he did not comply with the marriage agreement: He refused, although already excommunicated by the Catholic Church, to embrace the separated Armenian Church as his father Bohemond IV had promised he would do. In addition, he spent as much time in Antioch as possible. In 1224, as he set out again from Armenia for Antioch, he was arrested at Sis, where he was poisoned a few months later. Zabel, brokenhearted, fled to Seleucia. The Hospitallers, or Templars, had openly favored the heretical Armenian; to avoid the shame of surrendering Zabel in person, they handed the whole town over to the regent Constantine. Zabel was then forced to marry Constantine's son Hethoum (Hayton) I of Lambron, although for many years she refused to live with him. Finally she relented, and in 1226 the two were crowned together. Bohemond IV, still seething over the murder of his son Philip at the hands of Constantine, tried vainly to persuade the pope to arrange a divorce between Zabel and Hethoum so as to deprive Hethoum of the right to rule. The couple had at least five children: Leo III, who became king of Armenia on his mother's death in 1269; Thoros; Sibylla, who married Prince Bohemond VI of Antioch; Euphemia, who married John of Sidon; and Maria, who married Guy of Ibelin. In 1254–1255 Hethoum, an ally of the Mongols, journeyed to Karakorum and back by way of Samarkaland and Persia. His travels were chronicled by Kirakos Gandzaketse in an account that provides some of the best source material on early Mongolian life and culture.[1]

Zabibi
Queen, ruler of an Arabian state
(ca. 738 B.C.)

In ancient Mesopotamia the term ''queen'' was applied only to goddesses and to those queens of Arabia who served as rulers. If a king were ruling, both his spouse and his mother were also politically important. In 738 B.C. Samal of northern Syria formed a coalition of principalities to obstruct the advance of King Tiglath-pileser III of the New Assyrian Empire. The coalition was defeated, and Tiglath-pileser exacted tribute from rulers of all the important states of Syria-Palentine, including Menaham of Israel and Rezin of Damascus. Queen Zabel was among those Assyrian rulers required to send him tribute.[2]

Zauditu (also called Judith or Waizero)
Empress, titular ruler of Ethiopia
(1916–1930)

Zauditu was the daughter of Emperor Menelik II, ruler of Ethiopia from 1889 to 1913. Menelik had named his grandson, Lij Iyasu, as his heir, but the heir apparent refused to ready himself for the position. He refused all schooling after the age of 15 and, five years later, announced his conversion to Islam (1916). As he had not yet been crowned, the Ethiopian Church and the local chiefs removed him and named Menelik's daughter Zauditu as empress, with Ras Tafari as her regent and heir. Zauditu married Ras Gugsa. Her reign was marked by turmoil between the conservative pro-Church group, led by war minister Hapta Giorgis, and the liberal, pro-Western group, led by Ras Tafari. In 1923 Ethiopia joined the League of Nations, which later authorized an Ethiopian protest against Britain's plan for division. In 1924 slavery was abolished in Ethiopia. Eventually the country regained access to the sea that had been lost along both the Red Sea coast and the Gulf of Aden. Ras Tafari, not daring to usurp the throne from the empress, named himself ''king'' after the death of his old rival Giorgis (1928), but early the next year, Zauditu's husband Ras Gugsa organized a revolt, which was squelched by Ras Tafari's forces with great

effort. Empress Zauditu died in 1930, and Ras Tafari was immediately crowned emperor with the title of Haile Selassi I.[3]

Zenobia
Queen, ruler of Palmyra, Syria
(A.D. 266–272)

She was born Bat Zabbai, or Septima Zenobia. Arabians knew her as Az-Zabba. She became the second wife of King Odaenathus, ruler of Palmyra for Rome ca. A.D. 260 to 266. She bore three sons: Wahballat or Vaballath, Herennianus, and Timolaus. She reputedly instigated the murder of her husband and his heir by his first wife, and then became regent for her own son, ruling extremely effectively. Not content to remain under Roman cliency, she decided to extend her power. In 269–270, she moved into Egypt and then occupied most of Asia Minor. In 271 she had her son proclaimed augustus. Roman Emperor Aurelian, who had not taken her seriously up until her move into Egypt, mar-

Queen Zenobia. The Granger Collection, New York.

shalled his considerable forces and marched against her. He recovered Egypt and Asia Minor, then besieged Palmyra itself. After its surrender, Zenobia and her two younger sons were taken back to Rome and exhibited in Aurelian's triumphal procession (272 or 274). Wahballat's fate is unknown; Zenobia was granted a pension. She later married a Roman senator and lived into old age in Italy.[4]

Zoë

Empress of Byzantine Empire (1028–1050)

She was born in A.D. 980, the middle daughter of King Constantine VIII, ruler of Byzantium from 963 to 1028, and his wife Helena of Alypius. Psellus described Zoë as "very regal in her ways, a woman of great beauty, most imposing in her manner, and commanding respect." As her pock-faced older sister Eudocia had entered a nunnery, Zoë was named by her dying father to be married to Romanus III. The two inherited the reign when Constantine died in 1028, and Zoë exiled her other sister to a nunnery, probably at Romanus' suggestion. Romanus immediately lost interest in Zoë, even keeping her short of money. She took as her lover a peasant's son, handsome Michael IV, and together they conspired to murder Romanus in his bath. Zoë claimed the right to rule after Romanus' death, not for herself but for her adored Michael, whom she married and made emperor. Although Michael treated her badly, confining her to the women's quarters, he nevertheless convinced her to adopt his nephew, Michael V, as his successor. When Michael IV died in 1042, Michael V became ruler, but to avoid the possibility of a usurpation of his power, he made the mistake of exiling the aging Zoë to the island of Prinkipo. Indignation at the treatment of the rightful empress swept through the land, and mobs quickly assembled to protest her exile. Michael quickly brought Zoë back and made a great show of his regard for her, but it was of no avail: the mob tracked him down in a local church and gouged his eyes out after he had been forced to watch as the same treatment was given to his minister. Meanwhile, the youngest sister Theodora had been brought back by another faction, which had proclaimed her queen, while across town an-

Empress Zoë. Byzantine Visual Resources, Dumbarton Oaks, Washington, DC.

other crowd had pledged loyalty to Zoë. Eventually Zoë made the first move of reconciliation, welcoming her sister back with an embrace. The sisters ruled jointly for a while, although Theodora bowed to her older sister's seniority and, if Psellus was correct, did not show the slightest rancor about having spent the best years of her life in a nunnery. Then in 1042 Zoë, ever warm-blooded and impulsive, seized power again by marrying, at the age of 64, the 42-year-old senator, Constantine Monomachus, who ruled with her as Constantine IX. More tolerant with the passing of years, aware that her own charms had faded, Zoë ignored her husband's open affair with Sclerina, a niece of his second wife. He gave his mistress the title of Sebaste, and she took her place beside Zoë and Theodora at all court ceremonies. Zoë died in 1050, and when her husband died three years later, her sister Theodora at last ruled alone.[5]

Notes

Introduction

1. Robert Briffault, *The Mothers* (New York: The Macmillan Co., 1931), 279.

2. John G. Jackson, *Introduction to African Civilizations* (Secaucus: The Citadel Press, 1970), 95; Balmer, W. T., *A History of the Akan Peoples of the Gold Coast* (New York: Negro Universities Press, 1969), 176–177.

3. K. Madhu Panikkar, *The Serpent and the Crescent, A History of the Negro Empires of West Africa* (Bombay: Asia Publishing House, 1963), 327.

4. J. W. Nyakatura, *Anatomy of an African Kingdom, A History of Bunyoro-Kitara* (Garden City, NY: Anchor/Doubleday, 1973), 191; Roland Oliver, and J. D. Fage, *A Short History of Africa* (Harmondsworth, Middlesex: Penguin Books, 1970), 45, 129.

5. Panikkar, *The Serpent and the Crescent,* 162.

6. Jomo Kenyatta, *Facing Mount Kenya* (New York: Vintage Books, 1965), 8.

7. Wilfred Cartey and Martin Kilson, eds., *The African Reader: Independent Africa.* (New York: Vintage Books, 1970), 315.

8. "The Defiance of Women." *Sechaba* 1 (9 August 1967). For a general orientation on Africa, see also E. Jefferson Murphy, *Understanding Africa* (New York: Thomas Y. Crowell, 1969).

9. Hermann Kinder and Werner Hilgemann, *The Anchor Atlas of World History,* 2 vols., trans. Ernest A. Menze (Garden City, NY: Anchor/Doubleday, 1974), vol. 1, 33.

10. Ibid., 35.

11. Herodotus, *The Histories*, trans. Aubrey de Sélincourt (New York: Viking Penguin, 1988), 619.

12. Sir John Glubb, *A Short History of the Arab People* (New York: Dorset Press, 1969), 204.

13. Romila Thapar, *A History of India* (London: Penguin Books, Ltd., 1987), vol. 1, 269.

14. Ann Elizabeth Mayer, "Benazir Bhutto and Islamic Law," *The Christian Science Monitor* (6 February 1989), 18.

15. Thapar, *A History of India,* vol. 1, 103.

16. John Pemble, *The Raj, the Indian Mutiny, and the Kingdom of Oudh 1801–1859* (Rutherford: Fairleigh Dickinson University Press, 1977), 237.

17. Percival Spear, *A History of India* (London: Penguin Books, Ltd., 1987), vol. 2, 151.

18. Ian Buruna, "A Nation Divided," *The New York Times Magazine* (15 January 1989), 26–40, particularly 29.

19. Sheila Tefft, "Restlessness among Pakistan's Youth," *The Christian Science Monitor* (3 March 1989), 4.

20. Glubb, *A Short History of the Arab People,* 284.

21. Buruna, "A Nation Divided," 27–28.

22. Basil Gray, ed., *The Arts of India* (Ithaca: Cornell University Press, 1981), 77.

23. Glubb, *A Short History of the Arab People,* 46.

24. René Grousset, *The Empire of the Steppes, a History of Central Asia,* trans. Naomi Walford (New Brunswick: Rutgers University Press, 1970), 129.

25. A. T. Olmstead, *History of the Persian Em-*

pire (Chicago: The University of Chicago Press, 1948), 461.

26. Grousset, *The Empire of the Steppes,* 249.

27. Ibid., 356–357.

28. W. E. Garrett, ''Pagan, on the Road to Mandalay,'' *National Geographic,* 139 (March 1971): 343–365, especially 362.

29. Kinder, et al., *Anchor Atlas of World History,* vol. 1, 33.

30. Dennis Bloodworth and Ching Ping Bloodworth, *The Chinese Machiavelli, 3000 Years of Chinese Statecraft* (New York: Farrar, Straus and Giroux, Inc., 1976), 214–215.

31. Dennis Bloodworth, *The Chinese Looking Glass* (New York: Farrar, Straus and Giroux, 1967), 77–78.

32. Edwin O. Reischauer and John K. Fairbank, *East Asia: The Great Tradition* (Boston: Houghton Mifflin, 1958, 1960), 224–225.

33. Ibid., 556.

34. Peter Tompkins, *Mysteries of the Mexican Pyramids* (New York: Harper & Row, 1976), 165–175.

35. Edward Weyer, Jr., *Primitive Peoples Today* (Garden City, NY: Dolphin/Doubleday, n.d.), 143–158.

1. N. G. L. Hammond, *A History of Greece to 322 B.C.* (Oxford: Clarendon Press, 1986), 607, 621; A. T. Olmstead, *History of the Persian Empire* (Chicago: University of Chicago Press, 1948), 436, 483, 487, 499.

2. Steven Runciman, *A History of the Crusades,* 3 vols. (Cambridge: Cambridge University Press, 1952, 1987), vol. 2, *The Kingdom of Jerusalem and the Frankish East,* 20, 48, 78; Friedrich Heer, *The Medieval World,* trans. Janet Sondheimer (New York: Mentor/NAL, 1962), 124.

3. C. W. Previté-Orton, *The Shorter Cambridge Medieval History,* 2 vols. (Cambridge: Cambridge University Press, 1952, 1982), vol. 1, *The Later Roman Empire to the Twelfth Century,* 436–437; Hermann Kinder and Werner Hilgemann, *Atlas of World History,* trans. Ernest A. Menze (Garden City, NJ: Anchor/Doubleday, 1982), vol. 1, 143.

4. Runciman, *History of the Crusades,* 102–105, 199, 207, 251–252.

5. Edward E. Egan, Constance B. Hintz, and L. F. Wise, *Kings, Rulers and Statesmen* (New York: Sterling Publishing Company, 1976), 162.

6. T. K. Derry, *A History of Scandinavia* (Minneapolis: University of Minneapolis Press, 1979), 39; William L. Langer, ed., *World History* (Boston: Houghton Mifflin Company, 1940, 1980), 182–183.

7. Previté-Orton, *The Shorter Cambridge,* vol.

1, 385–389; Bernard Grun, *The Timetables of History* (New York: Simon and Schuster, 1979), 913.

8. Thomas J. Lewin, *Asante before the British* (Lawrence, KS: Regents Press of Kansas, 1978), 49, 74, 82; W. T. Balmer, *A History of the Akan Peoples* (New York: Atlantis Press, 1925), 167.

9. Egan et al., *Kings, Rulers, and Statesmen,* 159.

10. J. D. Mackie, *A History of Scotland* (Harmondsworth, Middlesex: Penguin Books, 1984), 80; Jane Porter, *The Scottish Chiefs* (New York: A. L. Burt Company, 1831).

11. Previté-Orton, *The Shorter Cambridge,* vol. 1, 460.

12. Egan et al., *Kings, Rulers, and Statesmen,* 153.

13. *The Cambridge Ancient History,* 3d ed., 2 vols. (Cambridge: Cambridge University Press, 1970–1971), vol. 1, 40, 62.

14. J. E. Manchip White, *Ancient Egypt* (New York: Dover Publications, 1970), 164–165.

15. K. Madhu Panikkar, *The Serpent and the Crescent: A History of the Negro Empires of West Africa* (Bombay: Asia Publishing House, 1963), 104.

16. John M. Thompson, *Revolutionary Russia, 1917* (New York: Charles Scribner's Sons, 1981), 14–23.

17. Jean Cooke, Ann Kramer, and Theodore Rowland-Entwistle, *History's Timeline* (New York: Crescent Books, 1981), 33; Langer, *World History,* 94.

18. Runciman, *History of the Crusades,* vol. 2, 176–177, 183–184, 188–190, 198–200.

19. The Associated Press, Dakar Senegal, ''Mystery Finally Solved: Rebellious Queen Sitoe Succumbs to Scurvy,'' *Houston Post* (27 October 1983): W 3.

20. Friedrich Heer, *The Medieval World* (New York: Mentor/NAL, 1962), 318.

21. Edward Gibbon, *The Decline and Fall of the Roman Empire* (Chicago: Encyclopedia Britannica, 1952), vol. 1, 646, 887; vol. 2, 14–16; Previté-Orton, *The Shorter Cambridge,* vol. 1, 139–140, 190.

22. Walter A. Fairservis, Jr., *The Ancient Kingdoms of the Nile* (New York: Mentor/NAL, 1962), 193; S. A. Cooke, F. E. Adcock, and M. P. Charlesworth, *The Cambridge Ancient History,* vol. 10 (London: Cambridge University Press, 1971), 42, 243, 778; Alvin M. Josephy, *The Horizon History of Africa* (New York: American Heritage Publishing Co., 1971), 61–63.

23. Panikkar, *The Serpent and the Crescent,* 113–114, 273.

24. Robert B. Asprey, *Frederick the Great: The Magnificent Enigma* (New York: Ticknor and Fields, 1986), 119, 160; Langer, *World History,* 515–516.

25. George Ostrogorsky, *History of the Byzantine*

State (New Brunswick, NJ: Rutgers University Press, 1969), 376.

26. Asprey, *Frederick the Great*, 160, 230, 275.

27. Ostrogorsky, *History of the Byzantine State*, 510, 518, 520, 526, 535.

28. Ibid., 508, 534, 579, 581.

29. Ibid., 489, 495, 519, 579, 581.

30. Egan et al., *Kings, Rulers and Statesmen*, 154; Langer, *World History*, 409–410.

31. Margaret Hodges, *Lady Queen Anne* (New York: Farrar, Straus and Giroux, 1969); J. P. Kenyon, *The Stuarts* (Glasgow: William Collins Sons and Co., 1970), 186–207; M. E. Hudson and Mary Clark, *Crown of a Thousand Years* (New York: Crown Publishing, 1978), 114–117.

32. Will Durant and Ariel Durant, *The Story of Civilization*, Part 8, *The Age of Louis XIV* (New York: Simon and Schuster, 1960), 3–45; Robert Harding, *Anatomy of a Power Elite* (New Haven, CT: Yale University Press, 1978), 127, 221.

33. Langer, *World History*, 475–476.

34. Previté-Orton, *The Shorter Cambridge*, vol. 2, 484.

35. Egan et al., *Kings, Rulers and Statesmen*, 151.

36. H. W. Codrington, *A Short History of Ceylon*, (Cambridge: Cambridge University Press, 1947); Egan et al., *Kings, Rulers and Statesmen*, 438.

37. Howard Mumford Jones, *The Literature of Virginia in the Seventeenth Century* (Charlottesville, VA: University of Virginia Press, 1968), 19–20.

38. Lucy Komisar, *Corazon Aquino: The Story of a Revolution* (New York: George Braziller, 1987).

39. Egan et al., *Kings, Rulers and Statesmen*, 156; Langer, *World History*, 247.

40. Diana Bowder, *Who Was Who in the Greek World* (New York: Washington Square Press, 1984), 101–102; Langer, *World History*, 96.

41. Hammond, *History of Greece*, 239; Olmstead, *History of the Persian Empire*, 253, 269, 433–434; Herodotus, *The Histories*, trans. Aubrey de Sélincourt (New York: Penguin Books, 1954, 1988), 8, 11, 14, 474, 545–546, 552–558; Bowder, *Who Was Who in the Greek World*, 106.

42. Olmstead, *History of the Persian Empire*, 426, 429, 432–435; Bowder, *Who Was Who in the Greek World*, 299–300; Will Durant, *The Story of Civilization*, vol. 2, *The Life of Greece* (New York: Simon and Schuster, 1939, 1966), 586, 593.

43. Frank R. Donovan, *The Vikings* (New York: American Heritage Publishing Co., 1964), 89; David Wilson, *The Vikings and Their Origins* (London: Thames and Hudson, 1970), 57, 122.

44. Langer, *World History*, 45; G. Ernest Wright, *Biblical Archaeology* (Philadelphia: Westminster Press, 1957), 162; Robert Dick Wilson, *A Scientific Investigation of the Old Testament*, revised by Edward J. Young (Chicago: Moody Press, 1959), 71.

45. Michael and Aubine Kirtley, "The Ivory Coast, African Success Story," *National Geographic* (July 1982): 94–125.

1. Merrill C. Tenney, ed., *Pictorial Bible Dictionary* (Nashville: Southwestern Company, 1976), 701.

2. Elise Bolding, *The Underside of History: A View of Women through Time* (Boulder: Westview Press, 1976), 396.

3. Maureen Seneviratne, *Sirimavo Bandaranaike: The World's First Woman Prime Minister* (Sri Lanka: Colombo, 1975); "Sri Lanka's Racial Riots Could Cost It Dearly," *U.S. News & World Report* (8 August 1983): 8.

4. C. W. Previté-Orton, *The Shorter Cambridge Medieval History*, 2 vols. (Cambridge: Cambridge University Press, 1952, 1982), vol. 1, *The Later Roman Empire to the Twelfth Century*, 457; William L. Langer, ed., *World History* (Boston: Houghton Mifflin Company, 1940, 1980), 232.

5. Langer, *World History*, 306.

6. Edward E. Egan, Constance B. Hintz, and L. F. Wise, *Kings, Rulers and Statesmen* (New York: Sterling Pblishing Company, 1976), 153.

7. Langer, *World History*, 475; Bart McDowell, "The Dutch Touch," *National Geographic* 170 (October 1986): 500–525.

8. K. Madhu Panikker, *The Serpent and the Crescent: A History of the Negro Empires of West Aftica* (Bombay: Asia Publishing House, 1963), 60.

9. Egan et al., *Kings, Rulers and Statesmen*, 125; Diana Bowden, ed., *Who Was Who in the Greek World* (Ithaca, NY: Cornell University Press, 1982), 405–406.

10. Bowden, *Who Was Who in the Greek World*, 406; John Anthony West, *The Traveler's Key to Ancient Egypt* (New York: Alfred A. Knopf, 1985), 428–429, 446.

11. Benazir Bhutto, *Daughter of Destiny* (New York: Simon and Schuster, 1989); or see: Benazir Bhutto, *Daughter of the East* (London: Hamish Hamilton, 1988); Tariq Ali, "Dynasty's Daughter," *Interview* (February 1989): 68–71, 124; Ann Elizabeth Mayer, "Benazir Bhutto and Islamic Law" *Christian Science Monitor* (6 February 1989): 18; James Brody, "In Step with David Frost," *Parade* (18 February 1989): 18.

12. Denis Mack Smith, *A History of Sicily*, 2 vols. (New York: Dorset Press, 1968), vol. 1, *Medieval Sicily*, 91–92; Langer, *World History*, 306.

13. Langer, *World History*, 321.

14. Egan et al., *Kings, Rulers and Statesmen*, 430.

15. Steven Runciman, *A History of the Crusades*, 3 vols. (Cambridge: Cambridge University Press,

1952, 1987), vol. 3, 256, 274, 279–280; Friedrich Heer, *The Medieval World* (New York: Mentor/ NAL, 1962), 319.

16. Langer, *World History,* 322.

17. Rene Grousset, *The Empire of the Steppes: A History of Central Asia,* trans. Naomi Walford (New Brunswick, NJ: Rutgers University Press, 1970), 397.

18. Charles Duff, *England and the English* (New York: G. P. Putnam's Sons, 1955), 51, 52, 63, 232; Jean Markdale, *Women of the Celts,* trans. A. Mygind et al. (Rochester, VT: Inner Traditions International, 1986), 27, 32, 253; Langer, *World History,* 120, 179.

19. Nora Chadwick, *The Celts* (Harmondsworth, Middlesex: Penguin Books, 1976), 169; Duff, *England and the English,* 42.

20. Gregory of Tours, *The History of the Franks,* trans. Lewis Thorpe (Harmondsworth, Middlesex: Penguin Books, 1974), 196, 221–222, 233, 247, 251, 254–256, 268, 272, 275, 279, 305, 370, 383, 401–402, 417, 426, 437, 453, 456–458, 480–481, 488–489, 491–492, 502–503, 505, 507, 514–515, 518, 524–526, 578; Richard E. Sullivan, *Heirs of the Roman Empire* (Ithaca, NY: Cornell University Press, 1960), 39–40.

21. *International Who's Who, 1987–1988* (London: Europa Publishing, 1987), 200; "Women in Politics," *World Press Review* (March 1988): 53.

1. C. Merrill Tenney, *Pictorial Bible Dictionary* (Nashville: Southwestern Company, 1976), 143; Walter A. Fairservis, Jr., *The Ancient Kingdoms of the Nile* (New York: Mentor/NAL, 1962), 193.

2. Nora Chadwick, *The Celts* (Harmondsworth, Middlesex: Penguin Books, 1976), 65; Henri Hubert, *The Greatness and Decline of the Celts* (New York: Arno Press, 1980), 159; Jean Markdale, *Women of the Celts,* trans. A. Mygind et al. (Rochester, VT: Inner Traditions International, 1986), 32; Ward Rutherford, *Celtic Mythology* (Wellingborough, Northamptonshire: Aquarian Press, 1987), 31.

3. Edward E. Egan, Constance B. Hintz, and L. F. Wise, *Kings, Rulers and Statesmen* (New York: Sterling Publishing Company, 1976), 430.

4. Ernst Breisach, *Caterina Sforza: A Renaissance Virago* (Chicago: University of Chicago Press, 1967); Christopher Hare, *The Most Illustrious Ladies of the Italian Renaissance* (Williamstown, MA: Corner House Publishers, 1972), 36, 135, 229–256.

5. Egan et al., *Kings, Rulers and Statesmen,* 162.

6. Ibid., 404.

7. William L. Langer, ed., *World History* (Boston: Houghton Mifflin Company, 1940, 1980), 279.

8. Hugh R. Williamson, *Catherine de' Medici* (New York: Viking Press, 1973).

9. Garrett Mattingly, *Catherine of Aragon* (Cambridge: Cambridge University Press, 1942); A. R. Myers, *England in the Late Middle Ages* (Harmondsworth, Middlesex: Penguin Books, 1952), 205, 237; M. E. Hudson and Mary Clark, *Crown of a Thousand Years* (New York: Crown Publishing, 1978), 77, 78; Melveena McKendrick, *Ferdinand and Isabella* (New York: American Heritage Publishing Co., 1968), 99, 100, 134, 140.

10. J. P. Kenyon, *The Stuarts* (Glasgow: William Collins Sons and Co., 1970), 100–143; Hudson, *Crown of a Thousand Years,* 105.

11. Langer, *World History,* 282; George Ostrogorsky, *History of the Byzantine State,* 497, 508, 510.

12. Zoe Oldenbourg, *Catherine the Great* (New York: Pantheon Books, 1965); Robert Coughlan, *Elizabeth and Catherine* (New York: G. P. Putnam's Sons, 1974); Will Durant and Ariel Durant, *The Age of Voltaire* (New York: Simon and Schuster, 1965), 216, 360, 477, 510, 516, 575, 606, 644, 646, 665, 675, 679, 730, 733, 744, 774, 776, 779, 785.

13. Charles Moritz, ed., *Current Biography Yearbook, 1986* (New York: H. W. Wilson Co., 1986), 88–91; *International Who's Who, 1987–1988* (London: Europa Publishing, 1987), 256; Roberta Okey, "Trekking Nature's Terrarium," *Americas* (Sept./Oct. 1987): 8–13; Greg Walter, "Interview," *People* (November 1983): 20, 46; Charles L. Sanders, "Interview," *Ebony* (January 1981): 16; *Newsday* (April 1982): 4.

14. Newcomer, James, *The Grand Duchy of Luxembourg* (Lanham, MD: University Press of America, 1984), 16; Langer, *World History,* 986, 1180, 1198; Egan et al., *Kings, Rulers and Statesmen,* 297.

15. Langer, *World History,* 279.

16. W. Scott Morton, *China: Its History and Culture* (New York: McGraw-Hill, 1982), 57; Edwin O. Reischauer and John K. Fairbank, *East Asia: The Great Tradition* (Boston: Houghton Mifflin Company, 1960), 117; Kenneth Scott Latourette, *The Chinese: Their History and Culture* (New York: Macmillan, 1934); Langer, *World History,* 146.

17. Georgina Masson, *Queen Christina* (New York: Farrar, Straus and Giroux, 1969); T. K. Derry, *A History of Scandinavia* (Minneapolis: University of Minnesota Press, 1979), 120, 128–131; Egan et al., *Kings, Rulers and Statesmen,* 449; Hugh Trevor-Roper, *The Golden Age of Europe* (New York: Bonanza/Crown, 1987), 32, 126, 140, 144, 174.

18. Langer, *World History,* 426, 473, 494.

19. Marina Warner, *The Dragon Empress: Life and Times of Tz'u-hsi (1835–1908)* (New York: Atheneum Press, 1986); Morton, *China,* 168–175.

20. Egan et al., *Kings, Rulers and Statesmen,* 316.

21. Langer, *World History*, 97; John Anthony West, *The Traveler's Key to Ancient Egypt* (New York: Alfred A. Knopf, 1985), 26, 420.

22. Langer, *World History*, 97.

23. West, *The Traveler's Key*, 446.

24. Emil Ludwig, *Cleopatra* (New York: Viking Press, 1937); Plutarch, *Makers of Rome*, 271–352, 360–361; Edward Gibbon, *The Decline and Fall of the Roman Empire* (Chicago: Encyclopedia Britannica, 1952), vol. 1, 122, 125, 685, 818; vol. 2, 85; H. G. Wells, *Outline of History*, vol. 1. (Garden City, NJ: Garden City Books, Doubleday, 1949), 469, 472–474; West, *The Traveler's Key*, 24, 26–28, 405, 429.

25. Plutarch, *Makers of Rome*, trans. Ian Scott-Kilvert (Harmondsworth, Middlesex: Penguin Books, 1980), 348.

26. Langer, *World History*, 95.

27. Ibid., 97; Egan et al., *Kings, Rulers and Statesmen*, 125; West, *The Traveler's Key*, 428–429.

28. Denis Mack Smith, *A History of Sicily*, 2 vols. (New York: Dorset Press, 1968), vol. 1, *Medieval Sicily*, 44–45, 47, 51, 55; Sidney Painter, *The Rise of the Feudal Monarchies* (Ithaca, NJ: Cornell University Press, 1951), 114; Steven Runciman, *A History of the Crusades*, 3 vols. (Cambridge: Cambridge University Press, 1952, 1987), vol. 2, *The Kingdom of Jerusalem and the Frankish East*, 428; C. W. Previté-Orton, *The Shorter Cambridge Medieval History*, 2 vols. (Cambridge: Cambridge University Press, 1952, 1982), vol. 1, *The Later Roman Empire to the Twelfth Century*, 510, 605–615; George Ostrogorsky, *History of the Byzantine State* (New Brunswick, NJ: Rutgers University Press, 1969), 411–412; Langer, *World History*, 224–225.

29. Previté-Orton, *The Later Roman Empire*, 510, 557; Langer, *World History*, 228, 306, 313.

30. Runciman, *The Kingdom of Jerusalem*, 183–184, 198–200, 305–306, 330–333, 345–349, 352, 358–360; Egan et al., *Kings, Rulers and Statesmen*, 16.

1. Josephus Flavius, *Life and Works*, trans. William Whiston (Philadelphia: Winston Company, n.d.), 150; Edith Deen, *All the Women of the Bible* (New York: Harper and Brothers, 1955), 69–74; David Alexander and Patricia Alexander, eds., *Eerdman's Handbook to the Bible* (Berkhamsted, Herts, England: Lion Publishing Co., 1973), 219–222; J. I. Packer, Merrill C. Tenney, and William White, Jr., *The Bible Almanac* (Nashville: Thomas Nelson, 1980), 44–52, 204, 427, 429.

2. William L. Langer, ed., *World History* (Boston: Houghton Mifflin Company, 1940, 1980), 411.

3. Romila Thapar, *A History of India* (London: Penguin Books, 1987), vol. 1, 226.

4. Edward Gibbon, *The Decline and Fall of the Roman Empire* (Chicago: Encyclopedia Britannica, 1952), vol. 2, 279, endnote 160; Langer, *World History*, 48; Peter Tompkins, *Mysteries of the Mexican Pyramids* (New York: Harper & Row, 1976), 351; Mark P. O. Morford and Robert J. Lenardon, *Classical Mythology* (New York: Longman, 1977), 2f, 257, 261, 453, 455, 488.

5. Langer, *World History*, 275; Hermann Kinder and Werner Hilgemann, *Atlas of World History*, trans. Ernest A. Menze (Garden City, NJ: Anchor/Doubleday, 1982), vol. 1, 169; Jean Cooke, Ann Kramer, and Theodore Rowland-Entwistle, *History's Timeline* (New York: Crescent Books, 1981), 47, 61.

6. Bamber Gascoigne, *The Great Moghuls* (New York: Dorset Press, 1971), 88; Sachchinananda Bhahacharya, *A Dictionary of Indian History* (New York: George Braziller, 1967), 321–322; Langer, *World History*, 356–358, 569.

1. René Grousset, *The Empire of the Steppes: A History of Central Asia*, trans. Naomi Walford (New Brunswick, NJ: Rutgers University Press, 1970), 329.

2. Edward E. Egan, Constance B. Hintz, and L. F. Wise, *Kings, Rulers and Statesmen* (New York: Sterling Publishing Company, 1976), 123.

3. William L. Langer, ed., *World History* (Boston: Houghton Mifflin Company, 1940, 1980), 307; Egan et al., *Kings, Rulers and Statesmen*, 430.

4. William W. Kibler, ed., *Eleanor of Aquitaine: Patron and Politician* (Austin: University of Texas Press, 1976).

5. *Britannica Macropedia* (Chicago: Encyclopedia Britannica Press, 1983), vol. 16, 244–245. For a comprehensive study of the period, *see* Mary Delane, *Sardinia: The Undefeated Island* (London, 1968).

6. Egan et al., *Kings, Rulers and Statesmen*, 277; John J. Putnam, "Napoleon," *National Geographic* 161 (February 1982): 142–189, particularly 168.

7. Francis Dvornik, *The Slavs in European History and Civilization* (New Brunswick, NJ: Rutgers University Press, 1962), 234, 349, 436; Langer, *World History*, 337–339; Egan et al., *Kings, Rulers and Statesmen*, 229.

8. Paul Johnson, *Elizabeth I* (New York: Holt, Rinehart and Winston, 1974); Mary M. Luke, *Gloriana: The Years of Elizabeth I* (New York: Coward McCann and Geoghegan, 1973); Lacey Baldwin Smith, *Elizabeth Tudor: Portrait of a Queen* (Boston: Little Brown and Co., 1975).

9. Zoe Oldenbourg, *Catherine the Great* (New

York: Pantheon Books, 1965); Robert Coughlan, *Elizabeth and Catherine* (New York: G. P. Putnam's Sons, 1974);

10. M. E. Hudson and Mary Clark, *Crown of a Thousand Years* (New York: Crown Publishing, 1978), 148–150; "Throne Power," *World Press Review* (February 1988): 38; "Life in the Grand Style for Europe's Leaders," *U.S. News & World Report* (21 June 1982), 23.

11. Langer, *World History,* 406–407; Egan et al., *Kings, Rulers and Statesmen,* 297.

12. Egan et al., *Kings, Rulers and Statesmen,* 338–339; Dvornik, *The Slavs in European History,* 48, 82.

13. Langer, *World History,* 475, 674.

14. Egan et al., *Kings, Rulers and Statesmen,* 156.

15. Ibid., 159; Friedrich Heer, *The Medieval World,* trans. Janet Sondheimer (New York: Mentor/ NAL, 1962), 318.

16. Egan et al., *Kings, Rulers and Statesmen,* 297.

17. Steven Runciman, *A History of the Crusades,* 3 vols. (Cambridge: Cambridge University Press, 1952, 1987), vol. 3, 329, 343, 393–395, 422.

18. Michael Psellus, *Fourteen Byzantine Rulers,* trans. E. R. A. Sewter (Harmondsworth, Middlesex: Penguin Books, 1982), 339–360; Edward Gibbon, *The Decline and Fall of the Roman Empire* (Chicago: Encyclopedia Britannica, 1952), vol. 2, 184, 327, 372–373; George Ostrogorsky, *History of the Byzantine State* (New Brunswick, NJ: Rutgers University Press, 1969), 344–345.

19. C. W. Previté-Orton, *The Shorter Cambridge Medieval History,* 2 vols. (Cambridge: Cambridge University Press, 1952, 1982), vol. 1, *The Later Roman Empire to the Twelfth Century,* 77–83; Ostrogorsky, *History of the Byzantine State,* 54; Langer, *World History,* 134.

20. Jasper Ridley, *Napoleon III and Eugénie* (New York: Viking Press, 1980); Eugen Weber, *France* (Cambridge: Belknap Press of Harvard University, 1986), 95, 97, 181; Langer, *World History,* 683.

21. Egan et al., *Kings, Rulers and Statesmen,* 162.

22. A. A. Vasiliev, *History of the Byzantine Empire* (Madison, WI: University of Wisconsin Press, 1952), 440–445, 487; Ostrogorsky, *History of the Byzantine State,* 408, 410–416, 577; Previté-Orton, *The Later Roman Empire,* 112; Gibbon, 426.

1. Charles Moritz, ed., *Current Biography Yearbook, 1987* (New York: H. W. Wilson Co., 1987), 169–172; Betty Beale, "Word from Washington:

Iceland's President Kicks Off Scandinavian Culture Extravaganza," *Houston Chronicle* (5 September 1982), sec. 7, 11; John Edward Young, "Iceland's 'Chef of State' Needs Plenty of Cod and Imagination," *Christian Science Monitor* (8 July 1987): 25.

2. Gregory of Tours, *The History of the Franks,* trans. Lewis Thorpe (Harmondsworth, Middlesex: Penguin Books, 1986), 222–587; C. W. Previté-Orton, *The Shorter Cambridge Medieval History,* 2 vols. (Cambridge: Cambridge University Press, 1952, 1982), vol. 1, *The Later Roman Empire to the Twelfth Century,* 156–157.

1. Krishan Bhatin, *A Biography of Prime Minister Gandhi* (New York: Praeger, 1974); Indira Gandhi, *My Truth* (New York: Grove Press, 1980); Tad Szulc, "What Indira Gandhi Wants You To Know," *Parade* (25 July 1982): 6–8; "Gandhi on Atomic Power," *Houston Post* (18 September 1983): A 3; "Clouds over India Dim Gandhi's Global Star," *U.S. News & World Report* (21 March 1983); Sheila Tefft, "Gandhi Murder Inquiry Released," *Christian Science Monitor* (29 March 1989): 4.

2. E. Papinot, *Historical and Geographical Dictionary of Japan* (Rutland, VT: Charles E. Tuttle Company, 1972), 115; George Sansom, *A History of Japan to 1334* (Stanford, CA: Stanford University Press, 1958), 82; Edwin O. Reischauer and John K. Fairbank, *East Asia: The Great Tradition* (Boston: Houghton Mifflin Company, 1960), 480.

3. Papinot, *Historical and Geographical Dictionary,* 117.

4. Ibid., 127, 399, 535.

5. Alison Plowden, *Lady Jane Grey and the House of Suffolk* (New York: Franklin Watts, 1986); M. E. Hudson and Mary Clark, *Crown of a Thousand Years* (New York: Crown Publishing, 1978), 82–85.

1. J. E. Manchip White, *Ancient Egypt: Its Culture and History* (New York: Dover Publications, 1970), 165–167; Walter A. Fairservis, Jr., *The Ancient Kingdoms of the Nile* (New York: Mentor/NAL, 1962), 133–134, 141, 165; H. G. Wells, *Outline of History,* vol. 1, 174; John Anthony West, *The Traveler's Key to Ancient Egypt* (New York: Alfred A. Knopf, 1985), 342–343.

2. John Pemble, *The Raj, the Indian Mutiny, and the Kingdom of Oudh, 1801–1859* (Rutherford, NJ: Fairleigh Dickinson University Press, 1977), 4, 210–211, 213, 222–223, 229, 234, 245–247.

3. Alban Butler, *The Lives of the Fathers, Martyrs and Other Principal Saints* (Chicago: Catholic

Press, 1961), vol. 4, 1290–1295; Prince Hubertus Zu Löwenstein, *A Basic History of Germany* (Bonn: Inter Nationes, 1964), 38.

4. Michael Psellus, *Fourteen Byzantine Rulers,* trans. E. R. A. Sewter (Harmondsworth, Middlesex: Penguin Books, 1982), 63, 308; George Ostrogorsky, *History of the Byzantine State* (New Brunswick, NJ: Rutgers University Press, 1969), 262, 264, 279, 283–284.

5. Robert R. Harding, *Anatomy of a Power Elite* (New Haven, CT: Yale University Press, 1978), 21, 143–149; Edward E. Egan, Constance B. Hintz, and L. F. Wise, *Kings, Rulers and Statesmen* (New York: Sterling Publishing Company, 1976), 159.

6. C. W. Previté-Orton, *The Shorter Cambridge Medieval History,* 2 vols. (Cambridge: Cambridge University Press, 1952, 1982), vol. 1, 158.

7. Philip K. Hitti, *History of the Arabs* (New York: St. Martin's Press, 1968), 83.

8. Douglas Newton, "The Maoris: Treasures of the Tradition," *National Geographic* 166 (October 1984): 542–553, particularly 546; Yva Momatiuk and John Eastcott, "Maoris: At Home in Two Worlds," *National Geographic* 166 (October 1984): 522–542.

9. Steven Runciman, *A History of the Crusades,* 3 vols. (Cambridge: Cambridge University Press, 1952, 1987), vol. 2, *The Kingdom of Jerusalem and the Frankish East,* 280, 332, 333, 335.

10. Jasper Ridley, *Napoleon III and Eugenie* (New York: Viking Press, 1980), 3–13.

11. René Grousset, *The Empire of the Steppes: A History of Central Asia,* trans. Naomi Walford (New Brunswick, NJ: Rutgers University Press, 1970), 131–132.

12. Ibid., 64–65.

1. Edward E. Egan, Constance B. Hintz, and L. F. Wise, *Kings, Rulers and Statesmen* (New York: Sterling Publishing Company, 1976), 152.

2. George Ostrogorsky, *History of the Byzantine State* (New Brunswick, NJ: Rutgers University Press, 1969), 175–182, 186–188, 192–197, 220–225; C. W. Previté-Orton, *The Shorter Cambridge Medieval History,* 2 vols. (Cambridge: Cambridge University Press, 1952, 1982), vol. 1, *The Later Roman Empire to the Twelfth Century,* 249.

3. William L. Langer, ed., *World History* (Boston: Houghton Mifflin Company, 1940, 1980), 855; Egan et al., *Kings, Rulers and Statesmen,* 61.

4. Egan et al., *Kings, Rulers and Statesmen,* 157.

5. Steven Runciman, *A History of the Crusades,* 3 vols. (Cambridge: Cambridge University Press, 1952, 1987), vol. 3, 329, 342.

6. Melveena McKendrick, *Ferdinand and Isa-bella* (New York: American Heritage Publishing Co., 1968); Langer, *World History,* 304–305.

7. Langer, *World History,* 694–697; Jasper Ridley, *Napoleon III and Eugénie* (New York: Viking Press, 1980), 144, 154, 158, 162, 167–168, 205, 246, 323, 492, 539.

8. Pieter Geye, *The Revolt of the Netherlands 1555–1609* (London: Ernest Benn, 1958), 218, 223, 227, 232, 239–243; Hugh Trevor-Roper, *The Golden Age of Europe* (New York: Bonanza/Crown Publishers, 1987), 53, 84–85, 89, 101.

9. Charles L. Mee, Jr., *Daily Life in Renaissance Italy* (New York: American Heritage Publishing Co., 1975), 70–72.

10. Langer, *World History,* 487–489.

11. Langer, *World History,* 299–301; Runciman, vol. 3, 456.

12. Runciman, vol. 3, 206, 288–289.

1. Francis Dvornik, *The Slavs in European History and Civilization* (New Brunswick, NJ: Rutgers University Press, 1962), 83–84, 129–130, 169, 222, 224, 436; William L. Langer, ed., *World History* (Boston: Houghton Mifflin Company, 1940, 1980), 337–340; Edward E. Egan, Constance B. Hintz, and L. F. Wise, *Kings, Rulers and Statesmen* (New York: Sterling Publishing Company, 1976), 361.

2. Egan et al., *Kings, Rulers and Statesmen,* 157.

3. Ibid.

4. Hugh Trevor-Roper, *The Golden Age of Europe* (New York: Bonanza/Crown, 1987), 162; Robert R. Harding, *Anatomy of a Power Elite* (New Haven, CT: Yale University Press, 1978), 39, 176, 188; Langer, *World History,* 410, 411.

5. Egan et al., *Kings, Rulers and Statesmen,* 162.

6. Ibid, 152.

7. Langer, *World History,* 494–495.

8. Sachchidananda Bhahacharya, *A Dictionary of Indian History* (New York: George Braziller, 1967), 321–322.

9. W. G. Aston, trans., *Nihongi: Chronicles of Japan from the Earliest Times to A.D. 697* (Rutland, VT: Charles E. Tuttle Company, 1972), 224–253; Edwin O. Reischauer and John K. Fairbank, *East Asia: The Great Tradition* (Boston: Houghton Mifflin Co., 1960), 468–469; George A. Sansom, *A History of Japan to 1334* (Stanford, CA: Stanford University Press, 1958), 16–17; E. Papinot, *Historical and Geographical Dictionary of Japan* (Rutland, VT: Charles E. Tuttle Company, 1972), 229–230.

10. Sansom, *A History of Japan,* 65; Papinot, *Historical and Geographical Dictionary,* 70, 232; Aston, *Nihongi,* 382–423.

11. Edward Gibbon, *The Decline and Fall of the*

Roman Empire (Chicago: Encyclopedia Britannica, 1952), vol. 2, 569, 577; Egan et al., *Kings, Rulers and Statesmen*, 267; Langer, *World History*, 314–315.

12. Langer, *World History*, 314–315; Egan et al., *Kings, Rulers and Statesmen*, 267.

13. Langer, *World History*, 418–419.

14. Friedrich Heer, *The Medieval World*, trans. Janet Sondheimer (New York: Mentor/NAL, 1962), 318; Egan et al., *Kings, Rulers and Statesmen*, 52.

15. Langer, *World History*, 406.

16. Melveena McKendrick, *Ferdinand and Isabella* (New York: American Heritage Publishing Co., 1968), 99, 130–136, 140, 141, 144, 146–147; Langer, *World History*, 406, 415, 428.

17. Heer, *The Medieval World*, 251; Egan, et. al., *Kings, Rulers and Statesmen*, 157, 430; Langer, *World History*, 298.

18. Langer, *World History*, 296–298; Egan et al., *Kings, Rulers and Statesmen*, 430.

19. Frederick C. Gamst, *The Qemant: A Pagan-Hebraic Peasantry of Ethiopia* (New York: Holt, Rinehart and Winston, 1969), 13, 14, 124.

20. Edward Gibbon, *The Decline and Fall of the Roman Empire* (Chicago: Encyclopedia Britannica, 1952), vol. 1, 271–272.

21. Diana Bowder, *Who Was Who in the Roman World* (New York: Washington Square Press, 1984), 70; *see also* Biblical references in Acts 25:13 and 23.

22. Gibbon, *The Decline and Fall of the Roman Empire*, vol. 1, 48, 52, 54–55, 58; Diana Bowder, ed., *Who Was Who in the Roman World* (Ithaca, NY: Cornell University Press, 1980), 89–90, 226–227, 270–271, 491–494.

23. Bowder, *Who Was Who in the Roman World*, 180–181, 271, 272; Gibbon, *The Decline and Fall of the Roman Empire*, vol. 1, 58, 60–61.

24. William Hoffman, *Queen Juliana: The Story of the Richest Woman in the World* (New York: Harcourt Brace Jovanovich, 1979); Langer, *World History*, 475; John Gunther, *Inside Europe Today* (New York: Harper and Bros., 1961), 114–115; Sydney Clark, *All the Best in Holland* (New York: Dodd Mead and Co., 1963), 76; Jennifer S. Uglow, comp. and ed., *International Dictionary of Women's Biography* (New York: Continuum, 1982), 250.

25. Capron Lewis, "Florida's Emerging Seminoles," *National Geographic* 136 (November 1969): 716–734.

1. Roland Oliver and J. D. Fage, *A Short History of Africa* (Harmondsworth: Penguin Books, 1970), 71; Edward Gibbon, *The Decline and Fall of the Roman Empire* (Chicago: Encyclopedia Britannica, 1952), vol. 2, 279–280; William L. Langer,

ed., *World History* (Boston: Houghton Mifflin, 1940, 1980), 202.

2. Edward E. Egan, Constance B. Hintz, and L. F. Wise, *Kings, Rulers and Statesmen* (New York: Sterling Publishing Company, 1976), 438.

3. K. Madhu Panikker, *The Serpent and the Crescent: A History of the Negro Empires of West Africa* (Bombay: Asia Publishing House, 1963), 60.

4. John Anthony West, *The Traveler's Key to Ancient Egypt* (New York: Alfred A. Knopf, 1985), 110, 134; Langer, *World History*, 37.

5. E. Papinot, *Historical and Geographical Dictionary of Japan* (Rutland, VT: Chas. E. Tuttle Co., 1972), 296, 527–528; W. G. Aston, trans., *Nihongi: Chronicles of Japan from the Earliest Times to A.D. 697* (Rutland, VT: Chas. E. Tuttle Co., 1972), 171, 248–273; George Sansom, *A History of Japan to 1334* (Stanford, CA: Stanford University Press, 1958), 54.

6. Sansom, *A History of Japan*, 89; Papinot, *Historical and Geographical Dictionary of Japan*, 237, 299–301; Edwin O. Reischauer and John K. Fairbank, *East Asia: The Great Tradition* (Boston: Houghton Mifflin Company, 1960), 484.

7. Egan et al., *Kings, Rulers and Statesmen*, 69; for an account of the times, but not Kossamak's part in them, see: Thomas J. Abercrombie, "Cambodia: Indochina's 'Neutral' Corner," *National Geographic* 126 (October 1964): 514–551.

1. Sachchinananda Bhahacharya, *A Dictionary of Indian History* (New York: George Braziller, 1967), 538; John Pemble, *The Raj, the Indian Mutiny, and the Kingdom of Oudh 1801–1859* (Rutherford, NJ: Fairleigh Dickinson University Press, 1977), 192; Percival Spear, *A History of India* (London: Penguin Books, 1987), vol. 2, 142.

2. William L. Langer, ed., *World History* (Boston: Houghton Mifflin, 1940, 1980), 306–307, 309.

3. W. Scott Morton, *China: Its History and Culture* (New York: McGraw-Hill, 1980), 63; Edwin O. Reischauer and John K. Fairbank, *East Asia: The Great Tradition* (Boston: Houghton Mifflin, 1960), 125–126; Langer, *World History*, 148–149.

4. Edward E. Egan, Constance B. Hintz, and L. F. Wise, *Kings, Rulers and Statesmen* (New York: Sterling Publishing Co., 1976), 438.

5. Edward T. James, ed., *Notable American Women 1607–1950.* (Cambridge: Belknap Press of Harvard University Press, 1971), vol. 2, 403–404; Langer, *World History*, 938.

6. Langer, *World History*, 410, 422, 429.

7. Egan et al., *Kings, Rulers and Statesmen*, 316.

8. Dennis Bloodworth and Ching Ping Bloodworth, *The Chinese Machiavelli: 3,000 Years of Chi-*

nese Statecraft (New York: Dell, 1976), 143, 148; Reischauer, *East Asia*, 94, 117; Morton, *China*, 50.

9. Steven Runciman, *A History of the Crusades*, 3 vols. (Cambridge: Cambridge University Press, 1952, 1987), vol. 3, 343, 403–407.

10. Ibid., 207, 230–231, 233, 278, 288, 343.

11. Jean Cooke, Ann Kramer, and Theodore Rowland-Entwistle, *History's Timeline* (New York: Crescent Books, 1981), 46, 61; Hermann Kinder and Werner Hilgemann, *Atlas of World History*, trans. Ernest A. Menze (Garden City, NJ: Anchor/Doubleday, 1982), vol. 1, 169; Langer, *World History*, 255.

12. Langer, *World History*, 700.

13. Ibid., 490, 491.

14. Egan et al., *Kings, Rulers and Statesmen*, 270.

1. Bamber Gascoigne, *The Great Moghuls* (New York: Dorset Press, 1971), 79–81; Percival Spear, *A History of India*, vol. 2, 29–30.

2. Edward E. Egan, Constance B. Hintz, and L. F. Wise, *Kings, Rulers and Statesmen* (New York: Sterling Publishing Company, 1976), 153.

3. Alice Kemp-Welch, *Six Medieval Women* (London: Macmillan, 1913), 93, 102; Egan et al., *Kings, Rulers and Statesmen*, 153.

4. Egan et al., *Kings, Rulers and Statesmen*, 152.

5. Ibid., 159.

6. Ibid., 152.

7. John G. Jackson, *Introduction to African Civilizations* (Secaucus, NY: Citadel Press, 1970), 268–269; Sir John Glubb, *A Short History of the Arab Peoples* (New York: Dorset Press, 1969), 24.

8. René Grousset, *The Empire of the Steppes: A History of Central Asia*, trans. Naomi Walford (New Brunswick, NJ: Rutgers University Press, 1970), 509.

9. Mary Flood, "First Female Cherokee Chief Ready for Job," *Houston Post* (7 April 1984): A 1, 26.

10. Francis Dvornik, *The Slavs in European History and Civilization* (New Brunswick, NJ: Rutgers University Press, 1962), 44, 53, 54.

11. Egan et al., *Kings, Rulers and Statesmen*, 52.

12. Ibid., 52, 159; William L. Langer, ed., *World History* (Boston: Houghton Mifflin, 1940, 1980), 299, 406–407.

13. Joseph Dahmus, *Seven Medieval Queens* (Garden City, NJ: Doubleday, 1972), 233–275. Egan et al., *Kings, Rulers and Statesmen*, 112–113, 447; Langer, *World History*, 334–336.

14. A. R. Myers, *England in the Late Middle Ages* (Harmondsworth: Penguin Books, 1976), vol. 4, 126–130, 193; Dahmus, *Seven Medieval Queens*, 276–327.

15. Steven Runciman, *A History of the Crusades*, 3 vols. (Cambridge: Cambridge University Press, 1952, 1987), vol. 3, 329, 394–395.

16. Langer, *World History*, 422, 429.

17. Pieter Geye, *The Revolt of the Netherlands, 1555–1609* (London: Ernest Benn, 1958), 70, 75, 78, 79, 87–92, 98, 100, 101, 154; George Masselman, *The Cradle of Colonialism* (New Haven, CT: Yale University Press, 1963), 27; Shepard B. Clough et al., *European History in a World Perspective* (Lexington, MA: D. C. Heath and Co., 1975), vol. 2, pp. 638, 713–715; Hugh Trevor-Roper, *The Golden Age of Europe* (New York: Bonanza/Crown, 1987), 66, 80, 82; Langer, *World History*, 407–408.

18. Denis Mack Smith, *A History of Sicily* (New York: Dorset Press, 1968), vol. 1, *Medieval Sicily*, 38–40.

19. J. D. Mackie, *A History of Scotland* (Harmondsworth: Penguin Books, 1984), 35, 45, 61–63, 135; Steven Runciman, *A History of the Crusades*, 3 vols., (Cambridge: Cambridge University Press, 1952, 1987), vol. 3, 401–402; Langer, *World History*, 214, 217, 218.

20. A. R. Myers, *England in the Late Middle Ages*, vol. 4, 205; Langer, *World History*, 396.

21. Egan et al., *Kings, Rulers and Statesmen*, 52.

22. Ibid.

23. *International Who's Who, 1987–1988* (London: Europa Publications, 1987), 963; Charles Moritz, ed., *Current Biography Yearbook, 1972* (New Haven: H. W. Wilson Co., 1972), 306–308; Egan et al., *Kings, Rulers and Statesmen*, 114.

24. Egan et al., *Kings, Rulers and Statesmen*, 152.

25. Ibid., 157.

26. Smith, *History of Sicily*, vol. 1, 87; Egan et al., *Kings, Rulers and Statesmen*, 274.

27. Egan et al., *Kings, Rulers and Statesmen*, 378; Langer, *World History*, 491, 492.

28. Langer, *World History*, 491, 698, 699; Jasper Ridley, *Napoleon III and Eugenie* (New York: Viking Press, 1980), 85; Egan et al., *Kings, Rulers and Statesmen*, 379.

29. Egan et al., *Kings, Rulers and Statesmen*, 298.

30. Langer, *World History*, 417, 486.

31. Ibid., 491–492.

32. Smith, *History of Sicily*, vol. 2, 325, 335–338, 341, 348; Langer, *World History*, 496, 497, 702.

33. Egan et al., *Kings, Rulers and Statesmen*, 52.

34. Ridley, *Napoleon III*, 142, 144, 152, 157; Langer, *World History*, 694–696.

35. Langer, *World History*, 695, 696–697.

36. Ibid., 695.

37. Langer, *World History*, 339, 342; Dvornik, *The Slavs in European History*, 83, 436; Egan et al., *Kings, Rulers and Statesmen*, 229.

38. Geye, *The Revolt of the Netherlands*, 38.

39. Edward Crankshaw, *Maria Theresa* (New York: Viking Press, 1969, 1971); Karl A. Roider,

Jr., ed., *Maria Theresa* (Englewood Cliffs, NJ: Prentice-Hall, 1973).

40. Egan et al., *Kings, Rulers and Statesmen,* 152.

41. Ibid; Langer, *World History,* 224.

42. Runciman, *History of the Crusades,* vol. 3, 32, 66, 84, 94–95, 104, 132–134, 320.

43. Egan et al., *Kings, Rulers and Statesmen,* 151.

44. Ibid., 152.

45. Christopher Hare, *The Most Illustrious Ladies of the Italian Renaissance* (Williamstown, MA: Corner House Publishers, 1972), 211; Robert R. Harding, *Anatomy of a Power Elite* (New Haven, CT: Yale University Press, 1978), 127, 129, 175, 226; Trevor-Roper, *The Golden Age of Europe,* 153, 158, 166, 172, 173; Langer, *World History,* 414.

46. John J. Putnam, "Napoleon," *National Geographic* 161 (February 1982): 165–170; Langer, *World History,* 644, 650; Egan et al., *Kings, Rulers and Statesmen,* 270.

47. C. W. Previté-Orton, *The Shorter Cambridge Medieval History,* 2 vols. (Cambridge: Cambridge University Press, 1952, 1982), vol. 1, *The Later Roman Empire to the Twelfth Century,* 359, 437; Langer, *World History,* 230.

48. Langer, *World History,* 303, 324, 327, 406, 427.

49. J. M. Hussey, ed., *The Cambridge Medieval History* (Cambridge: Cambridge University Press, 1966), vol. 4, pt. 1, 621.

50. M. E. Hudson and Mary Clark, *Crown of a Thousand Years* (New York: Crown Publishers, 1978), 78, 82–89; Trevor-Roper, *The Golden Age of Europe,* 26, 40, 190; Langer, *World History,* 395–396, 398–399, 417.

51. Hudson and Clark, *Crown of a Thousand Years,* 112–114; Langer, *World History,* 463, 465–467, 553.

52. James Cerutis, "Sea Islands: The South's Surprising Coast," *National Geographic* 139 (March 1971): 373–374.

53. George Ostrogorsky, *History of the Byzantine State* (New Brunswick, NJ: Rutgers University Press, 1969), 394, 396; Runciman, *A History of the Crusades* (Cambridge: Cambridge University Press, 1952, 1987), vol. 2, *The Kingdom of Jerusalem,* 359–360, 427–428; Previté-Orton, *The Shorter Cambridge,* vol. 1, 536.

54. Mackie, *A History of Scotland,* 133, 136–139, 149.

55. Ibid., 134, 136–139, 153–175, 202, 308. For a speculative insight into relationships among Mary and Darnley and Bothwell, *see* Olivia Orfield, *Death Trap* (Elgin, IL: Performance Publishing Co., 1979) (one-act play).

56. Egan et al., *Kings, Rulers and Statesmen,* 159.

57. Prince Hubertus Zu Löwenstein, *A Basic History of Germany* (Bonn: Inter Nationes, 1964), 30.

58. Doris Mary Stenton, *English Society in the Early Middle Ages* (Harmondsworth: Penguin Books, 1965), 35–36, 225; Hudson and Clark, *Crown of a Thousand Years,* 26–27.

59. Previté-Orton, *The Later Roman Empire,* 382, 608; Friedrich Heer, *The Medieval World,* trans. Janet Sondheimer (New York: Mentor/NAL, 1962), 318; Markdale, *Women of the Celts,* 32, 37, 91; Charles Duff, *England and the English* (New York: G. P. Putnam's Sons, 1954), 83.

60. Nora Duff, *Matilda of Tuscany* (London: Cambridge Press, 1909); Previté-Orton, *The Shorter Cambridge,* 457, 485, 491, 494, 496, 497; Sidney Painter, *The Rise of the Feudal Monarchies* (Westport, CT: Greenwood Press, 1982), 103–104; Langer, *World History,* 221–223, 232–236, 314.

61. Diana Bowder, ed., *Who Was Who in the Roman World* (Ithaca, NY: Cornell University Press, 1980), 335, 575.

62. Golda Meir, *My Life* (New York: G. P. Putnam's Sons, 1975); Michael Avallone, *A Woman Called Golda* (New York: Norton Publications, 1982).

63. Runciman, *The Kingdom of Jerusalem,* 177–178, 185–187, 191–193, 231–236, 247, 279–283, 311, 333–337, 360–361.

64. Egan et al., *Kings, Rulers and Statesmen,* 130; E. A. Budge, *A History of Ethiopia* (London: Methuen, 1928), 221–222.

65. W. B. Emery, *Archaic Egypt* (Harmondsworth: Penguin Books, 1987), 32, 65, 66, 68, 69, 94, 126.

66. David Bergamini, *Japan's Imperial Conspiracy* (New York: William Morrow, 1972), 282–283; Langer, *World History,* 916–917, 922.

67. Grousset, *The Empire of the Steppes,* 69.

68. E. Papinot, *Historical and Geographical Dictionary of Japan,* (Rutland, VT: Chas. E. Tuttle Company, 1972), 124, 417.

1. Walter A. Fairservis, Jr., *The Ancient Kingdoms of the Nile* (New York: Mentor/NAL, 1962), 182–187; J. E. Manchip White, *Ancient Egypt* (New York: Dover Publications, 1970), 188, 192.

2. White, *Ancient Egypt,* 158; I. E. S. Edwards et al., eds., *Cambridge Ancient History* (Cambridge: Cambridge University Press, 1980), vol. 2, pt. 1, 43; John Anthony West, *the Traveler's Key to Ancient Egypt* (New York: Alfred A. Knopf, 1985), 442; John G. Jackson, *Introduction to African Civilizations* (Secaucus, NY: Citadel Press, 1970), 107–108.

3. *Britannica Micropaedia* (Chicago: Encyclopedia Britannica Press, 1983), vol. 2, 758.

4. Herodotus, *The Histories,* trans. Aubrey de Sélincourt (New York: Viking Penguin, 1988), 115–117; A. T. Olmstead, *History of the Persian*

Empire (Chicago: University of Chicago Press, 1948), 55, 115, 321–322.

5. Herodotus, *The Histories,* 166.

6. Bamber Gascoigne, *The Great Moghuls* (New York: Dorset Press, 1971), 136–137, 141, 154, 158–160, 165–172, 178–179, 181.

7. Richard Gray, ed., *The Cambridge History of Africa* (Cambridge: Cambridge University Press, 1975), vol. 4, 8; David Birmingham, *Trade and Conflict in Angola: The Mbundu and Their Neighbors under the Influence of the Portuguese* (Oxford: Oxford University Press, 1966), 6, 226, 236–246, 268, 270.

1. René Grousset, *The Empire of the Steppes: A History of Central Asia,* trans. Naomi Walford (New Brunswick, NJ: Rutgers University Press, 1970), 272–274, 330, 349, 596; Steven Runciman, *A History of the Crusades,* 3 vols. (Cambridge: Cambridge University Press, 1952, 1987), vol. 3, 260, 293–294.

2. George Ostrogorsky, *History of the Byzantine State* (New Brunswick, NJ: Rutgers University Press, 1969), 283, 292; C. W. Previté-Orton, *The Shorter Cambridge Medieval History,* 2 vols. (Cambridge: Cambridge University Press, 1952, 1982), vol. 1, 265; William L. Langer, ed., *World History* (Boston: Houghton Mifflin Company, 1948, 1980), 195, 259, 260.

3. Langer, *World History,* 1024.

4. Grousset, *The Empire of the Steppes,* 274–275, 286, 329–332; Runciman, *A History of the Crusades,* vol. 3, 309, and Appendix III.

1. Ved Mehta, *The New India* (Harmondsworth: Penguin Books, 1978), 154–155; *International Who's Who, 1987–1988* (London: Europa Publishing, 1987), xvi, 1130.

2. Romila Thapar, *A History of India,* 2 vols. (London: Penguin Books, 1987), vol. 1, 103.

3. "Isabel Perón's Return Confirmed," *Houston Post* (27 August 1982): 3A; "Isabel Perón Pardoned," *Houston Post* (10 September 1983): 4A; "Intelligence Report," *Parade* (27 February 1983): 2; Edward E. Egan, Constance B. Hintz, and L. F. Wise, *Kings, Rulers and Statesmen* (New York: Sterling Publishing Company, 1976), 18.

4. William L. Langer, ed., *World History* (Boston: Houghton Mifflin Company, 1940, 1980), 250, 252.

5. Herodotus, *The Histories,* trans. Aubrey de Sélincourt (New York: Penguin Books, 1954, 1988), 326–328, 337–339; N. G. L. Hammond, *A History of Greece to 322 B.C.* (Oxford: Clarendon Press, 1986), 178.

6. Edwin O. Reischauer and John K. Fairbank, *East Asia: The Great Tradition* (Boston: Houghton Mifflin Company, 1960), 463; George Sansom, *A History of Japan to 1334* (Stanford, CA: Stanford University Press, 1958), vol. 1, 22, 45.

7. Diana Bowder, ed., *Who Was Who in the Roman World* (Ithaca, NY: Cornell University Press, 1980), 4–5, 46, 146, 413–414, 556–557; C. W. Previté-Orton, *The Shorter Cambridge Medieval History,* 2 vols. (Cambridge: Cambridge University Press, 1952, 1982), vol. 1, *The Later Roman Empire to the Twelfth Century,* 78, 86–88; Langer, *World History,* 134, 158–159.

8. Steven Runciman, *A History of the Crusades,* 3 vols. (Cambridge: Cambridge University Press, 1952, 1987), vol. 3, 278, 281, 284–286, 288–289.

9. Previté-Orton, *The Later Roman Empire,* 159.

10. Thapar, *A History of India,* vol. 1, 139–140.

11. Bowder, *Who Was Who in the Roman World,* 452.

1. Edward E. Egan, Constance B. Hintz, and L. F. Wise, *Kings, Rulers and Statesmen* (New York: Sterling Publishing Company, 1976), 302.

2. Ibid.

3. Ibid.

4. Ibid.

5. Peter Hardy, *Historians of Medieval India* (Westport, CT: Greenwood Press, 1982), 65, 91; Tariq Ali, "Dynasty's Daughter," *Interview* (February 1989): 124; H. M. Eliot and J. Dowson, *A History of India as Told by Its Own Historians* (Cambridge: Cambridge University Press, 1931), vol. 2, 185; Romila Thapar, *A History of India,* 2 vols. (London: Penguin Books, 1987), vol. 1, 269, 301.

6. René Grousset, *The Empire of the Steppes: A History of Central Asia,* trans. Naomi Walford (New Brunswick, NJ: Rutgers University Press, 1970), 260, 263, 272, 350; Steven Runciman, *A History of the Crusades,* 3 vols. (Cambridge: Cambridge University Press, 1952, 1987), vol. 3, 249–250; J. M. Hussey, ed., *The Cambridge Medieval History* (Cambridge: Cambridge University Press, 1966), vol. 4, pt. 1, 783; N.A., *Storm across Georgia* (London: Cassell, 1981), 40; John Buchan, ed., *The Baltic and Caucasian States* (Boston and New York: Houghton Mifflin Company, 1923), 173–174.

1. Percival Spear, *A History of India,* 2 vols. (London: Penguin Books, 1987), vol. 2, 76, 104, 107, 117, 132, 135.

2. Melville Bell Grosvenor, "South Seas' Tonga Hails a King," *National Geographic* 133 (March

1968): 322–344; *International Who's Who, 1987–1988* (London: Europa Publishing, 1987), xvi; Marjorie Dent Candee, ed., *Current Biography 1953* (New York: H. W. Wilson Co., 1954), 552–554; Luis Marden, "The Friendly Isles of Tonga," *National Geographic* 133 (March 1968): 345–367; Edward E. Egan, Constance B. Hintz, and L. F. Wise, *Kings, Rulers and Statesmen,* 450.

3. Joan Oates, *Babylon* (London: Thames and Hudson, 1979), 111; A. T. Olmstead, *History of the Persian Empire* (Chicago: University of Chicago Press, 1948), 118, 163, 321–322, 380; William L. Langer, ed., *World History* (Boston: Houghton Mifflin Company, 1940, 1980), 33; Herodotus, *The Histories,* trans. Aubrey de Sélincourt (New York: Penguin Books, 1954, 1988), 115.

4. Biblical records: I Chronicles 5:26, II Kings 15 and 16. In the Biblical coverage, Tiglath-Pileser is called "Pul" or "Pulu"; J. I. Packer, Merrill C. Tenney, and William White, Jr., *The Bible Almanac* (Nashville: Thomas Nelson, 1980), 134, 316, 500, 675.

5. René Grousset, *The Empire of the Steppes: A History of Central Asia,* trans. Naomi Walford (New Brunswick, NJ: Rutgers University Press, 1970), 128–129.

6. Steven Runciman, *A History of the Crusades,* 3 vols. (Cambridge: Cambridge University Press, 1952, 1987), vol. 2, *The Kingdom of Jerusalem and the Frankish East,* 362, 392–393, 404, 407, 423–449; vol. 3, 19–21, 30.

7. Denis Gray and Bart McDowell, "Thailand's Working Royalty," *National Geographic* 162 (October 1982): 486–499; *International Who's Who, 1987–1988,* xvi; Barabara Crossette, "King Bhumibol's Reign," *New York Times Magazine* (21 May 1989): 30–36.

8. Egan et al., *Kings, Rulers and Statesmen,* 438; Gray and McDowell, "Thailand's Working Royalty," 23.

9. Francis Dvornik, *The Slavs in European History and Civilization* (New Brunswick, NJ: Rutgers University Press, 1962), 491–492, 510, 526; Ian Grey, *Peter the Great: Emperor of All Russia* (Harmondsworth: Penguin Books, 1960), 4–30; Langer, *World History,* 514–515.

10. Sir John Glubb, *A Short History of the Arab Peoples* (New York: Dorset Press, 1969), 202–205, 210.

11. Romila Thapar, *A History of India,* 2 vols. (London: Penguin books, 1987), vol. 1, 225–226.

12. W. G. Aston, trans., *Nihongi: Chronicles of Japan,* 2 vols. (Rutland, VT: Charles E. Tuttle Company, 1979), vol. 2, 121–156; E. Papinot, *Historical and Geographical Dictionary of Japan* (Rutland, VT: Charles E. Tuttle Company, 1972), 605; George Sansom, *A History of Japan to 1334,* 3 vols. (Stanford, CA: Stanford University Press, 1958), vol. 1,

50; Edwin O. Reischauer and John K. Fairbank, *East Asia: The Great Tradition* (Boston: Houghton Mifflin Company, 1960), 475.

13. Grousset, *The Empire of the Steppes,* 132.

14. Ibid., 287; Langer, *World History,* 369.

15. Egan et al., *Kings, Rulers and Statesmen,* 153.

1. William L. Langer, ed., *World History* (Boston: Houghton Mifflin Company, 1940, 1980), 872.

2. John Buchan, ed., *The Baltic and Caucasian States* (Boston and New York: Houghton Mifflin Company, 1923), 173; Steven Runciman, *A History of the Crusades,* 3 vols. (Cambridge: Cambridge University Press, 1952, 1987), vol. 3, 74, 101, 126, 163, 247; Edward E. Egan, Constance B. Hintz, and L. F. Wise, *Kings, Rulers and Statesmen* (New York: Sterling Publishing Company, 1976), 411; J. M. Hussey, ed., *The Cambridge Medieval History,* 4 vols. (Cambridge: Cambridge University Press, 1966), vol. 4, pt. 1, 783.

3. René Grousset, *The Empire of the Steppes: A History of Central Asia,* trans. Naomi Walford (New Brunswick, NJ: Rutgers University Press, 1970), 165–166.

4. Langer, *World History,* 146.

5. Ibid., 253–254.

6. Penny Junor, *Margaret Thatcher: Wife, Mother, Politician.* (London: Sidgwick and London, 1983); Julian Baum, "Sizing up a Decade of British Radicalism," *Christian Science Monitor* (4 May 1989): 1–2.

7. George Ostrogorsky, *History of the Byzantine State* (New Brunswick, NJ: Rutgers University Press, 1969), 219, 232; C. W. Previté-Orton, *The Shorter Cambridge Medieval History,* 2 vols. (Cambridge: Cambridge University Press, 1952, 1982), vol. 1, *The Later Roman Empire to the Twelfth Century,* 249, 252–253.

8. Previté-Orton, *The Later Roman Empire,* 220; Edward Gibbon, *The Decline and Fall of the Roman Empire,* 3 vols. (Chicago: Encyclopedia Britannica, 1952), vol. 1, 607; vol. 2, 107, 630; Langer, *World History,* 165.

9. Robert Browning, *Justinian and Theodora* (New York: Praeger Publishers, 1971); Ostrogorsky, *History of the Byzantine State,* 25, 69, 73; Previté-Orton, *The Later Roman Empire,* 78, 185–188; Langer, *World History,* 186.

10. Will Durant, *The Age of Faith,* vol. 4 of *The Story of Civilization* (New York: Simon and Schuster, 1950), 427; Richard E. Sullivan, *Heirs of the Roman Empire* (Ithaca, NY: Cornell University Press, 1965), 103, 125; Ostrogorsky, *History of the Byzantine State,* 215, 219–223, 225, 250, 575; Pre-

vité-Orton, *The Later Roman Empire*, 249, 252–253; Langer, *World History*, 192, 194.

11. Michael Psellus, *Fourteen Byzantine Rulers*, trans. E. R. A. Sewter (Harmondsworth, Middlesex: Penguin Books, 1982), 143–162, 261–271; Ostrogorsky, *History of the Byzantine State*, 321, 326, 337–338, 576; Previté-Orton, *The Later Roman Empire*, 273–274, 277.

12. Previté-Orton, *The Later Roman Empire*, 258–259; Ostrogorsky, *History of the Byzantine State*, 284, 285, 293.

13. Ostrogorsky, *History of the Byzantine State*, 296, 314; Gibbon, *The Decline and Fall of the Roman Empire*, vol. 2, 320; Prince Hubertus Zu Löwenstein, *A Basic History of Germany* (Bonn: Inter Nationes, 1964), 21–24; Langer, *World History*, 176, 195, 230–231.

14. J. E. White, *Ancient Egypt: Its Culture and History* (New York: Dover Publishing, 1970), 169, 172, 173; John Anthony West, *The Traveler's Key to Ancient Egypt* (New York: Alfred A. Knopf, 1985), 226, 235, 338, 378.

15. A. T. Olmstead, *History of the Persian Empire* (Chicago: University of Chicago Press, 1948), 66; Herodotus, *The Histories*, trans. Aubrey de Sélincourt (New York: Penguin Books, 1954, 1988), 123–127.

16. Runciman, *A History of the Crusades*, vol. 3, 249, 251–252, 293; Grousset, *Empire of the Steppes*, 268–269; Edwin O. Reischauer and John K. Fairbank, *East Asia: The Great Tradition* (Boston: Houghton Mifflin, 1960), 267, 270, 273.

17. Reischauer, *East Asia*, 125–126; W. Scott Morton, *China: Its History and Culture* (New York: McGraw-Hill, 1982), 63; Langer, *World History*, 146.

18. Stanley Karnow, *Vietnam: A History* (New York: Viking Press, 1983), 100.

19. Ibid.

20. K. Madhu Panikker, *The Serpent and the Crescent: A History of the Negro Empires of West Africa* (Bombay: Asia Publishing House, 1963), 112–113.

21. West, *The Traveler's Key*, 444; White, *Ancient Egypt*, 142, 162; Previté-Orton, *The Later Roman Empire*, 273.

22. Morton, *China: Its History and Culture*, 168–175.

1. Bamber Gascoigne, *The Great Moghuls* (New York: Dorset Press, 1971), 245, 250; Sir R. Burn, ed., *Cambridge History of India* (Cambridge: Cambridge University Press, 1937), vol. 4, *The Moghal Period*, 462; Sir John Glubb, *A Short History of the*

Arab Peoples (New York: Dorset Press, 1969), 235–236, 244.

2. *Las ruinas de Tulum* (Mexico: Instituto Nacional de Antropología e Historia, 1969), 14.

3. T. K. Derry, *A History of Scandinavia* (Minneapolis: University of Minneapolis Press, 1979), 159, 163, 166, 178; William L. Langer, ed., *World History* (Boston: Houghton Mifflin Company, 1940, 1980), 441, 508.

4. Kevin B. Reilly, *The Kingdom of Leon-Castilla under Queen Urraca, 1109–1126.* (Princeton: Princeton University Press, 1982); Steven Runciman, *A History of the Crusades*, 3 vols. (Cambridge: Cambridge University Press, 1952, 1987), vol. 2, 249–250; Langer, *World History*, 250.

1. Robert C. Suggs, *The Island Civilizations of Polynesia* (New York: Mentor/NAL, 1960), 53–54.

2. Elizabeth Longford, *Queen Victoria: Born to Succeed* (New York: Harper & Row, 1964); Roger Fulford, *Hanover to Windsor* (Glasgow: Fontana/Collins, 1981), 38–113; Jasper Ridley, *Napoleon III and Eugenie* (New York: Viking Press, 1980), 579–588, 603–617, 622–623; M. E. Hudson and Mary Clark, *Crown of a Thousand Years* (New York: Crown Publishing, 1978), 132–135.

3. Edward E. Egan, Constance B. Hintz, and L. F. Wise, *Kings, Rulers and Statesmen* (New York: Sterling Publishing, 1976), 277; William L. Langer, *World History* (Boston: Houghton Mifflin Company, 1940, 1980), 425.

1. William L. Langer, ed., *World History* (Boston: Houghton Mifflin Company, 1940, 1980), 674, 986, 1136, 1172, 1179; William L. Shirer, *The Rise and Fall of the Third Reich* (New York: Simon and Schuster, 1960), 561, 640, 652, 721–723, 729.

2. Brian Hook, ed., *The Cambridge Encyclopedia of China* (Cambridge: Cambridge University Press, 1982), 189–190, 191; Dennis Bloodworth, *The Chinese Looking Glass* (New York: Farrar, Straus and Giroux, 1967), 90–92; Dennis Bloodworth and Ching Ping Bloodworth, *The Chinese Machiavelli: 3,000 Years of Chinese Statecraft* (New York: Dell Publishing Company, 1976), 214–215, 218, 258–259; René Grousset, *The Empire of the Steppes: A History of Central Asia*, trans. Naomi Walford (New Brunswick, NJ: Rutgers University Press, 1970), 107–108; W. Scott Morton, *China: Its History and Culture* (New York: McGraw-Hill Book Company, 1980), 87, 89; Edwin O. Reischauer and John K. Fairbank, *East Asia: The Great Tradition*

(Boston: Houghton Mifflin Company, 1960), 157, 170, 190.

1. Thomas J. Lewin, *Asante before the British* (Lawrence, KS: Regents Press of Kansas, 1978), 69–206; W. T. Balmer, *A History of the Akan People* (New York: Atlantis Press, 1925), 169–185.

2. Lewin, *Asante before the British*, 211–222.

3. Francis Dvornik, *The Slavs in European History and Civilization* (New Brunswick, NJ: Rutgers University Press, 1962), 278, 343, 378, 439, 442; William L. Langer, ed., *World History* (Boston: Houghton Mifflin Company, 1980), 442, 444, 446.

4.René Grousset, *The Empire of the Steppes: A History of Central Asia,* trans. Naomi Walford (New Brunswick, NJ: Rutgers University Press, 1970), 165–167.

5. Steven Runciman, *A History of the Crusades,* 3 vols. (Cambridge: Cambridge University Press, 1952, 1987), vol. 3, 134, 173–177, 179–182, 221; Prince Hubertus Zu Löwenstein, *A Basic History of Germany* (Bonn: Inter Nationes, 1964), 38.

6. George Ostrogorsky, *History of the Byzantine State* (New Brunswick, NJ: Rutgers University Press, 1969), 430, 433; Langer, *World History,* 281–282.

7. Edward E. Egan, Constance B. Hintz, and L. F. Wise, *Kings, Rulers and Statesmen* (New York: Sterling Publishing Company, 1976), 159.

8. Edwin O. Reischauer and John K. Fairbank,

East Asia: The Great Tradition (Boston: Houghton Mifflin Company, 1960), 206–208; Langer, *World History,* 365–366.

1. Steven Runciman, *A History of the Crusades,* 3 vols. (Cambridge: Cambridge University Press, 1987), vol. 3, 164, 172–173, 230; René Grousset, *The Empire of the Steppes: A History of Central Asia,* trans. Naomi Walford (New Brunswick, NJ: Rutgers University Press, 1970), 281–282, 360–363; Edward E. Egan, Constance B. Hintz, and L. F. Wise, *Kings, Rulers and Statesmen* (New York: Sterling Publishing Company, 1976), 21.

2. Jørgen Laessøe, *People of Ancient Assyria* trans. F. S. Leigh-Browne (London: Routledge and Kegan Paul, 1963), 113; A. Leo Oppenheim, *Ancient Mesopotamia* (Chicago: University of Chicago Press, 1977), 104, 169; A. T. Olmstead, *History of the Persian Empire* (Chicago: University of Chicago Press, 1948), 22; William L. Langer, ed., *World History* (Boston: Houghton Mifflin Company, 1940, 1980), 33.

3. Langer, *World History,* 872, 1078–1079.

4. Diana Bowder, ed., *Who Was Who in the Roman World* (Ithaca, NY: Cornell University Press, 1980), 586–587.

5. Michael Psellus, *Fourteen Byzantine Rulers,* trans. E. R. A. Sewter (Harmondsworth, Middlesex: Penguin Books, 1982), 55–59, 63–65, 75–81, 87–240 passim, 250; George Ostrogorsky, *History of the Byzantine State* (New Brunswick, NJ: Rutgers University Press, 1969), 321, 323, 326–327.

Bibliography

Alexander, David, and Patricia Alexander, eds. *Eerdman's Handbook to the Bible*. Berkhamsted, Herts, England: Lion Publishing Co., 1973.

Alexander, John T. *Catherine the Great, Life and Legend*. Oxford: Oxford University Press, 1989.

Asprey, Robert B. *Frederick the Great, the Magnificent Enigma*. New York: Ticknor and Fields, 1986.

Aston, W. G., trans. *Nihongi: Chronicles of Japan from the Earliest Times to A.D. 697*. Rutland, VT: Charles E. Tuttle Company, 1979.

Avallone, Michael. *A Woman Called Golda*. New York: Leisure Books, 1982.

Balmer, W. T. *A History of the Akan Peoples*. New York: Atlantis Press, 1925.

Bergami, David. *Japan's Imperial Conspiracy*. New York: William Morrow, 1972.

Bhahacharya, Sachchidananda. *A Dictionary of Indian History*. New York: George Braziller, 1967.

Bhatin, Krishan. *A Biography of Prime Minister Gandhi*. New York: Praeger, 1974.

Bhutto, Benazir. *Daughter of Destiny*. New York: Simon and Schuster, 1989.

_____. *Daughter of the East*. London: Hamish Hamilton, 1988.

Bloodworth, Dennis. *The Chinese Looking Glass*. New York: Farrar, Straus and Giroux, 1967.

Bloodworth, Dennis, and Ching Ping Bloodworth. *The Chinese Machiavelli: 3,000 Years of Chinese Statecraft*. New York: Dell Publishing Co., 1976.

Bolding, Elise. *The Underside of History: A View of Women through Time*. Boulder: Westview Press, 1976.

Bowder, Diana, ed. *Who Was Who in the Greek World*. Ithaca, NY: Cornell University Press, 1982.

_____. *Who Was Who in the Roman World*. Ithaca, NY: Cornell University Press, 1980.

Breisach, Ernest. *Caterina Sforza: A Renaissance Virago*. Chicago: Chicago University Press, 1967.

Browning, Robert. *Justinian and Theodora*. New York: Praeger Publications, 1971.

Buchan, John, ed. *The Baltic and Caucasian States*. Boston and New York: Houghton Mifflin, 1923.

Budge, E. A. *A History of Ethiopia*. London: Methuen, 1928.

Butler, Alban. *The Lives of the Fathers, Martyrs and Other Principal Saints*. Vol. 4. Chicago: Catholic Press, 1961.

Campbell, Joseph. *The Masks of God: Primitive Mythology*. New York: Penguin Books, 1969, 1976.

Candee, Marjorie Dent, ed. *Current Biography 1953*. New York: H. W. Wilson Co., 1954.

Chadwick, Nora. *The Celts*. London and Harmondsworth: Penguin Books, 1976.

Clark, Sydney. *All the Best in Holland*. New York: Dodd, Mead and Co., 1960.

Clough, Shepard B., David L. Hicks, David J. Brandenburg, and Peter Gray. *European History in a World Perspective*. Vol. 2, *Early Modern Times*. Lexington, MA: D. C. Heath and Co., 1975.

Codrington, H. W. *A Short History of Ceylon*. Cambridge: Cambridge University Press, 1947.

Cooke, Jean, Ann Kramer, and Theodore Rowland-Entwistle. *History's Timeline*. New York: Crescent Books, 1981.

Cooke, S. A., F. E. Adcock, and M. P. Charlesworth. *The Cambridge Ancient History*. Vol. 10, London: Cambridge University Press, 1971.

Coughlan, Robert. *Elizabeth and Catherine*. New York: G. P. Putnam's Sons, 1974.

Crankshaw, Edward. *Maria Theresa*. New York: Viking Press, 1969, 1971.

Dahmus, Joseph. *Seven Medieval Queens*. Garden City, NY: Doubleday, 1972.

Deen, Edith. *All the Women of the Bible*. New York: Harper and Brothers, 1955.

Derry, T. K. *A History of Scandinavia*. Minneapolis: University of Minneapolis Press, 1979.

Donovan, Frank R. *The Vikings*. New York: American Heritage Publishing Co., 1964.

Duff, Charles. *England and the English*. New York: G. P. Putnam's Sons, 1955.

Dukes, Paul. *Russia, a History*. New York: McGraw-Hill, 1924.

Durant, Will. *The Story of Civilization*. Vol. 4, *The Age of Faith*. New York: Simon and Schuster, 1939, 1966.

Durant, Will, and Ariel Durant. *The Story of Civilization*. Vol. 9, *The Age of Voltaire*. New York: Simon and Schuster, 1965.

Dvornik, Francis. *The Slavs in European History and Civilization*. New Brunswick, NJ: Rutgers University Press, 1962.

Edwards, I. E. S. et al., eds. *Cambridge Ancient History*. 3d ed. 2 vols. Cambridge: Cambridge University Press, 1970–1971.

Egan, Edward W., Constance B. Hintz, and L. F. Wise. *Kings, Rulers and Statesmen*. New York: Sterling Publishing Co., 1976.

Emery, W. B. *Archaic Egypt*. New York: Viking Penguin, 1987.

Fairservis, Walter A., Jr. *The Ancient Kingdoms of the Nile*. New York: Mentor/NAL, 1962.

Fernandez-Armesto, Felipe. *Ferdinand and Isabella*. New York: Taplinger, 1975.

Fraser, Antonia. *Mary Queen of Scots*. New York: Delacorte Press, 1969.

Fulford, Roger. *Hanover to Windsor*. Glasgow: William Collins Sons and Co., Fontana Edition, 1981.

Gamst, Frederick C. *The Qemant: A Pagan-Hebraic Peasantry of Ethiopia*. New York: Holt, Rinehart and Winston, 1969.

Gandhi, Indira. *My Truth*. New York: Grove Press, 1980.

Gascoigne, Bamber. *The Great Moghuls*. New York: Dorset Press, 1971.

Gernet, Jacques. *A History of Chinese Civilization*. New York: Cambridge University Press, 1982.

Geye, Pieter. *The Revolt of the Netherlands 1555–1609*. London: Ernest Benn, 1958.

Gibbon, Edward. *The Decline and Fall of the Roman Empire*. Chicago: Encyclopedia Britannica, 1952.

Glubb, Sir John. *A Short History of the Arab Peoples*. New York: Dorset Press, 1969.

Gray, Richard, ed. *The Cambridge History of Africa*. Vol. 4. Cambridge: Cambridge University Press, 1975.

Gregory of Tours. *The History of the Franks*. Translated by Lewis Thorpe. London and Harmondsworth: Penguin Books, 1974.

Grousset, René. *The Empire of the Steppes: A History of Central Asia*. Translated by Naomi Walford. New Brunswick, NJ: Rutgers University Press, 1970.

Gunther, John. *Inside Europe Today*. New York: Harper and Bros., 1961.

Hammond, N. G. L. *A History of Greece to 322 B.C.* Oxford: Clarendon Press, 1986.

Harding, Robert. *Anatomy of a Power Elite*. New Haven, CT: Yale University Press, 1978.

Hare, Christopher. *The Most Illustrious Ladies of the Italian Renaissance*. Williamstown, MA: Corner House Publishing, 1972.

Heer, Friedrich. *The Medieval World*. Translated by Janet Sondheimer. New York: Mentor/NAL, 1962.

Herodotus. *The Histories*. Translated by Aubrey de Sélincourt. New York: Penguin Books, 1954, 1968.

Hitti, Philip K. *History of the Arabs*. New York: St. Martin's Press, 1968.

Hodges, Margaret. *Lady Queen Anne*. New York: Farrar, Straus and Giroux, 1969.

Hoffman, William. *Queen Juliana: The Story of the Richest Woman in the World*. New York: Harcourt Brace Jovanovich, 1979.

Hook, Brian, ed. *The Cambridge Encyclopedia of China*. Cambridge: Cambridge University Press, 1982.

Hubert, Henri. *The Greatness and Decline of the Celts*. New York: Arno Press, 1980.

Hudson, M. E., and Mary Clark. *Crown of a Thousand Years*. New York: Crown Publishers, 1978.

Hussey, J. M. *The Cambridge Medieval History*. Vol. 4, Part 1. Cambridge: Cambridge University Press, 1966.

International Who's Who, 1987–1988. London: Europa Publications, 1987.

Jackson, John G. *Introduction to African Civilizations*. Secaucus, NJ: Citadel Press, 1970.

James, Edward T., ed. *Notable American Women, 1607–1950*. Cambridge: Belknap Press of Harvard University Press, 1971.

Johnson, Paul. *Elizabeth I*. New York: Holt, Rinehart and Winston, 1974.

Jones, Howard Mumford. *The Literature of Virginia in the Seventeenth Century*. Charlottesville, VA: University of Virginia Press, 1968.

Josephus Flavius. *Life and Works*. Translated by William Whiston. Philadelphia: Winston Company, n.d.

Josephy, Alvin M. *The Horizon History of Africa*. New York: American Heritage Publishing Co., 1971.

Junor, Penny. *Margaret Thatcher: Wife, Mother, Politician*. London: Sidgwick and London, 1983.

Karnow, Stanley. *Vietnam: A History*. New York: Viking Press, 1983.

Kelly, Amy. *Eleanor of Aquitaine and the Four Kings*. Cambridge: Harvard University Press, 1978.

Kemp-Welch, Alice. *Six Medieval Women*. London: Macmillan, 1913.

Kenyatta, Jomo. *Facing Mt. Kenya*. New York: Vintage/Random House, 1965.

Kenyon, J. P. *The Stuarts*. Glasgow: William Collins Sons, 1970.

Kibler, William W., ed. *Eleanor of Aquitaine: Patron and Politician*. Austin: University of Texas Press, 1976.

Kinder, Hermann, and Werner Hilgemann. *The Anchor Atlas of World History.* 2 vols. Translated by Ernest A. Menze. Garden City, NJ: Anchor Press/Doubleday, 1974

Komisar, Lucy. *Corazon Aquino, the Story of a Revolution.* New York: George Braziller, 1987.

Laessøe, Jørgen. *People of Ancient Assyria.* Translated by F. S. Leigh-Browne. London: Routledge and Kegan Paul, 1963.

Langer, William L., ed. *World History.* Boston: Houghton Mifflin, 1980.

Latourette, Kenneth Scott. *The Chinese: Their History and Culture.* New York: Macmillan, 1934.

Lewin, Thomas J. *Asante before the British.* Lawrence, KS: Regents Press of Kansas, 1978.

Longford, Elizabeth. *The Queen: The Life of Elizabeth II.* New York: Alfred A. Knopf, 1983.

_____. *Queen Victoria: Born to Succeed.* New York: Harper and Row, 1964.

Löwenstein, Prince Hubertus Zu. *A Basic History of Germany.* Bonn: Inter Nationes, 1964.

Ludowyk, E. F. C. *The Modern History of Ceylon.* New York: Frederick A. Praeger, 1966.

Ludwig, Emil. *Cleopatra.* New York: Viking Press, 1937.

Luke, Mary. *Gloriana: The Years of Elizabeth I.* New York: Coward, McCann and Geoghegan, 1973.

McKendrick, Melveena. *Ferdinand and Isabella.* New York: American Heritage Publishing Co., 1968.

Mackie, J. D. *A History of Scotland.* Harmondsworth: Penguin Books, 1984.

Markdale, Jean. *Women of the Celts.* Translated by A. Mygind, C. Hauch, and P. Henry. Rochester, VT: Inner Traditions International, 1986.

Masselman, George. *The Cradle of Colonialism.* New Haven, CT: Yale University Press, 1963.

Massie, Robert K. *Nicholas and Alexandra.* New York: Atheneum Press, 1974.

Masson, Georgina. *Queen Christina.* New York: Farrar, Straus and Giroux, 1969.

Mattingly, Garrett. *Catherine of Aragon.* Cambridge: Cambridge University Press, 1942.

Mee, Charles L., Jr. *Daily Life in Renaissance Italy.* New York: American Heritage Publishing Co., 1975.

Mehta, Ved, *The New India.* Harmondsworth: Penguin Books, 1978.

Meir, Golda. *My Life.* New York: G. P. Putnam's Sons, 1975.

Morby, John E. *Dynasties of the World.* Oxford and New York: Oxford University Press, 1989.

Morford, Mark P. O., and Robert J. Lenardon. *Classical Mythology.* New York: Longman, 1977.

Moritz, Charles, ed. *Current Biography Yearbook.* New York: H. W. Wilson Company, 1972, 1986.

Morton, W. Scott. *China, Its History and Culture.* New York: McGraw-Hill, 1980, 1982.

Murphy, E. Jefferson. *Understanding Africa.* New York: Thomas Y. Crowell, 1969.

Myers, A. R. *England in the Late Middle Ages.* Harmondsworth: Penguin Books, 1952.

Newcomer, James. *The Grand Duchy of Luxembourg.* Lanham, MD: University Press of America, 1984.

Nyakatura, J. W. *Anatomy of an African Kingdom.* Translated by Teopista Muganwa, edited by Godfrey Uzoigwe. Garden City, NJ: Anchor/Doubleday, 1973.

Oates, Joan. *Babylon.* London: Thames and Hudson, 1979.

Oldenbourg, Zoe. *Catherine the Great.* New York: Pantheon Books, 1965.

Oliver, Roland, and J. D. Fage. *A Short History of Africa.* Harmondsworth: Penguin Books, 1970.

Olmstead, A. T. *History of the Persian Empire*. Chicago: University of Chicago Press, 1948.

Oppenheim, A. Leo. *Ancient Mesopotamia*. Chicago: University of Chicago Press, 1977.

Ostrogorsky, George. *History of the Byzantine State*. New Brunswick, NJ: Rutgers University Press, 1969.

Packer, James I., Merril C. Tenney, and William White, Jr. *The Bible Almanac*. Nashville: Thomas Nelson Publishers, 1980.

Painter, Sidney. *The Rise of the Feudal Monarchies*. Ithaca, NY: Cornell University Press, 1951.

Panikker, K. Madhu. *The Serpent and the Crescent: A History of the Negro Empires of West Africa*. Bombay: Asia Publishing House, 1963.

Papinot, E. *Historical and Geographical Dictionary of Japan*. Rutland, VT: Charles E. Tuttle Company, 1972.

Pemble, John. *The Raj, the Indian Mutiny and the Kingdom of Oudh 1801–1859*. Rutherford, NJ: Fairleigh Dickinson University Press, 1977.

Plowden, Alison. *Lady Jane Grey and the House of Suffolk*. New York: Franklin Watts, 1986.

Plutarch. *Makers of Rome*. Translated by Ian Scott-Kilvert. Harmondsworth: Penguin Books, 1980.

Porter, Jane. *The Scottish Chiefs*. New York: A. L. Burt Co., 1831.

Previté-Orton, C. W. *The Shorter Cambridge Medieval History*. 2 vols. Cambridge: Cambridge University Press, 1982.

Psellus, Michael. *Fourteen Byzantine Rulers*. Translated by E. R. A. Sewter. Harmondsworth: Penguin Books, 1982.

Reischauer, Edwin O., and John K. Fairbank. *East Asia: The Great Tradition*. Boston: Houghton Mifflin, 1960.

Ridley, Jasper. *Napoleon III and Eugenie*. New York: Viking Press, 1980.

Roider, Karl A., Jr., ed. *Maria Theresa*. Englewood Cliffs, NJ: Prentice-Hall, 1973.

Runciman, Steven A. *A History of the Crusades*. 3 vols. Cambridge: Cambridge University Press, 1987.

Sansom, George. *A History of Japan to 1334*. Stanford, CA: Stanford University Press, 1958.

_____. *A History of Japan 1334–1615*. Stanford, CA: Stanford University Press, 1961.

Seneviratne, Maureen. *Sirimavo Bandaranaike: The World's First Woman Prime Minister*. Sri Lanka: Colombo Press, 1975.

Sitwell, Sacheverell. *Portugal and Madeira*. London: B. T. Batsford, 1954.

Smith, Denis Mack. *A History of Sicily*. 2 vols. New York: Dorset Press, 1968.

Smith, Lacey Baldwin. *Elizabeth Tudor: Portrait of a Queen*. Boston: Little, Brown and Co., 1975.

Smith, Vincent A. *The Oxford History of India*. London: Oxford University Press, 1958, 1967.

Spear, Percival. *A History of India*. Vol. 2. London: Penguin Books, 1987.

Stenton, Doris Mary. *English Society in the Early Middle Ages*. Harmondsworth: Penguin Books, 1965.

Sullivan, Richard E. *Heirs of the Roman Empire*. Ithaca, NY: Cornell University Press, 1960.

Tanner, J. R., ed. *The Cambridge Medieval History*. Vol. 12. Cambridge: Cambridge University Press, 1967.

Tauté, Anne. *The Kings and Queens of Great Britain*. London: Hamish Hamilton, 1976.

Thapar, Romila. *A History of India*. Vol. 1. London: Penguin Books, 1987.

Thompson, John M. *Revolutionary Russia, 1917*. New York: Charles Scribner's Sons, 1981.

Tompkins, Peter. *Mysteries of the Mexican Pyramids*. New York: Harper and Row, 1976.

Trevor-Roper, Hugh. *The Golden Age of Europe*. New York: Bonanza/Crown, 1987.

Troynt, Henri. *Catherine the Great*. Translated by Joan Pinkham. New York: Dutton and Co., 1980.

Uglow, Jennifer S., comp. and ed. *International Dictionary of Women's Biography*. New York: Continuum, 1982.

Warner, Marina. *The Dragon Empress*. New York: Macmillan, 1972.

Weber, Eugene. *France*. Cambridge: Belknap Press of Harvard University, 1986.

Weightman, Christine. *Margaret of York: Duchess of Burgundy 1446–1503*. Gloucester: Alan Sutton Publishing, 1989.

Wells, H. G. *The Outline of History*. 2 vols. Garden City, NJ: Doubleday, 1949.

West, John Anthony. *The Traveler's Key to Ancient Egypt*. New York: Alfred A. Knopf, 1985.

White, J. E. *Ancient Egypt: Its Culture and History*. New York: Dover Publishing, 1970.

Whitelock, Dorothy. *The Beginnings of English Society*. Harmondsworth: Penguin Books, 1974.

Williamson, Hugh R. *Catherine de Medici*. New York: Viking Press, 1973.

Wilson, Robert Dick. *A Scientific Investigation of the Old Testament*. Revised by Edward J. Young. Chicago: Moody Press, 1959.

Wolpert, Stanley A. *A New History of India*. New York: Oxford University Press, 1977.

Wright, Arthur F. *The Sui Dynasty: A Unification of China, A.D. 581–617*. New York: Alfred A. Knopf, 1978.

Wright, G. Ernest. *Biblical Archaeology*. Philadelphia: Westminster Press, 1957.